The History *of* Nations

SOUTH AMERICA

GHENT
EDITION

THE INCA (EMPEROR) AND COYA (EMPRESS),
ATTENDED BY THEIR CCUMILLU (DWARF),
SITTING IN STATE

Drawn from description furnished by the Inca Garcillasso de la
Vega, historian of Peru   —page 19

THE HISTORY OF NATIONS

HENRY CABOT LODGE, Ph. D., LL. D. · EDITOR-IN-CHIEF

SOUTH AMERICA

TRANSLATED AND EDITED FROM THE WORK OF

ALFRED JOSEPH DEBERLÉ

BY PHILIP PATTERSON WELLS, Ph. D.

LECTURER IN HISTORY AND LIBRARIAN OF THE
LAW SCHOOL, YALE UNIVERSITY

VOLUME XXI

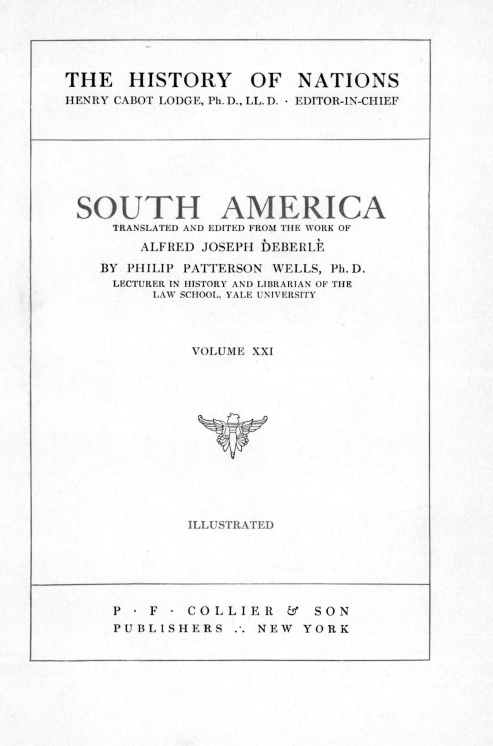

ILLUSTRATED

P · F · COLLIER & SON
PUBLISHERS ∴ NEW YORK

Designed, Printed, and Bound at
The Collier Press, New York

THE HISTORY OF NATIONS

EDITOR-IN-CHIEF

HENRY CABOT LODGE, Ph.D., LL.D.

Associate Editors and Authors

ARCHIBALD HENRY SAYCE, LL.D.,
Professor of Assyriology, Oxford University

CHRISTOPHER JOHNSTON, M.D., Ph.D.,
Associate Professor of Oriental History and Archaeology, Johns Hopkins University

C. W. C. OMAN,
Professor of History, Oxford University

THEODOR MOMMSEN,
Late Professor of Ancient History, University of Berlin

ARTHUR C. HOWLAND, Ph.D.,
Department of History, University of Pennsylvania

CHARLES MERIVALE, LL.D.,
Late Dean of Ely, formerly Lecturer in History, Cambridge University

J. HIGGINSON CABOT, Ph.D.,
Department of History, Wellesley College

SIR WILLIAM W. HUNTER, F.R.S.,
Late Director-General of Statistics in India

GEORGE M. DUTCHER, Ph.D.,
Professor of History, Wesleyan University

SIR ROBERT K. DOUGLAS,
Professor of Chinese, King's College, London

JEREMIAH WHIPPLE JENKS, Ph.D., LL.D.
Professor of Political Economy and Politics, Cornell University

KANICHI ASAKAWA, Ph.D.,
Instructor in the History of Japanese Civilization, Yale University

WILFRED HAROLD MUNRO, L.H.D.,
Professor of European History, Brown University

G. MERCER ADAM,
Historian and Editor

FRED MORROW FLING, Ph.D.,
Professor of European History, University of Nebraska

FRANÇOIS AUGUSTE MARIE MIGNET,
Late Member of the French Academy

JAMES WESTFALL THOMPSON, Ph.D.,
Department of History, University of Chicago

SAMUEL RAWSON GARDINER, LL.D.,
Professor of Modern History, King's College, London

P. W. JOYCE, LL.D.,
Commissioner for the Publication of the Ancient Laws of Ireland

ASSOCIATE EDITORS AND AUTHORS—Continued

PREFACE

DEBERLÉ'S *"Histoire de l'Amérique du sud depuis la conquête jusqu'à nos jours"* was first published at Paris in 1876. A third edition, revised and brought down to date by Albert Milhaud, was published in 1897. The first edition was plagiarized by an unknown Spaniard, who added some pages on the colonial system from Robertson's "America" and such minor variations of the text as might be expected from a journalist with some knowledge of South American affairs, and published the whole at Barcelona in 1878 under the title: *"Historia de la America del Sur, desde su descubrimiento, hasta nuestros dias, etc., etc., por un Americano."* The final chapter, on Patagonia, may pass for an original production of this "author." This Spanish version was innocently translated into English by Adnah D. Jones and published in London and New York in 1899 under the title: "History of South America from its discovery to the present time, etc., etc., by an American." The blunder was the more absurd because Milhaud's edition of Déberlé had been published in Paris only two years before, so that Jones' version was not only a fraud, but was more than twenty years out of date when it issued from the press.

Déberlé's book is the best short outline of the general history of South America. Milhaud added: an introduction summarizing briefly our knowledge of pre-Columbian America; a third part and supplementary pages to some of Deberle's chapters, briefly narrating the history of the twenty years preceding his edition; and a bibliography. In this translation all the matter relating to the years 1877-1910 has been collected in Part III, which has been freely adapted and rewritten for that purpose. Déberlé's text in Parts I and II has been translated, with such slight changes and omissions as the events of the last thirty years have made necessary; but errors of fact have been corrected, such as the statement that the Indians were under the jurisdiction of the Inquisition (Part I, Chapter III); and passages showing a decided bias on the part of the author have been modified in accordance with the results of the most recent research. This has been done in certain passages denouncing the Catholic Church and the Spanish Colonial System. Deberle sometimes wrote as might be expected of an anti-clericalist in the early days of the third French Republic, and failed to balance his account of the crimes of the *conquistadores* by the humane legislation first inspired by Las Casas.

Philip F. Abell

INTRODUCTION

SOUTH AMERICA BEFORE COLUMBUS

SCHOLARS and historians have busied themselves with the past of America before the arrival of Columbus, of pre-Columbian America as it is called. Existing races, legends, and archæological monuments furnish the basis for this study.

The first questions which demanded answers were: Was America peopled by men from the Eurasian continent? Has it experienced invasions and great immigrations? Are there in ethnic characteristics, customs, and technique of the arts and trades, points of resemblance between the men of America and those of other parts of the world?

Some think that they have found such resemblances and analogies, finding material for the comparison of the old American races and those of the ancient world. They cite similar funeral customs among the Mexicans, Peruvians, Egyptians, and Guanches; these diverse peoples all embalmed the dead and adorned them with necklaces. In Peru, as in Egypt, the embalmers placed small plates of silver in the dead man's mouth. In Europe, as in America, they have found *tumuli* used as monuments of the dead; in both continents the customs of burning and of burying the dead have existed side by side.

Moreover, the idea of the deluge, which is so widespread among Eurasian peoples, exists among the Americans. They, too, believe that a cataclysm destroyed all mankind except certain favored couples. There are resemblances between the American cosmogonies and those of ancient civilization in Europe.

Nevertheless, these arguments are held by some scholars to be insufficient proof of a common origin. These reply that such likenesses may spring from the parallel and independent development of human society on the two continents. To the claims of the monogenistic school, another school of scientific Americanists answers that the native race is autochthonous and has simply been modified by crossings. Others accept the theory of a plurality of races (Virchow, "*État générale des connaissances concernant l'anthropologie américane,*" 1877), and like Koleman in particular, arrive at this conclusion by the study of fossil American skulls ("*Die Autochthonen Amerikas:*" *Zeitschrift für Ethnologie,* 1883).

It would be difficult to prove the case either way beyond a doubt. Whatever may have been the origin of the American races it seems probable that they have been subjected to foreign influences, though it is very difficult to say at what time.

Immigration may have come from the northwest by way of Bering Sea; from the northeast by way of the Atlantic; from the Pacific islands, aided by the favoring ocean currents; and, perhaps, from that land of Atlantis whose existence was formerly questioned as legendary, but is now a permissible scientific conjecture in the light of geological knowledge.

The most has been made of some arguments in favor of foreign influence:

Esquara, the language of the Basques, has certain analogies with different North American tongues. Similar likenesses between the American and the Uro-Altaic languages have been noted by Forschammer ("*Vergleichung des amerikanischen Sprachen mit den Ural-Altaïschen hinsichtlich ihrer Grammatik*").

The calendar of the civilized American peoples (before the arrival of the Spaniards) is like that of the Hindus, Thibetans, Chinese, and Japanese. Another still more striking fact is that there are found among the archæologic monuments of Central America, where the elephant is unknown, objects representing elephants' trunks and heads, etc.

Some scholars go further and specify the Chinese, and perhaps the Japanese also, as the bearers of Asiatic customs and civilization to America. A country which may be identified as America was visited by the Chinese, as their annalists show. " Formerly the religion of Buddha did not exist in those countries; it was in the fourth year of the reign of Hiao-wu-te of Song (485 A. D.) that five *pi-khïéou* or monks of the country of Ki-pin, went to Fusang and spread the law of Buddha. They took with them the books, the holy images, and the ritual, and instituted monastic customs there which changed the morality of the people." Thus are explained the signal resemblances in cosmogony and in certain traits of civilization. Thus are explained certain analogous customs of the Peruvians and the Chinese, such as the detailed rules which determine all the outward actions of men, the annual fête held in honor of agriculturists, the high esteem in which agriculture is held, the system of irrigating canals, the payment of taxes in kind, the building of suspension bridges, the likenesses in architecture, the resemblance of the Chinese junk and the Peruvian barque. To the objection that the incas did not flourish till six centuries later, the only possible reply for the supporters of the Chinese theory is that at the time of Kublai Khan a fleet sent against Japan was thrown upon the coasts of South America. However this may be, miniature golden figures found among the tombs of the Muyscas represent the Mongolian type quite accurately.

The following are some of the evidences of western influence: it has been observed that the people of Central America, like those of ancient Egypt, have a red, or copper-colored, skin and are almost always beardless. The two countries are strangely alike in their pottery, obelisks, pyramids, equal months of thirty days each, a year of three hundred and sixty days with five intercalendar days added, at Thebes as in Mexico. The Mexicans of to-day wind about their bodies a striped fabric so as to form a petticoat falling below the knees. So did the Egyptians of former times, for this was the costume of Isis.

We can only state these facts and conflicting theories. In the present imperfect state of knowledge with respect to the history of primitive America it is too early to adopt any definite conclusion, but we cannot entirely neglect the results of the numerous investigators in this strange field.

For the period before the fifteenth century we can safely affirm as follows:

Man existed in America in the Stone Age, to use the terms of archæology, or in the quaternary, and perhaps in the tertiary ages, in the language of geologists.

The civilization of the old and new worlds, whether in contact or not, developed along parallel lines.

There are several American races: the most ancient peoples of the Andine chain seem to have come from Asia and have points of resemblance to the Mongols; the most ancient peoples in America are probably the Bocudos and Patagonians.[1]

[1] See M. de Nadillac's "*l'Amerique préhistorique*," from which the greater part of the foregoing information is taken; a work richer in documents than in criticism.

When the Spaniards landed in America they found the natives in two widely different stages of civilization, some civilized, others still barbarous and in many cases nomadic.

The civilized peoples were grouped in the high valleys and upon the tablelands of the Rocky Mountains and of the Andine chain. Perhaps they were able to develop their civilization there more readily because the less oppressive temperature was more favorable to mental activity, and natural barriers secured to them protection, peace, and the development of the arts which is dependent on peace. These civilized peoples were the Aztecs of Mexico, the Mayas of Central America, the Muyscas or Chibchas in the high valleys of Colombia and on the tableland of Condinamarca, the Quichas of Peru and Ecuador, and the Aymaras of Bolivia.

The nomads, for the most part living by the chase, are the Redskins of North America, the Caribs in the Antilles and on the nearby continental coasts, the Aruacs in Guiana, the Antis eastward of the Andes in the Amazon valley, the Carayus, the Panos, the Miravhas of the Brazilian tableland, the Tupis or Guaranis, the Guayturas, the Gaytacas or Puris, the Chworas in the region of Rio de Janeiro, and finally the Patagonians and the Araucans at the southern extremity of South America.

It must be said that selva and pampa, thick tangled forests and endless steppes, afforded poor centers for social groups, and these conditions may perhaps explain in part the social and political inferiority of the peoples of the plain.

The ethnic characteristics of the South American aborigines have been clearly noted by Élisée Reclus ("*Amerique du Sud*," t. I.) : " In general the natives of South America differ from those of the St. Lawrence and Mississippi valleys in the color of the skin. They are not red or copper-colored,[2] but, according to geographical situation and race, are of two distinct colors, olive brown and yellow with gradations of intermediate shades. If we consider large divisions we may say in a general manner that brown prevails among the Andeans and yellow among the Indians of the plains and of the mountains of Guiana and of Brazil.[3]

What is the cause of this difference in color between these groups of Indian nations? Doubtless it is not extraordinary. The contrasts of climate, occupation, manner of life, and nourishment

[2] Alex von Humboldt, "*Voyage au régions équinoxiales.*"
[3] A. d'Orbigny, "*l'Homme Americain.*"

contribute in different proportions to produce the difference in the color of the skin. We must remember as facts of great importance that the Andeans of the west live in a climate which is dry, or at least has a far lower degree of humidity than the eastern lands, that they are for the most part agricultural peoples, and that their food is chiefly vegetable. In the plains the tribes of hunters and fishers subsist chiefly upon flesh.

The shape of the skull and height of the figure differ, but the differences in these respects between the different nations and tribes do not give a sharp classification by which we can regularly group the Indians according to race characteristics. While differing in some respects, all the natives resemble each other in their thick, black, smooth hair, in the absence of a beard, shortness of chin, small size of the deep-sunken eyes, strength of the jaws, and beauty of the teeth. They are by nature of good figure, a fact attributable to the perfect freedom of movement which the mothers allow their children, who are almost always entirely naked.

They suffered one great disadvantage in comparison with the peoples of the old world. They had no domestic animals whose strength they could add to their own. Their extraordinary skill in taming wild beasts gave them pets, but added nothing to their powers; for this purpose they had only the lama and the dog, while the natives of other parts of the world had the camel, the horse, the ass, the ox, the dog, and the sheep.

In North America the Spaniards found an empire which they destroyed and a civilization which they extinguished: the empire and civilization of the Aztecs. When they entered South America they found another empire with a remarkable organization and a brilliant civilization, in the region which we now call Peru.

The empire of the incas was founded in the eleventh century. It succeeded that of a more ancient civilized people—the Aymaras, whose monuments are still extant. The language of the Quichua people, of whom the incas were the chiefs, was spoken in what is now Ecuador, Peru, Bolivia, and Chili. It was first reduced to writing by the Spaniards, who expressed it in Latin characters.

For the beginning of the history of the incas we have a legend: Manco Capac and his sister, Manco Oello Huaco, children of the Sun, left the region of Lake Titicaca toward the end of the eleventh century and moved northward, seeking a place for settlement. In different spots they tried to thrust a gold coin into the resisting

soil. At length the coin buried itself in the ground: Manco Capac
had found the place fixed by the fates for his residence. The town
of Cuzco was founded, he became king (inca), and his fourteen
descendants governed the empire which the Europeans discovered, that is to say the region which is included in the tableland
and coast of Peru, Ecuador, a part of Bolivia, and Chili as far as the
land of the Araucanians.

The incas worshiped the sun, but the theogony of the conquered peoples modified that of their conquerors so that we find
other coexisting cults, as in the east, that of Viracocha, who created
the sun and formed men out of stones. In the west that of Pa-
chaemac (soul or source of the world) was the god of the masses.

The social organization of the empire was two-fold—a caste
system and a system of communism.

The soil was divided into four portions of equal area. The
first was allotted to the laborers and their families, the second to
the infirm, and to widows and orphans, the third to the inca and
the official class, and the fourth to the sun, or in other words to
the priests. As the inca was both the political and religious head
of the empire he owned half the soil. Cattle and crops were owned
in common, each man taking what he needed, but the inca made
provision to prevent scarcity; to him belonged the gold and silver
from the mines of Cerro de Pasco and of Lake Titicaca.

The mass of the people tilled the soil and made clothing, arms,
and tools. The study of theology, mathematics, and astronomy,
of the sciences and the arts, of history, legislation and politics,
and the use of arms were the privileges of the children of the
inca and of the nobles. Education was regulated by the state
and marriage was obligatory.

The country was divided into four provinces: the northern,
southern, eastern, and western, governed by officers called curacas.
The highway system was remarkable, and there were inns and
storehouses for the use of the royal couriers to expedite their journeys so that the orders of the sovereign were promptly transmitted
and obeyed.

The Quichuas built fortresses and temples of a uniform architectural type; they could build dams and throw up earthworks;
they wove cloth and worked in metals. Their agriculture was enlightened, they built aqueducts, dug irrigating canals, and used
guano as a fertilizer. They were good sailors. They were not con-

tent to hug the shore, but struck boldly into the high seas and penetrated to the Gallapagos Islands, more than 600 miles to the west. Pizarro's pilot, Ruiz de Estrada, tells us that their ships were well built and could stand a heavy sea. They were rigged with two masts and square sails. It has already been remarked that the Quichuas divided the year into 365 days and knew how to calculate eclipses and the sun's motion.

The conquerors, to be sure, exaggerated the wonders of the country they had subdued, wishing to dazzle Europe by their story and the fame of their achievement. Nevertheless it is certain that they did find civilized regions. We hasten to add that they wasted them. The population, relatively dense when the Spanish arrived, was decimated by massacres, epidemics, and crop failures, brought on by a conquest too ignorant to appreciate the wisely arranged social order and the well organized government of the natives.

ALBERT MILHAUD.

CONTENTS

PART I

SPANISH AND PORTUGUESE SOUTH AMERICA
1492-1504

PART II

INDEPENDENT SOUTH AMERICA. 1824-1876

PART III

THE PRESENT SOUTH AMERICA. 1876-1910

APPENDIX

LIST OF ILLUSTRATIONS

TEXT MAPS

PART I

SPANISH AND PORTUGUESE SOUTH AMERICA 1492-1504

HISTORY OF SOUTH AMERICA

Chapter I

THE DISCOVERY OF AMERICA. 1492-1504

THE northern parts of the American continent were explored and even colonized by the Scandinavians at a very early date. Toward the end of the tenth century Eric the Red, an Icelander, settled in Greenland, which his compatriot, Gunnibiorn, had discovered a few years before. The corsairs who followed him established themselves in Newfoundland in the year 1000, and later in Nova Scotia and Massachusetts. Communications between Iceland and its colonies were kept up until the middle of the fourteenth century, when they ceased, because of political developments in Denmark. All traces of them were lost, but their memory survived.

In fact, while Jean de Béthencourt, a Norman gentleman, was conquering the Canaries (1402), other Norman adventurers covered the whole western coast of Greenland with new settlements. Modern scholarship has sought to trace these men as far as Brazil, and it is said that they sailed the entire length of the North American coast, and finally established a settlement in the province of Bahia, and that these important explorations were known in Europe. A sea captain of Dieppe is said to have reached the South American coasts many years before the first voyage of Columbus. However this may be it was the achievement of the immortal Genoese to fix the attention of the Old World upon the New.

It has been claimed, to be sure, that the achievement of the great navigator was nothing more than an official taking possession of that part of the world and the credit of its discovery has been denied him. On the authority of a legend four hundred years old the critics have proved to their own satisfaction that he was not the first to tread the soil of America. But the glory of Columbus shines brightest in the execution of his project. That is indubitably his own and no rival can make any pretensions to it.

He appeared in an age when enterprises to distant countries were the ruling passion, when the ambition of making discoveries incited to the perfecting of maritime science and trained new navigators, when the discovery of a sea route to India was a preoccupation in Genoa and Venice, in Spain and Portugal, in France and England.

The humble sailor, unknown, poor, and without influence, was seeking, as did so many others, a new road to Asia. The writings of the ancients, his comparison of these with the works of Marco Polo, scientific computations corroborated by traditions that he is said to have collected in a voyage to Iceland, led him to believe that by sailing westward he could reach the east coast of Asia. He did not suspect that America would bar his passage.

His long and heavy misfortunes are well known. This alien, dying of hunger and covered with dust, who stops on his way to Palos at the door of a monastery to beg a bit of bread and some water for his child, is the man destined to make for Spain an empire on which the sun was never to set. He reached Portugal, but was treated as a visionary by John II., and went to try his fortune in Spain where new trials awaited him. Struggling with misery and repulsed by almost everyone, he had to contend against incredulity, to put up with mockery, and to argue his case before an ecclesiastical council which answered his scientific reasoning with Biblical texts. He would have resumed his wanderings, staff in hand, had not love detained him. A lady of Cordova, Beatrix Enriquez, loved the great man in his poverty, shared his obscurity, and bore him a son, Fernando. For a space of eight years he contended against the scruples of bigotry which interposed themselves between him and the sovereigns. At last the queen's confessor pronounced judgment for the theologians that his project was an empty dream. Broken-hearted, Columbus set out for France, at the call of Charles VIII., when Isabella, giving way to the entreaties of Luiz de Santangel and of the Franciscan Juan Perez, two friends of Columbus, decided to recall him. Just at this time his brother, Bartholomew, whom, in despair of success in Spain, he had sent to seek aid of Henry VII., returned from England with a favorable answer. So near was America to falling to the lot of England or France!

Columbus appeared at Salamanca before an ecclesiastical council convened to pass upon his project and was attacked by texts drawn from Genesis, the Psalms, and the prophets; scientific arguments and the enterprise of genius were negatived by quotations from St. Chrysostom, St. Augustine, St. Jerome, and the other fathers who had stoutly denied the sphericity of the earth.

The Spanish queen secured for him a handful of adventurers; the city of Palos was ordered to furnish two caravels, a sort of light vessel without decks. Columbus and his friends equipped at their own expense a third, and soon all was in readiness for departure. He was to be viceroy of all the lands he might conquer, with the right to appoint governors thereof; also he obtained office of high admiral for himself, his descendants, and successors in perpetuity; and finally, a fifth of all the profits.

The little fleet sailed from Palos in the early morning hours of Friday, August 3, 1492, and three days after setting sail arrived at the Canaries, where it was obliged to remain a month to repair the damage that the ships had sustained. On September 6 Columbus again set sail from the port of Gomera, to escape three Portuguese ships which were cruising in those parts for the purpose, it is said, of seizing the great navigator.

The incidents of this voyage, the numerous dangers that were run, among which not the least were the ignorance and cowardice of the crews, give an extraordinary grandeur to the figure of Columbus. And we can understand how those of a mystical turn of mind were led to believe in him as a supernatural being. The manifold dangers were increased by the spirit of mutiny among the sailors. These poor men thought themselves lost in a boundless sea and the unknown filled them with terror. They would fain abandon the attempt to penetrate further the mysterious void and longed to return. Columbus consoled them, reanimating their courage, describing to them in the most brilliant colors the rich lands they were going to conquer.

By the first of October they were 766 leagues from the Canaries and their goal, the coasts of India, was not yet in sight. Despair took possession of the admiral's companions. The equatorial calms filled them with consternation, but the faith of Columbus was unshaken. At last, about ten o'clock on the night of October 11, when the gloomy and angry crews were muttering threats of casting him into the sea for a madman who would lead them to certain death, Columbus, as he anxiously scanned the empty darkness, thought he saw a light in the distance. That solitary light from the fire of some savage was the lowly pharos which announced the presence of a new world!

At two o'clock on the morning of the 12th Rodrigo de Triana, a seaman of the *Pinta,* which sailed ahead of the little fleet, at last saw land. A cannon shot, the agreed signal, resounded over the ocean and made the admiral tremble. They furled the sails and lay to to await the dawn. Daybreak disclosed in the midst of the sea an island resplendent with verdure. Men and women entirely naked, coming from the woods and scattering about on the shore, expressed by their gestures, fear and wonder at the sight of the ships brought to their shores by the waves during the night. Boats, manned by armed sailors, advanced toward them with flags displayed, strains of instrumental music, and the discharge of fire-arms. Columbus was the first to set foot upon the shore. Be-decked with all the insignia of his rank as admiral and viceroy and displaying his rich scarlet cloak he advanced, holding the royal standard in one hand and his sword in the other, knelt down and kissed the earth. The island was called Guanahani, but he named it San Salvador and took possession in the name of the Crown of Castile.

It was one of the Lucaya or Bahama group which extends as far as the coast of Florida and is situated more than a thousand leagues west of Gomera, whence the little squadron had sailed. Columbus, believing it to be an outpost of the Indies, which was always his goal, called the people Indians and this erroneous name has perpetuated the memory of his error. This also is the derivation of the name West Indies, which was for a long time used for America. These Indians had no weapons save lances tipped with bone or flint, and were ignorant of the use of clothing, but many wore little pieces of gold for ornaments in the ears and nostrils. When asked by signs where the precious metal came from they pointed to the south. The Spaniards reëmbarked confident of finding in that direction the fabulous countries of Cathay and Cipango, where the royal palaces were floored with sheets of gold. They began to cross the dangerous reefs (" keys "), which have given the Bahama group its name of Lucayan, and wandered among the channels which separate innumerable islands varying in size, but all alike in luxuriant vegetation.

They landed on three of them, to which Columbus gave the names of Santa Maria de la Concepcion, Fernando, and Isabel, never suspecting the existence of the great new continent of which they were the splendid outposts in the sea. Here also the islanders indicated that they got their gold from the south. Going on again in this direction he reached the Cuban coast, after three days' sailing. " It is the most beautiful island," he wrote in his notes, " that human eyes have ever seen, in which I should wish to live forever and in which I cannot conceive there is either pain or death." The land was cultivated in many parts, and the Spaniards thought that beyond the distant mountains which they saw would be found civilization, gold mines and the fabulous wonders of Asia. These thoughts inflamed their imaginations and excited the cupidity of all.

Alonso Pinzon, the captain of the *Pinta,* which was the best sailer in the squadron, left it, with the intention of being the first to reach the island of Hayti, where, according to the report of the natives of Cuba, the precious metal abounded. Columbus ignored the act as if it had been unintentional, and making sail toward the southeast arrived on December 6 at Hayti, to which he gave the name of Hispaniola, or Spanish Island. He missed the continent. The constant pressure to find the means of satisfying the greed of his companions and to fulfill the hopes of those who had assisted him induced him to put about when, had he held on his course, he would surely have reached the mainland. " The American archipelago," says Lamartine, " in baffling him and leading him astray from island to island, seemed to turn him aside wantonly from the goal which, unconsciously, he had almost reached. The phantom of Asia which had brought him to the American coast now stood between him and America to cheat him with a dream in lieu of the great reality." The natives of Hayti had much gold, which they received from their neighbors, and which they gave to the Spaniards in exchange for glass beads, pins and other objects of no value. This only inflamed the avarice of the Spaniards, who wished to know where the mines were situated. The natives pointed out to them a mountainous country to the eastward. Columbus skirted the coast and was about to land at the point indicated, when the *Santa Maria* struck a reef and sprung a leak. The Spaniards, with the help of the natives, succeeded in saving the cargo.

In his letters, Columbus is evidently affected by the goodness and generosity of these people, whose cacique, the first friend of the Europeans, was soon to become their first victim. " There is nowhere in the world," he wrote, " a better people or a better country.

They love their neighbors as themselves; their speech is soft and kindly and their lips wear always a smile of gentleness. They are naked to be sure, but sufficiently clothed with modesty and frankness." Columbus believed that he had at last found the source of the fabulous riches described by the travelers in Asia. He wished to return without delay to Spain to announce his success, and he feared that the traitor Pinzon had sailed for Europe to outstrip him and claim the glory of the expedition. He thought then of leaving part of his people in Hayti. Those who would volunteer to await his return were to learn the language of the natives, study their customs, explore the country and endeavor to discover the mines and serve as a base for a colony, whose existence was to be assured by his prompt return. Thirty-eight men, tempted by the wealth in which the island seemed to abound, voluntarily offered to remain in Hispaniola, at the head of whom he placed Diego de Aranda. For their better security a little fort was built, a deep ditch dug, ramparts erected furnished with palisades and flanked by cannon saved from the wreck of the *Santa Maria*. The work was finished in ten days, thanks to the zeal with which the poor islanders labored to raise this first monument of their slavery.

Columbus left on January 4, 1493, loaded with gifts from the cacique, and taking with him several Indians. Coasting along the island he met Pinzon, who had explored during the six weeks of his absence the north coast of Hayti. They put to sea together, and the voyage was favorable until February 14, when a violent tempest parted them again.

At last, on March 15, Columbus reëntered the port of Palos, whence he had sailed seven months and eleven days before. His journey to the royal court at Barcelona was a veritable triumph and he entered the town in great state.

"America," says Jean Reynaud, "saved Columbus, though he did not seek it. For, but for it, he would either have been lost in the vast extent of the ocean or forced to return in disgrace. Though thus fortunate for him, it is nevertheless the fact that the finding of the New World gave the lie to his system and cut short his bold project. He had overcome all obstacles to his exploration of India, but America was one which he had not foreseen and could never conquer. Here was a barrier stretched across the ocean pathway between the two extremes of the Old World upon which a ship must run aground. Here, we may say, begins the true life of Christopher

Columbus. Hitherto obscure, and rich only in the dreams of hope, it was suddenly filled with glory and magnificence, but also with reverses and misfortunes of every kind. The viceroy of the Indies, author of the most splendid achievement of modern times, founder of colonies and benefactor of Spain, deserves more pity than the humble traveler at the convent gate asking bread for his sick child." This story of the ingratitude of princes has been often told. We will here set down only so much as cannot be separated from our narrative.

On September 25 Columbus left the harbor of Cadiz for his second voyage. Three great ships and fourteen caravels made up the fleet which Spain now furnished him. He took with him

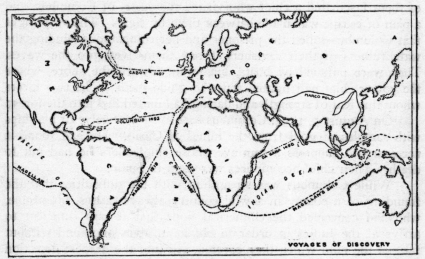

VOYAGES OF DISCOVERY

1500 persons, gentlemen, laborers, priests, adventurers attracted by the unknown and the marvelous, urged on by greed or religious zeal, by the spirit of trade or the love of glory. He discovered many of the Antilles on the way and gave them names of religious significance—Dominica, Mari-Galante, Guadalupe, Monserrat, Santa Maria la Redonda, Santa Maria la Antigoa, San Martin, Santa Cruz. These islands, which also bore the name Caribbean, were all inhabited by cannibals, who, in their raids, went as far as the Bahamas. After having discovered the Eleven Thousand Virgins and Porto Rico the fleet reached Hayti. The shore was deserted, the fort destroyed. The scattered bones of the Spaniards were whitening on the sand. The little garrison had abused the hospitality of the caciques to oppress the natives, seizing their gold, carrying off their daughters and their wives. The victims had attacked their oppressors, who were, moreover, divided among themselves, and numbers had overcome firearms. It was the first outbreak of hatred between the two races, one of which brought to the other the double gifts of slavery and extermination. Columbus departed from this blood-stained shore, and at some distance built Isabella, the first town built by the Spaniards in the New World, and the mother of so many other colonies. Later it received the name of San Domingo, after the father of Columbus. This was the scene of a romantic adventure. On board the ships were many young Indian girls who had been captured in the neighboring islands. One of them fascinated a chief who visited the vessel of Columbus, and a plan of escape was made between them by signs. The very night that Columbus sailed the prisoner and her companions, eluding the watchfulness of their ravishers, threw themselves into the waves. They were pursued by boats, but swam toward the shore, where the young chief had lighted a fire to guide them. The two lovers whom this feat of strength and daring had united fled into the forest.

On August 5, 1494, Columbus sent to Spain twelve of his ships with samples of gold from the mines of Cibao. He had found it necessary to suppress a mutiny, whose ringleaders he had put to death. Their chief accomplices were sent to Spain.

While Columbus was struggling with the difficulties that the founding of a colony in a wild country always causes, his people, who had conceived the chimerical hope that it was sufficient to arrive at the Indies in order to obtain in abundance and without fatigue the gold which they coveted, fell into the deepest dejection that very soon was turned into despair. Discontent became general, the spirit of insubordination spread, and a conspiracy was formed that might have been fatal to the admiral and the colony. Columbus discovered it, and repressed it with energy.

The discontented and envious, at the head of whom were Pedro Margarite and the monk, Boyle, returned to Spain on ships which they had seized in the harbor. Seconded by Fonseca, Bishop of Badajos, they accused Columbus of ambition and cruelty. By an ordinance of April 10, 1495, disregarding his contract with Columbus, the King authorized any subject to settle in Hispaniola and to undertake voyages of discovery and commerce in the New World.

During this time Columbus fortified Isabella, appointed a coun-

cil to carry on the government, explored the country, again put to
sea and discovered Jamaica, where, for the first time, he made use of
dogs against the natives, a cruel measure too often employed later;
visited the northern coast of Cuba, sailing among the numerous
islands, to which he gave the name " Queen's Gardens," in token of
the rich and spicy vegetation.   The Spaniards at Isabella had not
only broken over all discipline, but had exasperated the natives.   The
rashness and treachery of the young and hotheaded Ojeda drove
many of the chiefs to despair and to revolt.   Columbus, although
they had not been in the wrong, took severe measures against them.
After defeating them in battle he laid upon them a heavy tribute,
especially in gold.   Many prisoners were loaded upon four vessels
and shipped off to Spain like human cattle sacrificed to an infamous
traffic.   The war then degenerated into a sort of man hunt.   Dogs
were employed for this purpose in the woods, and they tracked,
mangled, and caught by the throat the wretched Indians, aiding the
tyrants greatly in their work of slaughter.

At the Spanish court the enemies of Columbus triumphed.
Juan Aguado, an officer of the king's household, was sent to examine into the condition of the colony, and Columbus judged it
necessary to return to Spain in order to justify himself in person.
He set out on March 10, 1496, after deputing his powers to his
brother Bartholomew, and arrived at Cadiz on June 11.   His presence excited the compassion of the queen.   He went to her at
Burgos in the dress of a Franciscan, his head bowed with affliction
and cares, and barefoot, as a suppliant of genius going to ask pardon
for his glory, as Lamartine puts it.   The queen took up his defense,
but two years were wasted in struggle against every kind of
intrigue, before Columbus could return to the work of discovery.

On May 30, 1498, Columbus set out from the port of
San Lucas de Barraneda with six ships on his third voyage, on
which he finally reached the continent.   Running south to the
equator, he then steered directly west in the hope of finding a mild
temperature.   He suffered severely from headache and made a vow
to give the name of the Trinity to the first land he should see.   The
vow had hardly been made when they sighted the shores of Trinidad
(July 31).   Coasting the island in search of a place to anchor, he
discovered to the south a low land that stretched farther than the
eye could see, and far along the coast the mouth of a great river,
whose impetuous flood penetrated for three leagues into the ocean

without mixing with its waters. He rightly conjectured that so large a river must traverse a vast continent. Nor was he deceived; the Orinoco with its fifty mouths, its numerous affluents and its course of 1500 miles, waters an immense country; its floods are terrible and in its overflowings it extends 60 miles from its banks. That low land, from the center of which he saw the river fall into the ocean, was the coast of Colombia, the continent of the New World. But he did not suspect that it was a new world. Always blinded by his dream of reaching the Indies, he believed it to be the prolongation of the east coast of Asia; and the great quantity of gold and the large number of most beautiful pearls that he obtained from the natives of the coast at the different points where he landed, the beauty and fertility of the country, the riches of its vegetable productions, the variety of birds, all confirmed him in this opinion. He believed that he had discovered the Terrestrial Paradise, and in his account of the voyage there is a long digression attempting to demonstrate that the Orinoco is the famous river that rises in Eden. Full of enthusiasm, he explored the coast for some twenty leagues to the westward, as far as the place where the city of Caracas was afterwards built. He left this enchanted country with regret, not without a promise to return and complete his important discoveries when he should have regained his health and revictualed his squadron. On his voyage to Hispaniola, where he arrived on August 30, he discovered the islands of Cubagua and Margarita, which afterwards became celebrated for their pearl fisheries.

He found the colony torn by anarchy. The colonists were divided into many factions, which frequently came to blows. Ojeda had chartered some ships on his own account in Spain, had gone on a cruise to make a descent on the southern coast of the island, and was in league with Roldan. Then Roldan had betrayed Ojeda, and once more submitted to the authority of Bartholomew Columbus, whose strong hand could hardly hold the mastery of the situation. The island had become a prison and a slaughter house for the wretched natives, who were treated with treachery, cruelty and frightful oppression, in which religious fanaticism sometimes surpassed greed. While Columbus was endeavoring to pacify the colony, Ferdinand and Isabella, informed of the miseries of the island, imputed them to him, and sent out Francisco de Bobadilla, who had Columbus arrested, confiscated his property, and sent him in chains to Spain.

When the sovereigns knew that the admiral was brought back a prisoner they were ashamed and public opinion was aroused at seeing the man to whom Spain owed a whole world arrive loaded with chains. Bobadilla, recalled in disgrace, was lost at sea after leaving Hayti, but Columbus did not recover his viceroyalty and could hardly get permission to make a fourth voyage.

He sailed in 1502, and added to his numerous discoveries Martinique, the harbor of Porto Bello and the coasts of Costa Rica and Honduras. Repelled from Hayti by his old companions, he had to contend with famine and sickness, and was saved only by the provisions that he obtained from the natives by predicting an eclipse. He returned to Spain in 1504, discouraged, broken by hardships and by age. Isabella had passed away. Ferdinand left him to die in Seville in poverty and disappointment. But he was at least spared the bitterness of living long enough to hear the new world which he had discovered called by the name of Amerigo Vespucci, a pilot who had accompanied him on one of his voyages.

It has been asked, and justly, whether Columbus did not allow himself to be misled too easily by the success of his first voyage, and whether he did all that the service of geographical science required in exploring these new lands. "Perhaps," writes Reynaud, "we shall have to accuse him for his constant eagerness to obtain gold, his lack of political ability, his injustice toward the unoffending natives of America, his lack of humanity and of genius if we must speak plainly. We must clearly distinguish his two functions, the bold explorer of the Atlantic and the founder of the first Spanish colonies in the New World. Columbus, despite the most hallowed principles of the law of nations, enslaved the unfortunate islanders who had welcomed him with open arms and thereby gave the signal for that work of crime and destruction which for so long a time stained the soil of America with blood and dishonored the annals of Christianity. He paid the inevitable price for glory to the spirit of his age by sharing the atrocious political morality with which that age was stained. The Spaniards in pillaging, enslaving and massacring at will in America were only exercising their rights under the law of nations sanctioned by the church, and enjoying the fruits of the famous bull of Pope Alexander Borgia, which gave over to Portugal the pagans of Africa and the East, and to Spain those of the West."

Chapter II

CONQUEST. 1493-1713

THE Bull granted in 1493 by Alexander VI. was explicit. " Of his own mere motion and certain knowledge and by virtue of his full apostolic powers," the Pope conceded to the Catholic sovereigns, Ferdinand and Isabella, the right of conquest, annexation and government of the western Indies. " Whoever opposes it ought to be considered as having incurred the anger of Almighty God and of the blessed apostles Peter and Paul." Neither Spaniards nor Portuguese, to be sure, gave to this famous demarcation the respect which was its due. Carried away by the lust of conquest, they broke through the barrier more than once. As for the former, strong in the plenary powers of the vicar of God on earth, they thought they had not only a right of conquest, but a right of property to dispose of America at their will. Hardly had it been discovered when they drenched it in blood. The grasping Spaniards fell upon their prey with savage eagerness. Two abominable acts mark that merciless work, that twofold crime which is known as the conquest and colonization of the New World: the destruction of the aboriginal race and the establishment of negro slavery upon that generous soil, so well fitted for liberty.

It has already been noted that the Spanish court, in violation of its contract with Columbus, had in 1495 granted to all its subjects the liberty to fit out vessels and go to seek fortunes in the land of gold. It calculated upon increasing its possessions without loosening its purse strings, and even on enriching itself at the same time by the stipulated share in the profits of the expeditions which was expressly reserved for the government. The subjects of Ferdinand and Isabella let several years elapse before exercising these powers. It was only in the last year of the century that they changed their minds. They were seized by the spirit of emulation when the Portuguese Vasco da Gama, by doubling the Cape of Good Hope, opened a sea route to the East Indies. All now longed eagerly to throw themselves into that pursuit which they had before called visionary. In the meantime England had made an attempt on the lines laid down by Columbus. In 1497 John and Sebastian Cabot, father and son, first saw the northern continent. They had been sent by Henry VII. with a small squadron and had discovered Newfoundland, skirted Labrador and in returning coasted as far south as Florida.

Alonso de Ojeda, who accompanied Columbus in his second voyage, led the way. He was bold to the point of rashness and had been page to Isabella. One day when the queen had climbed to the top of the Giralda tower in Seville to wonder at its great height, he threw himself upon a narrow beam which projected from the battlements, and whirling there upon one foot performed feats of strength and skill to please his sovereign. Assisted by wealthy speculators, he now equipped four ships and set sail in May, 1499, accompanied by Amerigo Vespucci. His landfall was at Maracapana, two hundred leagues east of the Orinoco, and coasting that part of the southern continent which was at first called Terra Firma, he reached Cape Vela. A few months before Alonso Niño and Cristobal Guerra had touched at the same place on a purely mercantile expedition. The brothers Pinzon, who had followed Columbus in his first voyage, left Palos in December, 1499, with four caravels. They made the land at Cape St. Augustine, the extremity of Brazil, discovered the mouth of the Amazon, and explored six hundred leagues of coast before reaching Hayti. A few months later Diego Lepe and Alonso Velez de Mendoza followed them, doubled Cape St. Augustine, saw that the coast extended much farther toward the southwest, and made the first maps of those regions. The Portuguese Pedro Alvarez Cabral, borne far to the west by the ocean currents on his voyage to India, came upon the Brazilian coast in the same year; anchoring on April 24 in a harbor called by the Portuguese Seguro, he set up on May 1, after the mass had been celebrated, a cross of wood bearing the arms of Portugal as a symbol of its sovereignty over the country, which was at first called Vera Cruz, and some years later Brazil. To Cabral belongs the honor of the discovery of Brazil, for his predecessors had sown no seed of colonization and had excited the enmity of the natives they fell in with. No one contested the honor, and Europe conceded the rights of the Portuguese crown over the new country. It is evident that even if Columbus had not succeeded, Cabral, thanks to the ocean currents which carried him out of his course, would have discovered America. Such is the basis of fame. Fame! Columbus himself was the most notable victim of her caprice, for did she not give the name of one of his subordinates to America? Amerigo Vespucci, who wrote the first narrative of travel in the newly discovered regions, was in truth a man of worth, a good seaman and a distinguished geographer, but in this matter fortune served him far too well.

Rodrigo de Bastidas and Juan de la Cosa, completing the investigations of Ojeda, doubled Cape Vela in 1501 and explored 100 leagues of unknown coasts, which, some years later, were to acquire sufficient notoriety from the misfortunes that Nicuesa and Ojeda himself suffered on them, and where, shortly after, Santa Marta, Cartagena and Nombre de Dios, on the Gulf of Darien, were founded. Portuguese enterprise continued active. As early as 1500 Gaspar Cortereal was dispatched to Greenland, Labrador and Newfoundland. But in a second voyage he was lost with his brother, who accompanied him.

Nicolas Ovando, who had succeeded Bobadilla in the government of San Domingo, subjected, in 1505, almost the whole island of Hayti. The barbarous measures which he employed against the natives made him infamous in history; he massacred the wretched people without mercy, insomuch that not enough were left to work the mines, whereupon the Bahamas were depopulated by his slave-catchers.

The coasts of Terra Firma, Honduras and the eastern part of Yucatan were traced by Juan Diaz de Solis and Yañez Pinzon in the following year. In 1512 Juan Ponce de Leon occupied Porto Rico, which had been granted to him as governor, and founded a colony in Florida. Yet a quarter of a century elapsed before the Spaniards actually took possession of Florida and of a great part of Louisiana.

The following year Vasco Nuñez de Balboa, an adventurer who had become the head of a little colony at Darien, climbed the mountains which stretch along the Isthmus of Panama searching for lands rich in gold and discovered the Pacific Ocean. Advancing fully armed into the waves to the depth of his knees, he had drawn his sword and taken possession of the South Sea in the name of his sovereign. On this expedition he had heard of Peru, a land of promise which kindled the imagination of all who heard of it, and he gave an enthusiastic account of it. An expedition was planned

CONQUEST

and he had by intrigue secured the command of it, when he was accused of imaginary crimes and sent to the scaffold by Pedro Arias de Avila, whom Ferdinand had made governor in his stead, and who coveted the advantages arising from Balboa's discoveries. This Avila found the country afterward known successively as Terra Firma of the West, New Granada and the United States of Colombia. He was followed by a crowd of adventurers, none of whom penetrated far into the country. About the same time Diaz de Solis explored the bay of Rio de Janeiro, was the first man to enter the Rio de la Plata, and on the shore at Maldorado fell into the hands of Indian cannibals, who devoured him and his companions (1516). Four years later Magellan discovered Patagonia and entered the Pacific through the strait which bears his name.

Up to this time the explorers only ventured along the coasts and kept within reach of their ships. From this moment a new race, that of the conquerors, throws itself upon its helpless prey. These bold robbers, employing sometimes force of arms, sometimes cunning and treachery, go forth annihilating the warlike nations and pillaging and enslaving the pacific tribes. Hernando Cortez, the most celebrated among them, a pupil in the school of Ovando, the terrible governor of San Domingo, had aided Velazquez to subdue the Island of Cuba. Commissioned to conquer Mexico, which Grijalva had just discovered and had not dared to attack, he set out in 1518 with between 600 and 700 Spaniards, eighteen horses and fourteen cannon of small caliber. In less than three years he subjugated the powerful empire of Montezuma. He was rewarded by Charles V., as Columbus had been by Ferdinand, and the civil administration of the conquered country was taken from him. When he returned to Spain he had added to his conquest the discovery of California and of the Vermilion Sea. He died there of disappointment. One day when he thrust himself through a crowd to get near the person of the king the latter asked who he was. " I am he," Cortez haughtily replied, " who has given you more provinces than you inherited cities from your ancestors."

The two great peninsulas which form the American continents were now known. The task of seizing their unequaled riches alone remained. From year to year all the European nations joined more and more in the plunder and monopolization of this vast territory, almost a third of the habitable globe. But this study is limited as its title indicates; of the conquests of the Old over the New World, we are concerned only with those which relate to South America properly so called. Its three immense plains, which are watered by the Amazon, the La Plata and the Orinoco, have been the theater of renowned deeds worthy of an epic.

Mexico and Peru were the jewels of North and South America, respectively, but there was another people whose civilization was comparable with that of the early Egyptians, and who held a territory of more than six hundred square leagues, with its political center on the plateau of Bogota. We refer to the Chibchas, whose destruction was so sudden and complete that after a few years it was hardly possible to trace even the traditions of the country. Their very name almost disappeared, for the conquerors, perpetuating an error of their earliest days in the land, called them Muyscas or Mozcas, a word which in the Chibcha tongue means individuals or persons. It was on these three powerful nations, rivals in civilization, that the first invaders threw themselves, passing by the swampy plains and impenetrable forests, which did not seem to hide the gold which they greedily sought.

While Hernando Cortez was triumphing in Mexico, Francisco Pizarro was preparing for the conquest of Peru with Diego de Almagro and Fernando de Luque. Pizarro had been a swineherd in his youth and could not read or write. Almagro was a foundling, who had taken the name of his native place, and Luque, a Dominican monk, was a schoolmaster at Panama. These three bold associates had lost no time in coming to America to seek their fortunes, and had combined their small means and vast ambition. Firmly united in adversity, good fortune was to divide them later, but while waiting for it they loved each other like brothers. From 1524 to 1527 they made expeditions into the hitherto unexplored regions to the south of Panama. After several unsuccessful attempts they got help from the Spanish government, Pizarro having gone to court to ask it. Three ships were fitted out. The invasion was preceded by religious ceremonies; they sought the blessing of heaven upon the work of extermination to which they were about to set their hands. The flags were blessed; officers and soldiers to the number of one hundred and eighty, one hundred and forty-four foot and thirty-six horse, attended mass and received the communion. Four priests, Fernando de Luque, Vincent de Valverde, Pedraza and Otiaz, accompanied the " army " by the express command of Charles V. Such was the detachment which set out to overthrow an empire. That empire measured 2500 miles in length and from 375 to 500 in breadth, being bounded on the north by the Blue River, whose bed is almost under the equator, and on the south by the river Maouly. In this territory are the present day republics of Ecuador, Peru, Bolivia, and Chili. Cuzco, the center of the territory, was its capital. Other important places were the tablelands of Quito and Lake Titicaca.

The expedition set sail in February, 1531, and occupied the island of Puna, whence the invasion of Peru itself could easily be accomplished. At the moment the country was given over to civil war. Two brothers, Huascar and Atahualpa, sons of the last inca, were fighting for the succession and for this reason alone did nothing to stop the strangers.

Fame was not slow to exaggerate the power of the Spaniards. The Peruvians were astonished by the arrival of these bearded men, armed with the thunder and riding upon beasts of terrible aspect. They took the newcomers for beings of a superior kind. On the march Pizarro received the envoys of Huascar, who asked his protection. Leaving behind him a little garrison to secure his retreat in case of need, Pizarro continued his march with sixty-two horsemen and one hundred and two foot. In the meantime Huascar had been defeated by Atahualpa, who sent two envoys with rich gifts to meet the Spaniards. Atahualpa, moreover, consented to meet Pizarro at Caxamarca, where he was encamped. On the day set for the interview (November 16, 1532) the inca unsuspectingly approached the Spanish quarters borne on a litter of massive gold, when the priest, Valverde, advancing with a crucifix in his hand to meet him, declared that as the Pope had granted Peru to Spain, he ought to acknowledge himself the vassal of Charles V. and become a Christian. Atahualpa seemed not to understand this harangue. Pizarro, who had drawn up his soldiers in order of battle along a wall, ordered a volley to be fired at the Peruvians, and taking advantage of the wild panic into which they were thrown by the noise of the firearms, rushed upon them, slew the bodyguard of the emperor and seized his person. This base crime which history ought to brand with infamy had its sequel some time later. Under the false pretext that Atahualpa had given orders for exterminating the Spaniards he was condemned to death. He demanded to be taken to Spain and presented to the monarch whose suzerainty he had acknowledged. They promised him life and liberty if he would receive baptism and fill with gold as high as a man could reach a room twenty-two feet long and sixteen wide. When he had fulfilled these conditions he was bound to a stake and strangled. This act of brigandage made the conquest of the country certain by increasing the prevailing confusion and anarchy.

Pizarro was made captain-general of Peru; Luque, Bishop of Cuzco, and Almagro, governor-general or *adelantado* of the 200 leagues of country from the boundary of Peru southward. Thus was Peru conquered. In less than a year all the region between Quito and Cuzco was subdued. On November 13, 1532, the Spaniards entered Cuzco, and it is still a day of mourning for the natives. Every year on that day one who crosses the cathedral square may see superstitious Indians kneeling in the dust, listening with ear pressed upon the ground for the murmuring of the traditional lake of destiny under the cathedral. Among the treasures without number which the conquerors expected to seize in the pillage of the capital was the golden chain which Huana-Capac had caused to be made on the occasion of the first cutting of the hair of her son Huascar. It was of the same size as an ordinary iron chain, weighed many thousands of pounds, was half a mile long and was used to enclose the great square at Cuzco at the time of the great equinoctial festivals of Raymi and Cittua. To save this gigantic piece of jewelry the people confided it to the deep waters of the Lake of Urcos. Forty Spaniards and two hundred Indians worked for three months searching the waters of the lake and finally draining it, but the golden chain of Cuzco could not be found.

The Peruvians, in fact, exasperated by the barbarous treatment of their conquerors, and feeling themselves powerless to recover their liberty, wished to keep their immense treasures from the rapacity of their executioners, and concealed them so successfully that they never could be found. The search for them continued and still continues, but time has kept the secret inviolate. In the outskirts of the little village of Endajes there is a deep and narrow conduit where treasures without number were buried. Some years ago a Spaniard named Vidagura wished, as so many others had. to explore the subterranean passage. He followed it to the end, which was very narrow. As he was sounding the wall a stone fell from the roof and closed the opening. The poor man was caught like a mouse in a trap.

But it was not their gold alone that the Peruvians snatched

from the soldiers of Pizarro. With the rage produced by despair, in order that their implacable enemies should not enjoy the sumptuous palaces, and the magnificent temples erected by their ancestors, they destroyed the grand monuments of their ancient civilization, a work in which they were stupidly seconded by the Spaniards. Two fine roads ran from Cuzco to Quito, a distance of not less than 1650 miles. They were paved, enclosed by high walls, crossing the deep valleys among the mountains by causeways and not diverging even to avoid the lakes. They disappeared with the rest.

Quito, which the Spaniards took in 1533, was given over to the torch and the sword, and the entire male population was exterminated, insomuch that one of the brutal lieutenants of Pizarro, who wished to make an expedition into the provinces of the interior, could get only women and children in answer to his summons for men to carry the baggage and cut a road through the forest. Suspecting a trick, he became enraged and had the whole herd of human beings slaughtered then and there. Possibly this was Benalcazar, to whom Pizarro delegated the government of Quito.

This Benalcazar occupied Pasto and Popayan, where he founded Guayaquil, penetrated the valley of Cauca and that of Bogota, and pushed on as far as the Caribbean Sea, having thus traversed the whole of New Granada. He arrived just when the country of Cundinamarca was being subdued by Quesada.

Gonzales Ximenes de Quesada had succeeded where Alfinger and his companions, who had set out from Coro in Venezuela seven years before, had failed. Alfinger had been unable to cross the Cordillera, and after suffering all the horrors of illness, cold and famine, was retracing his steps, having given to his companions for food the last Indians of his train, when he was slain in a fight. Quesada left Santa Marta in 1537, after organizing two expeditions to work in concert. One was to ascend the Magdalena, the other to follow the overland road. Forced to send his boats back to the coast with the sick, he had entered the Cordillera and had pushed steadily toward the south, crossing the present states of Santander and Boyaca. The chroniclers give full details of the sufferings and hardships endured by the Spaniards in this campaign. Forced to live for several weeks on herbs, plants and insects, they at last ate the leather of their belts and armor.

To return to Peru, while Pizarro was founding Lima, Almagro pushed into Chili, which had fallen to him in the division of the

spoils. He set out with five hundred and seventy Spaniards and
five hundred Indians, furnished by Manco-Capac, second of the
name and brother and successor of Atahualpa. The inca had ordered his brother, Paiello Topa, and the high priest, Véléhoma,
to go in advance and prepare the way. They handed over to him
en route 90,000 pesos of fine gold (about $450,000), which the
tributary nations of Chili had sent to the inca. Some days thereafter the high priest and one of the interpreters, weary of insults,
took flight. The latter was recaptured and quartered.

Almagro took the shortest route, by the Snow Mountains.
His lieutenant, Saavedra, preceded him, with orders to halt when
he had marched one hundred and fifty leagues from Cuzco. The
place where Saavedra established himself is now the village of
Paria in Bolivia. Many of the soldiers of the adelantado died of
hunger or exhaustion; others were slain by the arrows of the natives
who constantly harassed the expedition. A hundred and fifty
Spaniards and ten thousand Peruvians had succumbed or disappeared before the plains of Copiapo were reached. Almagro took
possession of the territory by issuing the formal proclamation, which
the Pope had caused to be drawn up by a special commission of
theologians and jurists, and which Ojeda had been the first to
employ in 1509. Armed from head to foot and bearing the insignia
of his rank, surrounded by his officers and some chiefs who had
come to do homage, thanks to the interposition of the Peruvian
ruler, he drew his sword, seized a handful of the soil and addressed
the natives as follows:

" I, Diego de Almagro, the servant of the most high and mighty
emperor, Charles the Fifth, king of Castile and Leon, his ambassador and captain, notify and give you to know, as best I am able,
that God our Lord, one and everlasting, created the heaven and
the earth, and one man and one woman of whom you and we and
all men in the world were and are descendants born, and all those
who shall come after us."

The adelantado explained that the successive generations of
men for more than five thousand years had been scattered in the
different parts of the world and were divided into many kingdoms,
since a single country could not contain them nor supply them with
the means of subsistence, and that God had given all these peoples
in charge to a single man named Peter, whom he had made lord
and chief of the human race to the end that all men wherever born,

or in whatsoever religion instructed, should obey him. This man and his successors were called popes, that is to say, admirable, great, father, protector. One of these pontiffs, as lord of the world, had granted Terra Firma and the Islands of the Ocean to the kings of Castile and their successors. Therefore he, Diego de Almagro, admonished his hearers to acknowledge the sovereignty and over-lordship of his sovereign and to allow the missionaries to preach the faith to them.

"His majesty, and I in his name," continued the adelantado, "will receive you in all love and charity and will leave you your wives and children free, without servitude, to enjoy all your rights of property; and further than this, his majesty will give you many privileges and exemptions and will show you many favors. If you refuse or willfully delay to obey my admonition, then, with God's help, I will invade your country by force and will wage war against you most cruelly, and will subject you to the yoke and obe-dience of the church and of the king, and will take your wives and children and make them slaves, and as such sell and dispose of them according to the good pleasure of his majesty. His majesty and I will take from you your goods and will do you all the harm and damage that I can, as rebels, who refuse to submit to their lawful sovereign. And I protest and warn you, all the blood that shall be shed and all the miseries that shall follow your disobedience must be imputed to yourselves alone, and not to his majesty, nor to me, nor to those who serve under my orders. Therefore, hav-ing made you this declaration and demand, I require that the notary here present give me a certificate thereof in the prescribed form."

The native warriors who witnessed this ceremony probably un-derstood very little of Almagro's harangue. In their ignorance they respectfully attended upon him as a messenger from their god, Viza-cocha. But when three plundering soldiers were killed in a brawl and Almagro seized the chief of the tribe, his brother, and twenty-seven warriors, and burned them all alive in revenge, the Indians swore eternal hatred to the invaders. Almagro consolidated his forces and attempted to penetrate the territory of the Promaucans, but suffered a serious reverse on the banks of the Rio Claro. In this critical situation he learned that a revolt had broken out in Peru and that Pizarro, shut up in Lima, was cut off from a party of his companions, who were themselves besieged near Cuzco by large forces. Almagro concluded that the time was ripe for revenge upon his old comrade and hated rival, so he broke camp and retraced his steps.

What had happened in Peru since the departure of Almagro for Chili? Manco-Capac, who reigned in Cuzco, although only in name and under the guardianship of Pizarro and the vigilance of his three brothers, was able, from his palace, which had become his prison, to correspond with some friends who remained loyal to the national cause. A plot was laid while Pizarro was busy founding Lima and dreaming of declaring his independence of Spain and of proclaiming himself child of the sun and successor of the incas. A festival was to be held in the neighborhood of the future capital and the sovereign of Cuzco was invited to attend it. The occasion seemed favorable for the execution of the plan which had long been matured. Hardly had Manco-Capac left the walls of Cuzco when the war cry resounded throughout the empire and two hundred thousand warriors flocked to the standard of the inca. The brothers of Pizarro, attacked in Cuzco, defended themselves with desperate valor, while he was himself savagely and repeatedly attacked in Lima.

Such was the situation of Peru when Almagro arrived. He brought increase of discord. The time had come when the conquerors were to fight among themselves for the privilege of excelling in cruelty and infamy. After a difficult march across the snow-covered Andes through terrible solitudes and storms more terrible, he arrived before Cuzco with the wreck of his army and without either horses or baggage. A considerable number of his partisans flocked to his standard. At their head he fell upon Manco-Capac and routed him; and then attacked the Pizarro brothers in Cuzco. The brothers had now held the place against the besiegers for nine months, and one of them, Juan, had died. Almagro forced them to surrender, but was soon afterward himself beaten and captured by Pizarro, who had him hanged in prison and afterward decapitated in the public square. Almagro was seventy-five years old at his death. Thus perished, in April, 1538, this ferocious, ambitious, and greedy adventurer, a man who possessed all the qualities of a brigand and among them only one that was praiseworthy, courage. He appointed a son, whom he had had by an Indian woman of Panama, as his successor in his government.

Pizarro remained sole master of Peru and, to find employment for his officers, sent them out in different directions. Knowledge of the interior of the continent was rapidly extended to the region east of the Andes; upper Peru was explored as far as the Grand Chaco, and new towns were added to those already existing in that region. To the north Gonzalo Pizarro, leaving Quito in search of the province of Canela, reached the banks of the Napo and descended it for the greater part of its course. Orellana, a member of the expedition, abandoned it and continuing the descent reached the Amazon, down which he voyaged in a small brigantine until he reached its mouth. Some years before, in 1531, the great rival of the Amazon, the Orinoco, had been explored by Diego de Ordaz, who had ascended it as far as the mouth of the Meta. This Ordaz had been one of the conquerors of Mexico and boasted that he had gathered sulphur for that enterprise in the crater of Popocatapetl, in commemoration of which exploit he was authorized to add to his coat of arms a flaming volcano. He had sought and obtained from Charles V. the government of all the country he could conquer between Brazil and the coast of Venezuela. He set out. Some Indians showed him emeralds as big as one's fist and pointed out the mountain which produced them. Shipwreck destroyed all his hopes, but the exaggerated descriptions of the riches he had seen helped to spread the belief in El Dorado.

The La Plata was not overlooked. In 1535 Pedro de Mendoza, a rich gentleman of Cadiz, who had offered to Charles V. to undertake at his own expense the discovery and conquest of Paraguay, had founded Buenos Ayres. At about the same time Agolas and Irala ascended the Parana, entered the Paraguay River, traced it up to the Lake Xarayes, on the banks of which he founded the city of Asuncion. The Tucuman, the Cuyo, the northern part of the pampas, were explored, and colonies founded there. In the general movement of that extraordinary epoch no part of America was overlooked. In Brazil the Portuguese laid the foundations of their power and covered the coast of the mainland with towns.

It was at this time that Pizarro thought to finish on his own account the conquest of Chili, which had been commenced by Almagro. He sent thither Pedro de Valdivia, who had helped to defeat the adelantado, at the head of two hundred Spaniards and a great number of Peruvians. His purpose was to plant a permanent colony and he took with him a certain number of women and priests. He fought his way to the banks of the Mapocho, where, in 1541, he founded Santiago.

During this time Pizarro had sent to Spain part of the treasures wrested from the vanquished, thus securing for himself the favor of Charles V., who enlarged the privileges which had been conferred on him, made him a knight of the Order of Santiago, and gave him the title of Marquis of Las Charcas. He was charged with the duty of establishing a regular government in the vast possessions he had conquered, and, although an unlettered soldier, he was able to replace by his keenness and good judgment the advantages of education. He divided Peru into districts, established magistrates in each, organized the administration, regulated the collection of taxes, the working of the mines, and the mode of treating the Indians. But he abused his victory, not hesitating about means so long as they tended to secure his authority. Surrounded by his mistresses, among whom was a sister of Atahualpa, he gave himself up in his palace at Lima to all kinds of excess, especially to gambling, which was a mania with him. In the midst of his orgies he issued the most tyrannical orders. His brothers, his friends, and his partisans had received, in the distribution of spoils, the richest districts, and all their inhabitants as slaves. They were like so many satraps asserting their absolute right to rob and oppress. The soldiers of Almagro, and those who were suspected of having favored his cause, were not only excluded from a share in the division of lands and offices, but were, besides, persecuted as suspected persons. They, therefore, swore to rid themselves of the despot and avenge their leader. On June 9, 1541, in broad day, some determined men set upon the conqueror in his palace, riddled him with sword thrusts and proclaimed the son of Almagro as governor general. The new master of Peru was defeated and slain in 1542 by Vaca de Castro, with whom he was fighting for power.

The reign of terror and absolutism, to which the unfortunate Indians were subjected, became doubly odious amid this intestine strife. Burning to enrich themselves quickly, and firmly persuaded that pillage was only a just reward for their labors and achievements the Spaniards heaped up ruins wherever they went, robbing their hapless victims, slaughtering them by thousands, reducing them to the most abject slavery, crushing them cruelly by forced labor, burdening them with endless tasks. Many of these unfortunate men, unwilling to give themselves up to utter ruin, marched with their caciques into the depths of the woods, and others, in their exasperation, gladly sacrificed their lives to avenge themselves. Thus died, assassinated in 1541 by the Indians of the province of Quispicanchi, Father Valverde, who in 1538 had succeeded Fernando Luque in the bishopric of Cuzco. The atrocities committed in the name of religion by Valverde had made that monster an object of terror.

Las Casas pleaded the cause of the oppressed at the Spanish court and Charles V. sent out as viceroy Nuñez Vela. Gonzalo Pizarro, who had returned to Peru after the death of his brother, marched against the viceroy, ejected him from Lima, pursued him beyond Quito, defeated and slew him under the walls of that city January 17, 1546. He afterward made his triumphal entry into Lima, and, refusing the crown which his soldiers offered him, contented himself with taking the title of captain general. Still later he marched against Diego Centena, who had put himself at the head of the royalist forces, and utterly defeated him at Guarina, October 16, 1547. Attacked in the following year by the president, La Gasca, who was sent from the mother country with unlimited powers, and deserted by his troops, he was beaten in his turn, condemned and executed as a rebel, and his head was exposed on the gallows at Lima. His house was razed to the ground, his partisans slaughtered indiscriminately, and his brother, Fernando, wasted away twenty-three years in the prisons of Madrid. Even such terrible reprisals did not put an end to anarchy, which continued until the reign of Philip II.

The hope of finding a country where gold was to be had in plenty, a country which seemed to vanish mysteriously from before those who sought it, filled the European adventurers with enthusiasm and made them dare all dangers and undergo incredible labors. This imaginary country which was reputed to be marvelously rich in gold and precious stones was supposed to be situated not far from the fabulous lake of Parima, in what is now Venezuela. Guaynacapac, one of the sons of the Inca Atahualpa, with some thousands of fugitives, was said to have penetrated and conquered the vast region between the Amazon and the Orinoco which was called by the generic name, Guiana. Here he had founded an empire much more powerful than Peru, whose splendor and wealth surpassed everything in the known world. In his capital, Manoa, were palaces whose colonnades were encrusted with emeralds, and temples with roofs of solid gold. Around the city spread the lake of Parima, with waves of molten gold and a bed of pearls, where diamonds were as plenty as pebbles. The monarch's august body was anointed each morning with a sweet smelling resin and then rolled in gold dust, and this unique and costly garment was washed off at bedtime. Juan Martinez, a Spanish soldier who had been condemned to death and then turned adrift upon the Orinoco in a canoe, pretended that he had entered Manoa and lived there seven months. The marvelous wealth which dazzled his eyes caused him to give the city the nickname of El Dorado.

The story of Martinez was deposited after his death in the archives of Porto Rico. From that time forward all the region lying between the upper Orinoco and the Marañon, or Amazon, was the scene of all the absurd tales with which the popular imagination was fed. Here were the warrior women, armed with the bow, that Orellana was forced to fight; new Amazons who led a wandering life on the banks of the great river to escape from the galling yoke of men. Here also, among other prodigies, were headless men with eyes in their shoulders and mouths in their bosoms. The numerous expeditions for the discovery of El Dorado, the land of gold, the romantic experiences of the explorers, the persistence of the belief in its existence until the last years of the eighteenth century when the Spaniard, Antonio Santos, undertook the last search for it, together make up a wonderful story even for that wonderful age. The companions of Pizarro were excited by the exaggerated stories of the Indians and first navigators and rushed into the search for these regions which rumor had filled with hoarded treasures. Orellana claimed that he saw them in his journey in 1541. He set out in 1549 with three ships, but lost two of them on the coast of Caracas and died there of mortification at his failure. Gonzalo Pizarro, instead of Lake Parima with its waves of liquid gold, made at least one interesting find. He discovered the American cinnamon tree, and ought to be remembered in the spice trade. Other captains, setting out simultaneously from Venezuela, New Granada, Peru, Brazil, and the Rio de la Plata, for the conquest of the provinces of the golden monarch, found only hardships, misery, and disappointment.

Pedro de Ursua, one of the bravest soldiers of the conqueror, who started from Cuzco at the head of some of his bold companions, was assassinated on the road by his lieutenant, Lopez de

Aguirre, who was desirous, according to some, of being the sole chief of the expedition, and according to others, of getting rid of an inconvenient husband, and thus being able to unite himself with the fair Inés (1560).

Unexpected discoveries were the result of these expeditions. Some Spanish deserters, who wished to go in search of El Dorado on their own account, found a large quantity of gold in the valleys of Caravaya; they first drove away the natives, and, abandoning dreams for reality, settled there and undertook to make the most of the riches that chance had put into their hands. This happened about 1550. The secret of the discovery was soon divulged; and the viceroy, desiring to acquire a large part of the profits that might result from it, hastened to send colonists, soldiers, engineers, and masons. Several small towns were built, and Charles V., in return for an ingot of gold weighing 218 pounds, sent by the men of San Gaban and San Juan del Oro, granted them the title of Imperial City and ennobled all their inhabitants. The working of the nineteen valleys that form the eastern part of Caravaya lasted more than two centuries, and produced many millions for the crown of Spain.

By the middle of the sixteenth century, as we have seen, more than half of America was already known; up to that date the Spaniards held the first place among the conquerors; the Portuguese followed them; but during the second half of the century both began to encounter rivals among the other nations of the old continent. Brazil, divided into captaincies since 1534, and given a general government in 1549, had seen, from the early days of its discovery, French traders come to traffic in dye wood in the Bay of Rio Janeiro. These adventurers lived on good terms with the tribe of the Tamayos who peopled that region. Their commercial or smuggling operations were very soon followed by an attempt at conquest. In 1555 a knight of Malta, Villegagnon, protected by Admiral Coligny and supported by the French Government, came with a large number of Calvinists to settle and fortify themselves on an island that even now bears his name. This personage, in whom were united a craving for adventure and a decided taste for religious controversy, did not lack talent. Unfortunately, his perfidy and excessive vanity, which he carried so far as to have himself addressed as King of Brazil, made him insupportable to his followers. He returned to Europe, execrated by the

Protestants as the Cain of America, but the colony, always allied with the Tamayos, held its ground and received, in 1559, a reinforcement of 300 men, led by Bois-le-Comte, and this allowed the French to form a new settlement on the west coast of the bay. Villegagnon had called the kingdom of his ambitious hopes "Antarctic France." The French Calvinists resisted repeated Portuguese attacks for years, but were completely crushed in January, 1567, after an heroic resistance. The greater part of their possessions were abandoned to the Jesuit Fathers, and a war of extermination against the Tamayos, irreconcilable enemies of the Portuguese, was carried on with fury.

Drake, the famous English seaman, trained in coasting voyages to France and Holland, was for the space of about twenty years the terror of the Spanish colonies. His first exploit was the taking of Nombre de Dios and Vera Cruz on the Isthmus of Panama in 1573. He passed the Straits of Magellan in 1578, laid waste the coasts of Chili and Peru, and, when he returned to England gorged with plunder, took with him an immense booty. Seven years later he sacked San Domingo, Cartagena, and Florida. In 1594 he went a-raiding again in the Caribbean, and in 1596 he burned Santa Marta and Rio de la Hacha on the coasts of New Granada. On this expedition a cannon ball demolished a chair in which he was sitting, but he escaped without injury. Anger and grief at the losses he suffered at Porto Rico and Panama caused his death, thus delivering the Spaniards from one of their most formidable enemies.

England, who appealed to the expeditions of the Cabots in order to claim a part of the American territory, had proposed to herself the double object of augmenting her own power and diminishing that of Spain. Such was the idea that Sir Walter Raleigh, the lover and favorite of Queen Elizabeth, cherished during his life. He also, like so many others, had allowed himself to be carried away by the chimera of El Dorado, which marvelous region he set out to conquer early in 1595. On March 22 of the same year he disembarked in the Island of Trinidad, seized the fort that the Spaniards had built and made prisoners of the commander and his officers. The Indians had seen twenty-three expeditions set out from this point, but their failure did not lessen Raleigh's zeal. He marched a hundred leagues, but was stopped by the rains and the overflow of the rivers. He returned, then, to

PIZARRO, ON THE ISLAND OF GALLO, DRAWS HIS SWORD THROUGH THE SAND AND DARES HIS DISCOURAGED COMPANIONS TO FOLLOW HIM TO THE CONQUEST OF THE GOLDEN-LAND THEY ARE IN QUEST OF

Painting by A. Lizcano

—page 18

Trinidad, and afterward to England, but not before he had put to ransom and pillaged the Spanish settlements on the coast. The next year he fitted out a second expedition, under Lawrence Keymis, who explored all that part of the coast included between the River Amazon and the Orinoco, without catching a glimpse of El Dorado, which he conjectured should be sought toward the Oyapock. Through him we know that the French at that time sought the coast of Guiana for dye wood. About 1604 they attempted a settlement there. What is now French Guiana was first called " Equinoctial France."

On October 14, 1596, a third expedition fitted out by Raleigh set sail under the command of Thomas Masham, but soon returned for lack of sufficient forces to maintain itself against the Spaniards, who were already beginning to fortify their possessions in these parts. In 1617 the obstinate Raleigh again set sail with a squadron of twelve ships. Betrayed to Spain by King James, to whom he had communicated his plans, his passage to Guiana was opposed; his son Walter and Keymis attacked and burned San Tomé, reducing it to ashes. Diego de Palamesa, who bore the title of Governor of Guiana, El Dorado and Trinidad, lost his life in this action, and the young Walter suffered the same fate. Keymis, instead of advancing, retreated to join Raleigh, and, unable to bear his reproaches, committed suicide. Raleigh returned to England heart-broken and entirely ruined. He was prosecuted on the complaint of Spain and accused of having violated Spanish territory. He replied that it was the Spaniards who should be accused of seizing a territory that belonged to England, since, during the reign of Elizabeth, his squadrons had been the first to take possession of Guiana in the name of England; and King James, he added, had sanctioned his action by granting to Charles Leigh and to Harcourt a part of the lands of Guiana, and consequently he had not exceeded the powers that the king had conferred upon him. All that he put forward in his defense and in favor of the rights of priority of his country was useless; Spain demanded his head and James, the royal pedant, was base enough to yield to the demand. The accusation of treason for which he had been condemned to death fifteen years before was revived against him and he was sent to the block. Before receiving the fatal stroke he took the ax from the hands of the headsman, examined its edge, and, having found it to his mind, said: " It is a sharp remedy, but it cures all ills." So died, at the age of sixty-six years, one of the greatest men England has produced, basely sacrificed to a rival nation.

Five nations were to contend persistently for Guiana—Spain, Portugal, France, England, and Holland. After spilling much blood and heaping up many ruins, these powers ended by dividing among themselves the disputed territory; but the wars of independence have completely eliminated the first two.

At the end of the sixteenth century there was very little of importance remaining to be discovered in South America; thus it is that, with few exceptions, the early years of the seventeenth century are much more remarkable for the part that the European nations took in the great movement of colonization, than for those hazardous expeditions characteristic of the first period of the conquest. We must, nevertheless, mention an attempt made by the Spaniards in 1584 to settle on the Straits of Magellan, near Cape Froward; the name of Port Famine, given by them to the site which they had attempted to occupy, has preserved the memory of their sufferings. Six years later the Jesuits, more fortunate, laid in Paraguay the foundations of that colossal power that lasted for more than two centuries, of which we shall have occasion to speak later.

In 1616 the Dutch navigator Jacques Lemaire, with the pilot Schouten, discovered the strait south of the American continent which bears his name, situated between Staaten Island and Tierra del Fuego. He doubled Cape Horn and crossed the Pacific, pointing out to mariners a shorter and safer route to those seas than the Straits of Magellan. New explorations were carried out at the same time in Brazil, where in spite of the royal prohibition by Portugal of exploration in the interior, the Paulists, in the prosecution of vast slave raids, reached the banks of the River Amazon and the frontiers of Peru. The nascent prosperity of this country could not fail to draw the attention of the other European nations. The French, who were always prowling along the coast, formed some ephemeral settlements at the mouth and on the banks of the Amazon. In 1544 Jacques Riffault, a buccaneer of Dieppe, seized the uninhabited Island of Maranham and made a treaty with the Indians. He then returned to France and organized a maritime company which fitted out a large expedition under the command of Daniel de la Ravardière, who founded on the island a colony named St. Louis in honor of Louis XIII., who had promised to support the enterprise. The colonists built a fort and extended their power over a considerable territory, but at last were defeated with fifteen hundred Indian allies in 1614, and completely expelled from the island in the next year.

In 1624 the Dutch under Admiral Villekens began the conquest of Brazil by attacking Bahia, which they took and pillaged. Repulsed by the Spanish troops, for Portugal was then under the power of Spain, they returned to the charge in 1630, took Pernambuco and made themselves masters of several provinces in succession. After several years of hard fighting they remained masters of the north part, and when Portugal had recovered her independence John IV. ceded it to them, by the treaty of 1641, in order to procure allies. But the violent and tyrannical conduct of the Dutch aroused the colonists, who expelled them in 1654, after a sanguinary struggle. Four men, representatives of the various races that compose the Brazilian population, had prepared and executed this great act of liberating their country from foreign rule. Vidal, a white man; Fernandez Vieira, a mulatto; Diaz, a negro; and Cameran, an Indian, are the men that Brazil considers as her liberators, and the real chief, the mulatto Fernandez Vieira, the true hero of the enterprise, who afterward resigned his power when the work of liberation was finished.

"No epoch in Brazilian history," says Ferdinand Denis, "is so heroic and dramatic. Now Vieira, after conquering most of the coast towns and being invested with dictatorial power, gives up his authority into hands which he deems stronger and more skillful than his own; again, on receiving a royal order to cease hostilities, he replies that he will gladly suffer the penalty of disobedience after he has restored to the crown its best dependency. It is Cameran, the Indian, a survivor of the great tribes which have been annihilated, whose presence and indomitable courage are needed on every battlefield, and who has so high a sense of his own rank as a savage chief that he never speaks the language of his conquerors, not that he does not understand it as well as his own, but because he fears that he cannot express himself with sufficient dignity. It is Enrique Diaz who, when he loses one hand, seizes his weapons with the other and rushes into the thick of the fight with all the impetuous courage of the African race."

On January 27, 1654, Brazil was at last delivered from the

foreign yoke. It long remained almost unknown to the other
European nations, who were rigidly excluded from all intercourse
with the colony. From French and English smugglers and an
occasional ship of war permitted by special favor to put in at a
Brazilian port Europe heard vaguely of events in these far-away
regions. It is this that makes the expedition of Duclerc, in 1710,
so notable. Portugal was then at war with France. Duclerc arrived in the neighborhood of Rio Janeiro in August, disembarked
with 900 men in Guatariba, was attacked by three thousand Portuguese and five thousand negroes or mulattoes, whom he defeated,
but on entering the city he encountered a murderous fire from the
houses, was overwhelmed by numbers, defeated, and killed, and the
greater part of his men died of hunger in the prisons. To avenge
this defeat, another expedition sailed from France in the following
year, under the command of Duguay Trouin, who forced the defenses of the harbor, captured the city, and levied an enormous
ransom upon it.

In Chili the war between the Spaniards and the Araucanians,
which had continued for more than a century, partly ceased by
the treaty of peace of 1641. The Araucanians retained their territory, undertaking not to permit any foreign nation to disembark
in it, and they fulfilled their promise; but hostilities were frequently
renewed, and it was necessary for another century to pass before
another treaty put an end to this war which had cost Spain so
many lives.

In 1667 French ships entered the Pacific Ocean for the first
time, and carried on a considerable trade until the Peace of Utrecht
(1713). During this period voyages of exploration were made by
the astronomer and botanist, Fueillée (1699-1707), by the engineer,
Fézier (1711), and by the Breton, Labarbinais Le Gentil (1715),
and they were the first to give to the world definite knowledge
about Chili and Peru. The archipelagoes of Chiloé and Chonos,
Patagonia and the Galapagos Islands, were studied anew in the
latter years of the seventeenth and the beginning of the eighteenth
centuries by two Englishmen, Narborough and Wood, and by the
Frenchmen, Degennes and Beauchesne-Gouin.

This epoch was marked by the ever-increasing progress of
colonization in the interior of the continent, especially in Brazil
and Paraguay, and on the banks of the Amazon and its tributaries;
the coasts, also, became better known. Only a hundred years later,

in 1799, Humboldt and Bompland undertook their celebrated journey, fixing the geography of the Orinoco, and of Colombia, Peru, and Mexico, a journey that did not terminate until 1805. The way had been opened for the investigations of science. From this date the more pacific triumphs of study take the place of the sanguinary triumphs of the conquest. Later, the emancipation of the Spanish colonies and of Brazil, opening up the widest field to the activity of all nations, will give rise to a multitude of observations and discoveries which will add to the known marvels those that are yet unknown. But now the army that spreads over America, not without facing great dangers, has not rapine and extermination for its object; it does not come to crush under its feet a whole world, nor for bloodshed; its chiefs are not the scum of the civilized nations, the bold and greedy adventurers of former times, outcasts, and filibusters from all countries; they are the chosen leaders of humanitarian science, geographers, botanists, astronomers, physicians—in a word, they are all men of wisdom and research, whose glory will at least cause no tears to be shed.

Chapter III

COLONIZATION. 1534-1810

THE story of the colonization of the New World is the second act of the passion and martyrdom of the miserable Indians.

"The raging Iberian lion hurled himself, centuries ago, from the pillars of Hercules upon the empire of Montezuma and Atahualpa, and devoured unhappy America," wrote the deputies signatory to the declaration of independence of Upper Peru (Bolivia) in 1825.

The old continent took possession of the new by virtue of the brutal axiom that might makes right. All means of monopolizing the prize and of squeezing out the last drop of its riches were considered just. There was no other conception than the complete subjugation of the people and the wealth of the country. The policy of sharing with a conquered people the advantages of the civilization and commerce of the mother country, to the profit of the latter, is very modern. As Rossi remarks in treating of colonies, the idea of raising to some sort of political life men of another race and language, who were regarded as infidels with whom there was nothing in common, not even color, could not have sprung from the minds of that age. What the age desired had been the desire of classical antiquity—absolute domination, with no choice to the aborigines but slavery or death.

Thus, but a small number of the natives in America survived the conquest. In some places, such as San Domingo, for example, they completely disappeared. The terrible military power of the Spaniards, the superiority of their tactics, the unscrupulous trickery of their diplomacy, overpowered alike organized states and scattered tribes. The former were a prey to the ambitions of rival princes, the latter were not united by any bond.

It was only after terrible struggles, lasting more than a century, that a uniform and general colonization could be carried out. The Spaniards long considered themselves as almost the sole masters of the New World. In South America, which alone interests us now, they held, before the war of independence: New Granada, Peru, Chili, Rio de la Plata, and the captain generalcy of Caracas, which have since been transformed into independent republics, a territory about sixteen times larger than Spain. The Portuguese held Brazil until 1821. The French, Dutch, and English held parts of Guiana. Patagonia, which has recently been a bone of contention between Chili and the Argentine Republic, was still in the hands of its native masters. Under the Spanish domination it was rated as a part of the viceroyalty of La Plata, though the wandering tribes who occupied it were then as now practically independent.

The conquerors posed as the bearers of the blessing of civilization and Christianity to the American peoples. The pretext was ingenious; their true aim, and they never had any other, was lust of gold, and the central power itself had no more noble motive than simple greed. The massacres which stain the record of the Europeans from the very beginning throw light on this point. Do we not know how these well disposed and peaceful tribes, who came trustfully before the conquerors, were betrayed, robbed, and butchered without mercy? The incas were put to death, empires overthrown, civilization blotted out, temples burned, statues broken, precious vessels melted down. The Quipos, or annals of the Peruvians, preserved in cords by a curious system of knots, which served instead of written records, were scattered to the winds, and the work of centuries disappeared. The destruction was as sudden as robbery, as ferocious as crime. The blessings these Spanish adventurers brought with them to America were ruins and ashes, tears and blood. They imposed their language, their customs, and, above all, their vices on this virgin soil which Nature had loaded with her gifts.

The vast territory of Brazil after 1534 was divided into hereditary and mutually independent captaincies, each stretching fifty leagues along the coast. They were granted as fiefs with extraordinary rights of lordship and certain prerogatives of sovereignty to men of influence, who undertook to colonize them at their own risk and to defend them against attack from within and without. At the head of the colonial government was a governor general. This system lasted for two centuries and was ably supported by the Franciscans, the Carmelites, and above all the Jesuits, who, it must be confessed, knew how to protect the Indians from the brutal ferocity of the colonists. In 1562 and 1563 their opportune intervention put a stop to the war between the Tamayos and the Portuguese. In 1640, thanks to their labors, the bull of Paul III. in favor of the natives of Peru was extended to Brazil by Urban VIII. The colonists of Rio Janeiro and the Paulists, in a rage, took up arms to drive out the Jesuits, who finally yielded and accepted conditions which substantially nullified the bull. Then, when their colleges became numerous and their missions were firmly established, they again raised their heads and sought to rule a state within the state. By the decree of September 3, 1759, they were finally expelled.

But the most active agency of colonization in Brazil was that of the Paulists, whose famous *banderias* (expeditions) explored vast territories, immense river systems, and the highest mountain ranges. They were always victorious, penetrated the most distant wastes, and made the first settlements there. These hardy adventurers, the offspring of white men and Indian women, whose exploits are recounted in Brazilian legends, were the real conquerors of the interior. Their business was to hunt the savages who had fled into the forest. Making what was called *descer indios* (onfall upon the Indians), these *sertanejos* of St. Paul slew without mercy those who would not submit to slavery and marched the rest off to be sold at a special slave-mart called the *Curral* (corral). A contemporary Brazilian writer, De Macedo, says:[1]

"Whatever disturbances were caused by the quarrels of the Jesuit fathers on the subject of the control and management of the Indians, whatever abuses they were guilty of in pursuit of worldly and material interests, it is certain that their influence, their conduct, their system, and their real or pretended schemes for power and temporal greatness deserve the blessings of mankind, when compared with the burnings of Indian villages, the horrible massacres, the enslavement of thousands of natives by *banderias* or *descidas de indios,* and the other dreadful crimes of those colonists who were then lauded as heroes, but whose monstrous cruelties are weighed in a just balance by the civilization of to-day."

The Jesuit, with all his faults, was a saint in comparison with the Portuguese colonist who murdered Indians by the hundred for mere lust of blood and delight in terrorizing the natives. Witness that Pedro da Costa Favella who, in 1665, at the mouth of the Urubri, burned thirty villages of the Caboquenas, shot eight

[1] "*Notions de Chorographie du Brésil,*" Leipzig, 1873.

hundred of their miserable inhabitants, and dragged the rest into slavery, in revenge for the death of a few soldiers engaged in the Indian slave trade, whom the Caboquenas had killed in defense of their own liberty. Whenever laborers were needed in town or country man-hunts were organized by the government. One such expedition, in 1628, met with a bloody resistance from the Indians. But what could naked men avail with spears and arrows against disciplined troops equipped with firearms? The unfortunates were slaughtered so pitilessly that the governor of Pará, Francisco Coelho de Carvalho, was disturbed by the public outcry, and hastily recalled the expedition. He repealed the decree which allowed the slave trade to be constantly carried on, and restricted it to two hunts a year, which must be first duly authorized. The decree was evaded and man-hunting continued as before, though without license.

Time changed this order of things somewhat. The all-powerful minister of Joseph I., the Marquis of Pombal, decreed the equality of Indians and Portuguese before the law, and enacted penalties against all who should keep up the degrading distinctions between natives and Europeans, which had been introduced by the Jesuits and the colonists. His erroneous notions of political economy unfortunately led him to restrict freedom of foreign commerce. Believing that restriction and monopoly would enrich his country, he created the company of Grand-Pará and Maranham and granted it lucrative privileges. On the other hand his reform ordinances were not always executed.

The Portuguese settlements in Brazil had excited the jealousy of the Spaniards as early as the beginning of the sixteenth century. It was truly said that the two nations were neighbors and rivals in both worlds. Spain was forced to create in America a system of colonization and administration suitable to counterbalance the Portuguese power. She sent out expeditions in order to hem Brazil in on all sides, and to this policy the discovery of Paraguay is in part due. The quarrels of the two nations over their boundaries were hushed from time to time only to break out again with more bitterness than before. The demarcation of Pope Alexander VI. served no other purpose than to open the way for forced and false interpretations of its meaning.

The Spanish possessions, like the Portuguese, were handed over to satraps who came from the peninsula, traded in men and goods, absolutely free of control, quickly amassed fortunes and returned in haste to Spain to enjoy in peace the fruits of their robberies.　At the head of each of the great administrative divisions there was a man of high rank called governor, president, or captain general.　He was commander of the army, exercised control over the local governors, was the chief dispenser of justice, and

was president of the *audiencia real* and the other superior courts. He was directly responsible to the king, but in time of war was under the immediate authority of the viceroy.　The residence of the viceroy was Peru.　For more than two centuries the *audiencia* of Lima included in its jurisdiction Buenos Ayres, distant more than 2500 miles.　It was only in 1776 that La Plata was erected into a viceroyalty with Buenos Ayres as its capital.　In 1718 New Granada, which had until then been dependent on Peru, had in like manner been erected into a viceroyalty.

Each province was governed by a prefect or *corregidor*. In theory he was appointed by the Spanish court, but, because of the great distance from Spain, the governor often assumed the right to fill vacant prefectures. The *corregidors* exercised both civil and military powers. In each provincial capital there was a council of magistrates (*cabildo*) made up of several *regidors* or life-members, a standard-bearer, a public prosecutor, an *alcalde provincial* (provincial mayor), an *alguazil,* or chief justice, and two *alcaldes,* or consuls. These last were drawn from the ranks of the nobles and annually elected by the *cabildo.*

The *audiencia real,* a true engine of oppression, was the court of last resort for all civil and criminal cases, except that in cases where the amount in controversy was more than $6000 an appeal might be taken to the Great Council of the Indies, which the kings of Spain used as their instrument for drawing up the collection of laws and ordinances known as the *Recopilacion de Indias,* and which never accomplished any practical good. Neither natives nor creoles could get justice from the *audiencias,* which were made up wholly of Europeans and did not scruple to banish those who were pointed out for punishment at their hands.

Each *audiencia* sat in two divisions—the chancery and the criminal court. In each division there was a president, a *fiscál* or king's counsel, a guardian of the Indians, and several auditors, all grossly overpaid. The other courts had jurisdiction of the finances, of vacant lands, and of commerce.

Of the ecclesiastical system, which included many dioceses, it is enough to say that there was at Lima a tribunal of the Holy Office which maintained inquisitors, commissioners, and many employees of lower rank in all the chief towns of the captaincy. Certain provinces, like those of La Plata, were in a chronic state of anarchy, every man striving for the supreme power; and the boldest or most unscrupulous, who won the prize and got rid of his rivals, by fair means or foul, was certain to get the sanction of the Spanish court. Nuñez Cabeza de Vaca, better known for his explorations in North America, a wealthy gentleman, stirred by the same spirit of adventure which had lately lured Mendoza to his ruin, had been granted by Charles V. the title of *adelantado* of the provinces of La Plata. He was ordered to tolerate "neither barristers nor attorneys," to win over the natives by kindness, and to permit free trade with them by everybody. His humanity toward the Indian slaves caused an insurrection of the colonists and royal officers, who shipped him off to Spain by force. There he cleared himself, but he never succeeded in regaining his office. Such was the fate of every man who followed the promptings of justice and mercy. On the other hand one Irala, a powerful man who got rid of a rival by the simple process of beheading him, was confirmed in the title of governor, which he had usurped. To do him justice, his rule was less violent and arbitrary than this beginning promised. He organized the *encomiendas* under his government with real ability. This name was given to those groups of Indians held by the first conquerors in servitude for a term of years, at the expiration of which the group became a part of the royal domain. Later another kind of *encomienda* was granted for a term of ten years to anybody who established a small farming village of Indians or creoles. Then were laid the foundations of the theocratic system of the Jesuits, which we shall have occasion to describe later. In 1558 Irala died. In 1573 the bishop of Asuncion usurped the right to appoint the governor of the colony. His appointee, a certain Garay, coolly put in irons the legitimate governor, who did not long survive. His nephew, invested for a moment with the semblance of authority, was murdered by the fanatical Indians. Garay, to be sure, soon met the same fate, for such was the inexorable law; the victor of to-day became the vanquished of to-morrow.

The Spanish treasury faced bankruptcy after the death of Charles V. The people were disaffected and clamorous. The government saw in America its only means of salvation. "The stress of need stifled all pity," says Farini, "and the demands of the hour allowed no thought of the future. It was not enough to torture the natives and dig up the soil of whole provinces in the mad search for gold and silver; but all offices were put up at auction. The purchasers did not fail to force their subordinates to pay, and these to force others, and so on down to the last link of the social chain, the laborer, who was a sort of beast of burden, carrying an enormous load, broken down by blows, and begrudged the miserable pittance which was contemptuously thrown to him. The mother country, in its commerce with the colonies, was not content with the lion's share of the profits, but must have them all. Thus, for instance, Chili must abandon the cultivation of the grape and the olive and consume only the wine and oil of Spain. The customs duties levied upon colonial products were enormous. The treasures of South America must be sent to the mother country and the Americans could not buy from other nations even those necessities which Spain did not produce. Only Spaniards might settle in the American colonies. These over-sea possessions were guarded with the strictest jealousy, and a foreign ship which wished to touch there must get a special permit from the court of Madrid. A ship in distress was no exception to the rule, and every vessel which put in for refuge from a storm was seized, even when it belonged to a nation in alliance with Spain, and the crew put in irons."

Spain, blind to everything but the inexhaustible revenue which these rich territories promised to yield, had from the first parceled out the country into *encomiendas* or grants. Thus she, too, created a feudal system in America. When the beginning of a common political organization could be made, the real power was in the hands of the holders of these fiefs and was used or abused at their pleasure. The *encomienderos* or grantees were the feudal lords of the conquered country. The Indians were by law their slaves, treated like beasts of burden, forced to perform the heaviest tasks without the slightest compensation. From the age of thirteen years every Indian must pay tribute, and if he had not the wherewith to pay he was sold as a slave. And this was not all. Many harmless customs were forbidden out of sheer brutality; and certain modes of dress which, in the eyes of the natives, were the mark of noble lineage or of a certain rank, were suppressed by force. For example: Certain families had enjoyed the privilege, since the time of Manco-Capac, of cutting the hair square in front, or of greatly elongating the lobe of the ear. Pizarro and his rough officers spared no ridicule of the high officers who made it a point of honor to maintain inviolate these priceless rights. Certain officers were distinguished from those subject to their authority by the length of their hair, which the shears must never touch. They were now compelled by law to cut it. Harsh measures were taken to suppress customs which doubtless were uncouth, or at least appeared so, but which should have been tolerated for a time. Such abuses of power had not the excuse of the necessity for establishing colonization on a firm foundation; on the contrary, they resulted in depopulation, the extermination of the natives by the sword and by

forced labor in the mines.　Another result was the African slave
trade, for the hands which war, harsh treatment and man-killing
toil destroyed by thousands every day, must be replaced somehow.

A philanthopist, the bishop Las Casas, came to the conclusion that the only effective means for saving the last remnants of
the native race was to use for the same purpose, and for a brief
period, another race, the negroes, who could better endure the fierce
heat of the tropics.　Alas! this brief period, which grew into forever,
availed nothing.　The Indians were forced to toil without ceasing.
Some tilling the fields under the rays of the murderous tropical sun;
others cast into the sea to search for pearls; still others buried in
the mines without hope of ever again returning to the upper air.
Under the pretense of bettering their lot, Charles V. established the
Mita, which was a sort of civil conscription that, instead of being
an advantage to the Indians, decimated them.　Each district was
annually required to furnish a number of men sufficient for the
service of those who were developing its resources.　Every mine-
owner and landholder could demand as many Indians as he needed.
Now, in Peru alone there were fourteen hundred mines in process of
development.　Every man between the ages of eighteen and fifty
years was subject to the Mita.　He whom the lot made choice of
knew the sad fate in store for him.　The calling of his name was a
sentence of death, for out of every five of these wretched victims of
greed only one, on an average, outlived the hardships of this dreadful service.　Before departing, all those chosen made last provision
as for death, and their relatives conducted funeral ceremonies before
them, as before a corpse.　But their tyrants were at least pious, and
a mass was said for their benefit, though it was but one burden the
more upon them, for they must attend it, and, above all, pay for it.
At the end of the service the priest took their oaths of fidelity and
obedience to the King of Spain, sprinkled them with holy water,
pronounced the accustomed formula, vete con Dios, and turned his
back upon them.　Then they were led to the rich gold mines.　Assigned to the task of excavation, they went down into the shafts and
galleries, where the sudden transition from the pure air to the
pestilential atmosphere of the mines brought on a kind of asthma,
of which they usually died within the year, if excessive toil, bad
food and despair did not kill them sooner.　In Peru alone the Mita
counted eight million victims.　During the term of his service the
Indian was entitled to receive four reals (about fifty cents) a

day, of which one-third was paid back to his master for food. The master contrived to get the remaining two-thirds also on account of advances for clothing or strong drink. When the term of the *Mita* expired the Indian who had by any chance survived must continue his service until his debt was paid.

As the adventurers who descended on America were *hidalgos,* too proud to walk, and as a horse was worth about eight thousand dollars, they forced men to carry them long distances, preferring to lose several Indians rather than one such costly mount. Every Spaniard on a journey had in his train as beasts of burden five or six Indians, chained together and heavily loaded. If one succumbed to fatigue on the way his head was cut off to save the trouble of opening the clasps of his collar, and his body was left on the road to be devoured by beasts of prey. According to Captain Palomino, when the masters of the New World went to explore and take possession of provinces and villages, this was their course of procedure: "If the people received the explorers as friends the Spaniards put them to the torture to compel a disclosure of hidden treasures. If, on the other hand, the natives fled, their houses were burned, their stores of provisions destroyed and they themselves tracked like fallow deer by dogs which were specially trained to that horrible hunting. The fields lay waste, and so severe a famine followed that the natives died by hundreds by the wayside."

The vanquished could not bury all their treasures and, above all, could not conceal their mines. This was a means of retribution for their wrongs as Ernest Charton has remarked, for this vast wealth ruined and corrupted the victors instead of profiting them. "During the three centuries of their occupancy of South America they did nothing but exploit the deposits of gold and silver. The labor of the natives was not enough to satisfy their greed, and they imported negro slaves. Yet there is no region where the vegetable kingdom is so rich, the soil so fertile and so well watered as near the equator. But the Spaniards neglected to investigate the resources of the provinces which they had conquered; they were ignorant of the names and even of the existence of many great rivers which might have become important arteries of commerce. They were entirely absorbed in the exploitation of the gold mines, were utterly careless of the future and despised that which could have opened to unborn generations an inexhaustible source of wealth. Spain, proudly proclaiming herself the mistress of two oceans and two continents, could do nothing but destroy; she created nothing great or lasting." [2]   The Spaniards let ruins heap up around them. Roads disappeared, bridges fell in, dams broke, irrigating canals choked up, and soon nothing was left of all that the genius of the native states had created under the incas.

Agriculture was neglected: America could produce excellent vines, worthy to be compared with the growth of Madeira and the Cape, and the olive could flourish there; but Spain forbade the cultivation of the vine and the olive in America in order to monopolize the American market for Spanish wines and olives. Every sort of manufacturing establishment was forbidden. Lumbering in the forests could promise large returns, but nobody thought of it, in the rush for immediate profits. As for the future, who cared about that? All energies were bent upon gold mining, the only industry that the state favored, because from it was drawn the most unfailing part of the public revenues. The soldier turned lord, dug the soil only to get the precious metals, and thought only of enriching himself at the expense of the gang of natives subjected to him by order of the king. As J. M. Guardia [3] says: " This is the hateful cruelty, infinitely worse and a thousand times more destructive than that of the conquerors, for which Spain deserves especial condemnation. No doubt she shed innocent blood in the conquest, but her abominable and absurd system of financial administration, which in cold blood sacrificed a whole race to enrich a handful of adventurers and vagabonds for the benefit of the government, is her unpardonable sin. The greedy and thriftless central government knew no pity and exploited, with detestable cunning, the most foolish of human passions. The intermarriage of the whites and the Indians was the only means for establishing a vigorous and united people and thus laying the foundations of future prosperity. Race prejudice, strengthened by the memories of the conquest, was arrayed against such intermarriage, and the central government came to the aid of race prejudice by excluding *Mestizos* (half-breeds) from all social advantages and places of honor. The creoles themselves were treated as inferiors. Consequently the administration of the conquered territories was exclusively in the hands of men who had no stake in the country and had no thought but the amassing of fortunes to be spent elsewhere.

[2] Quito, " *Tour du Monde,*" Vol. XV.
[3] " *Les republiques de l'Amerique espagnole,*" 1862.

Thus ruin crept in and all germs of a good system were destroyed. The Spanish Government was concerned only with its own profit and prohibited all commerce and even all intercourse with foreigners. In order to establish monopoly more firmly it adopted a rigorous system of sequestration and isolation. Thanks to this absurd system, South America was given over wholly to Spain, which has been the most backward of all European nations since the end of the sixteenth century."

We have described the *Mita*. Another instrument of oppression and tyranny was the *repartimiento,* which granted to the *corregidors* the privilege of selling to the Indians all articles necessary for their use. These officers cynically exploited the privilege, forcing the natives to buy of them, at high prices, utterly useless or worthless articles. The collection of the royal tribute also gave a chance for outrageous extortion.

Paul Marcoy, author of a very interesting " Journey in South America," [4] has given us a very unfavorable account of the Peruvian missions. " The catechumens, who were overworked, badly nourished, and heavily flogged, died like flies. To make good this deficit and to keep the ranks of the Christianized Indians full, the Reverend Fathers of Jesus sent an armed flotilla of monks and soldiers to scour the banks of the Amazon and the missions founded by their co-religionists and rivals in Brazil. While the monks carried off the neophytes, the soldiers pillaged and destroyed the empty, and henceforward useless houses. Such deeds were not at all extraordinary in newly conquered regions. When the campaign was over the naval expedition returned singing hymns, and the prisoners, who had been taken in the name of Christ, were divided among the undermanned villages. Sometimes they were taken to the central missions of Upper and Lower Huallaga, where they waited, like goods in a storehouse, until the demand for souls (and hands) became pressing at some point. The forcible transportation to Peru of the Oneaguas, who were at the time settled in Brazil, but had formerly come from Popayan and New Granada by way of the River Sapura, was the result of one of these raids. Finally Brazil grew weary of this apostolic marauding which hastened the process of using up the natives and thereby interfered with her own privileges, and conceived the idea of fortifying Yahuaraté and thus guarding her ter-

[4] *" Tour du Monde,"* 1886.

Hist. Nat.

ritory. A garrison was established there and this Gibraltar in little
was ordered to cannonade every flotilla which descended the river
without answering the sentinel's challenge and the priestly command, "Advance, friend, and give the countersign."

From an early date the Jesuits had cherished the idea of organizing a new community in America to bring riches and strength to
their order. They had already penetrated to Chili and the banks of
the Tucuman, when they succeeded in founding a college at
Asuncion in Paraguay toward the close of the sixteenth century.
Once there, they quietly and patiently awaited a favorable moment
for carrying out their designs. The struggle between governors and
bishops, who assumed to make the civil power entirely subordinate
to themselves, gave the Jesuits the expected opportunity. The com-
mandery system helped them. Under color of collecting the Indians
for such establishments, in 1609, they laid the foundations, on the
right bank of the Parana, of that theocratic and communistic state,
which is still famous under the name of the Missions or *Reductions*
of Paraguay. They converted the Guaranis in a mass, enrolled
them, as it were, transformed them into agriculturists and excluded
foreigners from the country. Thirty-two villages were formed and
contained forty thousand families. These wise managers of men,
at once apostolic missionaries and temporal administrators, skillfully
exploited the labor of the natives, who, in the words of Schoell,[5]
"knew no chiefs, no masters, we might almost say no God, save
the Fathers."

All trade was in their hands. They established, for the profit
of their order, a monopoly which yielded vast returns. Crétineau-
Joly says:[6] "The Jesuits were the guardians of the organized
converts on the Paraguay. Because of the incompetence of these
savages and the civilizing influence of religion upon them, many
kings of Spain, especially Philip V. by a decree of December 28,
1743, renewing and confirming earlier decrees, granted to the missionaries the right to sell the produce of the lands tilled by the
neophytes and the fruits of their labors." This decree of 1743 gives
but a faint idea of the administrative methods of the Jesuits of
Paraguay. In fact, a full disclosure of their business was vouch-
safed to nobody, not even to the kings of Spain: "We may conclude from the information that was given, from the proceedings

[5] "*Cours d'histoire des États européens.*"
[6] "*Clément XIV. et les Jésuites.*"

of conferences and other scraps of evidence, that, because of the incapacity and laziness of these Indians in the management of their property, each one was allotted a parcel of land to cultivate for the maintenance of his family. The remaining lands were held in common and the yield of grain, roots, and food stuffs, as well as of grass and cattle, was divided by the Indians, under the direction of the priests, into three portions: the first for the royal tribute, on which was charged the salaries of the priests; the second for the adornment and repair of the churches; the third for the feeding and clothing of widows, orphans, invalids, those who were employed on other tasks, and for other needs, for hardly one of those who received allotments of land for tillage got enough from it to support himself throughout the year."

The neophytes were formed into armies, drilled in the European fashion, and were often under arms to resist the numerous enemies of the Fathers. The profits of the Jesuits from their establishments were certainly very great, though it has never been possible to determine the amount exactly. They were adepts in the art of concealing in Europe what went on in their parishes. Each village was surrounded by a ditch to prevent the neophytes from going out and strangers from coming in. Governors, and even bishops, were denied admittance. All trade was carried on at designated places on the boundary of each mission, and the neophytes had no part in it, for they were rigorously kept from all intercourse with outsiders. Royal decrees had no force in the dominions of these able potentates, for they were absolute masters there, laughing at rules, ordinances and decrees, and, on occasions, hurling their troops against the governors themselves.

On January 2, 1767, the Jesuits of Paraguay were expelled from the Spanish possessions, as they had been from those of the Portuguese some years before, and their property was confiscated. The territory occupied by the parishes had been ceded to Portugal by Spain in 1750, and had been taken over by Portugal eleven years later. It can be said in defense of the Fathers that, in recruiting for their missions and settling wandering tribes in their villages, they almost always avoided the use of force. In most cases they secured their converts by tact. After their expulsion little attention was paid to Paraguay. Spain, with her usual administrative incapacity, forgot it.

To sum up: Oppression, violence and the lust for plunder gave the law to the Spanish colonies, and it was not only the Indians who found the yoke too heavy to be borne; the Indian mixed bloods had no less cause for complaint, and even among full-blooded Spaniards nobody was well treated but officials and churchmen. The Spanish policy was to grind the colonists down with taxes, heap insults upon them, and keep them in ignorance. As the saying was: " The creoles should have no education, save in Christian doctrine, that they may be kept in subjection." In the province of Velez (New Granada) the holders of fiefs reduced the Indians of Tunebos to such misery that whole families threw themselves from the summit of a cliff thirteen hundred feet high into the river. The tribes of the Agatoès and Cocomes committed suicide in a body in one night to escape from their tyrants. Many Indians hanged themselves in despair, to avoid falling into the hands of the Spaniards and becoming slaves. A Spanish intendant went, rope in hand, to the place where many such wretches had met to put an end to their lives, and threatened to hang himself with them if they persisted. The poor creatures scattered in terror, preferring life with all its hardships to the companionship of one of their tyrants beyond the grave. Whole tribes, worn out at last by so many infamies and cruelties, revolted. The inhabitants of Aconcahu, in the province of Canas, angered by an increase in the tribute of gold dust which they were forced to pay, seized one day the Spanish collector who was roughly demanding payment and gave him molten gold to drink, " *para saciar de este modo la sed insaciable del recandador* " (to slake by this method the unquenchable thirst of the collector), says Florez, who reports the fact in a pamphlet, " *Patriotismo y amos á la libertad.*" After this achievement they left their village and were never seen again. One night in December, 1767, the descendants of the first dwellers in the valleys of Caravaya, the Carangas and the Suchimanis, settled accounts with the Spaniards of San Gaban for a usurpation which had lasted two centuries. They burned the town and slew the inhabitants with arrows and clubs. It is said that when the viceroy Antonio Amat got news of it he swore on a piece of the true cross to exterminate all the savages of Peru without exception; but the actress Mariquita Gallegas, famous for her nickname of Périchole, for her intimacy with the viceroy and her edifying last days in a cloister, pleaded their cause, showing her lover that the duty of a Christian and a viceroy under these circumstances was to endow a perpetual obit for the victims and send missionaries to teach and baptize their persecutors. The lover yielded, it seems, to the reasoning of la Périchole.

In 1780 the patience of the victims was exhausted. The villainy and greed of the *corregidors* had reached such a pitch that, by virtue of the *repartimiento,* they forced the naked and beardless natives to buy at exorbitant prices all kinds of useless articles, such as razors and silk stockings, and even spectacles and maps. One day Condorquanqui, cacique of Taugasuga, seized and with his own hands hanged the *corregidor* of Tinta, who in one year had imposed three *repartimientos* of about one hundred and fifty thousand piastres each. This cacique was a descendant from the Inca Tupac-Amaru, who was beheaded by the Spaniards in 1562, and is still mourned in the dirges which the Indians compose for their public festivals. The cacique assumed the name of his ancestor and the costume of the incas and gave the signal for revolt. He had been carefully educated in a convent at Cuzco and was respected and esteemed for his private virtues, but he made the mistake of not making common cause with the creoles, who were also outraged every day in respect of their most sacred rights. He treated them as enemies and they turned against him. The Indians flocked to his standard, and although without arms, their desperate valor won many advantages for him, and all Upper Peru was aflame. The struggle lasted a year, when Tupac-Amaru after betrayal by another cacique to whom the Spaniards had promised the epaulettes of a colonel, a promise never kept by the way, was captured and taken to Cuzco. He was tried and condemned by José Antonio de Arèche. This scoundrel pronounced a horrible sentence, worthy of the most barbarous ages, which was executed to the letter. The wife of the cacique, his two sons and his brother-in-law, Bastidas, were put to death before his eyes; the executioner then cut out his tongue, his limbs were bound and he was torn in pieces by four horses. His body was burned and his head, legs and arms sent to the rebel villages. His house was burned; his property was confiscated; his family was declared infamous forever; one of his brothers was sent to Spain and kept in prison for twenty years. It was thought that this punishment would terrify the Indians, but it only aroused their hate.

With the fury that marks every degraded people which rises against their oppressors, they exacted a terrible retribution. On hearing of the atrocities of Cuzco, many who had until then remained neutral hastened to join the insurgents, who were united under the command of Andrès, a nephew of Tupac-Amaru, and of another chief, Catari, and who fought with the fury of despair. It is said that each victim sacrificed at Cuzco cost five hundred Spanish heads. Andrès laid siege to Sorata, where the families of the surrounding country had taken refuge with their wealth. The fortifications and artillery of the defenders were an almost insuperable obstacle to besiegers without firearms, but Andrès built a dam and collected the waters from the melting snows of the neighboring mountains in a great reservoir, and thus sent a great flood against the town, which carried away the walls and opened a wide breach to the Indians. Sorata had about twenty thousand inhabitants. Only one, and he a priest, was spared. The rebels avenged their cacique by cruelties which recalled those of the Judge de Arèche. The rebellion came to an end with the death of the principal chiefs, who were betrayed for money by their own servants, and tyranny was exercised without restraint, as before. Nevertheless, all the bloodshed had not been in vain. The *repartimiento* was abolished. The creoles, on their part, endured the government to which they were subject with no less impatience. They were weary of persecution and of seeing the interests of their country sacrificed to the greed of Spain, and had vague schemes of emancipation. About the time when their Indian brothers were striving to free themselves, Socorro, a province of New Granada, rebelled because of certain vexatious taxes. The patriots advanced to the very walls of Bogota, their banner inscribed with the words, " Long live the King; death to wicked governors." The archbishop, clothed in his pontifical robes and bearing the holy sacrament, intervened and quieted the movement. But some time after Socorro was decimated and the greater part of its inhabitants were sent to the unwholesome regions of the coast and died there.

Nevertheless some reforms were tried. It was too late. The foundations of the murderous domination of three centuries were shaken. The revolution in the United States had given them a new shock and the French Revolution completed the ruin. The [French] " Declaration of the Rights of Men," secretly printed in Bogota and furtively read, inflamed all hearts and gave birth to an earnest desire for independence. The government struck blindly on all sides, and this painful childhood of liberty had its martyrs and its heroes. Bolivar, still young and entirely unknown, was then traveling in

Italy, and on the Sacred Mount took oath to deliver his country from foreign domination. He kept his word. The people, a mixture of so many elements, was ready to shed its blood. Lawyers, small landholders, the lower ranks of the clergy, the young soldiers among the natives, shared the passion for liberty. When Spain went down in defeat the hour of separation had come. By their mistakes and crimes, the kings of Spain had themselves made ready for it.

Chapter IV

INDEPENDENCE—THE CREATION OF NEW NATIONS. 1808-1826

THE emancipation of the South American colonies from the rule of their respective mother countries forms the third period of their history, which opens for the Spanish possessions by the events at Caracas and Buenos Ayres in 1810, and for the Portuguese, by the declaration of the independence of Brazil and its transformation into a constitutional empire in 1822.

We have seen the state of public opinion in the colonies in the eighteenth century. Spain might still have prevented the catastrophe, but her blindness knew no limits. She continued to trample upon every interest and to break every pledge. It was ordained that she should remain, to the last, deaf to all warnings, that everything in her insane conduct should make the coming rebellion inevitable and justify it at the bar of history. The rising was unanimous.

The revolution of Aranjuez was the decisive event in this movement. On March 18, 1808, the Spanish people had dethroned the weak Charles IV., who had allowed the queen to place all public business in the hands of her lover Godoy, and had given himself over to the pleasures of hunting and the care of his stables. Ferdinand VII., the wicked and vile son of this guilty mother and imbecile father, was placed on the throne; and shameful quarrels broke out among these Bourbons, whom Napoleon degraded at pleasure. The imprisonment of this unhappy family at Valençay; the renunciation of their rights in consideration of annuities and pensions; the imposition of the Napoleonic dynasty; the French invasion; the wicked and stupid colonial policy of the different political parties which were struggling for power; all united to bring on the rupture and gave South Americans cause to think that insurrection was a sacred duty. The worst misfortune of oppressed peoples is content with servitude. They knew how to escape that fate. They would no longer share the lot of conquered Spain, that stepmother who, even in defeat, continued to subject America to her caprices. Moreover, who was Spain? The resolutions and proclamations of all the contending factions reached America together; some from Charles IV.; others from Ferdinand VII.; others from the upstart usurper, Joseph. Besides these there were many declarations of juntas: the Junta of Cadiz; the Junta of Seville; the Junta of Asturias; and others; all claiming to be legitimate and demanding obedience; not to mention the Council of Regency. This was anarchy. Now that the tyrant was weakened at every point his victim saw a ray of hope.

So in 1809, Quito, " the first-born of independence," rose for freedom. The movement was suppressed and two patriots forfeited their lives in the cause; but the attempt was repeated in the following year (August 2) and was this time successful.

One might suppose that the mother country at this time would wish to remove every cause of complaint from the colonies. She had received from them in 1808 and 1809 subsidies and gifts of considerable value, and doubtless she agreed to reward this fidelity in misfortune by wholesome reforms. A royal decree of January 22, 1809, had gone so far as to declare the Spanish-American provinces integral parts of the monarchy with rights equal to those of the peninsular provinces, but this was only a bait. The following year, the Junta of Seville said, in an address to the Spanish-Americans: " At last you are raised to the dignity of free men. The time is past when you were bent under an unbearable yoke and the victims of absolutism, avarice and ignorance. In electing your representatives in the national congress remember that your destiny is no longer dependent on kings, viceroys and governors, but is in your own hands." This high-sounding denunciation of the manner in which Spain had governed her colonies resulted in a decree restricting the number of representatives to one for each principal town; and even the one was to be drawn by lot from a list of three names chosen by the municipal councils in such manner as the viceroys might be pleased to prescribe.

The Central Junta had proclaimed free trade by the ordinance of 1809; but the ordinanace was almost immediately repealed by the Regency of Cadiz, which took the place of the Central Junta. This rash action bore fruit quickly, for as soon as it was known at Caracas the storm burst. In this captaincy the principles of the French Revolution had won more adherents than in any other colony. The municipal council grasped the reins of power, declared itself the

Supreme Junta of government (April 19, 1810) and, though it recognized Ferdinand VII., refused to obey the regency or respect its decrees. About this time agents sent from Europe to demand an oath of allegiance to Joseph, were greeted with the cry "Long live Ferdinand." The country was unanimously opposed to Napoleon, the *josephinos* (adherents of Joseph) and the *afrancesados* (France-

lovers). When a rumor spread that French troops threatened New Granada the province of Cundinamarca was put under arms (July). The viceroy was accused of wishing to sell America to Napoleon and was sent off to Cartagena. This town had risen some time before, as well as the provinces of Pamplona and Socorro. In the north the provinces of Tunja, Casanare, Antioquia, Choco, Neiva and Mariquita rose all at once while Quito was making the second attempt spoken of above. The viceroyalty of New Granada had disappeared before the end of 1810. Each provincial capital wanted to have its own junta independent of all other juntas. Now united action was indispensable to ultimate triumph, and the junta formed at Bogota recognized Ferdinand VII. as king and invited Caracas to do the same and make common cause with it. Caracas declared that the representatives of the provinces of Venezuela ought to be instructed to organize a free government. Accordingly the congress of Caracas, made up of deputies from the provinces of Caracas, Variñas, Barcelona, Cumana, Margarita, Trujillo and Merida, which had separated from Maracaibo, proclaimed (July 5, 1811) the independence of Venezuela, and organized a republic.

Similar occurrences happened at many other places in America. Buenos Ayres and Montevideo had been blockaded by an English squadron from 1804 till 1807, for Spain was then at war with England. Jacques de Liniers, a Frenchman in the Spanish service, had organized the brave creoles and driven off the invaders. The new-made soldiers, proud of their victory, were petted and flattered by those who had begun to conspire against the Spanish domination, including such men as Moreno, Castelli, Belgrano, Bulcarce, all eager readers of the revolutionary literature from the United States and France, which had been brought in during the English occupation. Thus the army of the revolution was ready made. At Buenos Ayres the uprising was carefully prepared. An assembly of six hundred notables deposed the viceroy Cisneros (May, 1810). Castelli and Belgrano led the patriot movement. The royalists were repeatedly defeated in spite of assistance obtained from Portugal, through the influence of the queen, the wife of John IV., and the dispatch of an army corps to their aid by the viceroy of Peru. The struggle was short-lived. The Spanish leaders were abandoned by their troops and captured. For a time Montevideo was a rallying point and headquarters for the royalists, but juntas were organized in Paraguay and in all the provinces of La Plata. Chili also rose successfully in 1810. In that country the patriots had very few muskets. Many bodies of troops were armed with ox-yokes, and for artillery wooden cannon were made which burst at the fourth discharge. Victory under such conditions proves the magic power of liberty.

Lower Peru remained submissive and gave the Spaniards an

effective base for resistance, but Upper Peru struggled desperately. The revolution broke out first in Charcas and then in La Paz, in May, 1809. A small army, sent from Buenos Ayres the next year, became the nucleus of a numerous patriot force, and Castelli and Belgrano entered Potosi in triumph. The royalist government at Lima had to contend with the partisans of independence in Quito, Upper Peru and Chili, and its scattered forces were worn out, even when victorious. On the other hand, the revolution was not received with equal enthusiasm by all classes, especially in the beautiful, idle and luxurious city of Lima. The Castilian nobles, official families, and high dignitaries of the church opposed it; the lower ranks of the clergy everywhere favored it. " They were especially disaffected; not one seemed to be attached to the royal government."[1] The youth of the upper classes were in many places invaluable allies of the revolution. Moved by a lofty patriotism, they cheerfully submitted to conscription where it was in force, as in Venezuela, while men of the lower classes had to be dragged to the army in chains. The negroes and Indians had been brutalized by slavery and schooled to obedience and they allowed themselves to be thus forced to serve indifferently for or against the cause which was to make them free men. In several places, Buenos Ayres for example, certain tribes took advantage of the struggle to renew their inroads, and carried on terrible raids. Thus the war of independence went on with alternations of success and failure in every quarter. If Spain, just at this time, had produced a man of sufficiently clear judgment to discern the inevitable course of events, to submit to necessary losses, and definitely concede to the revolutionists the territory actually held by them, he might by equitable reforms have kept the allegiance of the vast and rich countries which had not yet revolted. Like every great social agitation, this revolution threw up extraordinary men. The greatest and most illustrious was Simon Bolívar, the hero of South America. In him was personified that gigantic struggle of the oppressed against the oppressors, which was to last fifteen years. His country granted him the title of " Liberator " (el Liberador), and one of the states which owed its independence to him took his name.

Simon Bolivar was born in Caracas in 1785; he was the

[1] Letter of Morillo to his government, among papers seized by a privateer of Buenos Ayres on board the ship Leona, and reproduced in " Les révolutions de l'Amerique Espagnole. bar un citoyen de l'Amerique Espagnole." Paris, 1819, 2d ed.

youngest of the four children of Juan Vicente Bolívar y Ponte, colonel of the militia of the plains of Aragua, a rich and respected man. Simon was an orphan at the age of six years and inherited a fortune yielding forty thousand dollars a year. He was sent while still a youth, to Madrid to finish his education in the family of his uncle, the Marquis de Palacios. At the age of seventeen he asked the hand of the Lady Teresa, his cousin, daughter of the Marquis de Toro. He was sent away for travel and visited Paris, but soon returned to Spain. He was only eighteen when he married and brought his young bride to Caracas, but had the misfortune to lose her within five months after their arrival, by a violent attack of yellow fever. Her loss was a great affliction to him. In 1803 he again sailed for Europe, revisited France in 1804, and did not come back to his native country until 1809, passing on his return through the United States. After having taken part, at Paris and Milan, in the apotheosis of Napoleon as emperor and king, he found himself in the midst of an energetic people which had freed itself by its own initiative. In France he had let fall bitter words which excited the suspicion of the imperial police; and in the United States he was filled with admiration for the just and great Washington.

The revolution found him upon his estates in Aragua. He offered his services, and was sent to England with Luis Lopez y Mendez to solicit her protection. The two envoys were received very coolly, because the English Government, making common cause with the Spanish Cortes against the French domination, refused to support a movement hostile to Spain.

Bolívar returned to America, bringing a small quantity of arms and accompanied by General Miranda, an old and valiant soldier, also a native of Caracas, who, for conspiring to give liberty to his country, had been expatriated, and had been going about the world for five and twenty years in search of allies for the American cause. Miranda had served France in the armies of the Republic; and weary of delay he had in 1806 organized a small expedition from his own resources and those of his friends. He landed at Ocumare, and afterward at Coro, but was forced to reëmbark in haste by the ill reception that his compatriots gave him on that occasion. He now returned an old man, but with spirit unbroken, to place his sixty years at the service of his country, and was made commander-in-chief.

The Spaniards had regained control. An earthquake which destroyed nine-tenths of the houses in Caracas on Holy Thursday, 1812, terrified the people, and it was used as a means for restoring tyranny in the name of Heaven. Monteverde, a sea captain, a man of rough manners and great severity, was made leader of the royalists, succeeded in recovering Venezuela, and obliged Miranda to capitulate. The country again fell under the domination of Spain. Miranda had obtained a promise of an amnesty in favor of the patriots, but the promise was not kept, and the unfortunate old man was the first victim of the reactionary rule that followed. Monteverde sent him to die in the dungeons of Cadiz. It is painful to record that among his enemies was Bolívar, who bore him a grudge for theoretic pedantry, irresolution and failure, and possibly for rumored intrigues with England which Bolívar may have accepted as true. At any rate, Bolívar's conduct in this matter was deplorable. Monteverde succeeded in spreading terror through the province; and when the prisons were full he gave the signal for vengeance. Murder and brigandage were forthwith erected into a political system. The country was filled with unfortunate wretches cast out of the city after having had their noses or cheeks slit, their ears cropped, or their nails torn out by the roots. The cause of independence seemed lost in Venezuela, and was in hardly better case in New Granada.

Chili was also weakened. At Quito the reaction was in control until the brave Mariño should come at the head of a new expedition, destined to wrest that country again out of the hands of the Spaniards. By good fortune La Plata was now completely emancipated, and the armies of Artiga and Lopez held the Spaniards in check on the frontiers of Chili and Peru. Here the cause of Spain was lost forever.

Bolívar had taken refuge in Curaçao with his cousin, Félix Ribas, where he collected all the refugees and led them to Cartagena. His project was to use the resources of this province, which remained free, to liberate Venezuela and save New Granada at one and the same time. The congress of Cartagena adopted it with enthusiasm. President Torrices furnished him with money, arms, supplies, and a force of five hundred men under Manuel Castillo. Bolívar led his three hundred Venezuelans and Ribas was second in command. The little army left Cartagena in January, 1813, but soon Castillo wanted to march on his own account toward the east, while Bolívar received orders from Congress to carry and hold Barancas, a town on the banks of the Magdalena. Bolívar did not know how to remain inactive, and disobeyed these orders, promising himself to obtain pardon for this fault by a glorious success.

He first seized Tenerife, a town situated on the right bank of the Magdalena, then Mompox, and lastly Ocaña, dividing, beating and dispersing the enemy. His invasion of Venezuela freed New Granada, and the cruelties of Monteverde now proved to be the salvation of the revolutionary cause in the former territory, for they drove the moderates into the patriot camp. Recruits poured in from all sides and Bolívar had two thousand men when he penetrated the Andes near Pamplona. After he had effected his junction with Ribas on Venezuelan soil many thousands of volunteers flocked to his standard. Ribas brought in six hundred men from New Granada, sent by the Congress of Tunja, and at the same time Colonel Briceno, who had been sent with a separate force toward Guadalito, arrived with a body of cavalry. Without loss of time Bolívar attacked the royalists at La Grita and afterward at Merida, making himself master of the district of this name; with equal promptness he occupied the province of Varinas. In the meantime Mariño, a young student who had reached the highest military rank and was considered one of the pillars of the revolution, defeated Monteverde, made himself master of the provinces of Cumana and Barcelona, and took the title of general-in-chief and dictator of the eastern provinces of Venezuela. Favored by this diversion, although it was opposed to his views of unity, Bolívar divided his army into two parts; taking command of one, he placed Ribas in command of the other, and pursuing the Spaniards closely, crushed Monteverde and marched on Caracas. In August, 1813, he entered the capital in a triumphal chariot drawn by twelve young women, amid the wildest enthusiasm, and was saluted by the title of " The Liberator." In a few months he had marched 375 miles and fought fifteen battles, besides numerous smaller actions. His glory would have been complete if, in this memorable campaign, he had not retaliated by sanguinary executions for the horrible cruelties of Monteverde. To be sure, the Spaniards had declared that not one of the patriot rabble ought to be suffered to live, and had actually killed women and children lest they should act as spies.

The liberation of Venezuela appeared to be complete. Bolívar occupied almost half of the captaincy-general and Mariño the rest.

The Spaniards held only a few unimportant points, and Monteverde was blockaded in Puerto Cabello. There seemed to be no reason to expect a turn of fortune.

Bolívar had taken the title of dictator of the western provinces of Venezuela, and was in no haste to reëstablish the civil government; but the echoes of public opinion convinced him of his error, and he convoked an assembly. To it he gave an account of his operations and plans, and tendered his resignation. This was not accepted and his dictatorship was continued until Venezuela should be able to unite with New Granada.

The royalists had not lost all hope, and now armed the slaves, promising them liberty. At the head of these bloodthirsty brutes the ferocious Puy won distinction. He seized Varinas and shot five hundred patriots there. Puy was lieutenant of Boves, the most dreaded of the adversaries of Bolívar. This Boves was a Castilian by birth, had been successively sailor, coastguard, and peddler, and had been imprisoned for his crimes. He enlisted in the royalist ranks without much knowledge of the issue or intelligible motive, and held the rank of captain of militia at the time of the defeat of the Spaniards. He appealed to the idlers, the fugitives from justice, the negroes and the mulattoes, and with these organized a body of troops which, from their ferocity, deserved their name of " The Infernal Legion." In its ranks were many *llaneros* (barbarians from the plains, herdsmen, and butchers). They were accustomed to tame the most vicious horses, lived in the saddle, and were unrivaled as cavalrymen. These men of the plains despised the mountaineer who lowered himself by going on foot, as well as the European, who was wearied by a gallop continued for sixteen hours. They ride bareback and have no other dress than a sort of short breeches. Stretched out over their horses, with lance in rest and whirling lasso, they fall upon the enemy, surprising and overwhelming him with the rapidity of lightning. No regular cavalry can resist the onset of these Cossacks of the Colombian steppes, who always leave behind them such terrible traces. The cupidity of these nomads had been excited by the promise to distribute the lands of the conquered among them, and Boves's force soon amounted to eight thousand men. Their detested intervention occasioned reprisals and twelve hundred prisoners were slaughtered in one day. The war was henceforth waged with frenzied cruelty, each side striving to outdo the atrocities of the other.

The energy of Boves was more than once paralyzed by the apathy of the Spanish generals, and Bolívar succeeded in defeating him several times in succession, as well as his lieutenants, the mulatto Roseta and the guerrilla chief Yañez. The dictator had the imprudence to risk himself on the vast plains, where he was surprised by the cavalry of Boves. Bolívar's whole force was crushed at La Puerta on June 14. Mariño, beaten almost at the same time, was driven back into Cumana. The conqueror entered Caracas so quickly that the dictator had only sufficient time to get on board a ship, thus trusting the safety of the republic to the mercy of the elements. Ribas rallied the patriots and managed to keep the field. Boves finally defeated him at Uriqua, but the victor received a spear wound during the battle and died on the field. His ferocious soldiers paid him suitable funeral honors by an indiscriminate slaughter of women, children and old men. Ribas was captured and shot and his head was sent to Caracas to be publicly exposed (December, 1814).

Bolívar had been able to reach Cartagena, which, with the province of Santa Marta, had been formed into a separate republic with Torrices as president. New Granada was very much divided. It will be remembered that a provisional junta had been established in Bogota since July, 1810. The provincial deputies assembled in congress had drawn up a federal constitution, which had not been approved by all the provinces, the dissidents electing a junta called the Junta of Cundinamarca. In 1812 this assembly published its plan of a constitution, which was no better received than the other. Anarchy reigned supreme. A third congress assembled in Tunja on September 10, 1814, and Bolívar offered his services. He was ordered to march against Bogota and its dictator, Alvarez, and he obtained a formal promise that the dissident provinces would join the confederation, provided that the old capital should be the seat of government. The Congress, once installed in Bogota, immediately set about preparing means to repulse the Spanish force which was expected to appear very shortly. Napoleon had fallen; Ferdinand VII. had returned to Madrid; and very soon news arrived that he was sending a squadron, with 10,642 men under the command of Morillo, to succor the royalists. The speedy arrival of this important reinforcement had been communicated to all the viceroys. The Madrid government hoped that the mere announcement would terrify the rebels and force them to submit in a body. This was reckoning too much on the prestige of the Spanish arms, which were already known not to be invincible. Moreover these events coincided with the capitulation of Montevideo, the last refuge of the mother country in the old viceroyalty of Buenos Ayres, which was from that moment transformed into an independent state. The new republic had formed a squadron and the seamen of La Plata had beaten the Spanish fleet. By the surrender of Montevideo and its garrison of 5500 men Spain lost her last foothold on the eastern coast. This misfortune had been partly counterbalanced by successes in Chili, which, in 1814, had again fallen under the yoke of the Spaniards, and been given over to all the horrors of merciless repression, though the guerrilla chief, Rodriguez, constantly harassed the royalists and kept the patriot cause alive. In Peru the provinces of Cuzco, Huamanga, and Arequipa, which had hitherto continued tranquil, declared for the cause of independence under the influence of Belgrano and the government of Buenos Ayres. Even Lima was held by the royalists with great difficulty.

The patriot leaders in New Granada and Venezuela had united. Castillo, Cabal, and Urdaneta acted for New Granada; Bolívar and Mariño for Venezuela. Troops were sent to the south to check the government of Quito, and in the east Urdaneta was charged to restrain the devastating incursions of Puy. Bolívar, appointed captain general of New Granada and Venezuela, descended through the province of Magdalena at the head of three thousand men, surprised Mumpox, where he shot four hundred prisoners, and demanded reinforcements from Torrices in order to attack Santa Marta. These reinforcements the latter obstinately refused him, thinking it more important to uphold the independence of Cartagena against Bogota than to repel the enemy. Bolívar wished to force the president to submit, and, instead of continuing his march, returned to Cartagena, thus losing precious time. In the meanwhile the enemy was approaching and the common danger averted a fratricidal struggle. He united his troops with those of Cartagena and embarked alone for Jamaica, whence he hoped to bring succor. When he was preparing to return with reinforcements he received news that Cartagena had surrendered after an heroic resistance of four months. The second period of the War of Independence thus terminated still more unfortunately than the first. Morillo entered Cartagena on December 6, 1815. It paid dearly for its refusal to support the common cause, for the city was nothing but a heap of ruins, since the whole strength of the enemy had been directed against it. By the loss of Cartagena New Granada was again opened to the enemy.

At first Morillo professed pacific intentions, but almost immediately, yielding to the advice of Morales, he gave orders that, with respect to the rebels, "all considerations of humanity" should be forgotten. Summary executions, wholesale deportations, imprisonments, forced contributions and seizures of property began everywhere. In the meantime the patriots kept the field with gallant pertinacity. After an important victory at Puente on February 16, 1816, Morillo allowed himself to be defeated by Urdaneta and Torrices, his position becoming very critical for the moment; five hundred Spaniards went over to the patriots, some privateers captured his convoys, and one of his ships blew up. Brion, a rich Dutch merchant of Cartagena, who served the government of Caracas first as captain of a frigate and afterward as admiral, brought back Bolívar, Mariño, and fifteen hundred resolute men, with one thousand negroes furnished by Pétion. The treachery, tyranny, and cruelty of Morillo threw into the ranks of the rebellion very many men now convinced that his capitulations and promises of pardon were only snares. For example: Bogota, by a formal treaty promising a general amnesty, opened its gates to the Brigadier Latoire; but Morillo did not hesitate to break the pledge given in his name. Torres, Lozano, Torrices, Cabal, Miguelde, Pombo, Caldas, and more than two hundred other patriots were shot, their families exiled, and their property confiscated. Though Morillo was endowed with incontestable military qualities, he was absolutely lacking in those necessary for pacifying a country. By exasperating the vanquished he made submission impossible. He came to reconquer America and made its loss certain. He believed in the efficacy of odious and arbitrary measures, conceived by him, and entrusted for execution to a "permanent council of war," a "council of purification," a "junta of sequestration," and courts martial.

The Spanish flag again floated over all the territory of New Granada, and this fortunate success blinded Morillo. He exaggerated his power and believed he could make it invincible and lasting by a reign of terror which he hoped to extend to bleeding Peru. He even dreamed of crushing Buenos Ayres. Bolívar undertook to dissipate his illusions. The Liberator secretly set sail from Cayes at the head of an expedition composed of two ships of war and thirteen transports, fitted out for the most part at the expense of Brion. On March 2 Brion defeated the Spanish flotilla, taking two vessels. On the 3d Bolívar disembarked on the Island of Margarita, which had fallen into the hands of the mulatto Arismendi, and there the insurgents in a mass meeting four days later proclaimed the Republic of Venezuela "one and indivisible" and Bolívar as its chief. Arismendi presented to the dictator a gold-headed reed, "emblem of the supreme authority in a country that can bend under the blast of adversity, but never break."

The Scotchman MacGregor at the head of 600 men was ordered to go to the succor of Mariño and Piar, who were holding out in Guiana, while Paez, operating from the province of Apure as a base, ejected Morillo from it. The Indian Paez, who had passed his youth among the *llaneros,* proposed to draw his old companions from the reactionary party, and unite them to the cause of independence. He succeeded, for the Spanish government, thinking there was no further need of their services, had contemptuously disbanded them without the least compensation. They were undeceived by this ingratitude and went over to the revolutionary party, becoming the most efficient instrument of its final success. By his loyal and generous character Paez had become the idol of these untamed natures. His exploits are those of a legendary hero, and most marvelous stories are told of him: that he repulsed the Spanish infantry by letting wild oxen loose against them; that he stopped pursuit by setting fire to the plains; that he captured several gunboats with his cavalry in the waters of the Apure by swimming; that with his terrible lance he killed as many as forty enemies in the fight, and when he fell upon a band of fugitives he completed the rout by his powerful voice and the fear that he inspired. Endowed with prodigous strength and unconquerable energy, he shared the amusements and the dangers of his men. At the head of the ferocious *llaneros* of the plains of the Apure, he began those brilliant exploits that were later to make him the terror of the Spanish armies.

Bolívar was deserted by fortune and found himself obliged to beat a retreat once more. He took refuge in Jamaica, where he narrowly escaped death by the poniards of the royalists; but nothing could abate his courage. He was active, resourceful, with an expedient for every emergency, and the moment had arrived when, after having touched the bottom of the abyss he was to rise and issue from it. The disobedience of some chiefs, his rivals, had been very fatal to the cause of independence and would have been much more so if the Spanish leaders had not also quarreled among themselves to such an extent that Morillo had been compelled to arrest two general officers, Morales and Real. After many conferences, Arismendi, Via, Paez, Rojas, Monagas, Sedeño, and Bermudez agreed to recognize Bolívar as general-in-chief. He called together a general congress in the Island of Margarita. Barcelona became the seat of the provisional government, of which he took the direction with the title of President of the Republic of Venezuela. Hither Morillo came to besiege him, but was himself defeated. The Spanish camp fell into the hands of the republicans, and the squadron escaped total destruction as by a miracle, for Bolívar boldly burned his own ships to cut off the enemy at the harbor mouth. Fortune once more smiled upon the patriots. They got the upper hand at many points and the royalists were discouraged. Nevertheless, Bolívar and Mariño could not agree. The one wanted to lay siege to Cumana, while the objective of the other was Caracas. The departure of Mariño weakened Bolívar; but by good fortune insurrectionary outbreaks increased in New Granada, the provinces of Antioquia, Quito, and Popayan were overrun by guerrillas, and Piar, with the help of Brion, invaded Guiana. Piar did his part well. Scouring the plains with his *llaneros* lancers he won two important victories and defeated Morillo in person. The Spanish army, in desperation, made ready to evacuate Caracas when a reinforcement of four thousand men so strengthened it as to justify an attempt to drive Mariño from the province of Cumana. The Island of Margarita had become the base of the Venezuelan navy. Morillo advanced against it and in two months his four thousand men perished there.

Bolívar had established his headquarters at Angostura. His rapid movements confused the enemy, for when beaten at one place he reappeared victorious in another. His popularity had not been diminished by his defeats and volunteers flocked to his standard from England and France, whom he organized as a model legion more than two thousand strong. At the same time he accredited *chargés d'affaires* to Washington and London. In England Lopez Mendez, charged to contract loans and enlist men, had no difficulty in procuring either. Venezuela had enrolled no less than nine thousand foreign soldiers. The Spaniards despaired of conquering the Liberator and attempted to assassinate him. Twelve men entered his tent one night, but he escaped half dressed from their daggers.

At the end of the year 1818 the republicans were in an excellent position. Bolívar convened a national congress at Angostura, opened it in person on February 15, 1819, and laid before it a proposed constitution. He was confirmed in the presidency of the republic and resolved to strike a decisive blow. His plan was to threaten many points at once and especially to make a feint upon Caracas, but march upon southern New Granada, which the Spaniards had held quietly for two years. Morillo got no inkling of it. Mariño was to occupy the eastern provinces and capture Cumana and Barcelona while the dictator carried on this campaign. Bolívar set out with his staff and about two thousand men, but he was counting upon the foreign troops, Paez and his *llaneros,* and volunteers from New Granada. The patriots of Casanare had risen once more and recognized the authority of Santander, a friend and agent of Bolívar, who had to effect a juncture with them, take Bogota with their help, and return to Venezuela with new forces. But he must cross the Andes in the rainy season, venture into rugged and sterile regions traversed by mountain torrents, cross deserts where the tortures of thirst were increased by the mirage, penetrate forests where trees of a prodigious height intercepted the light of day and dropped with continuous rain, and march hour after hour over flooded plains waist deep in water. On the heights his troops encountered icy whirlwinds and snow. They had climbed above all vegetation and their path was marked for them by the bones of travelers who had perished by the way. After seventy days of cruel suffering the little army gained the western slope of the mountains in a pitiable state and with greatly reduced strength. Much of the war material had been perforce abandoned; the horses had all perished, and the men marched as in a stupor. But the end was attained and these heroes were soon to receive the reward of their valor. On July 1, in the valley of Sagamoso, Bolívar encountered 3500 Spaniards, attacked and routed them, and the same night Tunja fell into his hands. The decisive victory of Boyaca opened the gates of Bogota to him (August 10, 1819). This brilliant campaign had lasted just seventy-five days. Bolívar now carried out the long projected union of

New Granada and Venezuela in one republic, left Santander as vice president, and set out again for Angostura. His march was a continuous triumph. The congress, under the presidency of Antonio Zea, sanctioned the union of the two provinces, which took the name of " The Republic of Colombia, one and indivisible," in honor of Christopher Columbus (December 17).

Before proceeding further let us cast a rapid glance on the political situation of the different South American countries: First, what had happened in Brazil? The House of Braganza, flying from the French, had disembarked in Rio Janeiro on January 17, 1808. It found this colony stirred like the rest by ideas of liberty, and ready for revolution. Dreams of emancipation were cherished there, as in the neighboring Spanish colonies. A plot had been hatched in 1789 among the youth who read the French authors of the period. The leader, Joseph de Sylva-Xavier, had paid for his patriotic devotion on the scaffold and his followers had been exiled. Rio Janiero now became the capital of the Portuguese monarchy and Brazil ceased to be a colony. Its ports were opened to commerce and many reforms were adopted which gave the country a degree of prosperity before unknown; but at the same time ideas of independence spread. The titular rank of a kingdom was granted to Brazil by the prince regent, who thereafter reigned under the style of John IV., but this gave only momentary satisfaction. In 1817 the republicans of Pernambuco attempted an insurrection which was drowned in blood. Other risings in different places were occasioned by royal exactions, increased taxes, and the bad administration of justice. The time was at hand when the antipathy of Portuguese and Brazilians would give rise to arbitrary and extravagant measures soon to be followed by terrible scenes of violence like the massacre on the Exchange in February, 1821.

In Paraguay the revolution was accomplished without bloodshed on May 14, 1811. Here was formed a so-called republic under the rule of a dictator for life, Dr. Francia, a strange being not unlike Louis XI. This suspicious despot followed the example of the Jesuits by absolutely forbidding all intercourse between Paraguay and the rest of the world.

The provinces of La Plata had definitely separated from the mother country. Nothing could check the work of their emancipation and it was finally accomplished in 1813 in spite of the war with the Spaniards in Upper Peru, the armed intervention of the

Portuguese in Brazil, the efforts of the royalist party to prolong
the anarchy, the rivalry of the chiefs, the insubordination of the
army, and the intrigues of the reigning houses of Europe, excited
by a perfect rage for domination.   The house of Braganza, taking
advantage of the captivity of the Spanish princes, asserted the
rights of Charlotte de Bourbon to the proposed kingdom; France
offered as candidate the Duke of Orleans and the Prince of Lucca;
others suggested Francisco de Paula, the brother of Ferdinand
VII.   These conflicting claims caused much bloodshed.   The first
ten years of the revolution passed amid incessant struggles, but the
magic words " country " and " liberty " united men of all parties in
the hour of danger, and the young republic came forth victorious
over all the obstacles that were raised against her on every side.
More than once the patriot cause seemed to be lost.   Torn by factional strife in the capital itself; attacked in the Banda Oriental by
Artigas, who wished to make himself the head of this territory;
threatened with disruption by the efforts for separation of the provinces, which were ill-disposed to bear the yoke of Buenos Ayres, and
the simultaneous arrival of a Spanish squadron and attack of a Brazilian army; exposed, in consequence of the victories of General
Pezuela in Upper Peru and of Colonel Osorio in Chili, to invasion
on both these frontiers, the new nation, under the guidance of
Puyredon, saw all these dangers disappear one by one.   Artigas,
who had seized for himself Santa Fé and Montevideo, was acknowledged by the government of Buenos Ayres as the head of the Banda
Oriental in 1815, and in the following year he repulsed an aggressive attempt of the Portuguese to seize all the country as far as the
La Plata, obliging them to enter into negotiations with the republic
of Buenos Ayres.   The Act of Independence of the United Provinces of Rio de la Plata, including at that time the provinces of
Upper Peru (Bolivia) was proclaimed on July 9, 1816, at Tucuman, by the Congress legislating " upon the great and noble subject
of the independence of peoples."

   This republic might have lived tranquilly if the project of
the great powers of Europe to erect the territory of La Plata into
a kingdom for the Prince of Lucca had not come to carry anarchy
to its highest point.   Puyredon, who held the supreme power, was
accused of favoring these designs, destructive to liberty, and from
that moment all was confusion and disorder.   Every province in the
republic set up as an independent state and hostilities broke out

between rival cities. The northern provinces began the war called the " War of the Federalists " and marched against the " Unionists " of Buenos Ayres. Artigas, in a severe battle at Cepeda, defeated the monarchist party, and a treaty of peace was concluded at El Pilar, February 23, 1820, by which it was agreed that a confederation should be formed under a central government; and the important constitutional change thus brought about was celebrated by public rejoicings. If Spain had not been fully occupied with internal complications she would, no doubt, have attempted a decisive blow here as she did in Colombia. As it was she bequeathed to Brazil the mission of perpetuating the war, by the pretensions of the House of Braganza to the possession of the Oriental Republic of Uruguay, which usurpation was consummated in 1822. After the Treaty of El Pilar the federal republics of the United Provinces of La Plata formed six divisions: Buenos Ayres, Mendoza, Tucuman, Cordoba, Salta, and Corrientes, with about 1,012,000 inhabitants. The federal army amounted to 30,000 men, of whom 14,718 were cavalry, 13,693 infantry, and 1296 artillery, besides militia and herdsmen of the plains.

La Plata was not content to selfishly seek its own independence; for, in spite of the difficulties it had to overcome, the young republic offered and furnished aid to the neighboring countries which desired to be free. Puyredon had kept up active communications since 1815 with Bolívar, and was in touch with O'Higgins. This famous Chilian patriot, when besieged in Rancagua and unable to hold out any longer, had sewn a black stripe upon his banner, fired his last guns, shotted with coin instead of grape, and then, by the light of the burning town, cut his way through the enemy sword in hand, and arrived at Santiago followed by 300 dragoons, all that remained of his army (1814). Chili bore with resignation the system of persecution organized by the commandant San Bruno; but influential men were preparing the revenge of liberty, and the government of Buenos Ayres was in correspondence with them. It maintained equally close relations with all the chiefs of the insurgent bands in Upper and Lower Peru. Thus was formed an alliance against which the last efforts of Spain were soon to dash themselves to pieces.

An army of 4000 men, under San Martin, the Governor of Mendoza, had been sent to the aid of Chili. San Martin entered the country by a pass in the Andes, theretofore considered impracticable. He won the battle of Chacabuco February 14, 1817, and established O'Higgins in power. The bloody battle of Maypo (April 5, 1818) finally freed Chili from the Spanish yoke. The joy in Santiago over this victory was so great that one old man fell down dead at the news, and many citizens suddenly became insane.

From this moment the Chilians did not content themselves with defending their own territory but, together with the men of Buenos Ayres, flew to the aid of the neighboring peoples who were still enslaved by Spain. A Spanish fleet carrying two thousand soldiers was defeated by the united forces of the two republics, and shortly afterward the Chilian fleet, under the command of Lord Cochrane, an English officer, was strong enough to command the sea and land five thousand men on the coast of Peru (1820). Lord Cochrane and San Martin, sent to liberate Peru from Spanish rule, took Lima on July 28, 1821; Peruvian independence was proclaimed on the same day; and on August 3 San Martin made himself supreme dictator of the country. The protectorate of the liberty of Peru and the command in chief of the insurgent army were given to San Martin.

From the foregoing account it is evident what the situation of the Spanish-American colonies was when the revolution of 1820 occurred in the mother country. When it broke out Ferdinand VII. was making ready at Cadiz a great expedition, with which he intended to reduce his rebellious colonies to obedience and subjugate them for all time. Twenty-two thousand men were mobilized and waited in mutinous discontent for the embarkation, which never came, because means of transportation were lacking. These men, who had been destined to oppose the revolution in America, proclaimed it in Andalusia, and carried it to victory in Madrid. Bolívar proposed to Morillo that the struggle, which had already lasted too long, should cease, and an armistice was concluded at Trujillo, November 25, 1820, between the Spanish and Colombian generals, and ratified the next day by Bolívar and Morillo, who had a solemn interview at the village of Santa Anna, dined at the same table and slept one night in the same room.

The Spanish Cortes was displeased, recalled Morillo and replied by insulting proposals to the attempts at negotiation. Three and a half months after the truce was signed Bolívar denounced it to Latorre, the successor of Morillo. On June 24 he advanced upon the Spanish headquarters and captured them, after a brilliant charge by Paez's lancers. That same night Bolívar occupied Valencia. Caracas and La Guayra again fell under his power. Cartagena and Cumana surrendered.

A congress assembled at Cucuta laid the foundations of a new government. The constitution, which was proclaimed August 30, 1821, was modeled on that of the United States. It abolished the inquisition, assumed the debts of Venezuela and New Granada, confided the legislative power to an assembly of two houses, and the executive power to a president elected for four years. Bolívar was again invested with the supreme authority. In 1822 the United States acknowledged the independence of Colombia, and treaties of alliance and union were signed with Peru, Buenos Ayres, Chili, and Mexico. By the end of 1823 the last Spanish garrison in Colombian territory, that of Puerto Cabello, laid down its arms. The Liberator was then at Lima, where the royalists were stirring up strife. He had hurriedly crossed the Andes once more to save the cause of independence. The Colombian General Sucre had defeated the viceroy near Pinchincha in 1822, and entered Quito and Guayaquil. The representatives of these provinces voted their annexation to Colombia, thus increasing the population of that republic to 2,615,000. The memorable victories of Junin and Ayacucho, in 1825, assured the deliverance of Peru. The surrender of Callao completed it; and the year 1826 witnessed the departure of the last Spanish soldier from the soil of South America, destined thenceforward to be free. Spain lost forever the rich provinces that she had till then exploited without pity; and her shameful defeat was a just retribution for her conduct toward the peoples she had ruled with such cruel tyranny. The liberating army had come to the end of its victorious career. The whole empire of the incas was set free, and among the standards taken from the Spanish troops, who for fourteen years had fought against the emancipation of Peru, there was one of priceless value. It was that with which Pizarro three hundred years before had entered the capital of Atahualpa.

The history of South America from this time is told in the second part of this work, which describes the development of the vast empire that took the place of the Portuguese colony, and the laborious organization of nine republics out of the fragments of the Spanish colonial empire. If Brazil, with the aid of the monarchies of Europe, could make the transition without undue shock to her institutions, the Spanish-American republics, surrounded by dangers and obstacles from the cradle, were not so fortunate. Before condemning too severely the turbulence of these young nations, most of which are still in the experimental stage, we should be mindful of the condition of ignorance and degradation in which Spain had systematically kept her subject peoples; of the great financial difficulties she had bequeathed to them; of the seeds of fanaticism planted by her inquisitors; and of the mental confusion and lack of experience in the peaceable exercise of liberty which resulted from this long-endured and degrading oppression.

PART II

INDEPENDENT SOUTH AMERICA. 1824-1876

Chapter V

THE UNITED STATES OF COLOMBIA (NEW GRANADA). 1824-1876

A DECREE of June 23, 1824, divided the territory of the Colombian Republic into twelve departments: Orinoco, Venezuela, Apure, Zulia, Boyaca, Cundinamarca, Cauca, Magdalena, Isthme, Ecuador, Assuay, Guayaquil. These were subdivided into provinces, districts and parishes. But this organization was short lived. When put in force the constitution had been most fiercely attacked. Two parties soon formed, the "Unitaries," who wanted to maintain a national union, and the "Federalists," who demanded local independence in a loose league.

When Bolívar, who was invested with the dictatorship of Peru, returned to Colombia, in June, 1826, the internal peace of the country was gravely compromised. In the name of the public safety, he made himself dictator in Colombia also. The army was devoted to him and applauded this resolution, but the civil element suspected him of yielding to the temptations of power and of desiring to follow in the footsteps of Napoleon. His accusers pretended that Colombia was saved from monarchy under Bolívar only by the fact that he was surrounded by many patriots devoted to the national cause, who would not in any wise lend themselves to his despotic scheme. It has been said that, like Cæsar, Bolívar sought on all sides for an Antony, who, under the pretext of the public welfare, should force him to seize the reins of government and absorb all authority.[1] It is even alleged that it was but the refinement of hypocrisy for him to warn his fellow citizens to be on their guard against himself. This warning was repeated on all occasions. History has preserved his fine answer to the Congress of Angostura, which offered him the presidency of the Colombian republic in 1819: " The sword will be useless in peace. A man like me is dangerous in a popular government, a constant menace to the sovereignty of the people. I prefer the title of citizen to that of liberator, because

[1] G. Hubbard. *"Histoire Contemporaine de l'Espagne."* Paris and Madrid, 1869, 2 vols.

77

the latter has its origin in war and the former in the law." In 1824 he wrote to the president of the Senate to resign his powers: " I desire to convince Europe and America of the horror with which supreme power inspires me, under whatever name it may be designated; my conscience is irritated by the atrocious calumnies that the Liberals of America and the Serviles of Europe accumulate against me." In presenting to the congress of Bolivia a plan of a constitution for that country, he said: " Legislators, liberty is from this day indestructible in America. The wild nature of this country is in itself sufficient to repel every form of monarchical government. We have here neither great aristocratic powers nor high ecclesiastical dignities. Without such support tyrants cannot found a stable empire, and if any ambitious men dream of seizing supreme power let the fate of Dessalines, Christophe and Iturbide be a warning of the end in store for them. The upstart princes who are so vainglorious as to wish to build thrones on the ruins of liberty, simply dig their own graves, and will only teach posterity that men could be found who preferred their own insatiable ambitions to the pursuits of honor and glory." It seems impossible that a man who coveted a crown could have expressed himself so unequivocally. Another time, at Bogota, this toast was given at a banquet: " If monarchical government is ever established in Colombia, may Bolívar be our emperor." One of the generals of the war of independence leaped to his feet and cried: " When Bolívar lets himself be saluted as emperor may his heart's blood flow like the wine from my glass." The Liberator immediately embraced his old companion in arms, saying: " If the sentiments of this man of honor are shared by all the inhabitants of Colombia, our independence and liberty will never be in danger." Though Bolívar wished to retain the dictatorship during his life, it is certain that he considered it the only means of attaining the complete deliverance of America and the aggrandizement and preponderance of his country; and in this he was on the fatal downward road to despotism. But we persist in believing in his sincerity, good faith, and patriotism. He has been called a political hypocrite. This is a great injustice to a high-minded patriot, whom the example of Bonaparte could not corrupt. He should not be measured by the standards of Washington, but is a creole hero who should rather be compared with Sertorius. Such is our judgment upon him. Let us forget his boasting, his pride, his deceitfulness, and remember his activity, his bravery, his pas-

THE STATUE ERECTED IN HONOR OF SIMON BOLIVAR, "EL LIBERADOR,"
IN THE CITY OF CARACAS, VENEZUELA

From a Photograph

sion for the glory and independence of his country, his disinterestedness and his generosity.   He emancipated all slaves, including 1200
on his own estates.   His blood, his life and his wealth were all
sacrificed to the cause which he had undertaken to champion.   We
may criticise his acts and his passion for domination, but we should
believe in the purity of his motives.   His thoughts turned early
toward France and the principles of her immortal revolution, and
the Declaration of the Rights of Man changed him from a
thoughtless and dissolute youth into a citizen and a hero, like
other heroes not without weaknesses, faults, and even crimes.   That
at certain times the men about him could talk of monarchy without
rebuke, as in like circumstances Washington spoke to his friend,
John Jay, is beyond question.   The thought was in men's minds
and found expression in words.   From words to deeds, though but
a step, is an irrevocable and terrible step.   This step Bolívar never
dreamed of taking, and therefore all free peoples will hold his name
in honor forever.

While he was in Peru the Liberator attempted to realize the
great project that he had conceived in the year 1822, namely, an
assembly of plenipotentiaries of the American states to deliberate,
"under the auspices of victory," upon their common interests, to
think over the means of defending themselves against Spain or any
other nation that threatened their independence, opposing, at last, a
vast American federation to the Holy Alliance and to the threatening principle of intervention proclaimed by the European cabinets.
This assembly might, in Bolívar's opinion, serve as a council in
serious disputes, as a rallying point in common dangers, as a faithful
interpreter of public treaties if controversies should arise, and finally
as an arbitrator.[2]   This project was during the year 1825 the object
of an active correspondence between Colombia, Peru and the other
new Spanish-American governments, and even with the United
States and Brazil.   Bolívar was the more urgent because the
restoration government in France threatened at that time to support,
in the name of divine right, the cause about to be abandoned by
Spain.[3]   He went so far as to ask the Congress to form itself into

[2] Note from the council of government of Peru to the executive power of
La Plata, May 2, 1825.

[3] The intervention of the Holy Alliance in America to reduce the Spanish
colonies to obedience prevented by the promulgation of the " Monroe Doctorine"
by the United States on December 2, 1823, and by the opposition of England to
the project.

a Committee of Public Safety independent of its electors, and to organize and place under its orders a powerful squadron and an army of 100,000 men.   Mexico and Guatemala received the project with enthusiasm; Chili and Buenos Ayres, which asked time for consideration, as well as Brazil, which had declared war against La Plata, and the United States were contented with the simple part of spectators; as to Paraguay, she was a stranger to everything that passed beyond her frontiers.   On June 22, 1826, the conferences were opened at Panama, in that magnificent position from which American diplomacy could attend to and protect the interests of ten new states and constitute a republican federation opposed to the old monarchical organization of Europe.   The congress was scarcely opened when the effects of the climate made themselves felt in an alarming manner, the plenipotentiary of the United States and two secretaries of the British commissioner dying almost at the same time.   Under the menace of a danger that increased every moment, the representatives of Colombia, Peru, Guatemala and Mexico hastily signed a treaty of perpetual union and confederation, and adjourned *sine die,* but later events postponed to a distant day the realization of this ambitious project.   Bolívar's hopes were dashed, and he sadly compared the Congress of Panama to an insane pilot on the shore attempting to guide a tempest-tossed ship at sea.   His secret aim had been to organize Colombia, Peru, Bolivia, La Plata and Chili into an immense republic, of which he should be the supreme head, the American continent being thus divided into four great states: Mexico, aggrandized at the expense of Guatemala; the United States; Brazil; and, lastly, under the name of the United States of South America, the rest of the southern continent.   A dispatch to Santander, vice-president of the Colombian republic, from Vidaure, the Peruvian minister of foreign affairs, proved that the project was known at Panama.   In a letter to Bolívar, Vidaure, who presided over the Congress, expressed his indignation.   The words of his dispatch to Santander show his deep distrust: " I was shocked to hear the nephew of the Liberator, Señor Briceno Meridez, a plenipotentiary to the great American congress, speak of his coronation. His old aide-de-camp, Masquera, the intendant of Guayaquil, exhibited an equal devotion to his royal highness," and he adds: " How deep was my grief and my surprise when, in these circumstances, I heard Señor Gual say to me: ' Colombia will have a population as great as that of Mexico.' "   From that moment Vidaure

determined to utterly overthrow this project, " so strong in the imaginations of the abettors of tyranny, but in fact without any solid foundation." He wrote for the opening of the congress a speech which was approved by the representatives of all the free states, but which, he says, caused the envoys of England and Holland to say to him: " Your life is in great danger. Bolívar has torn off the mask; he wishes to be emperor and establish a new dynasty." According to Vidaure, Bolívar's project was defeated by the haste with which the treaties were concluded.

These facts give us a clear view of the Liberator at this time. It is certain that the union of the three republics of Bolivia, Peru and Colombia under the title of confederation, with a capital, the seat of a perpetual and inviolable chief, was almost realized. The system of centralization had many enemies, who were treated as factionists, anarchists and disturbers of the peace. At their head was Paez, Bolívar's old companion in arms, who represented Venezuela in the Colombian senate. He demanded the absolute autonomy of this country, which had given him the command of its military forces. The vice-president, Santander, though he publicly and apparently opposed the federalist, or separatist party, secretly supported it. It is said that his purpose was to deceive this party, then to annihilate it by intrigue, and afterward to step into Bolívar's place. In any case the Liberator himself, who well knew where his enemies were, proposed to get rid of them by attacking them separately and opposing one to another, but his calculations did not obtain the result that he expected. In March, 1826, Bolivar had obtained from Congress an accusation against the administration of Paez. The old chief of the *llaneros,* supported by Mariño, endeavored to excite a rebellion. Quito, Guayaquil, Maracaibo, and Puerto Cabello hoisted the banner of revolution. Then it was that the Liberator came from Peru to reëstablish order. He marched against the rebels, easily subdued many of the revolted cities, had the dictatorship offered to him by the municipalities and granted an amnesty. By a decree of August 3, 1827, he convoked a great National Assembly of Colombia, to meet in the city of Ocaña March 2, 1828, to determine whether the constitution ought to be reformed, and if so to proceed to its reformation. This decree succeeded in reëstablishing a sort of momentary calm. In reality, by convoking this congress, Bolívar only intended that the extraordinary powers which he had seized should be confirmed. Intrigue presided at the elections. Of the 108 deputies elected only sixty-four appeared at Ocaña; the remainder were suspicious of Bolívar's intentions and remained at home. The Congress assembled. Discord broke out from the first session. The friends and partisans of the president accused Santander of extravagance, and, making the most of the necessity for a strong government, presented a plan of constitution in which the federalists thought they discovered the foundations of a throne for the Liberator. These fears spread, and the Bolívarists clearly saw that their numbers decreased day by day. The withdrawal of twenty of them made the deliberations of the Congress impossible, and it broke up in the midst of great popular excitement. The Liberator, being a few leagues from Ocaña, from whence he directed the action of his partisans, feigned surprise. By a proclamation in which the Congress was indirectly blamed, he incited the provinces to adopt extraordinary measures. In Bogota, Cartagena and Caracas, which he visited in succession, popular assemblies organized by his tools were convoked and opened, in which deliberations were carried on under the protection of bayonets; and the municipalities besought him to take supreme power and save the country. The republic was passing through a terrible crisis.

During this time Peru overthrew the semi-monarchical constitution known under the name of Bolívar's Code, which the Liberator had imposed upon her. The Congress of Lima declared in 1827 that Bolívar, as president for life, was incompatible with liberty. General La Mar, who was appointed president, blockaded the coasts of Colombia, and thus foreign war was added to internal discord. Bolivia, for her part, aided by Peru, overthrew General Sucre, who had been imposed on this republic at the same time as Bolívar's Code. Negotiations followed. Peru and Bolivia threw off the control of Bolívar and regained possession of themselves; the edifice that the Liberator had proposed to raise had collapsed.

As for Colombia, he held it under his authority with difficulty. His conduct in the midst of such grave complications had not been such as to disperse injurious suspicions. It was thought that he was too much preoccupied in getting unlimited power, and his ardent pursuit of despotic centralization opened the door to all manner of suspicion. This mistrust grew day by day. Absolutism and despotic centralization were asserted to be his sole objects. The federalists, or republicans, did not cease to watch him,

and to increase their strength against him. They resolved
to make an end of it and free themselves once for all from
his attempts at supreme power. On the night of September 26,
1828, they attacked his palace and killed the sentinels, and he
would have fallen under their poniards but for his presence of
mind. The conspirators had relied on the people, but they pronounced in favor of Bolívar, in whom they always saw the legendary
hero of emancipation, the Liberator. Many were executed, and
Santander, who was accused of being the mover of the plot, was
imprisoned and afterward exiled. The enemies of the Liberator
did not acknowledge their defeat. General Cordoba, an old friend
of Bolívar, rose in the province of Antioquía and was killed in the
midst of his soldiers. Insurrections broke out in Popayan and Rio
Negro, and a much more serious movement began on November 25,
1829, in Caracas, the native city of the Liberator, where an assembly
of a thousand notables, public functionaries and generals agreed
that Venezuela should be separated from Colombia and that Paez
should take upon himself the provisional dictatorship. The Senate
protested in vain against the dismemberment of Colombia. Bolívar
saw that his star was waning and employed means and resources
unworthy of a great man in order to prevent it; he exhibited himself
as exposed to the daggers of the friends of liberty, and struck a
medal commemorative of the attempt of September 26. In the
message that he sent to Congress on January 20, 1830, he again
tendered his resignation, so many times offered. He complained
bitterly that he had been suspected in the United States, in Europe,
and even in his own country, of aspiring to a throne. Reëlected
once more, he proclaimed that the Congress should adopt the most
energetic measures to prevent the dismemberment of Colombia. He
started at the head of 8000 men for the province of Maracaibo,
where Paez was awaiting him with superior forces and occupying
an impregnable position; this obliged Bolívar to pause. Suffering,
restless and discouraged, the Liberator hesitated as to the part he
should take, when the provincial assemblies were called together by
the Congress in order to avoid the division that they feared. For a
moment the congress thought of conferring on the Liberator the
presidency of the republic for life; but would he accept it? After
many negotiations, Bolívar renewed his offer of abdication. The
new constitution was achieved. On May 4 the Congress elected
Mosquera president of Colombia, offering Bolívar at the same time,

in the name of the Colombian nation, the tribute of their gratitude and admiration and an annual pension of 30,000 pesos payable at the place where he should fix his residence.

The departure of Bolívar excited keen regret. On taking leave of his old companions in arms, the emotion of General Urdaneta and his officers was so great that those present sobbed aloud. The very day of his departure the army raised Urdaneta to power, but he could not maintain his position. This was the last effort of the Unitaries. They were finally defeated by the separatist party, whose triumph was signalized by the recall of Santander, who had been banished from the republic for life by Bolívar. A decree of June 10 reinstated that " illustrious victim of despotism " in all his grades and military honors and in his rights of citizenship. On his arrival at Cartagena, Bolívar learned with sadness that the separation of Venezuela was an accomplished fact. Ecuador also, under General Flores, had declared itself independent; the Colombian edifice thus lost its two lateral columns. So perished the unity which had been the constant aim of all Bolívar's efforts. The tragic end of Sucre, who was mercilessly shot by the orders of his captor, Ovando, completed the affliction in which Bolívar was plunged. Overwhelmed with grief, humiliated in his glory, and deceived in his hopes, he died December 17, 1830, from a languid sickness, which had overtaken him in San Pedro, near Santa Marta. He was only forty-seven years old at the time of his death. His farewell to the Colombians, dated the 10th of the same month, shows us the cruel anguish that embittered his last moments. His last words were " Union! Union! "

This last appeal of the Liberator was not heard. The Colombian Republic, which had been born at his *fiat,* brought forth at his tomb three states—New Granada, Ecuador, and Venezuela.

Venezuela was formed of the departments or provinces of Venezuela, Zulia, Maturin and Orinoco; Ecuador of Ecuador, Guayaquil and Assuay. New Granada, which later was changed into the Granadine Confederation, and still later took the name of United States of Colombia, was composed of the five provinces of Cundinamarca, Isthme, Boyaca, Cauca and Magdalena, to which have been added Antioquía, Guaneta, and the territories of Guajira and Mocoa. The history of the republics of Ecuador and Venezuela is dealt with in other chapters; and in this we shall concern ourselves only with that of New Granada, or the United States of Colombia.

General Francisco de Paula Santander was elected the first president of the republic of New Granada while he was absent in the United States. He was inaugurated on October 8, and called upon the Granadines, of whatever opinion they had been in the days of internal discord, to sacrifice their resentments upon the altar of the country, " that there should be but one party, that of liberty, under the institutions to which we have sworn obedience." Santander reëstablished order, and on March 1, 1835, at the opening of the third congress of the republic, he could draw a pleasing picture of the moral and material situation of the country. According to a census taken at this time, the population amounted to 1,687,000, a very small number in comparison with the area of the republic. Under Santander's presidency the Colombian debt, which had been contracted with many English houses in 1822 and 1824, was divided among the three republics. The Holy See officially recognized the republic of Granada; and treaties were made with Venezuela and Ecuador to determine their respective boundaries. In order to draw attention to the Isthmus of Panama, across which, from the year 1834, he had desired to build a railway that would spare navigators the voyage of 4500 miles around Cape Horn, and thus open direct communication with all the countries washed by the Pacific Ocean, Santander declared Panama and Porto Bello free ports for the space of twenty years for all nations not at war with New Granada, but prohibited the importation of slaves at either port. The railway connecting the two oceans was opened in 1855. A special treaty secured the perpetual and exclusive privilege of transporting war material by this route to the United States; and in exchange that government guaranteed to Colombia her sovereignty over the isthmus against any foreign government. This treaty was renewed in 1865. In 1836, when he gave up his office, Santander witnessed the outbreak of the strife, which he had till then restrained. When he died, four years later, civil war was desolating the country. We may say that it lasted a quarter of a century, during which the republic experienced all varieties of revolution and of government, vacillating between conservatism and extreme socialism.

The efforts of those who desired a radical organization of the federal type triumphed in 1858, and the republic in consequence was transformed into the Granadine Confederation. Doctor Mariano Ospina, elected by the conservative party, laid before Congress many bills tending to preserve the little centralization that remained; but these laws seemed to the federalists a covert attack on their system. Protests were heard. The state of Santander rejected the resolutions of Congress; that of Cauca, where the conservative ex-president, Tomas Mosquera, recently elected governor and converted to democratic politics, was all powerful, did the same. The states of Bolívar and Magdalena soon followed their example. Ospina proclaimed martial law in the Confederation and decreed a levy of troops; but his ideas on the subject of government did not permit him to use them. In his message to the Congress had he not philosophically declared that it was necessary to make a trial of all theories in order that the country might know practically the different systems of government? To this doctrine he soon returned, and accordingly folded his arms and waited patiently for the meeting of Congress in 1860. Neither did the Congress show itself very much disposed to defend the central authority by force, and early in 1861 the revolutionists were masters of the coast towns.

On the expiration of the term fixed by law, Ospina resigned the presidency and enlisted as a private soldier among the defenders of the constitution. Julio Arboleda, the ablest conservative leader, was chosen in his stead. Arboleda was a man of energy, a distinguished orator, and perhaps the most remarkable poet Colombia has produced. He was descended from a family all of whose members had achieved distinction in the war of independence. His father, desiring, in spite of the fever which devoured him, to fulfill a mission that Bolívar had entrusted to him, had poisoned himself with arsenic in an attempt to arrest the paroxysms of his malady; his two uncles, the scholarly Caldas and Miguel de Pombo, had been shot by the Spaniards at Bogota; his cousin Ulloa had suffered the same fate; one of his aunts chose rather to die of hunger than to surrender to the Spaniards, and other kinsmen had fallen on the field of battle. All these deeds, recited by an heroic mother, had aroused an ardent love of liberty in the heart of her child. His life had been most adventurous; when he was elected deputy a revolution broke out that carried him to prison. After being set free with difficulty he was besieged in his house, escaped, and returned at the head of an army, only to be defeated and condemned to death. A turn of fortune brought him back in triumph; a military *coup d'état* dispersed the Congress; Arboleda found himself at the head of a victorious army, was elected president of the

Senate, and was shortly after invested with the presidency of the republic. Arboleda did not expect to enjoy his honors long. "In this proud and valiant nation," he said, on receiving the oath of his friend Mallarino, "it is as easy to pass from exile to power, as from power to the bar of the Senate."[4] He soon had to plunge again into civil war, his chief adversary being his kinsman, Mosquera, who on June 18, 1862, seized Bogota, after a combat of five hours. The conqueror took the title of provisional president of New Granada, which thenceforth was called the United States of Colombia. He decreed that natural law should be the only code of the republic, proclaimed the separation of church and state, prohibited the parish priests from exercising their ministry without the authorization of the civil power, and confiscated the property of the monasteries. Without delay he followed up the struggle against the conservatives. Arboleda, betrayed by his companions in arms, was assassinated November 22 in the defiles of Berruecos, not far from the place where Sucre had formerly met a similar fate, and his lieutenant, Leonardo Canal, surrendered December 30.

The civil war was at an end and all resistance overcome when the Assembly elected to draw up the new constitution, which was finally voted on April 25, was opened at Rio Negro on February 9, 1863. It ratified the federal organization of the republic under the name of the United States of Colombia, which has become the official name of New Granada. General Mosquera was intrusted with the executive power until such time as the first constitutional Congress should meet, and the new president could take the oath before it. Mosquera resigned his authority, April 1, 1864, to Doctor Manuel Murillo Toro. Mosquera, though supported by a victorious and devoted army, had refused to be a candidate, because of the article of the constitution which forbade the reëlection of the president; but he remained the leader of the democratic party. A young man, aged twenty-two, son of a governor of Bogota who had been shot by his orders in 1861, fired at him in the middle of the road, and in broad day, with the intention of killing him. Mosquera was, nevertheless, the idol of the people, who applauded him in the clubs, where he uttered against France in regard to the Mexican expedition, and against Spain in regard to her conduct in Peru, burning words, in which there was always

[4] Elisée Reclus, "*La poésie et les poétes dans l'Amerique Espagnole.*" *Revue des Deux Mondes,* Feb. 15, 1864.

the thought of again uniting New Granada, Ecuador, and Venezuela in one nation under a republican, democratic, and federal form; of reconstituting, in a word, the Colombian edifice as in the early days of independence. Propositions of this nature had been made to the president of Ecuador without other result than the rupture of diplomatic relations between the two countries and the breaking out of hostilities, Mosquera defeating the Ecuadorians under the command of the now aged Flores in the battle of Cuaspud in December, 1863.

The president, Manuel Murillo Toro, one of the chiefs of the ultra liberal party, brought to his office the noblest and most honorable intentions, but he had to overcome almost insuperable difficulties. The sources of public credit were almost exhausted; the salt works, one of the chief sources of the wealth of the country, were very badly managed, and produced nothing; and the property of the clergy, by which the government calculated to pay off the debt, was sold at a low price. Such was the position of affairs, and it was aggravated by the corruption of public officers. In the struggle with the clergy Murillo found new difficulties. The hostility of the democratic party toward the Court of Rome had gone so far as the confiscation of ecclesiastical property, and had just been energetically condemned by an encyclical of the Pope, which induced Mosquera to propose to Congress a bill which was passed on April 26, 1864, by which every ecclesiastic was obliged to take an oath of fidelity to the constitution, and to obey no bull, decree, ordinance, or resolution of officials, churches, congregations, or councils resident abroad without previously obtaining express authority from the executive power. Murillo made extraordinary efforts to enforce this law with as much mildness as possible. It was one of the last acts of Congress before separating on May 18, 1864. In spite of the good intentions of the president, there was little internal tranquillity, and the states did not use their authority in an altogether blameless manner. The instability of their governments went so far as to compromise their relations with foreign powers. Murillo, in his message of February 1, 1865, used solemn words. The country had just escaped from a civil war, "the most disastrous of those registered in our sanguinary annals," said he. Peace had been desired. But how was this to be attained? Fresh disturbances very soon occurred in the city of Buenaventura and in the provinces of Magdalena, Cauca, Tolima, and Cundinamarca. In Panama, the most disturbed district of the confederation, a regiment mutinied on March 9, and made Doctor Gil Colunje president of the state, after overthrowing General Santa Colonna. In June the mulatto, Correoso, a friend of Mosquera, endeavored, although without success, to overthrow Doctor Gil Colunje. Panama, Magdalena, and Bolívar, displeased at seeing part of their customs dues going into the hands of the central government of Bogota,

ECUADOR COLOMBIA · AND VENEZUELA

desired to secede from the union and set up for themselves an independent republic. Lastly, a conservative uprising had been attempted in Cauca by General Joaquin Cordova. Murillo, dreading the return to power of his old opponents, who were supported and worked upon by the clergy, declared martial law, put himself at the head of the army, and, not without many combats, defeated and dispersed the rebels.

Mosquera was again recalled to power at the age of seventy-four years and succeeded Murillo on April 1, 1866. Faithless to

the constitution which he himself had drawn up, he immediately
yielded to the temptations of despotism, refused to show how he
intended to employ the loans that he had raised in England, and decreed a series of arbitrary measures, hostile to the constitutional
sovereignty of the federal states.   The legislatures of the several
states for the most part refused to submit to his will.   Being short of
money, Mosquera seized in the churches the gold and silver vessels
used in the celebration of divine worship.   The Congress in its session of 1867 annulled as unconstitutional the decrees published without its concurrence.   Mosquera appealed to the people, and, at a
review, made a violent speech to the garrison of Bogota.   The Congress stood firm and demanded an account of the state of the
exchequer; to which demand Mosquera replied by declaring that
he took upon himself the discretionary power, and prepared to arrest Doctor Murillo, who had time to take refuge at the French
legation.   The Congress gave way at length, voting the bills in
the form in which they had been presented.   Mosquera made a
great show of this reconciliation, organized a triumphal procession,
leading the deputies through the principal streets of the capital,
himself at their head in full uniform, with head erect and covered
with ribbons and decorations.   The *fête* was concluded with a
banquet.   It was not long, however, before harmony was again
disturbed, and Mosquera decreed the dissolution of the Congress,
proclaimed martial law in the confederation, and separated Bogota
from the state of Cundinamarca to make a federal district.   Four
deputies were about to be shot, when General Acosta, the second
vice-president, resolved to attempt a counter-revolution.   Mosquera
was arrested on the night of May 22 and sent to prison.   He
was accused of malversation and abuse of power, adjudged guilty
of having suppressed the freedom of sale of salt, of having
prohibited the circulation of newspapers, and of having sold to
Peru the alliance of Colombia, and was deprived of his presidential
authority and of his civil rights, and condemned to exile for four
years.   Mosquera immediately went to Lima; his partisans submitted, and a comparative calm succeeded these stormy years.   The
first vice-president, Gutierrez, was elected president and entered on
his duties on April 1, 1868.   He was succeeded by General Salgar.

Doctor Murillo Toro, the successor of General Salgar, was
elected for the term from April 1, 1872, to March 31, 1874.   He
was the first civilian who had been elevated to the presidential

dignity for the second time, a rank unfortunately too frequently reserved for generals. He immediately turned his attention to the railways, telegraphs, and schools, to material improvements and the taking up of the uncultivated lands. In his message in 1873 he congratulated the English and American governments on having given a great example of justice by submitting their differences to a tribunal of arbitration. " This precedent," he added, " ought to be considered as an important conquest of justice for the peace of the world and the security of nations." Was this not an invocation to the states of Colombia, so ready to wage war among themselves, to enter upon this pacific path and in future to settle their differences amicably? Murillo Toro, doubtless, had in mind the neighboring countries, especially Venezuela; for the eternal question of the frontiers was just then threatening to disturb the good relations existing between the two peoples.

At this period (1873), the republic of Colombia was making visible progress in consequence of the regular working of her institutions; industry and education had attained an enviable state of progress; the large sums due to the United States were paid, the foreign debt had been reduced to $10,000,000, and the law of June 10, 1872, for the funding of the home debt, had produced excellent results. From that time it could be foreseen that in consequence of the prudent and successful reforms introduced into the financial system the budget of expenses and receipts would balance without difficulty at a not distant date. The revenue amounts annually to more than $3,000,000 ($3,993,494 in the year's expenditure of 1872-1873), leaving a surplus over expenditure. The commercial movement in 1873 was: imports, $12,515,659, and exports $10,477,631. The maintenance of peace, the expansion of industry, and the opening of new means of communication facilitating exportation have contributed to augment the customs dues, the country being able with them to provide for the expenses occasioned by the law of June 5, 1871, for the taking up of waste lands.

Under the presidency of Dr. Santiago Perez the scientific and industrial progress which had characterized the country from 1870 was accelerated. At Bogota the streets were lighted with gas, chemical works were erected and railway lines projected to unite the heart of the country with the ocean and the valley of the Magdalena. But political strife broke out again.

It was impossible, in the confusion, for the people to elect a president, and accordingly Congress chose Aquilleo Parra. The conservatives would not recognize him, and the bishops raised the faithful in insurrection against him, clamoring for the restoration of religious teaching in the schools. Each party put an army in the field. The states of Cundinamarca, Boyaca, Santander, and Magdalena furnished 26,000 men to the conservatives, but the liberals got double that number from Cundinamarca, Santander, and Cauca. At Los Chancos, General Trujillo finally defeated the clericalists. The war had not been bloody, which was a proof of progress.

The struggle that had been kept up between the Catholic clergy and the civil power was terminated in 1874. A command published by the Archbishop of Bogota forbade ecclesiastics to interfere in any manner with politics. It would be well if this injunction were obeyed throughout South America. At the present time questions of material progress alone excite public attention, and the Colombians have not in vain passed through the period of disorder and agitation that we have endeavored to describe. The effects of the tranquillity that reigned in men's minds after 1865 were so happy, from the point of view of the general prosperity, that the customs receipts doubled in the short period of eight years, from 1865 to 1873.

Colombia is a magnificent country, remarkably well situated for the commerce of both hemispheres. Its capital, Bogota, is a beautiful and spacious city, whose squares are all adorned with fountains; there are 60,000 inhabitants, and it has besides magnificent houses and five very fine bridges, a remarkable cathedral, an astronomical observatory, a museum of natural history, a school of medicine, a botanical garden, a library, an academy, three colleges for men and one for women, a seminary, four hospitals, twenty-seven churches and a Protestant place of worship, and a theater. A new house of Congress was built in 1871. Near Bogota are the two natural bridges of Icononzo, formed by great rocks which have fallen across the torrent of the Summa-Paz in such fashion as to sustain each other. The highest of these bridges makes an arch about fifty feet long by forty wide.

The state of Cundinamarca, whose capital is Bogota, abounds in gold. Near the village of Muzo is one of the richest emerald mines known; these emeralds without any reason are called *Peru-*

vian emeralds, and under this name are sent to all parts of the
world. Cartagena, the chief fortress of Colombia, is the ordinary
station of the squadron; the trade of this city is considerable, especially in all kinds of metals. Cartegena, with its narrow and gloomy
streets, its extensive galleries supported by low, heavy columns, and
the flat roofs that project over the fronts of the houses, has something of the aspect of the cloister.

Dr. Saffray, who journeyed through the country in 1869,
shows that it possesses all the elements of prosperity; a vast
extent of coast line on two oceans; great navigable rivers and
streams without number; a fertile soil where, according to the elevation, all the vegetables are easily grown. Cocoa, indigo, cotton and
vanilla grow wild. Trees valued for dyes, cabinet making, medicinal uses, resin, and rubber, abound in the extensive virgin forests,
and its coasts furnish mother-of-pearl, pearls and tortoise shell.
The majestic Cordillera of the Andes ramifies over its territory,
giving to its many valleys the riches of its mountains: gold, platinum, silver, lead, iron, copper, porphyry, marble, grindstones, coal,
salt and precious stones.[5] Its admirable geographical position,
which allows direct communication with the North, its resources
of all kinds, its institutions, the activity and other qualities of its
inhabitants, show, we repeat, that Colombia is fitted to take, in the
future, a place in the first rank among the peoples of South America.

[5] *"Voyage à la Nouvelle-Grenade." Tour du Monde,* Vol. **XXVI.**

Chapter VI

THE UNITED STATES OF VENEZUELA
1829-1876

NEW GRANADA had acted wisely in not attempting to hold Venezuela by force in a union which Bolívar himself had not been able to consummate. Venezuela, with an area twice as large as France and a restless and heterogeneous population of Spanish creoles, civilized and uncivilized Indians, negroes, mulattoes, *mestizos* and *zambos,* would have been hard to subdue and harder still to hold. This population, thinly scattered along the coasts or wandering over immense plains whose bounds are imperceptible to the eye, along the rivers, on the numerous lakes and on the tableland of the Venezuela-Granadine chain at an altitude of 1800 or 2000 feet, did not exceed 1,000,000. To people a single one of the states forming part of this republic, New Andalucia for example, it has been calculated that at least twenty years of peace and the emigration of 200,000 European agriculturists would be necessary.

Venezuela had and has well-defined limits, which were those of the old captaincy-general of Caracas, formed by the four departments of Zulia, Orinoco, Venezuela and Maturin—on the north the Caribbean Sea, west and southwest New Granada, east the Atlantic Ocean, southeast British Guiana, and south Brazil. This vast territory of 407,725 square miles was then divided into twelve departments, which were subdivided into provinces, cantons, and parishes.

The dying Bolívar witnessed the triumph of Paez. His eyes had hardly closed before a Congress sat at Caracas. Paez, his dreaded comrade of the war of independence, became the first president of the republic of Venezuela, in 1831, after the establishment of its constitution. The late chief of the *llaneros* very soon made an end of the last partisans of Colombian unity, whose principal chiefs submitted on condition of preserving their military rank. Paez, by prescribing certain economies, proved his moderation and

administrative ability. The duties on imports and exports were
modified and liberalized; certain privileges of a decidedly monarchical character, which Bolívar had too easily granted to the
clergy and the army, were abolished, and the equality of all citizens
in the eye of the law was proclaimed. Paez revived agriculture and
industry, and he began negotiations with Spain for the recognition
of the republic, which did not take place until 1845. Slavery was
abolished in 1834.

The presidential authority conferred upon Paez expired January 20, 1835; he transmitted it to Dr. José Vargas, and retired
afterward to his estates. He left the country in a state of relative
prosperity. By electing a civilian for its new president, the republic
set an example which, unfortunately, it did not follow. Vargas, a
jurisconsult who had made the law his chief study, could only
govern by the law, and the sword was returned to the scabbard.
The army felt its influence waning, and its chiefs organized a conspiracy. On July 8 a dozen generals seized the president in
his residence at Caracas, and put him on board ship with the
vice-president and sent them to the Danish island of St. Thomas.
Paez left his retirement, raised a body of troops and marched on
Caracas. On the 15th he addressed a proclamation to the people
and the army in which he said: " While I was head of the state I
caused the constitution of 1830 to be respected and executed; in
1831 I renewed, as president, the oath to respect it; my duty com-
mands me to defend this compact, although it be with danger to
my life." Paez, with the support of the people, made himself master of the capital before the end of the month, and Vargas, who was
immediately recalled, entered again upon the exercise of his functions. Nevertheless, the struggle continued in the province of
Cumaná until the beginning of the following year, 1836.

Paez was called to the presidency for a second term in 1839,
and in 1842 Soublette succeeded him in the presidentship. This was
a period of tranquillity in the history of Venezuela. When, in 1846,
the war between the men of color and the creoles broke out, Paez
was invested with the powers and title of dictator. After the struggle was over he procured the election of Tadeo Monagas as president, in January, 1847, but soon had cause to repent of his choice.
At the head of some of his partisans, Paez attempted to overthrow
his successor, and captured Coro, July 2, 1849. But he was poorly
supported, was defeated, and surrendered with his two sons to

General Sylva on August 14. He was taken to Caracas, where he was a prisoner until May, 1850, when, having recovered his liberty through the energy of Senator Rendon, he took refuge in New York.

In the new presidential elections Gregorio Monagas, Senator Rendon, and Vice-president Guzman stood as candidates. None of them obtained the majority required by the constitution, that is, two-thirds of the number of votes, and the new president had to be appointed by Congress. As this Congress had been elected under the pressure of Tadeo Monagas, after its predecessor had been dispersed by violence, it was not difficult to foresee that the election would fall on the brother of Tadeo; and in fact it did sanction the usurpation of the Monagases who, cleverly alternating in the presidency, held power until 1858. On March 15 of this year a revolution put an end to the domination of this family and of the Federalist party.

A provisional government, of which General Julian Castro was appointed president, granted an amnesty to the exiles. After many doubts Paez returned to his country, but after the defeat of the conservative party in its contest with the Democrats, he being unwilling to serve as a pretext for civil war, again went into exile in June, 1859. On the day following the fall of the Monagases the Conservatives had restored the old constitution, modified by some liberal reforms, and Castro had already published the new constitution, which had been framed in Valencia by a constituent assembly. This did not satisfy the Liberals and Democrats, who raised the banner of federalism in order to free themselves from the domination of the old oligarchical party of Venezuela, the Conservatives. Several provinces responded to their call. Castro resigned power in order to break with his political friends, but afterward recovered the presidency, appointed Liberal ministers and published a Federalist programme. This clever maneuver, nevertheless, did not have the success that he expected. Deserted by everyone at the moment when the two rival parties were coming to blows in Caracas, he was by turns arrested and set at liberty, and finally disappeared. The Conservatives, sole masters of the field, placed Dr. Pedro Gual, the first *designado* or vice-president, at their head, who caused Castro to be tried as a traitor, and afterward pardoned him. Gual suppressed the insurgent movements, thwarted the new attempts of the Monagases and reëstablished public tranquillity. Manuel Felipe de Tovar being elected president received the republic in a fairly satisfactory condition from the vice-president, but the Federalists did not give up the contest. Tovar took measures against them with not very successful results. All eyes were again turned toward Paez. The old general had been accredited to the United States as envoy extraordinary and minister plenipotentiary in October, 1860, but was now recalled. In March, 1861, he reached Caracas. Tovar gave him the command of the army; but as he attempted to limit his authority Paez tendered his resignation. This withdrawal caused so much excitement that Tovar was obliged to abdicate on May 8. Gual again took the direction of affairs and restored Paez to his position, investing him with the widest powers. Fresh differences or dissensions arose between Paez and Gual himself, who openly favored the Liberal party, and Paez gave in his resignation for the second time. On August 27, a colonel named Echezuria, hitherto unknown, being ambitious of becoming a general, put himself at the head of the garrison of Caracas, marched to the Government House, made prisoners of Dr. Gual and the ministers, and proclaimed Paez dictator. This dictatorship was born of the divisions among the Conservatives, whose four sections were fighting among themselves, and merely added one more complication to the endless dispute between the Unitarians and the Federalists. Paez soon found himself powerless to put down the Federalist movement, and its chief promoter, General Juan José Falcon, assumed the position of head of the government in the provinces occupied by him. This weakness was shown in the negotiations that he found it necessary to begin with Falcon.

Indeed, the illustrious leader in the War of Independence was worn and old, and really left the exercise of power to his associates, who made use of the prestige attached to his past life to govern according to their own views and passions, and who did not scruple to compromise his reputation in low and underhand intrigues. His friend Rojas governed, acted and spoke in his place. He was the power behind the throne. Paez had appointed him Minister of the Interior at the same time that the ambitious Colonel Echezuria received the portfolio of war. Rojas returned to despotism, multiplying the most arbitrary and vexatious measures. This system, decorated as usual with the title of conservative, made Paez unpopular, and produced results entirely different from those that were expected. Maracaibo separated from Caracas, August 20, 1862, and formed itself into a free state. Soon the Federalists were almost the sole masters everywhere. Paez lacked financial resources and his forces were fluctuating in number and untrustworthy. For example: Echezuria, the Minister of War and Marine, the same who had proclaimed Paez, now conspired against him and was imprisoned; Generals Rubio and Michelena, sent against Falcon, went over to his side. Other personages on whom he counted for governorships and other duties, refused their support on account of Rojas, who was the object of general censure. And as if this critical state of things were not enough, diplomatic relations with Spain were broken off in consequence of the insulting words of the Minister of Foreign Affairs to the *chargé d'affaires* of that country. While this was taking place, Falcon defeated the government troops.

In the month of April, 1863, the confusion had reached its height; the western provinces proclaimed federation at the same time that armed parties overran and raised the eastern provinces. The capital was, so to say, blockaded by the insurrection. On April 23, Paez was obliged to treat with the Federalists; on May 22 it was stipulated that the supreme administration of the state should be confided to a junta, to which each province should send four members, half appointed by Paez and half by Falcon. This junta met in Victoria, the capital of the province of Aragua, June 15, and the two rival chiefs resigned their authority. Two days thereafter the junta appointed Generals Juan Falcon and Guzman Blanco, provisionally, president and vice-president. The last had powerfully contributed to the triumph of the Federalists. The revolution was terminated without effusion of blood; nevertheless the pacification was not complete. The Unitary generals, Martinez and Cárdenas, shut up in Puerto Cabello, formed a provisional government with General Cordero at its head. Falcon entered Caracas on July 26 amid popular demonstrations, introducing the vice-president into the new cabinet as Minister of Foreign Affairs and Finance.

The elections for the Constituent Assembly, charged to reorganize once more the republic of Venezuela, were to take place October 11. In the meantime the chief of the new Federation, making use of his dictatorial powers, appointed a Council of State and sent governors of his own choice to the provinces. On August 18 he published a Declaration of Rights, granting every kind of liberty to the Venezuelans and abolishing capital punishment. Unfortunately financial difficulties were pressing, and already a loan was spoken of. As Paez had by his side a councillor who was the real dictator, so also had Falcon close to him a man disposed to dominate; General Blanco seemed to wish to be a second Rojas, and it was even suspected that a certain understanding existed between these two persons, by whom peace had been negotiated. Rojas, on his fall, had had himself appointed a general, notwithstanding that he had never served in the army, and it was supposed that he was preparing the means of his return to power.

On December 24 the Constituent Assembly, which had been elected on October 11, met at Caracas. In his message Falcon declared that nobody had been imprisoned or exiled, that his conduct had been dictated by the sentiment of generosity, and that the fullest guarantees were secured to all the citizens. He then resigned to the representatives of the nation the dictatorial authority with which he had been invested. Falcon, the mover of "the great crusade of liberty," was invited "to continue to carry on the general government of the federation with the rank of President of the United States of Venezuela," and afterward the honorary title "The Great Citizen-General" was given to him. The powers of Guzman Blanco were also confirmed, and he was elected president of the Assembly.

The legislative authority was commissioned to draw up a uniform code of laws applicable to the whole confederation; and also to select an uninhabited tract of country for a federal district, where the national capital should be built. The new Assembly immediately took up the question of the national finances, which were in great confusion. Nevertheless, in 1862, in spite of civil war, the general commerce with France amounted to $2,783,600, of which $1,853,000 were imports of French goods—textiles, novelties, wines and liquors. Indeed, the revenue, which was raised almost exclusively from customs duties, was greater than that of New Granada, although the population of the latter was more numerous; in 1864 it exceeded $6,400,000, while the budget called for only $4,000,000. Unfortunately this revenue was pledged to secure various creditors, which absorbed a large part of it, and no new taxes could be laid in excess of those decreed in 1862 and 1863, without destroying commerce.

Under these circumstances the Congress decided, January 14,

1864, to vote a loan of $15,000,000, which Guzman Blanco was commissioned to negotiate in Europe.

Those who suppose that these new-born American republics lose or neglect, in the midst of their continual revolutions, all thought of economic betterment are much mistaken. In this same troubled year, 1863, two lines of steamers were established, one between La Guayra and Ciudad-Bolívar, calling at the island of Margarita, Barcelona, Carupano, Cumana, and Trinidad, and the other the River Aroa; a contract entered into between La Guayra and Santo Tomás extended the line of navigation to Puerto Cabello, where the foundations of a lighthouse had been laid; the construction of the eastern railway was actively prosecuted; the works for lighting the capital by gas were completed, and a school of engineers and another of arts and trades were established in Caracas. In the previous year Venezuela made a successful figure at the London Exhibition, ranking next after Brazil. Nevertheless, we are far from asserting that political agitation has not exercised a pernicious influence. Industry and agriculture have especially suffered in this country by the continual stress of civil war. Only one important enterprise prospered, namely, the gold mines of Yuruari, discovered in 1849 and actively worked since 1858.

Falcon had left Caracas while the constitution was under discussion, leaving the direction of affairs to the second *designado,* General Paredes. He did not return until April, 1864, to close the legislative session, and watch more closely the incidents of the Spanish-Peruvian war, which had just broken out. Lima begged for the support and assistance of the American states, and, notwithstanding the crisis that the republic was passing through, it answered that the government of Venezuela would not break " the common bond that united her with the other republics of the American continent, if they were obliged to defend themselves for the preservation of their autonomy and institutions." Therefore, Venezuela had a representative at the conference which began in Lima toward the end of 1864.

Falcon formed a new Cabinet, created a ministry of Public Credit, under Alvarez Lugo as the first minister, and reduced the effective strength of the army to 2800 men. Thereafter, the two vice-presidents being absent, he left the cares of government to one of the ministers, General Trias, and retired to Coro. It is difficult to understand such an abandonment of responsibility. There was a dispute with Spain; the Conservatives were restive; the states were endeavoring to throw off their dependence on the central power; in the month of August the governors of Aragua and Apure were overthrown; General Sotero, the Governor of Guarico, rebelled against Caracas and had some imitators; in Guiana General Arismendi, chief of the customs house of Ciudad-Bolívar, raised a body of troops and placed some small vessels at the small mouth of the Orinoco; and in the capital, unseasonable measures with respect to the price of bread aroused the people, who were irritated against foreigners by the events in Peru, and provoked some riots. The president, leaving his retirement, was able with great difficulty to get together 1000 men, but he could not maintain them. The treasury was empty, and exchange on London was suspended. The financial mission entrusted to Blanco had not produced the results that were expected, and credit was so low that a merchant demanded cash payment in coin before filling an order for saber scabbards. In this critical situation the elections, which should take place according to law on October 21, 1864, were suspended, and Falcon thought that he might enter into negotiations with the state of Guiana. The state of Guarico could be reduced by force, but that of Maracaibo maintained its independence. Blanco, on his return from Europe, took (November 6, 1864) the government that Falcon, who was engaged against the rebels, left to him. A loyal ministry was formed, which procured some resources for the treasury by various extemporized measures, and caused the elections to be held. Falcon was reëlected president and proclaimed by Congress March 18, 1865, a month after the opening of the new Congress; but doubtless he was not ambitious to risk his popularity in inextricable difficulties; so he left Blanco to face the storm in his place, gave the command of the army to Trias, and retired to his quiet residence of Coro. His reëlection affirmed the definitive triumph of federalism. Paez saw that his part was played out, and again went into voluntary exile in the United States, a noble wreck, the sport of adverse winds, cast away upon a foreign shore. He died in New York in 1873, at the age of eighty-three years. A few months later, in 1874, Rojas died in France, where he had settled.

The country would have found peace if the conquerors had not become disunited after repulsing the common enemy. On the day following the electoral contest grave disorders broke out. In Barcelona, General Carvajal, after overthrowing the president of the state, attempted to set up the old Tadeo Monogas, who was more than eighty years old, as chief. In Maracaibo, Venancio Pulgar rebelled, was defeated, and owed his safety to the speed of his horse. Falcon took the direction of affairs in July, 1865, but his presence in Caracas in no way changed the situation. In November the state of Apure expelled its president, and the insurgents assassinated the captain and crew of an American ship plying upon the river that gives its name to this province. And as if these complications were not sufficient, Chili, at war with Spain, demanded the assistance of the republic. On March 2, 1866, Guzman Blanco, in the absence of Falcon, opened the legislative session; his message demonstrated the absolute want of funds in the federation. The Congress ordered the ministers to present their respective accounts within twenty-four hours. The Minister of Finance, Landaeta, alone presented his. The penury, he said, was so great, that he had not had sufficient money to pay for the printing of those of his colleagues. Landaeta said that bankruptcy was imminent, and declared that smuggling, favored by officials of all ranks, destroyed the resources of the treasury. The hostile attitude of the Congress recalled Falcon to Caracas. He wished to watch more closely the approaching elections for the vice-presidency. His two candidates, Generals Marquez and Colina, were elected, and in the new cabinet the highest position was given to his brother-in-law, General Pachano. He even succeeded in getting a vote of confidence from the Congress. At last he was able to calm the popular excitement resulting from the bombardment of Valparaíso. Falcon dreaded a war with Spain, because the Venezuelan coasts were much more exposed to attacks from the Spanish squadron than those of Chili and Peru. The Congress gave him full liberty to maintain peace or to break with Madrid. At bottom, the presidential authority was precarious. At the end of June the insurrection extended to the west. A campaign of three months, led by Falcon in person, was ended by a treaty. Peace was bought by distributing among the insurgents $1,000,000. In the bad condition of the finances this sacrifice was a terrible blow to the already weakened popularity of the government. Even the capital was very much excited. The provisional government, to which the president had delegated his powers on leaving Caracas, had suspended treasury payments. Blanco, the representative of the republic in Paris and London, criticised this measure and was recalled. At the same time the

majority of ministers resigned.   The anarchy was complete.
Colina, who commanded a small army near Caracas, hastened to
take charge of affairs, and persuaded the ministers who had resigned to resume their powers.

Nevertheless Falcon, as he had formerly done, put off the
duties of his position and remained at a distance from Caracas. He
did not appear to be disquieted either by the disturbances in Barcelona or the attacks on Maracaibo, at one time by the emigrants
who had returned to the national territory, at another by the Conservatives.   Many provinces had shown themselves ready to break
the federal compact completely.   The Congress, alarmed at this,
before separating, conferred almost unlimited power upon the president.   This was in June, 1867.   In October an insurrection broke
out in the State of Caracas itself, which was put down by Falcon
after a short struggle; but the opening of the year 1868 was very
threatening.   Only La Guayra and Puerto Cabello paid into the
national treasury the product of their customs houses with any regu-
larity; while the other states appropriated to their own use the proceeds of the customs houses situated in their territories.   The republic could not satisfy its creditors, and its penury had reached its
limit.   Under such circumstances Falcon fell.

The Unitarian party, which had been vanquished in 1863, conquered in 1868, led by J. R. Monagas, who was raised to the presidency, but was soon overthrown in its turn.   Monagas died in
November.   In December Fulgar was elected provisional president.
The year 1869 was very agitated.   On April 27, 1870, Guzman
Blanco, becoming master of Caracas after three days' fighting, proclaimed himself "general-in-chief of the constitutional army of the
Confederation."   On July 13 he was granted extraordinary powers
and the title of provisional president of the republic by a Congress
which met in Valencia.   This provisional government lasted until
February 20, 1873, when he was finally elected.   In this interval
he had to overcome a formidable insurrection, led by General Salazar, the second *designado*.   The struggle had been very bitter in
the eastern districts, where many strong places, which it was necessary to take by assault, were held by the rebels.   The defeat of
Salazar, who was taken prisoner and shot in June, 1872, secured
the triumph of Blanco, and put an end for a short time to the
civil war.

On March 1, 1873, the president, addressing the Congress

of the United States of Venezuela, assembled for the first time
in the new palace in Caracas, expressed the opinion that if a new
war did not again disturb the country, and arrest it on the path of
progress, in a few years it would reach a high degree of prosperity;
that during his dictatorship no new debt had been contracted; and
that the financial position was exceptionally favorable. He said that
he intended to submit to Congress a new civil code, a penal code, a
commercial code, a code of finance, and a military code. He concluded by calling for an important modification of the constitution,
demanding that the constitutional term of office of the president and
other officers should be reduced from four to two years. This
measure would, in his opinion, offer a guarantee of liberty and put
an end to revolutions, because, instead of overthrowing the established government by force of arms, it would be found more prudent
to await the lapse of so short a period. The president, if his proposition should be adopted, would gladly renounce the third and
fourth years of his term in order to give his country this proof of
abnegation and to show how far removed he was from personal
ambition. This proposition was not accepted by the legislators of
Caracas.

The government has been equally active in the development of
all the important material enterprises, and of public instruction. Its
decrees on the subject of emigration have produced good results;
thousands of colonists have left France, as well as Spain and Germany, to carry to Venezuela the coöperation of their strength and
intelligence.

During the presidency of Guzman Blanco Congress made very
important changes in religious and ecclesiastical affairs: the suppression of the monasteries was decreed in 1874 (May 2); and a
national church was established (1876).

Chapter VII

THE REPUBLIC OF ECUADOR. 1831-1876

THE territory of Ecuador extends from east to west between Brazil and the Pacific Ocean. Bounded on the north by the United States of Colombia, and on the south by Peru, it forms one of the richest and most beautiful countries of the world. In the interior mountain ranges extend as far as the eye can reach and here are the highest volcanoes on the globe. At a lower level there are vast tablelands, and along the coast great plains covered with a wealth of tropical vegetation. There, as so often elsewhere in South America, Nature is more ready to respond to the advances of man than is man to make use of the bounty of Nature.

The sparse population is not sufficient for the prosperity of an extensive territory where the means of communication are so imperfect. A fertile land lavishes its treasures in vain if hands are wanting to gather them, and means to transport them; accordingly vast riches lie hidden in the mountains and virgin forests, the working of the mines is abandoned, and agriculture is completely neglected. "A number of valuable trees offer the tribute of their succulent fruits, or their wood, desirable for building and cabinet-making; here rise the cotton tree, the ebony, the cedar and the Peruvian bark tree, whose majestic trunks are enlaced with the savory granadilla or the perfumed vanilla; there the cinnamon tree, the indiarubber tree, the plants which yield spices and scents, medicinal balsams, resins, gums and lacquers, mixed with the tobacco, tamarind and laurel; the hollows in the trees conceal clusters of honeycomb, and at their feet often grow edible tubers and roots. All this wealth is the spontaneous product of the soil; the vegetable kingdom grows and fructifies without the aid of labor. It seems as if man is ignorant of or disdains these gifts of Nature." [1]

The population of Ecuador is grouped, for the most part, on the elevated tablelands of the province of Quito. The city of this

[1] Ernest Charton, "Quito."

name, the residence of the last incas and the capital of the republic, has 3500 inhabitants, and is situated over 10,000 feet above the level of the sea. Pinned, so to say, on the side of a mountain, between the two craters of Pichincha, which exhibits a column of smoke, sometimes broken by a slight eruption, it overlooks the streams and great river valleys of the two slopes which descend to the Pacific and the Atlantic. This city, so rich in historical memories, is best known in France for the visit made there in 1736 by the scientists sent out by the Academy of Sciences at Paris to measure a degree on the meridian. It is a dull and backward town from the point of view of civilization; its chief festivals are the interminable processions that traverse the steep streets and in which all the women of the city take part. Some religious buildings in the Moorish style are the sole enduring traces of the Spanish domination. It possesses a beautiful observatory, the first that has been erected on the line dividing the two hemispheres, a public library, a normal school, a famous university, and manufactures of cotton, linen, and flannel. Quito reckons among her sons distinguished painters, among whom is mentioned a half-breed named Santiago, who was eminent in the seventeenth century; wood-carving is carried on by some Indians and half-breeds, great makers of images of the Virgin and of Christ. Charton praises the nobility of type, the variety of their dress and the innate good taste which, even in the lowest classes, is shown in the cut of their garments and the harmonious and picturesque combination of colors; nowhere, even among the more gifted races, is artistic feeling found in equal degree.

After Quito, Guayaquil, with 30,000 inhabitants, is the most important town of the republic. The port of Guayaquil has an almost complete monopoly of the trade in so-called " Panama " hats, whose manufacture is peculiar to Ecuador. The best are made in the village of Monte Cristo, of the leaf named toquilla. Cuenca, the capital of the province of Assuay and the third city of the state, has 25,000 inhabitants; it carries on an important trade in grain, has several sugar refineries and a cotton mill. In its neighborhood traces of the great highway of the incas may be seen.

On the dissolution of the republic of Colombia, in 1831, Ecuador included the three departments of Ecuador, Guayaquil, and Assuay. The new republic was divided into seven provinces, which later were increased to twelve: Pichincha or Quito, Im-

ECUADOR   · 107

babura, Chimborazo, Leon, Esmeraldas, Guayaquil, Manabi, Assuay, Loja, Tienguregua, Los Rios and Oriente, forming the three
departments of Pichincha, Guayas, and Assuay; more commonly
designated by the names of their capitals—Quito, Guayaquil, and
Cuenca.

Unlike the other two fragments of the old republic of Colombia, the political parties in Ecuador were not Federalists and Unitarians, but Conservatives and Democrats. According to law the
inhabitants of Ecuador are all equally free, and neither titles, nobility, nor honorary distinctions are recognized. Slavery was finally
abolished in 1854. But it does not follow that the lot of the
aborigines was greatly improved thereby. They are always employed in the bearing of heavy burdens and left alone in their
misery and ignorance. They are forcibly enrolled to serve as private soldiers, because the whites refuse to serve the army except as
officers. "By a just retribution this tyranny has been disastrous
for the oppressors themselves," says Charton; "the Spaniards, by
trying to keep to themselves the privilege of working the riches
of the country, have decimated the aboriginal races and kept foreigners away. . . . Industry and agriculture are in want of
hands, colonial enterprises, which might give such strength and
greatness to the country, cannot be developed or even established,
and territories of wonderful fertility lie completely uncultivated."

From the date when it was formed into an independent republic Ecuador has been almost continually disturbed by civil wars
and wars with the neighboring states. From the beginning it was
in armed conflict with New Granada for the possession of the
provinces of Popayan, Buenaventura, and Pasto, so favorable for
its communications with the Pacific. The Granadine troops repulsed an invasion of Pasto led by President Flores, and on December 8, 1831, a treaty was signed which sanctioned the union of the
provinces in dispute with New Granada, but was not ratified by
Ecuador until four years later. Juan José Flores, the companion-
in-arms and friend of Bolívar, found support among the partisans
of the Liberator. His triumph might have changed the fate of New
Granada, but after his defeat he had to confine himself to the
achievement of his ambitions for the independence of Ecuador,
of which he was the first president. He led the Conservative
party, and had to fight against the Liberals, under Vicente Rocafuerte. In 1834 a revolutionary movement broke out in Quito, and

declared Flores an outlaw. He was defeated in Guayaquil, but in a short time gained an advantage over his opponent, whom he made prisoner in Quito. The victory of January 18, 1835, was decisive, although some generals attempted to keep the field, and three of them came forward to attack the government that same year. One of them was taken and shot with twenty-three of his soldiers. The other two fled over the frontier. Flores was never without such rivals to contend with. He and Rocafuerte were again reconciled (May, 1835), and an Assembly, which was specially called for the purpose, met on August 9 in Ambato, and gave a constitution to Ecuador. Rocafuerte was elected president, and Flores appointed commander-in-chief of the army.

Rocafuerte was born at Guayaquil in 1783 and had studied in France, at the college of Saint-Germain-en-Laye. In 1803 he met Bolívar at Paris and they became friends. Animated by liberal ideas, imbued with revolutionary principles, and fortified by reading the publicists of the eighteenth century, he returned to the bosom of his suffering country to take part in her first attempts at emancipation. He was a deputy for the province of Guayaquil in the Spanish Cortes in 1812, but was soon obliged to flee from the Peninsula. He traveled through Europe, visited the United States, and afterward resided in Mexico. He was a distinguished writer, and always showed himself an ardent defender of democratic ideas; as president, he proved himself a good administrator; reduced the chaotic finances to order, organized public instruction, established colleges, a military school, and an agricultural institute and appointed a commission to draw up a civil and a penal code, which the legislature discussed and passed in 1837. He renewed diplomatic relations with Spain, and Ecuador was the second Spanish-American republic whose independence was recognized by the old mother-country. In religious matters his policy was highly liberal and in harmony with modern ideas; he never made a compromise with fanaticism, nor contracted unworthy alliances with the clergy, as after him, some vulgar politicians did, in order to convert them to their personal views. In his message of 1839 he expressed his opinion with the greatest freedom on the necessity of establishing religious toleration, not only with respect to matters of conscience, but also as a means of favoring immigration and promoting the progress of the republic. Under his able direction the country passed through a period of calm and prosperity. In the same year (1839)

Flores succeeded Rocafuerte, who was appointed governor of Guayaquil.

The most important act of the second presidency of Flores was the decree of March 27, 1839, which opened the ports of Ecuador to the commerce and ships of Spain, and which had as a consequence, in 1841, a formal treaty of peace and friendship between the two nations. A convention, which met at Quito, revised the constitution of 1835, and substituted for it a new one, proclaimed on March 31, 1843. Rocafuerte, who was a member of the Assembly, energetically protested against the mutilation of the Compact of Ambato. His firm and patriotic language on this occasion stirred up so much enmity that he judged it opportune to leave the country; he voluntarily expatriated himself and fixed his residence in Lima, whence he undertook the task of supporting his principles by his pen.

At the beginning of 1843 Flores was reëlected for the third time; the conflict between him and the Liberals became more decided every day. A revolution which broke out in Guayaquil on March 6, 1845, overthrew him. Rocafuerte, who had led the movement, did not reap any advantage from it, and it was Vincente Roca, a mulatto, who was raised to the presidency. Rocafuerte was elected for the province of Pichincha, in the convention which met at Cuenca, was afterward senator for four provinces, was appointed in 1846 president of the Senate, and helped to introduce trial by jury in criminal causes. Flores agreed to leave the territory of the republic with the title of commander-in-chief and the annual pay of 80,000 francs; and several attempts made by him to enter Ecuador and again seize power failed completely. He has been even charged with the project of attacking Ecuador with an army recruited in Europe. Rocafuerte was charged by Congress to come to an understanding with the states of Peru, Bolivia, and Chili, for repelling any expedition of this kind, and at the same time was appointed plenipotentiary for Ecuador in the American Congress that was to meet at Lima. He fell ill on his arrival in that city in December, 1846, and died there May 7, 1847, bequeathing his library to the college at Guayaquil. In him his country lost a great citizen, and America an enthusiastic defender of her independence. The Congress ordered the removal of his body to Guayaquil.

A dispute arose with New Granada which gave rise to some

military movements, but it was ended by a treaty signed in Santa
Rosa de Carchi on May 29, 1846. Roca made a treaty of commerce
with Belgium and a convention with England for the abolition of
slavery. On the expiration of his term of office, in October, 1849,
parties not being able to agree, the executive power was provisionally entrustd to the vice-president, Manuel Ascasubi. The excitement was great, and still more so when the clerical party had succeeded in electing Diego Noboa to the presidency, and he recalled
the Jesuits and gave shelter and protection to the Conservative
fugitives from New Granada. Noboa replied to the threats of
New Granada by sending some troops to the frontier; but General
José María Urbina, who commanded them, only put himself at their
head to overthrow the president. The unpopular ruler was deposed
by a Junta assembled at Guayaquil in July, 1851, was arrested and
expelled from the territory of the republic. Urbina was appointed
dictator and established the government in Guayaquil, the ultra-
democratic party triumphing in his person. Flores sought to reap
an advantage from the irritation of the Conservatives, and attempted a *coup de main* with the connivance of the Lima government. He anchored in the waters of Guayaquil at the head of a
squadron on March 14, 1852, with the avowed purpose of reëstablishing Noboa as the sole legitimate president, but was betrayed
by his crew and fled to Peru. His failure naturally had no other
result than to strengthen Urbina. The latter resigned in 1856,
and General Robles succeeded him, defeating the Conservatives.
Robles, by a law of December 6, 1856, established a decimal system
of money, weights and measures, for the republic. This important
reform of commercial law was effected in 1858.

The Clerical or Conservative party redoubled their efforts.
Grave difficulties arose in home affairs, and quarrels with the
neighboring states became more bitter. A dispute with Peru, a
not very scrupulous neighbor, about some waste lands on the
frontiers, led to the blockade of the ports of Ecuador, in spite of
the offers of mediation of New Granada and Chili (November,
1858). Robles and Urbina, " the twins," as they were called, put
themselves at the head of the army; General Guillermo Franco,
appointed to defend Guayaquil, signed a treaty with the leader of
the Peruvian squadron August 21, 1859, by which the blockade
was raised, but the president refused to ratify this convention; two
insurrections broke out, one in Guayaquil and another in Quito, a

provisional government being formed in each city. Robles and Urbina were obliged to flee, and sought refuge in Chili. The revolutionaries in Guayaquil placed in power General Franco, who took the title of Supreme Head, named a ministry, and allied himself with Peru; but this power, which had to contend with a French squadron, could not aid him. On the other hand, the Conservatives of Quito put at their head a professor of chemistry, Gabriel García Moreno, a son-in-law of Flores. This old general, entrusted with the command of the army, defeated Franco at Babahoyo, August 8, 1860, and entered Guayaquil on September 14 following. Prosecuting, for the advantage of the country, the interminable quarrel with Peru respecting the boundaries, he invaded the cantons of Napo, Canelos, and Quijos; Peru was at that time fully occupied elsewhere and could not protest against this act. The triumvirs of Quito on July 8, 1861, called a National Assembly, which elected Dr. Moreno as president, while Flores received the important title of Governor of Guayaquil.

Moreno, a well-educated man, who united very fine qualities to the defects inherent in his country and race, had been proscribed in his youth. He employed the years of his exile in London and Paris in studying the institutions and administrative organization of the old world, hoping to be able some day to take back to his country the fruits of his observations and labors. He belonged to one of the oldest Spanish families, and the Conservative party, appreciating his superior intelligence, set all their hopes on him. On coming into power, Moreno found the finances in a wretched state. The public revenue did not amount to $1,000,000; the treasury was driven to makeshifts to obtain money, and was borrowing at 20 per cent. and public officers were unpaid. Moreno gave up his salary of $20,000 to be applied to works of public utility. His activity was directed to the most urgent material reforms. To him are owing the construction of roads from the mountainous regions to the coast, the formation of a new port in El Pailon, between the mouths of the Rivers Mina and Esmeralda, the establishment of a telegraphic line between the capital and Guayaquil, and the foundation of the mint and the hospital of Quito. He was well supported at first, but gradually saw his popularity decreasing. The forced currency of paper money caused discontent, and a concordat with Rome, which made over part of the public authority to the Church, gave rise to bitter criticism. It was soon known that the president, despairing of overcoming the difficulties of the situation without foreign help, had sought the protection of France. Rumors of annexation to Spain had afterward become so persistent that the Peruvian Minister of Foreign Affairs thought it his duty to invite, by his circular of August, 1861, the Spanish-American governments to unite, in order to prevent such annexation.

His private correspondence with a French diplomatist, published in Lima, raised a veritable tempest against him. All America was indignant, and there was talk of forming a league to overthrow him as a traitor to American independence. Peru, which felt herself threatened more than any other country, increased her efforts to combat him. The election of a new president of Peru, at the moment when diplomatic relations were broken off and war was probable, freed Ecuador from all danger on that side; but New Granada was very unfriendly. Her government put forward many grievances. In their view, Moreno was not only the man who demanded European intervention, but also the ultra-Conservative, who, recently, in the struggle between the Democratic party of Mosquera, and the Conservative party of Arboleda, had sturdily fought for the latter, promising to recognize him as the head of the Neo-Granadine Confederation. On August 15, 1863, Mosquera asked the Ecuadorians to overthrow the established government, and to join with him to federalize the three nations which previously had formed the Republic of Colombia. In this sense he proposed, on September 29, a treaty that Moreno refused to sign. Mosquera, advancing toward the frontier, declared in a proclamation that he desired to liberate " our brother Democrats of Ecuador from the theocratic yoke of Professor Moreno." The President of Ecuador was authorized by the Chambers, who supported him with patriotic enthusiasm, to declare that the country was in danger. On November 22 the aged Flores, at the head of 6000 men, invaded the territory of New Granada, explaining this blundering strategy by the necessity of carrying the war into the enemy's country rather than give up to invasion one of the richest provinces of Ecuador. On December 6 he found himself in front of the army of Mosquera, in Cuaspud. Before the battle Mosquera said: " They are 6000 men, but I have 4000 soldiers." The rout of the Ecuadorian army was lamentable; it lost 1500 in killed, wounded, and missing, and 2000 prisoners, and all its artillery. The republic seemed lost and thought of throwing itself into the hands of Peru; but Mosquera showed himself generous. Called away by other duties, he contented himself with imposing a treaty of peace on the vanquished, which was signed December 30, 1863, at the farm of Pensaqui. This compact was limited to placing the relations of the two countries in their previous state; Mosquera abandoned the use of force to convert Ecuador into an integral part of the United States of Colombia.

Such trials did not tend to raise the prestige of the Conservative party. The power of the president, shaken by two successive defeats, appeared from that moment unable to assure the security of the country. Moreno showed himself ready to resign his office, but in March, 1864, the Congress decided that he must keep it, and he would have recovered his prestige in public opinion if he had not weakened it by proposing new laws, which sacrificed the rights of the state to the interests of the Church. Thus the modifications introduced the preceding year into the concordat entered into with Rome in 1862, the publication of which had been suspended, were suppressed. By the president's influence the Congress bent before the will of the Holy See, that is to say, it left the clergy under the immediate jurisdiction of their ecclesiastical superiors. The contract entered into with the Jesuits for the supervision of a certain number of colleges was approved, and the opening of schools of the Brethren of the Christian Doctrine, supported by the taxpayers, was decreed. Nevertheless, when, after ratifying the treaty of peace with New Granada, passing a law of expropriation for the opening of public roads, organizing the police, voting the budget and reducing, for reasons of economy, the standing army to less than 1000 men, the Congress closed on April 18, 1864, Moreno thought himself sufficiently secure at home. But the situation was less reassuring abroad. Although peace had been arranged with the United States of Colombia, the tempest was always rumbling on the side of Peru. Solely to clear himself, Moreno sent a plenipotentiary to the Congress of Lima, instructed to examine a project of union between the American republics; when Spain, threatening Peru, occupied the Chincha Islands, he followed an ambiguous line of conduct, which formed a painful contrast to the proofs of sympathy that the other states of America lavished on the Peruvian cause.

Peru, engaged in her war with Spain, was not to be feared for the moment; but the rupture encouraged the hopes of the party hostile to Moreno, whose most active chief, Urbina, had taken refuge on the Peruvian frontier, encouraged and even aided by the Cabinet of Lima. Under such conditions, Moreno had to oppose new revolutionary movements, which sprang up one after another. The first broke out in Guayaquil in May; the second in the city of Quito itself, at the end of June. In August, Urbina threw the vanguard of his partisans on the Ecuadorian territory. The aged Flores was preparing to march against him, when death seized him in Guayaquil, removing in him one of the last survivors of the War of Independence, the father of the Ecuadorian republic, the man who during forty years had exercised so lamentable an influence on affairs. Moreno put himself at the head of the troops. The struggle was short. In November the province of Loja, the headquarters of the insurrection, was pacified, and Urbina was driven into the Peruvian territory. The president, among other measures of repression, ordered the execution of General Maldonado, the chief organizer of the movement in Quito; and after his victory he proclaimed an amnesty, from which the leaders of the insurrection alone were excepted.

Public works, forcibly interrupted, were actively recommenced, in spite of the deplorable condition of the exchequer. A new emission of legal tender paper money permitted the sanitary works in Quito to be continued, the establishment of a road to unite this city with Guayaquil, and the rebuilding of the edifices destroyed by the earthquake of 1859. An English company undertook to open an important road of communication in return for a concession of the lands adjoining it. The president, who saw the end of his term of office approaching, was impatient to finish the useful works with which he wished to endow his country. Unfortunately, everything was projected but nothing yet finished. By a clever policy he put an end to the enmity of the Peruvian Cabinet, and made terms with New Granada. At this period the use of postage stamps was introduced. Commerce appeared to revive, and the country was quiet.

The elections came on. Those of the provincial and cantonal chiefs and councilors, which took place in December, gave a majority to the Conservative or Government party; the presidential elections were, a few months later, to secure it the victory. The opposition put up as a candidate a man of influence, the late president of the Senate, Gomez de la Torre; nevertheless, Jerónimo Carrion, who was the nominee of Moreno himself, gained the day on May

1, 1865, by 21,733 votes against 8211 obtained by his competitor. It appears that the president used means of doubtful legality to secure the success of his candidate. Moreno received the government of Guayaquil, which he was to hold on quitting the presidency. In the meantime Urbina maintained himself continually on the Peruvian frontier; he took by surprise, on May 31, the *Guayas*, the only vessel of war possessed by the republic, put the crew to death, procured, besides, three small steamers, and blockaded the port. Moreno went against him, seized an English steamer at anchor in the port, paying three times its value upon the remonstrances of the consul, and put on a crew of 150 men, and succeeded in arming another merchant steamer. Then he put to sea, attacked the Urbinists, defeated them, seized their squadron and shot ninety-seven prisoners. The correspondence of Urbina, which was taken with his baggage, compromised many Liberals. Some were condemned to death, and the property of others was confiscated. Peru, also, was struggling under the efforts of rival parties. Moreno thought this a favorable moment to revenge himself on that country.

A new minister plenipotentiary being appointed to Quito, he refused to recognize him unless the Peruvian Government admitted itself a debtor to the Republic of Ecuador for $1,500,000 as an indemnity for the support that Urbina had found at Lima. This did not in any way prevent Ecuador adhering, in the following year, to a treaty of alliance, offensive and defensive, already signed between Chili and Peru, to resist Spain, and on this occasion a postal convention was signed with the Cabinet of Valparaíso, which for some years had broken off diplomatic relations with Ecuador.

The presidency of Carrion was at first tranquil enough. A man of modest habits and simple tastes, Carrion left his estate for the first time when he came to Quito to take possession of power. He understood the difficulties of the position from the beginning. Carrion was the nominee of Moreno, who reckoned upon continuing his work under his name, and making him act in conformity with his wishes; but Carrion left politics to his friend Bustamante. This minister was justly unpopular, and took advantage of his position to make himself absolute. Two senators and three deputies were arrested on the very steps of the Congress House. Carrion and Bustamante, accused of this deed, decided to dissolve the Chamber by force, but this *coup d'état* failed miserably. The minister fell, and Carrion had no other alternative than to associate

Moreno with himself in the government. The latter continued to be the most popular chief of the Conservative party, was made commander-in-chief of the troops, and made use of them to rebel against Carrion. On the night of November 5 Congress declared that the president had made himself " unworthy of the high position to which the popular confidence had raised him." Before this sentence, which Moreno himself came to pronounce, Carrion resigned his office. According to the constitution, the vice-president, Arteta, was invested, in the interim, with supreme power. Espinosa was elected president on January 29, 1868. In the following year General Veintemila rose against Espinosa with all the artillery which was under his command, but was killed in entering the city of Guayaquil.

In 1869 the constitution underwent modifications, in virtue of which the power passed into the hands of Moreno for the period of six years. The support given to the missions, undertaken by the fathers in Quito, in September, 1874, and above all the sending to the Pope of more than $200,000 from the funds of the state, excited men's minds, and insurrections broke out in various places, which the government met by declaring martial law in the provinces of Guayas, Assuay, and Manabi. At the end of his second term in the presidency, Moreno, in defiance of the constitution, solicited the suffrages of his fellow-citizens for the third time. This was his death warrant. On August 6 three assassins fell upon him, clove his skull with the stroke of a cutlass, and riddled him with bullets. Such was the tragical end of this man who deserves condemnation for having been peremptory by instinct and on principle, and too violent and extremely severe in his repressive measures. It is right to acknowledge, nevertheless, that during the years of his dictatorship very great progress was made. The receipts of the exchequer rose in the year of his death to $3,000,000. The registered debt was to be extinguished in 1876, and the floating debt did not amount to more than about $1,400,000.

In spite of military insurrections, in spite of being continually threatened and coveted by its neighbors, on account of its weakness, the Republic of Ecuador had prospered in some degree, seeing its commerce develop and its means of communication increase. There were more than 187 miles of high roads, 250 miles of bridle roads, a railway begun, and many wire bridges, to replace the swing bridges of osier, on which travelers are suspended over the abysses.   Its dissensions, the financial disorder, the scarcely repaired disasters of the terrible earthquake of 1859, were not sufficient to prevent Ecuador from bearing witness to her sympathy for stricken France.   Her subscription for the liberation of French territory from Germany exceeded $5000.   The country had hardly entered on the path of economic progress; it was evident that, with time, this republic might become one of the most prosperous countries of young America.

The strategic position of its capital, the mildness of its climate, the fertility of its soil, which in richness rivals that of Peru, the communication that the River Amazon allows it to open with Europe, all promise it an agreeable future; but, on the other hand, it is necessary for the people to be rescued from the state of dull ignorance and superstition in which intolerant priests and friars keep them, and on the other that new immigrants come to replace or at least to replenish the primitive population, which has been decimated or dispersed by a stupid administration.   The Ecuadorians are well fitted for manufacturing.   By very primitive methods, they produce carpets remarkable for the quality of the weaving, the beauty of the designs, and the brilliance of the colors.   The introduction of machinery has permitted the abilities of this people, reduced for a long time to supply by patience, ingenuity, and application, the insufficient means and instruments of fabrication, to be utilized. Agriculture, for the study of which a school has been founded, progresses slowly; but the means of communication, which join the elevated tablelands of the Andes with different points on the Pacific coast, through the woods and valleys, will permit of the introduction of the means of cultivation in the clearing of new ground. Finally, the Republic of Ecuador can hope for no solid future without European colonization, and she seems at last to understand it. Immigration, which has long been opposed, ought to be encouraged. The immigrants will then bring the help of their hands and their brains to this country of which Europe still really knows nothing but its faults.

Chapter VIII

THE ARGENTINE REPUBLIC. 1820-1876

THE Argentine Republic seems destined to rival the United States in growth and activity. There is no better field awaiting exploitation by mankind. Its capital would be the New York City of South America were it not for the revolutions that are constantly interrupting its agricultural and commercial life; but it is satisfied with being the Athens (at least such is its boast), proud as it justly is of its men of letters and poets, Mitre, Echevarria, Mármol, Gutierrez, Sarmiento, and others. Except Brazil, the Argentine Republic is the largest country on the southern continent, and the settled area is larger than Spain, France and England. It also excels in the number and importance of its rivers, which are all navigable for steamboats. The La Plata, which gives its name to this country, is one of the finest rivers in the world, and its estuary is a small sea widening out from 25 to 187 miles. It runs from north to south, fed by numerous tributaries, among them the Paraná, which can be navigated for 750 miles from the ocean.

This vast region is bounded on the north by Bolivia, on the east by Paraguay, Brazil and Uruguay, on the west by Chili, with which country it marches to the southern extremity of the continent. It is divided into three distinct parts: the first, closed between the Paraná and the Uruguay, which comprises the provinces of Entre Rios and Corrientes and the old territory of Misiones, is the Argentine Mesopotamia; the second skirts the chain of the Andes, and includes the mountainous provinces of Mendoza, San Juan, Rioja, Catamarca, Tucuman, Salta, and Jujuy. The third, which extends between the first two, with vast plains and natural pastures, where 15,000,000 cattle, 4,000,000 horses, and 80,000,000 sheep roam at will. This is the region of the Pampas, almost perfectly flat. There the untamed Indian, a terrible enemy, leads his warlike and wandering life, and the indefatigable Gaucho, armed with the lasso, constantly pursues the wild herds. The region includes the territory of the Argentine Chaco, the non-mountainous part of the provinces of Santiago del Estero, Cordoba and San Luís, and the whole of Sante Fé and Buenos Ayres; the last is the center of political and commercial life, and the experimental field of emigration. In addition to these provinces there are ten "territories." The fourteen provinces mentioned form so many independent states, as far as concerns their internal government, and collectively they form the Argentine Republic, the legislative authority of which lies in a Congress composed of two chambers. The deputies are elected by the people at the ratio of one for every 33,000 inhabitants, and there are two senators from each province and from the capital elected by the provincial legislatures, and in the capital by a special body of electors. The executive power is in the hands of the president or vice-president, who are chosen for six years, and are not reëligible until the lapse of a full presidential term after they give up their offices. They are elected by special electors chosen by the people of the several provinces. The federal judicial power is represented by a court of justice with jurisdiction of suits between different provinces or different officers of the same state.

The regular census of the population, taken for the first time in the month of September, 1869, made a total of 1,877,490 inhabitants, including the nomadic Indians of the Chaco, the Misiones, the Pampas, and Patagonia, reckoned at about 93,000. The population doubled in the twenty years ending 1895, and in consequence of this steady progress of the country many flourishing agricultural colonies settled at different points. Acclimatization is easy for Europeans, the country is one of the most healthful in the world, and its winter is like spring in southern France. The name of Buenos Ayres comes from the excellence and mildness of the climate. Few countries are so rich in food stuffs and the raw materials of industry, and the only interruptions of prosperity are the frequent revolutionary outbreaks.

The Treaty of El Pilar, signed in 1820, recognized the equality of all the provinces and their right to take part in forming the national government. The rout of the monarchical party had been complete, but Artigas was not to enjoy his triumph. A rebellion of Ramirez, one of his generals, obliged him to seek refuge in Paraguay, where the dictator, Francia, kept him shut up in a village. He was resigned to his fate, devoted himself to agriculture, was like a father to the poor, and died in 1826. As for Ramirez, he fell mortally wounded, July 10, 1821, under the walls of Buenos Ayres.

On the 21st of the same month a provincial administrative authority was formed, composed of a governor, General Rodriguez; a
Minister of Foreign Affairs and of the Interior, Rivadavia; a Minister of War and Marine, Cruz; and a Minister of Finance, García.
Rivadavia, an upright citizen, an able diplomatist and an enlightened administrator, had long represented the insurgent provinces
of La Plata in Paris and London. All the weight of public business
fell upon him. Various decrees referring to the establishment of
the representative system, the inviolability of property, the publication of the acts of the government, the liberty of the press and the
laws on civil, political and religious toleration and amnesty, and
the law relating to foreigners, are due to his initiative. Public instruction especially engaged his attention. Every district had its
elementary school; a university and various schools, a savings bank
and a benevolent society were founded; and navigation and the
working of the mines were favored. It is especially worthy of
notice that Buenos Ayres was at that time the first to set the example of suppressing letters of marque.

There was some tranquillity during these first years of development, but Brazil lost no opportunity of disturbing it. Because
of intestine struggles in Montevideo she had occupied it under
pretext of reëstablishing order, and had annexed the territory as
the Cisplatine Province (1821). A party opposed to the supremacy
of Buenos Ayres and of Brazil alike was formed in Montevideo,
which was destined to triumph later and transform the old Banda
Oriental, after a long war, into the Republic of Uruguay.

The independence of the Argentine provinces was a fact that
Spain alone disputed. It was recognized by the United States in
1823, and acknowledged, two years later, by England. In 1824
General Las Heras, the old champion of liberty, was elected to
succeed Rodriguez.

Rivadavia, at that time provisional governor, proceeded to
the installation of the new president, and voluntarily laid down
his office. One of the first subjects discussed in the General Congress of the United Provinces was the establishment of a permanent form of government. The constitution of December 24,
1826, confirmed the system of centralization under the name of the
Argentine Republic, and gave new strength—while appearing to
weaken it—to the pretension of Buenos Ayres to appoint the governors. Nothing more was needed to set the match to the powder
magazine. The concession to the provinces of the right to name

three candidates did not satisfy them. The war, which had been declared for some months between Brazil and Buenos Ayres, made new taxes necessary and a call under arms of all citizens between sixteen and forty years of age. These measures produced disturbances in Tucuman and Catamarca.

In the meantime Rivadavia, who had been raised to the supreme magistracy (February, 1825), was the soul of the Congress and the bond of friendship between the republic and foreign nations. In the midst of numberless difficulties he had negotiated a loan with England, and invited and favored immigration. He fitted out a small squadron under the command of the English admiral, Brown, against the Brazilian fleet, then blockading Buenos Ayres, which defeated the enemy in detail, but was not able to drive him away completely. Unfortunately the opposition of the provinces to the constitution of 1826 created new obstacles for him. Stanislas Lopez in Santa Fé, Bustos in Cordoba and Quiroga in the west, refused to recognize the supremacy of Buenos Ayres, wishing to establish a federal instead of a centralized system, and the people, aroused by them, refused to send their deputies to the Congress. The government of Buenos Ayres had never found itself in a more critical situation than at the beginning of the year 1827. Besides it was in open hostility with Colombia, or at least with Bolívar, on account of the separation of the provinces of Upper Peru, which were formed into a free state under the name of Bolivia, and whose independence Buenos Ayres was not disposed to recognize. The population of Buenos Ayres and of some small provinces was in reality left alone to fight with Brazil. The battle of Ituzaingo (February 20) gave the victory to the Argentine armies; but although it was possible to hold the Brazilians in check, and even to defeat them in detail, the political disorganization of the state and the distress in which the country was plunged did not by any means permit of following them up and gaining a complete victory. Under these circumstances García was appointed to carry proposals of peace to Rio Janeiro; but, overstepping the instructions he had received, he made a preliminary convention of May 13 by which Montevideo with its territory and all the Banda Oriental was ceded to Brazil. This convention excited great irritation in Buenos Ayres. The government disapproved of it as an attack upon the honor and independence of the nation, and the president, at the same time that he communicated this resolution to Congress, presented also his resignation (June 28).

Rivadavia, an open partisan of a centralized republic, thought that, in the present state of men's minds, his continuing in the presidency was one more obstacle to conciliation. Vincente Lopez, elected provisionally to succeed him, took the oath on July 7, but was not able, under such grave circumstances, to form a Cabinet immediately. In the end General Balcarçe consented to accept the Ministry of War, and Anchorena that of Finance. Afterward a species of truce was established between the parties; oblivion of the past was spoken of, and a great desire was shown to sacrifice private ambitions for the good of the country and to avenge the insult that the García treaty had given to the Argentine flag. By unanimous vote, Unitarians and Federalists declared for the continuance of the war with Brazil. The enthusiasm was admirable. The president, the Cabinet ministers and the government officials gave up part of their salaries; others, like Rivadavia, undertook to triple, during all the time the war lasted, the taxes levied upon them. Private subscriptions flowed into the treasury, the women offered their jewels, and all, as far as their means allowed, contributed to encourage men's minds and alleviate the precarious state of the national finances. The enthusiasm was communicated to the separatist provinces, and this crisis produced the salutary effect of disposing men's minds to conciliation. Thanks to the prudent firmness of Colonel Dorrego, who was elected by the Federalists, the city of Buenos Ayres voluntarily renounced its claim to be the capital and center of government of the republic. A federal diet met in Santa Fé, to continue the negotiations with Brazil, and showed itself equally decided to make what sacrifices were necessary to suitably support the honor of the nation. The two belligerent countries felt equally the necessity of putting an end to a state of things so disastrous for both. A treaty of peace was concluded on August 27, and was ratified on September 26 by the Congress of Santa Fé. Brazil, already fatigued by a conflict of ten years, abandoned her prey, and the countries which were the objects of the strife, being invited to proceed without delay to the election of their deputies, met in a constituent assembly, and proclaimed the independence of Montevideo and the Banda Oriental.

But soon the factional strife broke out again, and the struggle recommenced. The Unitarians under the influence of Lavalle, the conqueror of Ituzaingo, again demanded the supremacy of Buenos Ayres and a republic one and indivisible. Dorrego held the reins of government with a firm hand; he had had the good fortune to reconcile Buenos Ayres with the provinces, and the happiness of carrying out the glorious peace of August 27. But his federalist principles were sufficient cause for hostility to him in Buenos Ayres. The return of the army added to the complication of the situation. On December 1, Lavalle, at the head of a division, seized the Government House, and seconded by Admiral Brown, had himself appointed provisional dictator of the state by the notables assembled in the Cabildo. Dorrego marched to Santa Fé and demanded the support of the federal Congress; Lavalle pursued and overtook him, and had him shot December 9. This abominable and barbarous crime was the signal for a general rising. Congress declared the assassin, Lavalle, an outlaw, and he replied by a declaration of war; at the end of 1828 the republic was given up to all the horrors of anarchy. During the two following years the struggle between Federalists and Unitarians continued with fury, the former under Lopez and Quiroga, and the latter under Lavalle. The Federalists received a considerable reinforcement consisting of a band of Gauchos, devoted to a personage who was soon to acquire a terrible notoriety, Don Juan Manuel Ortiz de Rosas.

Rosas was at that time thirty-five years old; he had passed his youth on the estates of his family among half-savage shepherds. He had strongly marked features, lively and penetrating blue eyes, red and white complexion like a European, and tall stature like a Gaucho. He appeared for the first time on the political stage in 1820, at the head of his *colorados,* as an auxiliary of Rodriguez and the Unitarian party; seven years later he rallied his peasants again, but this time to aid the Federalists.

Dorrego had made him a general. When he learned the tragical end of his chief he hastened with his troop of Gauchos, gave battle to Lavalle, and routed him. The Federalists saluted him as their deliverer, and on December 8, 1829, he was appointed governor and captain-general of Buenos Ayres. In 1831 Lavalle again took the offensive in the province of Entre Rios, and was defeated there as Paz was at the same time in the province of Cordoba. This double misfortune was a mortal blow for the Unitarians, and the provinces of Cordoba, Corrientes, Mendoza and Santiago del Estero had already adhered to the federal compact when Rosas opened the session of 1832. It was stipulated that each state should preserve complete independence in internal affairs, and that the direction of foreign affairs and matters of war, common to the whole of the republic, should be delegated to the governor of Buenos Ayres. On taking authority Rosas said with great frankness: "You have chosen me to govern according to my ability and conscience, and I obey. My convictions will be my guide, and it will be my duty to make them prevail."

The Unitarians, who were pitilessly hunted down, gave proofs of indomitable obstinacy. Rosas employed all the resources of despotism to exterminate them; and the press, which was gagged, was silent before the arbitrary acts of the tyrant and his lieutenants; the soldiers gave no quarter, and organized bands of ruffians administered beatings to suspects. It is to be noted that from that time all documents bore the following epigraph: "Long live the Argentine Confederation. Death to the Unitarian savages!" The generals who had seconded Rosas filled him with a vague suspicion. Quiroga was assassinated in the neighborhood of Cordoba; Lopez, of Santa Fé, was invited to go to Buenos Ayres, and died there of a mysterious malady; and Cullen, his brother-in-law, was put to death, as also were the Generals Reynafé and Heredia. A campaign skillfully carried on against the Indians of the southern Pampas, which put an end to their incursions into the territories of Buenos Ayres, came in time to increase the prestige of Rosas. The multitude, who decidedly saw in him a hero and a man sent by Providence, threw themselves into his arms and made him a dictator.

The assassination of Quiroga, which was charged to the Unitarians, greatly excited popular indignation. On March 8, 1835, the day after the representation of a parliamentary comedy skillfully planned beforehand, the chamber of Buenos Ayres put all public authority into the hands of Rosas, with the title of governor and captain-general of the province, for five years. The dictator had not yet gained his object, and a plebiscite was necessary to confirm the election. A state entry was arranged for him, the idolatrous multitude drew his carriage, the frenzied Gauchos bore him in triumph, and the blessings and thanksgivings of the clergy filled the air. Such was the beginning of a dictatorship that lasted until 1852 and was able to hold England and France in check. Every five years, at the expiration of his term of office, Rosas hypocritically begged the chamber to take into consideration his weak state of health and to allow him to return to rural life. They renewed his powers, and the farce was played. In their admiration, the Gauchos called him the Washington of the South

Laborious, clear-sighted, and always attentive, he saw everything and managed everything; the army, police, finances, diplomacy, administration and the press. The treaties of 1829 made
the governor of Buenos Ayres the representative of the states of
La Plata with foreign powers, who learned to know Rosas in the
famous "affair of La Plata," which aggrandized him in the eyes
of the Americans and so much occupied Europe, and France in
particular. The July [1830] government of France had promptly
acknowledged the independence of the old Spanish colonies, but its
diplomatic agents were in conflict with Rosas, who had refused to
receive one of them, M. Laforet, under the pretext that he had given
offense to Chili. In Uruguay, President Oribe, attacked by Ribera,
who had made common cause with Lavalle, accepted the interested
help of Rosas, notwithstanding the protests of the French minister.
The arbitrary imprisonment of French citizens caused the blockade
of Buenos Ayres in 1838 by a fleet from Cherbourg. The dictator
stood firm and set himself up as the defender of American independence against Europe.

In the meantime Ribera expelled Oribe and declared war
against Buenos Ayres; Lavalle called upon the Argentine people to
revolt. Corrientes and Entre Rios took up arms against the dictator. Rosas, threatened on all sides, redoubled his cruelties against
his adversaries, and had seventy persons shot in one day. His lieutenants acted with the ferocity of wild beasts. In Santiago del
Estero the governor, Ibarra, made his name forever hated in the
whole district.[1] The diplomatic conferences lasted two years. At
length Vice-Admiral Mackau signed a treaty with Rosas, October
29, 1840, indemnity being promised to the injured Frenchmen;
but at Paris both the chambers and the press complained that this
treaty abandoned France's allies of yesterday to the vengeance of
Rosas. Lavalle, defeated November 16 in Santa Fé, was afterward
defeated in Lujan, and at length, being surprised in Jujuy, was
shot (1841). Oribe expelled the Unitarian general, Paz, from
Uruguay, and his victories in the provinces of Santa Fé and
Cordoba were followed by daily massacres. On the anniversary of
the election of Rosas his followers went through the streets, and
falling upon those persons who were suspected to belong to the vanquished party, pitilessly slaughtered them. The Unitarians being
defeated everywhere, Brown received orders to blockade Monte-

[1] As to this monster, see "*Les Aventures et Malheurs de la Señora
Libarona.*" (*Tour du Monde,* Vol. III.)

video; while Oribe, refusing the mediation of England and France, invaded Uruguay, laying siege to the capital by land.

Rosas had for some time conceived the idea of taking the Oriental Republic into the body of the Argentine Confederation, and Oribe zealously seconded his ambitious views.   Montevideo, defended by General Paz, had in its service a French legion under Thibaut, and an Italian legion under Garibaldi; but in spite of everything the city was about to yield when the French plenipotentiaries intervened.   Rosas refused to put an end to hostilities, and the fleets of France and England blockaded Buenos Ayres, September 18, 1845, and forced the passage of the Paraná, free entrance to which had always been refused to foreign ships.   This armed intervention was founded on three powerful reasons—the interests of commerce, the protection due to French citizens, and the coöperation of Brazil,[2] which was afterward withdrawn.   Montevideo had 2000 French residents, and Buenos Ayres 10,000.   The two chief interests at stake, commerce and humanity, had more to gain from peace than from war.   The negotiations opened with Rosas by the allied powers resulted in 1849 in treaties which secured the free navigation of the Paraná, the *status quo ante bellum* and the independence of the Oriental Republic.   At Paris the National Assembly refused to ratify the treaty made by Admiral Le Predour in the name of the republic, and in 1851 France decided to send an expeditionary military and naval force to the waters of the South Atlantic.

The tyranny of Rosas was nearing its end.   The dictator, who had been able to make head against two European powers of the first rank, fell before an insurrection of the provinces, supported by Brazil, which dreaded the time when it would have him for a neighbor.   His tyranny and his obstinacy in negotiations, which, by causing the blockade of the Argentine ports, interfered with the commerce of the La Plata and perpetuated the war with Montevideo, had at last wearied his own generals.   Justo José de Urquiza, the governor of Entre Rios, having been twice sent to pacify the revolted cities, at last embraced their cause.   Urquiza, a simple Gaucho sprung from the ranks of the people, owed his elevation to his strength of character and superior intelligence.   He began his military career under the command of Rosas, who appointed him gov-

[2] Rouher.   "Proceedings of the [French] National Assembly, December 29, 1850."

GAUCHOS FOLLOWING THE CASSOWARY OR SOUTH AMERICAN OSTRICH
WITH THE BOLO

Painting by Albert Richter   —page 118

ernor of Entre Rios in 1842, and distinguished himself against Ribera in Uruguay. Had he at length unraveled the crafty policy of Rosas? Did he see that he was using his patriotism for the furthering of a personal ambition? Certain it is that he turned against the dictator. When the latter wished in 1851 to repeat the comedy of his abdication, Urquiza published an eloquent manifesto against Rosas's bad faith. The insurgent leader obtained the alliance of Brazil, Paraguay, Corrientes, and Uruguay, forced Oribe to capitulate on October 8, and delivered Montevideo. On January 8, 1852, "the grand army of liberty of South America" crossed the Paraná and marched against Buenos Ayres, following the bank of the river. Rosas saw the danger; declared Urquiza "a traitor, madman, and Unitarian savage"; demanded a new investiture from the Chamber of Representatives, and had himself declared exempt, during the war and for three years thereafter, "from all limitations, ordinary as well as extraordinary. His forces, concentrated around the capital, amounted to 25,000. The liberating army numbered 28,000, and these two forces were the largest armies which had yet fought in South America. The battle of Monte Caseros (February 3, 1852) ended in a few hours the power of the chief of the Gauchos. Rosas had time to fly; an English steamer landed him in Ireland, with his daughter, Manuelita, on April 26. He afterward settled in Southampton, where he learned in 1861 that the tribunal of Buenos Ayres had condemned him to death.

The government created by Rosas had lasted twenty years. Although he had been raised to power as a Federalist, he had not always respected the rights of the provinces. The cause of his fall even at that late day was not so much the tyrannical measures by which he maintained his authority as the lion's share in the division of the proceeds of the customs which his policy gave to the capital. Rivadavia, the direct product of the ideas of the French Revolution, endeavored to make unity the basis of liberty; Rosas, the executioner of the Unitarians, centralized everything, and his despotic hand weighed upon every part of La Plata.

Urquiza entrusted the administration of Buenos Ayres to the old and esteemed Dr. Lopez, and convoked a constituent assembly in Santa Fé, in which the province of Buenos Ayres was not represented. Its pretensions to preponderance and political supremacy were tenacious, and its newspapers and assemblies revived Unitarian ambitions. Lopez gave in his resignation, and General Pinto,

president of the Chamber of Buenos Ayres, took power provisionally. Urquiza arrived and dissolved the Chamber, and by a dictatorial act, entrusted the government to one of his generals, who
was overthrown shortly after by a popular movement which declared the city free, and appointed Valentin Alsina captain-general,
October 30, 1852. The province of Buenos Ayres rose against the
city, demanding its immediate incorporation in the confederation,
and the provincial militia took up arms. Urquiza joined them, laid
siege to Buenos Ayres, and blockaded its port. At the same time
he signed a treaty with France and England, which secured the
free navigation of the Argentine rivers. Want of union in the
besieging army, the attitude of the fleet, which fraternized with
the population, and the unanimous resistance of the natives, as well
as of the Europeans, obliged Urquiza to retire precipitately, and
give up an attempt openly condemned by the national feeling.[3] He
offered his resignation to Congress, which refused to accept it.

The Congress had voted the constitution promulgated May 1,
1853, and delegated the executive authority to Urquiza. Peace
was an absolute necessity. The new president established his
government in Paraná, whither the representatives of foreign
powers followed it, and recognized the province of Buenos Ayres
as forming a state independent of the rest of the confederation,
with a national representation in two chambers, and a government
elected every three years. The relations between the two separate
factions in the Argentine family remained unfriendly until the
signature of the treaties of December 20, 1854, and January 8,
1855, which succeeded in reëstablishing confidence and assuring
public credit. The dissentient state received the diplomatic and
consular agents of friendly powers and of the Federal government
itself.

Under the enlightened, tolerant, and firm administration of
Dr. Obligado Buenos Ayres built sumptuous edifices, its monu-
mental customs house, theaters, and palaces, illuminated its streets
with gas and opened railways, while the Argentine Confederation,
under the presidency of Urquiza, saw order and prosperity return,
and its commerce and industry acquire a great development. The
plan of a railway between Cordoba and Rosario was studied, and
a geographical and statistical examination of the confederation
was undertaken, the rivers of the interior were explored, and nu-

[3] Balcarçe, "*Buenos-Ayres: Sa situation presente,*" etc. Paris, 1857.

merous agricultural colonies were settled in the provinces of Santa
Fé and Entre Rios.

In the meantime Urquiza did not lose the hope of forming
the federal bond again; but the negotiations opened with this object
found no echo in Buenos Ayres. This great city was then accused
of wishing to regain its lost empire, to be the center of monopoly,
and to repudiate the ideas of free navigation and commerce.[4] Some
modifications of its international relations resulted from this, of
which the government at Paraná took advantage to abandon the
pacific attitude which it had hitherto preserved. On March 18,
1856, it denounced the treaty of 1854, and by a later law established
differential duties on imports. The commerce of Buenos Ayres
was directly attacked, and the city complained. The relations
between the two states were embittered. In May, 1859, various
movements demanding the voluntary or forcible union of Buenos
Ayres with the Confederation took place in the provinces; both
parties set their national guards on a war footing, and although
the ministers of France, England, and the United States offered
their mediation, Buenos Ayres refused all accommodation, and entrusted its defense to General Mitre, who was defeated by Urquiza.
The battle of Cepeda, gained by the Federal troops on October 23,
was followed by a treaty, by the terms of which Buenos Ayres
reëntered the Confederation (November 11, 1859). On March 1,
1868, Urquiza, whose presidential term was ended, gave up his
office to Dr. Santiago Derqui. On May 1 following Mitre was
appointed governor of Buenos Ayres, and to celebrate the conclusion of peace between the various states of the confederation
national rejoicings brought together in Buenos Ayres, on July 9,
President Derqui, General Urquiza, and General Mitre, who received the title of brigadier-general from the nation.

The Argentine union had scarcely been formed when a rebellion
broke out in the province of San Juan; the governor, Virasoro, was
assassinated in his house, with five of his friends, and Dr. Abera-
stein, elected to occupy his post, fell into the hands of Colonel Sáa,
who was sent to punish the revolt, and was shot. This summary
execution excited indignation in the state of Buenos Ayres, and
Mitre, after asking in vain for the disapprobation of the act of
Colonel Sáa from the president, Derqui, applied to Congress. This

---

[4] *"Organisacion de la Confederacion Argentina";* and the following
journals for 1856: *Le Pays, Le Constitutionnel, Les Débats.*

subject was complicated by the quashing by the Argentine chamber of the election of the deputies for Buenos Ayres, which took place under the provincial and not under the federal law. About this time a terrible earthquake completely destroyed Mendoza.

Buenos Ayres made the denial of admission to its deputies a cause for war, suppressed the monthly payment to the treasury of the $100,000 from May 1, 1861, in order to preserve the control of its customs house; on the other hand, the federal authority presented various restrictive claims. The interminable conflict between state rights and national rights, between Unitarians and Federalists, broke out more ardently than ever. After exhausting all means of conciliation, Urquiza, general-in-chief of the forces of the Argentine Confederation, and Mitre, at the head of the troops of Buenos Ayres, began the campaign; but this time Urquiza, discontented with the policy of his successor, did not undertake the struggle willingly, and while he consented to it as a matter of form, he negotiated secretly with Mitre. The latter, after winning a victory on September 17, 1861, at Pabon, thanks to the Italian legion commanded by the ex-Garibaldian, Piloni, invaded the province of Santa Fé and penetrated to Rosario with 12,000 men, after receiving the adhesion of the province of Cordoba. Urquiza, from the beginning of the struggle, had returned to his usual residence at San José. His unexpected retirement had caused the dissolution of the Argentine army, which, deserted by its officers, without provisions, baggage, or munitions, had to undergo unheard of sufferings during its long retreat. President Derqui was reduced to impotence, solicited the hospitality of an English steamer, and took refuge in Montevideo; a few months later Mitre signed a peace with Urquiza, who remained governor of Entre Rios.

On May 1, 1862, Mitre opened the new provincial legislature in Buenos Ayres, and in his message he boasted of the triumph of the Liberal party, the reëstablishment of peace, the increasing prosperity of commerce, the satisfactory condition of the finances, the construction of new railways, and the material and administrative progress. The chief of the victorious party was elected president of the Argentine Republic, entering upon the exercise of his powers in the month of October, and the city of Buenos Ayres became again the seat of government by the terms of the provisional agreement.

Complications now arose in foreign affairs. The three republics of La Plata—the Argentine Confederation, Uruguay and

Paraguay—found themselves engaged in quarrels, in which the neighboring empire of Brazil was not slow to interfere, and which resulted in a bloody and general war. The three republics were always jealous of one another. Buenos Ayres was constantly working against the independence of its rival, Montevideo. The Argentines had not given up the idea of drawing Uruguay into their sphere of action and of forming a single state, of which Paraguay, also, would be an integral part. From this desire arose the efforts of the parties who came into power in Buenos Ayres to aid, in Montevideo, the parties most like themselves. In this situation of affairs Flores left Buenos Ayres with troops raised there to undertake an insurrection against the government of Uruguay. As for Paraguay, boundary disputes were a continual menace in that quarter. In 1864 underhand projects of territorial aggrandizement were the cause of an agreement between the cabinets of Buenos Ayres and Rio Janeiro against Uruguay. Paraguay, thinking that the equilibrium of the states of La Plata was threatened, protested against any armed intervention of Brazil in the internal affairs of Montevideo; this protest caused a general conflagration, and gave the sad spectacle of an empire, already dreaded for the extent of its territory, successfully embroiling three republics which should always unite for mutual help. On May 4, 1865, a triple alliance was formed against Paraguay, or rather against its president, Lopez, who was described as a despot and tyrant. Mitre, who does not deserve our sympathies in this business, was appointed generalissimo of the allied troops. His first care was to repulse a Paraguayan invasion, after which the allies, whose plan was to modify the government established in Paraguay, followed Lopez into his own territory.

This struggle is well known, and is recounted in the following chapters. The Argentine Republic entered upon it without the sympathy of Chili and Peru, and while it continued had to fight against a succession of internal disturbances. Urquiza exercised a dictatorship in Entre Rios almost independent of the federal government of Buenos Ayres; the provinces on the right bank of the Paraná endeavored to break the federal compact by force of arms, and we must add to these difficulties the depredations of hostile Indians. The legislature of Buenos Ayres openly censured the continuation of hostilities, and recruiting for the army was carried on everywhere with great difficulty.

Nevertheless, the presidential message of May 6, 1866, was congratulatory on the progress of immigration from Europe, which, in the first four months of the year, amounted to 4780 persons. It showed an excess of eighteen per cent. in receipts for 1865 over the preceding year, and a considerable increase in the exportation of raw wool. The financial crisis was none the less serious. Fifteen months' pay was due to the army corps sent against Paraguay. Mitre brought back with him some 4000 Argentines—more than half of the contingent—giving, on his return, new vigor to the operations carried on at home against the rebels.

In the midst of these grave events the cholera, which broke out on the battlefields of Paraguay, scourged Buenos Ayres for the first time, and before its frightful ravages political activity was suspended. Mitre, desirous of advancing military affairs, again set out for Paraguay on July 22, 1868, the troops employed in the pacification of the provinces having returned to the front in June, raising once more the Argentine contingent to some 8000 men; but the insurrection in the provinces of the Andes was scarcely extinguished in one place when it broke out in another. In La Rioja the government was overthrown fifteen times in seven months. In Entre Rios, Urquiza, the largest landed proprietor of the district and absolute master of the country, preserved an enigmatical attitude. Buenos Ayres, when the cholera reappeared at the end of the year with more virulence than ever, was panic-stricken, and drove the municipal authorities from power. Moreover, the federal government was not harmonious. The Minister of Foreign Affairs, Elizalde—the most decided partisan, after Mitre, of the Brazilian alliance—finding himself in complete disaccord with Paz, joined with the Minister of Justice in tendering his resignation. Thus war, disagreements with Chili, insubordination in the provinces, a financial and industrial crisis, and a violent epidemic make a summary of the year 1867.

A fact worthy of notice, and almost peculiar to these young and ardent nations, is the rapid increase of population in the midst of such chaos. European immigration, especially French, is considerable, there is great activity in the port of Buenos Ayres, and foreign commerce reaches the amount of $80,000,000, of which $24,000,000 is with France; some railways are in operation and others in course of construction; an electric telegraph unites Montevideo with Buenos Ayres; many roads are planned, and schools are founded: and the confederation took part in the French Universal Exposition of 1867, winning several prizes.

At the beginning of 1868 the death of the vice-president recalled Mitre to the control of civil affairs. On October 12 he resigned the presidency to Dr. Sarmiento, who had been elected on June 12, and who, as a publicist, had attacked the tyranny of Rosas in the press and been present at the battle of Monte Caseros as chief of staff to Urquiza. Later, as inspector-general of schools, he had given a great impulse to popular education and endowed the capital with important scholastic foundations. As senator and minister in 1860, he secured an appropriation of five millions for schools, which permitted him to plant the germs of civilization even in the Pampas. His initiative had also influenced the telegraphic service, the official survey and valuation of land (Cadastre), and the clearing of the vast plains. When he was governor of San Juan in 1862, he founded in that country a small school and a public library, and when the election to the presidency fell upon him he was the representative of the republic with the Government of the United States. One of his books ends with these words: "Without education there is no liberty," and bears as a motto: " Have schools and you will not have revolutions." Sarmiento put into practice these just expressions, he worked without ceasing, and in every way for the advancement of his country, and always earnestly sought to favor the education of the people.

On February 3, 1870, the anniversary of the battle of Monte Caseros, Urquiza received the new president at San José and gave proof of his allegiance to the national government by brilliant entertainments. This conciliatory step of the old Federalist caused a secret irritation in those who had long been accustomed to recognize him as their head. Two months later, at the end of an April day, he was stabbed in his own house. At the same hour Lopez Jordan raised a rebellion in Concepcion and entered the legislative chamber, which, in panic, was compelled to proclaim him governor. Sarmiento sent troops against Entre Rios; Lopez Jordan awaited them firmly, prolonging the contest until the following year, when it was ended by the defeat and flight to Brazil of the last of the chiefs. The old Gaucho party, that now includes only the retrograde and anti-liberal element, did not consider itself as finally conquered; and although it has lost its reason for existence in the present state of political and social development of the republic, it has continued its agitations in these latter times. In 1873 Lopez Jordan, who had again appeared in arms in Entre Rios, kept the field until the month of December, when he was crushed.

The intrepid president of Paraguay had been killed in a last combat, March 1, 1870; and on June 20 a treaty was signed between Brazil and the Argentine Republic on one part, and Paraguay, exhausted, devastated, and ruined, on the other; but very soon the Argentine statesmen were able to measure the results of this unrighteous war. The conquerors could not agree, and on September 30, 1871, the Argentine legation left Rio Janeiro in obedience to a recall by the cabinet at Buenos Ayres. A boundary question in regard to Paraguay caused the rupture, and it seemed as if the allies of yesterday were about to come to blows. Mitre was sent to Rio to reopen negotiations, and at the close of 1872 a peaceful arrangement was made.

A terrible scourge, the yellow fever, terrified Buenos Ayres at the beginning of 1871. The customs house, the bank and all public buildings had to be closed. By April 30 26,000 persons had perished in the course of 100 days. In the same year the Congress settled the question of the capital, which had been in suspense for a long time, by declaring that the government should abandon Buenos Ayres and fix its seat at Villa María, between Rosario and Cordoba; but the president put his veto on this project, for the reason that the seat of government in that town would be exposed to danger while the war with the state of Entre Rios continued. At the same time (October 15) a great national exhibition was opened in Cordoba, which marked a new era in the annals of the agricultural and industrial development of the republic.

Sarmiento's term of office ended in 1874. His last message to Congress was a consolatory statement of the condition of the country. The increase in the receipts of the treasury had kept pace each year with the rapid progress, in material as well as intellectual affairs, shown by the development of popular education and postal correspondence; by the increase in immigration; by the great consumption of paper, that so exactly gives the measure of the intellectual movement of a country; by the progress in means of communication in all parts of the territory; and, lastly, by the extent of country covered by telegraphic lines. In 1868 the receipts of the treasury amounted to $12,000,000, and in 1873 they were nearly $20,170,000. At the same date (1868) the number of immigrants was 39,000, and this number increased to 80,000 in 1873. In 1868 the postoffice distributed 4,000,000 pieces of written and printed matter; in 1873 the figures were 7,787,400, and the postal routes covered 81,000 leagues, and 1,000,000 letters were delivered by the letter carriers alone. In 1870 6400 telegrams were transmitted over lines extending 129 miles; in 1873 there were 170,079 telegrams, and the length of wires 2618 miles. In 1868 the colleges had 1006 students; there were 4000 in 1873. In 1852, the date of the fall of Rosas, twenty schools were sustained by the state of Buenos Ayres, and in the interior the number was still less. To-day there are 1117 public schools. In 1868 San Juan was the only province that had a public library; now there are 140; some can be found in the smallest villages. In 1868 there were only four steamers a month sailing for Europe; to-day there are 19, so that one leaves Buenos Ayres every two days. In 1868 the importation of paper did not reach 12,000 reams annually. In 1872 and 1873 it amounted to 200,000 reams. There were 5630 machines employed in industry in 1868, and 70,000 in 1873.

Speaking of public works, the message enumerated the buildings erected in Buenos Ayres for the national government; those containing the offices of accounts, the laboratories of chemistry and physics annexed to the national college, and more recent buildings for the offices of the master of the port, the telegraph and the postoffice. In Rosario and Santa Fé a national college, a telegraph office and a customs house were built; in Cordoba an observatory and an academy of sciences. The president took pleasure in pointing out the progress of ornamental architecture in the towns and their suburbs and in the villages: "On our lines of railway and the banks of our rivers the numerous chimneys of our factories now rise. Does not this sight give the traveler a good idea of the development of our industries?"

The presidential election in 1874 was warmly contested. Dr. Nicolás Avellaneda, the winner in the balloting in April, had Mitre for a competitor. His installation took place on October 12 under somewhat critical circumstances. Mitre had not accepted the result of the voting, which was said to have been vitiated by fraud. A military insurrection, fomented and directed by the party that called itself constitutional, which had lost the election, broke out. Mitre, with a considerable force, threatened Buenos Ayres; other chiefs, Arredondo, Rivas, and Borges, joined him, and on Novem-

ber 6 the insurgent flotilla cast anchor in sight of the port. The
government forces, under the command of Sarmiento, were victorious, and Mitre surrendered. In December the province of
Buenos Ayres was pacified, and Arredondo was completely routed.
Peace seemed to be reëstablished when a tragical event occurred.

At the inauguration of the new president, Nicolás Avellaneda,
some old pretensions were revived. The Jesuits had fled from
Buenos Ayres at the same time as the Spaniards. The state had
converted the establishments deserted by them into academies and
hospitals; the reverend fathers returned quietly, and took good care
not to arouse suspicion, patiently waiting till their time should
come. After the election of Avellaneda, who seemed no less a
friend of the order than the Archbishop Eneiro, they unmasked
their batteries. The passions of the clergy were aroused, and pul-
pits resounded with violent attacks against "the robbers of the
clergy, the Liberals, the Freemasons," etc. The archbishop formally demanded the restitution of the real estate which was converted into state property in 1816. The public was excited beyond
expression at such an impudent request. On March 1, 1875, the
students marched with a banner bearing this motto:

"A Protest against the Jesuits,"

and presented themselves before the house of these fathers. Considering it to be national property, they begged permission to cross
its courts. The door opened. The student carrying the banner,
a youth of twenty years of age, named Suzini, led the way over
the threshold, when the Jesuits, who lay in ambush, threw him to
the ground, and completely decapitated him by the sharp blades of
their knives and daggers. The comrade who followed him was
stabbed in the breast, a third received a frightful stab in the abdo-
men, and others rolled bleeding to the ground. The multitude,
beside themselves, broke loose, and threw themselves on the priests
and beat them to death on the spot; the building was given over to
fire and pillage, after which, with shouts of "Death to the Jesuits,"
the people marched to the archbishop's palace, which was searched
from garret to cellar, but the ultramontane prelate had fled, and it
was impossible to find him anywhere. Such are the facts, still little
known in Europe, and which we can only mention here.

Chapter IX

THE ORIENTAL REPUBLIC OF URUGUAY
1828-1876

THE treaty of August 27, 1828, which recognized the independence of the Banda Oriental, the chance spoil of Brazil, was ratified on October 4 of the same year. This old province of the viceroyalty of Rio de la Plata, on being definitely separated from the Argentine territory, elected deputies, who, sitting as a constituent congress, appointed as provisional president, General Rondeau, an old warrior of Peru, and lately one of the governors of Buenos Ayres. On July 18, 1830, the constitution was proclaimed. By it the government of the Oriental Republic of Uruguay was composed of an executive power exercised by a president, elected for four years by the two chambers sitting as one house, reëligible only after the lapse of a full term after his quitting the office, and assisted by four ministers, namely, those of the Interior, of Foreign Affairs, of Finance, and of War and Marine; a legislative power exercised by the Senate, over which the vice-president of the republic presides, and the Chamber of Deputies; the judiciary power, exercised by special judges with three grades of jurisdiction, corresponding to the French tribunals of first instance, appeal, and cassation. The Supreme Court of Justice, composed of five judges, acts as a court of final appeal and appoints some magistrates of the inferior courts. Criminal causes and offenses of the press are tried by jury. The French code forms the basis of the legislation on this subject.

Uruguay is the smallest state of South America, but it is not the least important from the point of view of commerce. Its population, which, according to the official census of 1865, was only 346,000, amounts, according to recent calculations, to nearly 1,000,000. This is not surprising if we take into account the large immigration of Europeans which has recently taken place, especially of Spaniards, Italians, French, English, and Germans. Montevideo, which the native poets call the Troy of South America, is admirably situated between the wide estuary of the La Plata and the Atlantic Ocean, and at its commodious port, where there is room for more than 200 vessels, almost all the steamers bound for Buenos Ayres call.

The Oriental Republic has always been coveted by Brazil, which bounds it on the north, and of the Argentine Confederation, from which it is separated by the River Uruguay on the west. On the south and east it is washed by the La Plata and the Atlantic. Its geographical position is eminently favorable to the development of its resources, since the greater part of its frontiers are formed by the sea and large rivers navigable by ships of the greatest burden. Wool and hides, as in the Argentine Confederation, are the principal industry of the country, which is divided into thirteen departments—Salto, Paysandú, Soriano, Colonia, San José, Montevideo, Canelones, Maldonado, Cerro Largo, Tacuarembó, Minas, Florida, and Durazno.

After a very short period of peace the newly emancipated state saw rival factions disputing for power, and the Indian tribes carrying devastation and death to the towns in the interior. Among these, the tribe of the Charrúas had always been distinguished for their unconquerable hostility. Diaz de Solis and his companions, the first Europeans who had ventured to enter the La Plata, had been devoured by them in 1516, and since then they had never ceased to carry on a war of extermination against the conquerors. Faithful to the traditions of their ancestors, these formidable savages sacked and burned the farmsteads, stole the cattle, killed the men, and carried off the women and children. Fructuoso Ribera, who was raised to the presidency, resolved to make an end of them, and little by little they were almost annihilated in many hard-fought battles; the few who escaped pursuit hid themselves in the depths of the wilderness; and this was the end of a nation which, like the lion in the fable,[1] had it known how to paint or write would have transmitted heroic annals to posterity.

Meanwhile, Uruguay saw the beginning of a sad period of *pronunciamientos*. Ribera was suddenly attacked in his headquarters, and very nearly killed; a colonel named Gurzon rose with his regiment, drove out the ministers, seized power himself and ap-

---

[1] La Fontaine's Fables, iii., 10. The lion contemptuously comments on a picture representing a man victorious over a gigantic lion.

pointed General Lavalleja commander-in-chief of the army. Ribera, with a loyal negro battalion and a few hundred white men, marched against the insurgents and defeated them. Ten officers were executed. The sentence of exile pronounced against the authors of these disorders was suspended three years later by a decree of amnesty, which was universal, even including General Lavalleja himself.

Manuel Oribe was elected president March 1, 1835, and Ribera, who was at first appointed by him to command the army, was soon replaced by Ignacio Oribe. Ribera became the personal enemy of his successor, made common cause with the Argentine Unitarians, who had fled to Uruguay, and united under his banners many French and Italians who were settled in Montevideo. Oribe obtained the help of Buenos Ayres, and Rosas, whose fixed idea was to annex the Oriental Republic to the confederation, hastened to intervene, disregarding the protests of the resident French minister. Ribera was beaten in 1837, and obliged to take refuge in Brazilian territory, whence he kept up guerrilla warfare. When the French squadron blockaded Buenos Ayres the next year, he entered Montevideo and had himself elected president, and his competitor, Oribe, took refuge with Rosas.

Oribe was appointed by Rosas general of brigade, placed at the head of the Argentine forces, and soon beat the Unitarian allies of Ribera. While the Argentine fleet, opposing the squadron of Uruguay, commanded by Coe and afterward by Garibaldi, was blockading Montevideo, Oribe, refusing the offer of mediation made by England and France, invaded the Banda Oriental, and at the end of 1842 defeated the army of Ribera near Arroyo Grande, made himself master of all the open country, and marched on the capital, to which he laid siege by land on February 16, 1843. His soldiers devastated the country, and he himself gave it up to pillage. It was not enough to lead a foreign invasion of his bleeding country; he made those whom he conquered suffer a despotism like that exercised by Rosas. The people abhorred him; he avenged himself cruelly, and his name has been given up to public execration; he is known on both banks of the La Plata by the name of The Headsman (*Corta-Cabezas*). The foreigners resident in Montevideo fought against him in the Italian legion, the French legion, and the Basque regiment, under Garibaldi and Colonels Thibaut and Brie. Paz and Pacheco and Obes directed the defense. Those men, representing the principles of liberty and humanity, performed prodigies of valor. Garibaldi, surprised in a sally that he made to San Antonio, by 12,000 cavalry and 300 infantry, beat them off for a whole day with only 180 Italians, and retreated in good order upon El Salto. The desire of protecting the independence of the Oriental Republic had been the principal reason put forward to justify the intervention of France, England, and Brazil; but the real motive was the free navigation of the Paraná, which was secured after the naval victory of Obligado won in November, 1845, by the combined squadrons of England and France. We have already seen in the preceding chapter how this disastrous struggle terminated. Oribe, being closely penned up by Urquiza, suffered a decisive defeat on October 8, 1851, by which the liberation of Montevideo was secured.

The country could then take breath, but the injury done to the national finances was great. All progress had been suspended and all improvement had been put off to a less turbulent time. Hitherto stock-raising, which constituted the principal wealth of Uruguay, had been limited to horned cattle, horses and mules; sheep-breeding for the production of wool was now acquiring considerable importance. With the increase of sheep farms the value of rural property increased very much. Many French, English, and Germans bought immense tracts of land suitable for pasture, on which are now found herds of 50,000 and 60,000 head. Nothing is more common than to see droves of 10,000 cattle and 6000 horses. Selected animals imported from Europe, ranging on vast and fertile pastures, whose freshness is constantly maintained by clear streams under a temperate and salubrious sun, multiply at a rate which exceeds all calculation. Thus the statistics for the first three quarters of 1866, notwithstanding the fact that it had been a very turbulent year, showed that 452,834 cattle and 21,404 horses were slaughtered and salted.

In the same year the shearing of 60,000 sheep on a single estate produced 137,425 pounds of wool, and 54,000 head on another gave 194,700 pounds. The cultivation of the yerba maté (Paraguay tea), sugar-cane, and cotton, of the principal cereals, of tobacco and indigo, yields the colonists large crops in a country where nature has displayed such a prodigious bounty and exuberance of fertility. Conditions would have been perfect but for the eternal divisions and subdivisions of parties, and the enmity caused by them. The

Colorados or Liberals constantly keep up the greatest antagonism to the *Blancos* or Conservatives, but, in spite of all this chaos, a certain material progress made headway, and this is one of the most curious phenomena of these turbulent nations, in which life is so vigorous. Uruguay, in the midst of its incessant disturbances, has not remained indifferent to peaceful industrial victories. Her products attracted little attention at the Universal Exhibition of Paris in 1855, which occurred shortly after her disasters, but took a prominent place in the exposition at London in 1862; and in the Paris Exposition of 1867 they won a gold medal and other well-deserved honors.

Uruguay on January 2, 1859, entered into a treaty with Argentina and Brazil to guarantee Uruguayan independence and neutrality in case of war between those two powers, who are forever intervening for some motive or other in her internal affairs and accusing each other of wishing to aggrandize themselves at her expense.

The presidential election of 1860 was peaceful. Pereira counted on having his son appointed as his successor, but he was defeated by a man old in years, although still strong and active. This was Bernardo Berro, an old subaltern of Oribe, and a member of the *Blanco* party. The majority of preceding governments had been distinguished for their arbitrary acts; the memory of the dark scene of Quinteros, in which Pereira had, without mercy, put to death General Diaz, General Freire, and Colonel Tajes, most distinguished officers, was still fresh in all minds. The new president, who disapproved of such severity, delivered on February 15, 1861, on the opening of the chambers, a moderate and pacific speech, and had a law passed which was not successful in bringing back the exiled *Colorados*. On the contrary, they assembled on the Argentine frontier in readiness to throw themselves at the first opportunity on the conquering party and wrest the power from them.

At first neither order nor labor was disturbed, and scarcely anybody attached any importance to the almost daily changes of obscure ministers whom Berro abruptly dismissed when it appeared that they would acquire some influence. The regulation of the English and French loans, to the payment of which the receipts on stamped paper were allotted, led to some diplomatic difficulties. Causes of friction with the powers of the Old World were of various *kinds* and arose continually from some slight incident or other. Because a warrant officer had received some sword cuts and a seaman had been ill-treated in Montevideo, Italy and England made threats. Due satisfaction was given to these powers, but unwillingly and without dignity, in such fashion that this weakness of the government was made manifest. For some months a provisional ministry had been at the head of affairs, and on January 21, 1863, President Berro endeavored to form a more homogeneous and representative Cabinet, but the political situation was not materially altered. The president followed with restless eyes the progress of the plot that the Uruguayan exiles were hatching in Buenos Ayres, became shaken and unnerved, and had recourse to those violent measures against the press and those acts of severity against individuals which never save any government from danger and often hasten its fall.

On April 19, 1863, General Venancio Flores, exiled leader of the *Colorado* party and ex-president of Uruguay, who had been admitted into the Argentine army and taken part in the battle of Pabon, disembarked on the east coast and called upon the country to rise. The divisions in the opposite party and the discontent produced by a feeble administration, made the enterprise easier. The terrified Chambers declared Flores guilty of high treason. The government, seized with panic, took measure after measure, sending troops in all directions and thus dispersing its forces. Montevideo was restless and torn by faction; the country people sunk in indifference and disposed to bear the yoke of the conqueror, either *Blanco* or *Colorado*. The ill-dissembled connivance of Buenos Ayres gave much strength and importance to the movement. At the beginning of August Flores was some three leagues from Montevideo, where he was attacked and defeated by the old General Medina; but before his whereabouts was generally known, Flores took the offensive, marched forty-five leagues in thirty-six hours, fell upon General Diego Lamas and completely routed him.

Berro was nearing the end of his term and his discouragement was extreme. He was accused by the ultra-Conservatives of a secret understanding with Flores; in conflict with the Chambers which he finally dissolved; confronted by an empty treasury and unable to feed or clothe his army; and impatient to leave the power in other hands. His successor, Anastasio Aguirre, who like himself, belonged to the *Blanco* party, took office on March 1, 1864.

The crisis had reached its height, and it seemed for a moment that the foreign diplomatic agents resident in Montevideo would intervene. But this was a vain hope; the situation became more complicated; certain international difficulties relating to territory caused the Argentine Republic and Brazil to combine against Uruguay, and then it was that Paraguay, threatened by that alliance and finding herself threatened by the claims of the allies, took part in the conflict. The fate that awaited her is already known. Not content with raising the greatest obstacles for the Cabinet of Montevideo, Brazil and the Argentine Republic favored the insurrection. Brazil especially would not have been displeased to see a government which was hostile to her replaced by another which, owing much to her, would naturally show itself more complacent. Emboldened by that attitude, Flores, who was master of the west, founded a government and collected taxes there. Toward the month of June an arrangement appeared possible between Brazil, the Argentine Republic, Flores, and Aguirre, but, as the Cabinet it was desired to impose on the latter was wholly composed of the friends of Flores, Aguirre refused the combination and war became inevitable. The Brazilian ultimatum was sent to Uruguay on August 4, in which all the grievances of the Cabinet of Rio Janeiro since 1858 were recapitulated. It demanded indemnities for natives of Brazil who had suffered in the civil wars, and fixed the term of six days, at the expiration of which an appeal to arms would be made. Brazil rejected the arbitration of a third power, and commenced hostilities.

Montevideo improvised an army of defense, enlisting all citizens between sixteen and sixty years of age, including those imprisoned for crime, and when her resources were exhausted appealed to the legations and the foreign naval forces to guarantee the safety of the city and the port. Aguirre had allied himself with Lopez, but the latter did not think the moment opportune for intervention. Flores was declared an outlaw, and responded to the empty threat by an assault on the capital of Florida, seized Durazno, and appeared before Salto, which the Brazilian squadron was bombarding.

The declaration of war by Paraguay against Brazil at this juncture did not prevent 6000 Brazilians from joining Flores and attacking Paysandú, which was given up to pillage. The fall of this town exasperated Montevideo. The overthrow of the government

was demanded and committees of public safety were set up. On
January 4, 1865, the republic was declared to be in mourning
and the treaties with Brazil were publicly burned. In its panic
the *Blanco* party proposed humiliating measures, rejected the
arbitration of Mitre, and refused to do anything for peace.
Terror had reached its height. The rich fled, the poor died of
hunger, provisions did not arrive, 8000 Brazilians were encamped
close to the walls of the city, and thirteen steamers blockaded the
port. On February 15 Aguirre resigned his authority to Villalba,
who was elected the same morning by seven senators, all who could
be got together.

Villalba saved Montevideo by a convention that secured the
triumph of the *Colorados*. On the 21st he resigned his authority
to a lieutenant of Flores, and on the 23rd Flores made a triumphal
entry into Montevideo, while a ship carried away Aguirre and the
other chiefs of the *Blanco* party. Public festivities took place, and
some weeks were spent in singing the "Te Deum," in theatrical
performances, banquets, speeches, and distribution of medals and
flags. Flores took the title of provisional governor of the republic, formed a ministry, censured the acts of his predecessor
with respect to the Cabinets of Buenos Ayres and Rio Janeiro, and
published a decree relative to banks. Another decree stirred up
bitter criticism; it restored to the religious associations, and especially the Jesuits, who had been expelled by an order of January 26,
1859, the power to establish schools. Flores made a treaty of offensive alliance with Brazil and the Argentine Republic against the
President of Paraguay, the ally of the *Blancos*, so that the triumph
of the *Colorados* was the beginning of a general war among the
states of the La Plata.

On June 23 Flores delegated the executive power to the
Minister of the Interior, Vidal, and started for the front with his
two sons, young officers of sixteen and twenty-five years of age
respectively. A decree of the 14th had ordered one man out of
every ten in the national guard to be drawn by lot for the purpose
of forming an army corps to march against Paraguay. This new
levy was ill received, and could not be immediately enforced.

Vidal succeeded in putting the finances in better condition, and
introduced important improvements into the postal system. A
project for the survey and valuation of lands (*Cadastre*) was
formulated. His government sought to preserve an absolute neu-

trality in the Hispano-Chilian quarrel, which then fixed the attention of all America, and this resulted in a short-lived rupture with Chili.

The allies, after some slight successes, were defeated September 22 at Curupayti. After this check Flores quitted the camp without dissembling his disapproval of the conduct of the operations, left the remains of the Uruguayan contingent under General Castro, and returned to Montevideo, where the provisional government had to contend with the disobedience of the prefects of departments and the insubordination of the famous *Libertad* battalion, commanded by one of the sons of Flores. The latter visited the provinces and infused energy into the whole administration. Material prosperity and the commercial importance of Montevideo increased rapidly. The cholera, which attacked the capital twice in 1867, continued to decimate the inhabitants. The cities that had suffered in the civil struggle repaired their losses. Numerous bodies of emigrants from Latin Europe continued to settle in Uruguay, and even Germany and Switzerland sent whole colonies. A submarine electric telegraph united Montevideo with Buenos Ayres, and railway concessions were granted, which would ultimately give the country means of communication hitherto unknown in the republic. The stock-exchange and the general postoffice at Montevideo were completed; the customs buildings were enlarged; a hospital, an orphan asylum, a penitentiary, and a market were built. General commerce exceeded $30,800,000 a year, and 2865 vessels of about 335,000 tons entered and left the port of Montevideo annually. These figures may give an idea of the activity of business in the midst of the gravest political complications. In a single month $291,344 was collected in duties, a figure which had never before been reached. A commission was appointed to revise the commercial code, the civil and criminal laws and the code of procedure. The civil code was finished and published at the beginning of 1868.

Representative government had not yet been established. Flores, yielding to the pressure of public opinion, warned by the attitude of the United States, which was little inclined to recognize a dictatorship, and perhaps weary of such a heavy responsibility, ordered general elections to be held, and they took place without disturbance at the end of 1867. He had promised to resign his authority into the hands of the newly elected chamber on February 15, 1868. Flores had many enemies; he was accused of having sold the independence of Montevideo and the entry to the River La Plata to Brazil. His life had already been attempted and his palace undermined, and now he was assassinated at the beginning of 1868. General Lorenzo Batlle, who belonged to the *Colorado* party, succeeded him on March 2, and although he saw the end of the war with Paraguay, he had to maintain an energetic struggle with the *Blancos,* who were in insurrection under their most influential leaders until January, 1872. An armistice was then signed between the insurgent forces and Dr. Gomensoro, president of the Senate, and *ex officio* provisional governor of the republic. At length a treaty was concluded on April 6 of this year through the intervention of the Argentine Republic, and there were public rejoicings for three days to put the seal to this reconciliation. The elections were approaching and clubs were formed in which lists of candidates were drawn up. These organizations were the genuine expression of the parties such as they were at that period; Red (*Colorado*), White (*Blanco*), and Radical. The Radicals were young men desirous of forming a new Liberal party, doing away with the old parties who had kept the republic divided for so long. The new Chambers met to canvass the votes in February, 1873. The Senate elected as its president Dr. José Ellauri, and on March 1 he was called to the presidency of the republic. During his administration Uruguay was placed in direct telegraphic communication with Europe by the installation of a transatlantic cable.

Ellauri, like his predecessors, saw his authority attacked by arms, and in December, 1874, the troops collected and organized to put down the insurrection, refused to march and demanded the dismissal of the ministry. Don Pedro Varela was chosen to replace Ellauri in March, 1875, and found financial and commercial affairs in great confusion. A year had scarcely elapsed when he resigned, and in 1876 Colonel Lorenzo Latorre took the title of provisional governor of the republic. The succeeding years of Uruguayan history were marked by the accession to power of the Red party and the opening of the country to foreigners, who come in at the rate of 15,000 to 20,000 a year, mostly Basques and Italians.

Chapter X

THE REPUBLIC OF PARAGUAY. 1811-1876

PARAGUAY is an exception in the turbulent history of the American republics. An unbroken but sterile peace reigned during the first part of the nineteenth century in this hermit nation, where internal crises never became acclimated. After her escape from Spanish rule and until she was crushed in 1865, she lived without shocks, not daring to raise her head, and completely separated from the other nations. Her government, despotic and jealous, and hostile to the foreigner, knew how to control her in its own way. We do not envy any people the particular kind of peace brought about by the Asiatic tyranny of a Francia. This strange personage swaddled this new-born nation in such tight bands that she could not move, and therefore could not grow. He isolated her from the rest of the world, favored by the remoteness of the country from the sea. Woe to the traveler who dared to tread the Paraguayan soil, since he expiated his rashness by a detention that might last ten years, as in the case of the botanist, Bonpland.

In the month of May, 1811, Paraguay had her revolution, which was effected without bloodshed. The movement was not only directed against the age-long authority of the mother country, but also against that recently improvised at Buenos Ayres. From an assembly which met in the following month was evolved an executive junta with Fulgencio Yegros for president, and Francia for secretary. The first was a man of little education and little aptitude for business. We shall soon see what were the qualities of the second. The junta decreed the independence of Paraguay, which was soon acknowledged by Buenos Ayres in the Treaty of Asuncion, and two years afterward a new Congress of 1000 deputies met. The junta was replaced by two consuls, Yegros and Francia. Two curule chairs had been erected for them, called respectively Cæsar's and Pompey's. On entering on the duties of the office Francia occupied the first, leaving the other for his companion in power. It was not very difficult for the former to concentrate all the branches of the administration in his own hands. He appointed a Secretary of State, endeavored to establish order in the finances and reorganize the army, and deprived the Spaniards of civil rights, with the object of winning over the sympathies of the aborigines. But he was not a man to share his power, and the Congress, composed for the most part of simple and ignorant men, accepted the idea of a sovereign magistracy as the only means of saving the republic, which was threatened from abroad; and on October 8, 1814, he was appointed dictator for three years. But this power, because limited in time, could not completely satisfy Rodriguez de Francia, and on May 1, 1816, the newly convoked Congress proclaimed him supreme and perpetual dictator.

José Gaspar Rodriguez de Francia, who was to make Paraguay feel, for a quarter of a century, the weight of one of the most singular tyrannies recorded by history, ruled over a population trained to obedience by the Jesuits, stupid, ignorant of arts and industry, and with a mere rudimentary knowledge of agriculture. He was then fifty-nine years old, of medium stature, lean and vigorous, with black and penetrating eyes. He claimed French descent through his father, who was invited by the Spanish government of Brazil to Paraguay to introduce the manufacture of tobacco, and married there. Francia had been destined in his youth for an ecclesiastical career, and commenced his studies in the seminary of Asuncion, finishing them in the University of Cordoba, in Tucuman. After receiving the degree of Doctor of Canon Law and an appointment to a chair of theology, he renounced orders, studied jurisprudence, and became a lawyer. Clever, eloquent, disinterested, always ready to defend the weak against the strong and the poor against the rich, he soon came into notice, and was successively elected a member of the municipality, then corporation counsel and mayor. We have seen how he became secretary of the state junta, consul and dictator. He was a curious composite of good and bad qualities and carried into the dictatorship the same disinterestedness that he had shown in private life. Though generous with his personal wealth, he was economical with the public funds, and would accept no more than $3000 of the $9000 that the Congress had assigned for his household. He made it a rule not to receive any presents, and paid for all that were presented to him or returned them to the sender. He had heard in his youth of the despotism of the Jesuits, of their ambition, of their dark and hidden intrigues. He was educated by the Franciscan friars, but had cause

to dislike them, and very early conceived an insurmountable aversion
for the outward forms of religion, which he considered gross trickery.   At the beginning of his dictatorship he went to mass every
day, but very soon he ceased to appear at church and dismissed his
chaplain; from that time he took pleasure in ridiculing the priests,
whom he accused of impudently selling mysteries that they themselves did not understand.   " The priests and religion," said he,
" serve more to make men believe in the devil than in God "; and
declared that if the Pope should come to Paraguay he would make
him his chaplain.

Rodriguez de Francia reëstablished the system of isolation
adopted by the old missions.   Under pretense of preserving his
country from the contagion of anarchy and at the same time with-
drawing it from the project of absorption that was attributed to
Brazil, he prohibited, under the most severe penalties, all communication between the inhabitants of Paraguay and their neighbors,
and forbade any foreigner to enter the country.   In 1826 he decreed
the penalty of death and deprivation of burial against all who, calling themselves envoys from the court of Spain, should cross the
frontier of Paraguay without previous authorization, and against
all natives who, on receiving any letter from foreign parts upon
political affairs, should not immediately present it to the tribunals.
These excessively severe measures may have been occasioned
by the conduct of the Cabinet of Madrid toward an agent of
the dictator appointed to carry out, with the assistance of Queen
Charlotte, certain negotiations whose real object is not very well
known, in which some have chosen to see a piece of deception,
and others a project which was to result in the reacquisition of
Paraguay by Spain.   The fact is that, at this time, either through
anxiety or weariness with the negotiations, or simply to consolidate
his authority by getting himself reappointed to power, the dictator
convoked a species of national assembly, which, on September 24,
1826, ratified a declaration of independence submitted by him because of the rejection of his proposals by the Spanish government.   After a military conspiracy had been opportunely discovered, a colonel named Avendaño was condemned to death,
and under these circumstances Francia was entreated to resume the
authority that he had laid down (November 4).   He consented at
last, but not without some pressure, and solely, he said, while waiting for the return of the Marquis de Guarano, his envoy to the

Spanish government, whom he named as his next successor. His schemes were thus accomplished and the country again fell under the yoke of the terrible doctor.

Francia has found apologists. This country, kept in absolute subordination among states stirred by all the storms of politics, in consonance with the ardent youthfulness of their peoples; this country, the model of passivity, has excited the admiration of the partisans of order at any price. Abuse of authority, prosecutions, tortures, proscriptions, and the thousand odious means employed by that exacting master to satisfy his insatiable thirst for unlimited power, have been forgotten. The internal organization of the country, its military power and industrial progress under his leadership are eulogized. Undoubtedly his system resulted in forming a nationality of part of the Indian race, which has remained nomadic and uncivilized in the rest of America, and produced a great military power, as was shown by the very duration and intensity of the war which destroyed it; but even conceding all this, and without endeavoring to prove that a different system might lead to the same result, how can we fail to see that all these pretended benefits of tyranny are reducible to the capricious regulation of a stifling monopoly.

In a word, what productive thought did this wonderful soil of Paraguay, which without cultivation yields two crops annually, inspire in Francia? Taking up the mercantile traditions of the Jesuits, he seized the crops and stored them for the account of a government which absorbed all functions, public and private, possessed two-thirds of the land, and disposed at will of the soil and its inhabitants. He undertook the exchange of products, and became a merchant in imitation of the priest-brokers. When hands were needed for the harvest he had recourse to the draft, applying the system of forced labor on behalf of the state. Nevertheless, he had to acknowledge, in time, that complete sequestration was impossible, since it must necessarily deprive him of resources that were indispensable. He opened then a point of communication on the Brazilian frontier, and established under the vigilance of his soldiers a sort of exchange for commercial transactions; but, fearing that this innovation would produce vexatious results for his secretive policy, this man averted the danger by monopolizing the trade. It was necessary to obtain a formal license, signed and delivered by him, in order to undertake these operations. Besides,

PARAGUAY

he settled the tariff on goods thus imported and sold them, constituted himself the sole purveyor of European articles, which were deposited in a kind of bazaar under military guard, and the quantity of these articles that each purchaser could acquire was determined with care.

Of course this strange economic system was not calculated to aid the development of agriculture, commerce, and industry. It led to the prohibition of individual effort and of progress. Thanks to it, every profitable enterprise was paralyzed. The price of a plain cotton handkerchief of English manufacture was twenty reals (one dollar). But did not Francia keep a store of produce, arms, and ammunition? For him that was the essential thing. Everything shows that his sole preoccupation was less to develop productive forces than to subordinate their strength to the ends of a policy of absolute monopoly. His ambition was to be able to dispense with intercourse with foreign countries.

He possessed a very miscellaneous library, in which were found, with the works of Voltaire, Rousseau, and Montesquieu, treatises on medicine, mathematics, and geography, and a French dictionary of arts and trades, which he valued very much and frequently consulted. From this book he got the idea of establishing manufactures and workshops, lavishing money and threats at the same time in order to stimulate the zeal of the workmen engaged on that task. Once he condemned an awkward blacksmith to hard labor, another time he had a gallows erected and gave an unfortunate shoemaker the alternative of being richly rewarded if he succeeded in his task, or being hanged if he failed. Francia prescribed the system which must be employed in the cultivation of the fields. Abundant crops, which were easily obtained from the extraordinary fertility of the soil, appeared to justify the agricultural pretensions of the dictator, and agricultural economy took a step in advance, but it was a short one. Everything remained in a rudimentary state. A stake served for a plow, wheat was ground in mortars, a sugar mill was a piece of wood moved by oxen; cotton was cleaned of its seed by hand, then spun on a spindle and put into the hands of some traveling weaver, who carried his loom on the back of a mule and hung it from the branch of a tree.

This very peculiar man once conceived the idea of beautifying Asuncion. Behold him drawing plans with his own hand, and mingling with the workmen, overseeing their labors. But in this his inexperience was demonstrated, and instead of being improved the capital was turned upside down. He was, however, more fortunate in laying out roads and in putting the fortified towns and Asuncion in a state of defense. A new city, Tebego, was founded under his auspices in the northern parts as a military post, intended to keep in check the Indian savages. In addition the dictator had fortified himself against every attempt at internal rebellion or foreign aggression by creating an armed force capable of imposing restraints on the neighboring states as well as on his subjects and the Indian tribes.

As to the natives scattered in the old Missions, he went on little by little bringing them under the yoke and obliging them to work on the land, incorporating them in the general body of citizens, and thereby increasing his military strength. His forces at length reached the number of 20,000 militia and 5000 regular troops, both well drilled in the use of arms and provided with excellent cavalry. The dictator's bodyguard was composed of picked grenadiers or gendarmes. They performed the duties of police, and guarded the old palace of the Spanish governors when the dictator lived in isolation after ordering the demolition of the houses surrounding it. There in retirement with his drunken mulatto barber, who served as confidant to this modern Louis XI., and as gazette to make the public acquainted with his projects; with his half-breed secretary Patiños, an insolent scribe, who revenged himself on the public for the ill-treatment received from his master; and waited on by four slaves, two men and two women, Francia, always restless and uneasy, seeing nothing but conspiracies everywhere, lived mysteriously, after the austere and simple manner of a monk, never sleeping successively in the same room, in order that it should not be known where he passed the night. At the age of seventy he married a young Frenchwoman. He concealed his sympathy for France, but greatly admired Robespierre and Napoleon. Curiously dressed, as he supposed to resemble the latter, in a costume copied from a German caricature, consisting of a blue coat with gold lace, Spanish epaulettes, white breeches and waistcoat, silk stockings and broad-toed shoes, and armed with a large sword and pistols, he himself drilled his troops, who, if they were subject to severe discipline under arms, had a liberty that bordered on license when they were not.

With such an army, and a population completely subjugated,

Francia could satisfy his dominating and cruel instincts. From the beginning he had imprisoned, deported to his colony of Tebego, shot or hanged every man who resisted his terrible inquisitorial system, on the old pretext that a plot against his person was treason to the state. Yegros, who had been his companion in the consulate, was one of his first victims. He was accused of favoring the projects of Ramirez, who meditated invading Paraguay from Entre Rios, and was condemned to death in 1819 with forty other citizens. More than 300 persons, imprisoned for the same cause, were condemned in a body to pay very dearly for their liberty, after eighteen months of daily tortures. Francia had no mercy for his prisoners, and had his special manner of putting them to the torture, renewing their sufferings, and making his vengeance a sort of feast. His cat-like nature grew more cruel at the sight of the terror of these miserable wretches, and his eyes, like those of a jackal looking for prey, followed them even to the scaffold. Some have deduced from this that, like his brothers, he had a tendency to madness; he was certainly subject to frequent attacks of hypochondria, and he was in that condition when he decreed the proscriptions and his most ferocious follies. Unfortunate was he who at such a time addressed him in writing or by word of mouth and omitted to call him Most Excellent Lord and Perpetual Dictator! Unfortunate was he who, in order to speak to him, approached him too closely and did not keep his hands well in view to show that he had no hidden arms, for the disease of suspicion gave him no respite, and everywhere he saw nothing but treason, daggers, and assassins. He had a countrywoman arrested because she approached the window near which he was working, and ordered his troops to fire on anyone who dared to look at his palace. An Indian very nearly paid dearly for that order, which was given under the idea that this poor woman might be another Charlotte Corday; but we must say, in acquittal of Francia, that he revoked it. A numerous escort accompanied the dictator when he went out. As soon as he put his foot outside the palace the bell of the cathedral tolled and the inhabitants went into their houses saying " His Highness (*El Supremo*)!" If any one, too slow in hiding, met the dreaded company, he threw himself face down upon the ground, not daring to lift his eyes to that cold countenance which imposed the silence of fear.

Death came upon him when he was at the height of his power, after a few days' illness, during which he went on attending to business, refusing all assistance and forbidding entrance into his room to anyone who was not called by him. He was asked in vain to appoint a successor to preserve the country from anarchy; he answered bluntly that there would be no want of heirs. That he did not end his life with a crime was owing to an accident; in a fit of anger against his *curandero,* a sort of quack doctor who attended him, he jumped out of bed, seized a sword and rushed upon him, but fell down, struck by a fit of apoplexy. No one dared to help him, against his orders, and he died on the morning of September 20, 1840, at the age of eighty-three years. He had a splendid funeral, and a mausoleum was erected to him, but was destroyed during the night by unknown hands.

Thus ended this strange personage, a mysterious genius whose silhouette is distorted into caricature; an insoluble problem for Europeans, whom one of his victims, the Swiss traveler Reugger, has compared to the man of Brumaire. It may at least be said in favor of the despot of Asuncion, that he had no Waterloo and did not prepare a Sedan. Napoleon was a real retrogression for the France of 1789, and Francia was a progression for the Paraguay of 1811. The advantage is on his side; since it was not a question of a civilized and clever nation, nourished by the brains of great geniuses and full of enthusiasm and heroism, but of a heterogeneous, degraded, brutalized, and ignorant people accustomed for the most part to the discipline of the Jesuits, and apparently ill fitted to do without a master. The Napoleonic tragi-comedy was acted on a much larger theater, and as there was no lack of hired applause around the Francia of the Tuileries, the multitude did not perceive his insane pride, his violence or his ridiculousness, and knew nothing of his proscriptions, and almost nothing of his judicial murders. The fits of hypochondria of the American dictator cost a few tears; those of the Corsican emperor cost rivers of blood and ruined the French nation. Therefore the comparison does not seem to us quite exact; tyrant for tyrant, the first is the better.

When it was found that Francia was really dead, the half-breed Patiños quietly summoned the chief commanders of the barracks. The event was kept secret for some hours, which they employed in making some arrests and doubling the guard of the public prison, where 700 prisoners were confined in narrow cells. But Patiños was not to survive his master; he was suspected of aspiring to the succession, was arrested by order of the very junta that he headed under the modest title of secretary, and to avoid the punishment that was awaiting him he hanged himself in prison. Juan José Medina attempted to seize power with the help of some citizens, but this usurped authority was not recognized by the troops. A congress, convoked on May 12, 1841, conferred the executive power for three years on two consuls, Carlos Antonio Lopez, the nephew of Francia, and Mariano Roque Alonzo.

The new government hastened to conclude a treaty of commerce and alliance with the province of Corrientes, which was then at war with Buenos Ayres, and decreed the gradual abolition of slavery. In March, 1844, Lopez received from Congress the title of President of the republic for ten years, and inherited the absolute power of his uncle. Like him, Lopez showed himself very jealous of his authority; but he was resolved to terminate the isolation in which hitherto Paraguay had been held, and all his efforts tended to stimulate commercial interests and to establish relations with foreign nations. In 1857 he signed treaties of friendship, commerce, and navigation with France, England, Sardinia, and the United States, and during his government foreign vessels were able to reach Asuncion. In 1861 an important step in the progress of the country was taken. Before the astonished multitude a railway from the capital to Villa Rica, the most important center of agricultural production, was opened. Lopez decreed the dissolution of the missions of Paraguay, always under the communistic organization, and brought the Indians under the common law, giving them the status of citizens (1848). He continued to organize the country with activity, formed a public treasury, established schools of primary instruction, an iron foundry at Ibicuy, and a military and naval arsenal at Asuncion. Sometimes he had petty disputes with England, the United States, and Brazil; but he was able to oppose and to overcome with great ability the difficulties that arose, and to repel energetically the aggressions of the neighboring states and the pretensions of Rosas, who persisted in considering Paraguay a mere dependency of the Argentine Republic. At last he was accepted as arbitrator or mediator in the war between the Argentine provinces and Buenos Ayres. Early in 1854 the National Congress, after examining and approving the acts of the presidential administration, reëlected Lopez for another ten years, and he, using a right that the constitution gave him, appointed his son, the Brigadier D. Francisco Solano Lopez, to the vice-presidency of the republic, on September

10, 1862, before his term expired. The retired and solitary life that he led destroyed his health, and he died when he was about to complete his sixtieth year.

Solano Lopez, who was then thirty-five years old, had completed his studies in Europe, and had in his early years visited France. His father had introduced him when very young into public affairs and appointed him Minister of War and Marine. The Congress assembled October 26, 1862, and ratified the choice of the dead president. The son was even more free than his father from the narrow traditions of Francia, and thus from his accession to power he supported the progressive movement of Paraguay, which had for so long been ignorant of or hostile to all the benefits of civilization. Through his energy the cultivation of cotton was much extended during the civil war in the United States, and he exempted from all import duties all machines and tools destined for agriculture and industry. The treasury advanced to natives and foreigners considerable sums for enterprises of general utility. We should also mention that a number of young men were periodically sent to Europe to complete their education in the old world. In June, 1863, on the return of some of these young men who could be immediately employed, the government conceived the idea of choosing thirty more students from the colleges of the republic and sending them to France, where they would perfect themselves for the professions of the magistracy, the army, the administration, industry, and commerce. In spite of a few despotic practices that the President Solano Lopez had inherited from his predecessors, and which he did not appear much inclined to give up, the Republic of Paraguay saw a hitherto unknown era of prosperity opening before her.

Then it was that the terrible war broke out between this country and three allied neighbors, Brazil, the Argentine Republic, and Uruguay, during which the president and people of Paraguay gave proofs of their indomitable energy. The obscure and undecided question of the frontiers had made the relations between Paraguay and the neighboring states difficult for some time past. The cause of the constant hostility always existing between the republics of this region was the desire to control the navigation of the Rio de la Plata and its tributaries, and, above all, the idea that was constantly being revived of uniting in one nationality the different peoples in the great river basin of which the Rio de la Plata is the vast outlet. This idea was not unconnected with the disturb-

PARAGUAY

ances in Uruguay and the Argentine Republic at that time. This placed Paraguay in a strained situation, and Lopez thought it prudent to put his country in a state of defense. This was clearly within his rights, but he went further. After securing the adhesion of the notables of Asuncion, Lopez did not hesitate to take the offensive. On November 11, 1864, he seized a Brazilian packetboat, with the Brazilian governor of Matto Grosso on board; on December 15 an army corps of 10,000 men invaded that province, and on January 1 took the fortified towns of Albuquerque, Corumba, and Dourado, and marched on Cuyabas. On the other hand, small skirmishes took place with the Argentine patrols, since Lopez wished to use force in his dealings with Buenos Ayres as he had with Rio Janeiro. The Congress, which met in Asuncion, approved his policy by acclamation on May 5, 1865, invested him with the title of marshal, and empowered him to raise a loan of $24,800,000 and issue paper money. Lopez had every reason to act quickly and give his adversaries no time to organize. On August 14 four Paraguayan vessels entered the harbor of Corrientes and seized two Argentine ships, while 2000 men took possession of the city and set up a Federal administration instead of the Unitarian *régime*. Lopez thought he could thus take advantage of the rivalries of the parties. Until now the contest was only with Brazil and the Argentine Republic. The Banda Oriental united with these adversaries after the victory of Flores at Aguirre. The three nations signed a treaty of alliance at Buenos Ayres on May 6, which, by the way, did not receive the sympathy of the other American republics, by which they undertook to carry on the war against Lopez alone, whom they called a tyrant, and set themselves the task of liberating a sister people groaning under a cruel despotism. On June 11 the Brazilian squadron and the Paraguayan flotilla met, and after a sanguinary fight, which gave an opportunity for the Paraguayans to give proofs of their courage, the advantage rested with the Brazilians. By way of compensation, the Paraguayan division operating against Uruguay entered the province of Rio Grande on the same day and occupied important positions. One part of this division was afterward overwhelmed by numbers, and was defeated by Flores. The other part, numbering 6000 men, was besieged in Uruguayana and surrendered to the allies without firing a shot, through the treason of Colonel Estigarribia, as is supposed.

Before this double reverse, which completely destroyed one of his army corps, Lopez, fearing that demoralization would spread among his troops, fell back by a very able retreat upon the territory of the republic. He fortified himself on the north bank of the Paraná, collected provisions there, took the town of Itapua for his base of operations, and immediately established reserve depots in Humaita and Asuncion. Then he waited for the allied army, which was not afraid to force into its ranks the prisoners taken from the enemy. During a whole year Lopez fought the Brazilian general, Porto-Alegre, and was generally successful. His troops, led on by ardent patriotism and excited to fanaticism by religious exhortations, offered themselves for slaughter with blind bravery. He took the greatest care of them, calling into his service English and American surgeons. He was obliged to retreat before superior numbers, and had to abandon his camp at Stapira, with the batteries that he had placed near the Paraná, and on April 23, 1866, to take up a position under the protection of the fort of Humaita. Here he waited and defeated the Argentines commanded by Mitre, who had unfortunately been tempted to take part in the fratricidal struggle. The defeat was a heavy blow to the assailants, and led to some attempts at negotiation which had no success, notwithstanding the efforts of Chili to promote them.

Although the exhaustion of Argentina and Uruguay was very great, the war began again with new butchery, and became more painful and cruel through the terrible epidemic of cholera which spread in both camps. At the end of 1867 Lopez was able to reëstablish his communications between Asuncion and Humaita, where the batteries sank some Brazilian vessels of war which attempted to force the passage. At that period the war was carried on by skirmishes, almost always adverse to the enemy, in which a young Englishwoman, named Eliza Lynch, took a very active part, at the head of some battalions of Amazons. She had ardently taken up the cause of the president, of whom she was violently enamored. A Brazilian army corps crossed the frontier of the province of Matto Grosso to invade Paraguay from the northeast, but was repulsed and closely pursued. The retreat was made under such difficulties that it took thirty-five days to cover a distance of 100 miles.[1] In the middle of 1868 another Bra-

[1] The story of this tragic episode has been told by one of the officers of the expedition. The "Retraite de Laguna," by Alfred d'Escragnolle Taunay. Rio Janeiro, 1871.

zilian fleet succeeded in breaking through the obstructions and ascending to Humaita, yet was detained there until the allies, reinforced by numerous contingents, had obliged Lopez to abandon the formidably entrenched camp of Humaita and retire to Tebicuari and Timbo (July 25). Lopez had to recruit his army, which was exhausted by so many sanguinary combats, but he was soon able to take the offensive again. By a bold march he advanced 25 miles south of Asuncion, and established himself at Villeta. Overcome once more by numbers he retired behind the trenches of Angostura, whence he was dislodged after six days' sanguinary struggle, on December 27, leaving in the hands of the allies six pieces of artillery and 1000 prisoners. By this blow the capital fell into the hands of the enemy.

Lopez seemed lost, and was reported to have fled to the United States, but the indomitable marshal, far from being beaten, had no other thought than taking his revenge. Rallying the wreck of his army, he called for new contingents and established himself in Piribebuy, which he made his provisional capital. The allies, on their part, thinking they had obtained a decisive victory, began to be divided, disputes between the generals arising every day. As soon as the Emperor of Brazil knew that Lopez had begun the campaign again, he sent fresh troops (1869), and put his son-in-law, the young Comte d'Eu, grandson of Louis Philippe, at the head of the allied armies. The Comte d'Eu marched against Lopez, who had fixed his headquarters in Ascurra, and after seizing the railway from Asuncion to Villa Rica, offered him battle on August 12, 1869, pursued him, and in the following month crushed him almost completely near Caraguatay.

A provisional government, composed of Loizaga, Rivarola, and Diaz de Bedoya, was set up in Asuncion on the 15th by the allies. At the same time a decree of the Brazilian government outlawed the hero, who thus, step by step, disputed his country with the enemy, and all who fought under his command. That iniquitous measure, which could have no other foundation than the savage Prussian axiom, " Might makes right," did not check Lopez, who was firmly resolved to defend the integrity of the Paraguayan territory to the last. Having only a small force of infantry and cavalry and some thirty small field pieces, he marched to San Isidoro, at the foot of the Cordilleras of Coaguaru, and entrenched himself there. He was dislodged from this last position and pursued to the mountains of the northwest by General Camera, where he procured the help of 5000 Indians, but it was in vain. Surrounded on all sides, he did not hesitate to make a desperate attempt to cut his way out, and the small Paraguayan army sustained its last attack, May 1, 1870, on the banks of the Aquidaban, where it was completely destroyed. Among the slain were President Lopez and Vice-President Sanchez, who had fallen in the vanguard. Thus ended the gigantic struggle of this small and intrepid people. It had lasted five years, and in it Lopez displayed the energy, tenacity and strength of mind of a patriot and a hero. He was brave, intelligent, of humane sentiments, and earnestly devoted to the future welfare of his country, which a war, as savage as it was useless, had ruined and depopulated.

Paraguay was entirely at the mercy of the allies and completely devastated. Its population, which in 1857 was reckoned at about 1,337,000, was reduced by war, executions, epidemics and famine to about a sixth of that number, and these were for the most part women and children. Its income had fallen from $2,600,000 to $400,000, and the instruments and objects of productive industry were everywhere destroyed; the railway had no rolling stock, workshops, nor stations; the public edifices were falling into ruins; provisions were scarce, and seed lacking. The wreck was so complete that even the government could not find the titles to its property. The very foundations of the nation had to be laid anew.

A preliminary treaty of peace between Brazil and the Argentine Republic, on the one part, and the provisional goverment of Paraguay on the other, was signed on June 20. On November 25 a Congress, elected by universal suffrage, proclaimed a constitution, modeled on that of the United States. A president, elected for three years, a vice-president, a Cabinet, composed of five ministers, a Senate, and a Chamber of Deputies were entrusted with the powers of the state. Some judicial and administrative reforms were made, the standing army was abolished, foreigners were admitted to all the rights and privileges of natives, including the right to hold office, except the high political and administrative posts.

At the beginning of August Cirilo Antonio Rivarola was made president. Grave dissensions arose between him and the Congress. At the end of 1871 he decreed the dissolution of the Assembly, which resumed its sessions outside the walls of Asuncion. The president called on the Brazilian and Argentine garrison for help; but the plenipotentiaries considered all foreign intervention as contrary to the constitution and an attack on the national independence and dignity. Rivarola resigned his authority, and the vice-president, Salvador Jovellanos, was raised to the presidency of the republic for a term of three years (December 12, 1871). Juan Bautista Gil succeeded him on October 11, 1874, after a long service as finance minister, during which he had spared no effort to reëstablish the national credit.

Paraguay has not yet fully recovered from its terrible disasters. According to the definitive treaty of peace made in January, 1872, with Brazil, the frontier between the two countries is formed by the course of the Paraná from the mouth of the Iguazu to the cataract of Seven Cascades; thence it follows the line of the watershed along the sierras of Maracayu and Amambay, thence to the Paraguay River, following the course of the Apa. The treaty establishes free navigation under all flags on the rivers Paraná, Paraguay, Uruguay and all their affluents. Other special treaties have settled the rules for the extradition of non-political criminals, the advantages given to the subjects of the allied countries, and free commerce between Paraguay and the Brazilian province of Matto Grosso. Paraguay promised to pay a war indemnity of $200,000,000 to Brazil, $35,000,000 to the Argentine Republic, and $1,000,000 to Uruguay. In return Brazil undertook to protect the government of Asuncion from all aggression, whether native or foreign, and for this reason it was stipulated that the Brazilian troops should continue to occupy the territory of the republic for ten years.

Chapter XI

THE EMPIRE OF BRAZIL. 1808-1876

BRAZIL was until recently organized as an empire, and also differs very much from the old Spanish colonies in manners, customs, and language. It resembles them closely in its economic problems, and there is the same disproportion between man's labor and the astonishing fertility of the soil. Although Brazil had the advantage of many of the republics in an established, determined, and settled political system, the Lusitanian empire nevertheless had its periods of popular excitement, crisis, and conflict. But the shocks which affected its internal and external life, though sometimes grave, were always within well-defined limits, and party strife went no further than to change a ministry.

Brazil is one of the largest of all nations, and occupies half of South America. France has but one-eighth of its area, and three times its population. Admirably diversified in its natural resources, it is in the best situation for taking part in the intellectual and commercial affairs of the world. Thus the Atlantic coast line is 5300 miles in length, and there is a large number of islands, some of considerable extent and fertility, and others notable for their geographic and political importance. Each of the harbors of Bahía, Angra dos Reis, and Rio Janeiro are capacious enough to shelter all the navies of the world. Its boundaries are: on the north French, English, and Dutch Guiana, the Republic of Venezuela, and the United States of Colombia; on the south Uruguay, Paraguay, and the Argentine Republic; on the west, the same republic, Paraguay, Bolivia, Peru, and Ecuador.

So vast an extent of territory cannot present a uniformity of climate. It is strewn with lakes; furrowed by innumerable streams and gigantic rivers, among them the largest and deepest on the globe, the wonderful Amazon, which runs for more than 1625 miles through Brazilian territory and with its tributaries is navigable for a total length of 18,750 miles; and bristles with mountains, some of which reach a considerable height. Brazil is essentially a hot

country, but though the heat of the sun is great on the equator at
Pará, it is much less in the central districts, and on the coast it is
moderated by regular breezes, until as one goes southward the climate becomes mild and healthful, especially on the great plains of
the Rio Grande, which are said to be among the best regions of the
globe, and are the Italy of the western hemisphere.   This, at least,
is the opinion of the French physician, M. Segaud, author of
"Du Climat et des Malades du Brésil."   Although Brazil about
1873 passed through one of those terrible epidemics of yellow
fever which are due in part to the bad conditions in which the South
Americans live, statistics proved that in the most populous cities, including Rio Janeiro, the mortality was lower than in the most sanitary capitals of Europe.[1]

All travelers who have visited the country have exhausted the
resources of imagery in trying to describe its magnificence, and
the splendor of its forests is beyond description.   Its mineral resources are equally rich, and it has given to Europe vast quantities
of the precious metals.   But, as in all other parts of South America, laborers and the spirit of enterprise are lacking.   Under the
empire Brazilian society, as a daughter of the conquest, was founded
upon slavery.[2]   The whites drove the Indians into the forests and
held the negroes bowed under the lash.   The great principle of *far
niente*,[3] brought to the country by the first settlers, is so well suited
to the mildness of the climate, the fertility of the soil, and to the
indolent and sensual nature of their descendants that it has become
the supreme law of their being.   Fortunately, for some years past,
the Old World has been sending laborers to this rich and little-
known land, who, as colonists, will be the principal agents of the
prosperity of the country.   Many thousand Europeans arrive annually in Brazil, settling in the country and the towns.   In the absence
of white women they form unions with Indian and negro women,
and beget children able to bear the fierce heat of the tropics.   It
is only by a continual infusion of European blood, by the rehabilita-
tion of labor, perfecting itself in ideas and habits, and by the vivify-
ing action of railways on the countries through which they pass, that
civilization will prosecute her conquests and take possession of those
immense spaces, solely given up to the forces of Nature.   It should

[1] Macedo, " *Nations de chorographie du Brésil.*"
[2] Slavery was abolished in Brazil in 1888.
[3] *Dolce far niente.*   It is sweet to do nothing.

be said that the contempt that the colored man has for every kind of work is not the result of the climate alone; its origin is chiefly the belief, very common in countries where slavery exists, that work is dishonorable.

In the first part of this work we have seen how the court of Portugal, flying from the French army in 1808, came to seek an asylum in its opulent colony of the New World. The presence of John VI. on Brazilian soil, until then subject to the utmost rigor of the colonial system, resulted in breaking down the barriers that kept all the ports closed to foreign nations. Brazil ceased to be a colony, and seven years later, by the decree of December 17, 1815, it became a kingdom. Ideas which moved Europe could now be brought to Brazil freely and without concealment. This was evident when the revolution of Pernambuco broke out in 1817, the first step toward national independence. A learned priest, Juan Ribeiro, inspired by the writing of Condorcet, and, in his own words, " breathing only for liberty," was the president of a provisional government. In order to set an example of endurance he had followed the insurrectionary army commanded by the merchant Domingo José Martins with bare feet and legs. This experimental republic lasted only two months and a half, and Ribeiro, like his master, Condorcet, committed suicide. The Royalists carried his head on a pike through the streets of Pernambuco. The other leaders suffered the extreme penalty of the law; and a cruel and implacable policy of repression was carried out by the Count of Arcos.

Nevertheless, the fact remained that the rights of the country had been discussed. The sojourn of John VI. in Brazil was constantly disturbed by insurrectionary movements, caused by the increase of taxation, the wretched administration of justice, the costly luxuries exacted by the sovereign, and his partiality for the Portuguese, whom he offensively enriched with fat offices. The enmity between Brazilians and Portuguese was constantly breaking out, and it was in vain that John VI. was proclaimed on February 5, 1818, King of Portugal, Brazil, and Algarve; the causes of the quarrel continued. Besides, important events had taken place in Europe. The Portuguese nation, impoverished and oppressed to satisfy the luxury of Rio Janeiro, tired of seeing that it had in a sense become the colony and Brazil the mother country, that its wealth was poured out to be spent in America, and that America gave nothing in exchange, demanded the return of the court to Lisbon. This demand was the cause of the loss of Brazil. When the revolution broke out at Oporto, in 1820, the object of which was to give a constitutional government to Portugal, Pernambuco became again disturbed. Bahía and the province of Pará proclaimed the constitution promulgated by the Cortes, while the court of Rio Janeiro was dreaming of sending an Anglo-Brazilian expedition against Portugal. The weak and melancholy John was placed between his wife, the ugly and ambitious Charlotte, who was the soul of the Absolutist party and had a special court which formed a center of opposition to the government of her husband, and his eldest son, Dom Pedro. The latter advised John to make some concessions, and John had at last the good fortune to follow the prince's advice to calm the popular excitement. By a formal decree he accepted the bases of the future constitution, a decree which was read by Dom Pedro himself to the multitude assembled in the theater of San Juan. Then, tired of a country which he had never liked, the unhappy monarch embarked April 26, 1821, for Portugal, leaving the regency of Brazil in the hands of the hereditary prince, the young Pedro, who then was scarcely twenty-two years old. His departure took place just after a catastrophe. Five days before the electors assembled in the Exchange of Rio Janeiro to choose their deputies to the Portuguese Cortes had manifested a desire to oppose the departure of the sovereign, or at least that he should make a formal promise that Brazil should always be on an equal footing with the mother country. They were suddenly attacked and shot down at close range by the auxiliary division, which completed its foul work by general pillage. Thirty victims died on the spot.

During the stay of John VI. in Brazil some successful attempts were made in colonization, the civilization of the savage tribes, and the exploration of the great rivers and the discovery of mines. Agriculture and manufacturing industry were encouraged; a school for teaching mathematics and military science, a hospital, and schools of anatomy, surgery and medicine were founded. A colony of French artists, chief among them Lebreton, Debret, and Taunay, and some Italian musicians were invited to Brazil. This was the impulse to a school of fine arts, a great number of notable edifices, and a theater.

The blind and stupid Portuguese Cortes reëstablished the colonial system for Brazil, and, relying on the garrisons of the cities, sent out impolitic and irritating decrees, and soon commanded the

prince regent to return to Europe.   Dom Pedro declared on January
9, 1822, that he would remain in Brazil.   Rio Janeiro, Pernambuco,
San Paulo, and Bahía took up arms and drove out the Portuguese
garrisons.   The regent, with a match in one hand and leaning on
a gun carriage with the other, announced that he would fire the first
shot against the intrenchments of the auxiliary division if it did
not immediately embark; he went in person to put down a Royalist
insurrection in Minas Geraes.   At Rio, during his absence, the
party of the past attempted a counter revolution, and his return was
greeted by enthusiastic acclaim.   On May 13 he received from the
representatives of the provinces the title of " Perpetual Defender of
Brazil," and on October 12 the National Assembly acclaimed
him " Constitutional Emperor."   A decree of August 1 had completed the rupture of every colonial bond between Brazil and the
Portuguese nation.

The young prince was impatient to bear the scepter, and accepted
all the consequences of a revolution so consonant with his ambitions.
On taking leave of him, his father had said: " Preserve Brazil to
the Portuguese crown as long as possible, and then take it for yourself."   This advice was too much in accord with the opinions of
Pedro for him to neglect it by failing to profit by the blunders of the
Lisbon government, blunders which directly increased his popularity.   He wrote to his father that his motive in becoming constitutional emperor was to preserve Brazil for the House of Braganza.
Whatever may be said as to his sincerity it is certain that Brazil,
which was very hostile to the Portuguese domination, would have
become a federal republic if it had not become an independent
monarchy.   In one way or the other it was destined to break the
yoke.   England had her hand in the business.   Lord Cochrane received the command of the imperial fleet, and the court of St. James,
by its ambassador, persuaded John to accept the facts with resignation, representing that after his death Brazil would naturally become
once more a part of the Portuguese monarchy, and Pedro did not,
as is generally believed, renounce his claims to the Portuguese throne
on ascending that of Brazil. But the son of John VI. was not the
man that the circumstances required to found an empire.   He was
by education completely possessed by all the prejudices of the old
courts of Europe, gay, impetuous, the slave of his impressions,
without firmness of purpose, very often undecided in his resolutions,
and wholly unfit for the part of a constitutional king.   At first, to

gain the good will of the people, he showed himself disposed to accept free institutions, and went so far as to have himself proclaimed Grand Master of the Freemasons; but as soon as he felt himself securely in power he returned to his absolutist ideas, ordered the masonic lodges to be closed, surrounded himself with favorites, and compromised his reign forever by his decree for the dissolution of the first constituent assembly (November, 1823). The constitution which he promulgated (March, 1827) and which he himself drew up, could not, in spite of its liberalism, overcome the resentment of the nation.

Pernambuco and Pará resisted, appealing to the unrecognized sovereignty of the people. Pernambuco declared itself a republic, inducing the provinces of the north to join and form the Confederation of the Equator; and Parahyba, Ceara, and Rio Grande do Norte obeyed the call. This attempt was repressed with savage energy by a reign of terror and the infliction of barbarous punishments. Discontent became general and was aggravated by the rising of the Cisplatine province, which demanded independence. There was no doubt of the connivance of the government of La Plata, and Dom Pedro declared war against the Argentine Republic at the close of 1825. England helped to stir up the quarrel. This campaign was a series of fruitless battles and mortifying defeats. To these difficulties there were added the attempts of the numerous and powerful Federal Republican party, and the claims and threats of the mother country. Portugal had not willingly resigned herself to the loss of the rich colony whose revenues were more than ever necessary. John VI., betrayed by his wife and his son, Miguel; surrounded by conspiracies; wearied by the dissensions in his cabinet, and enfeebled by his sufferings, dragged on a miserable existence, and was thought to be epileptic. On May 13, 1825, at the instance of Sir Charles Stuart, the representative of the British government at Lisbon, he signed, between two nervous attacks, letters patent acknowledging the independence of Brazil and its separation from Portugal; but in ten months the two crowns were again united on the head of Dom Pedro by the death of the unfortunate king. After holding both kingdoms a few months later Dom Pedro ceded the crown of Portugal to his daughter Maria, seven years of age, who was betrothed to her uncle Miguel. British diplomacy had again intervened and forced Pedro to abdicate the more honorable of the two crowns. It was a cruel disenchantment for him, and from that day he understood how precarious was his situation. He desired that the Princess Isabel Maria should act as regent during the minority of Maria; but England insisted that the regent should be Prince Miguel, and Dom Pedro yielded. Miguel went through London on his way to Portugal. He took the oath to the charter promulgated by Dom Pedro; but, urged on by the Clerical and Absolutist party, he dissolved the Cortes, seized the throne on his own account, and repelled all idea of marrying the young queen, who was not even allowed to disembark in Portugal, and had to return to Brazil under the protection of England. Miguel yielded to the influence, more or less avowed, of this nation, which gave the lie to its protests of neutrality by firing on a body of 600 partisans of Dom Pedro when they were entering Terceira, the only point in the kingdom that remained loyal to Doña Maria. The policy of England was to lessen the chances of the undesirable reunion of Portugal and Brazil by postponing indefinitely the accession of Doña Maria.

Pedro I. declared, notwithstanding the anarchy that reigned in his states and the difficulties of the situation, that he would maintain the despised rights of his daughter by force of arms, but the Brazilians were afraid of seeing their resources exhausted in defense of a dynastic question that in reality did not at all interest them. Under such conditions the treaty which terminated the unfortunate campaign in the south was signed, and the independence of Montevideo acknowledged. The emperor was accused of sacrificing the best port on the La Plata and a fortress very important for the security of the frontiers and the development of Brazilian commerce.

His second marriage was another cause of complaint. He had been a widower since 1826, and now (1829) married Maria Amalia of Leuchtenberg, the daughter of Eugène Beauharnais, and his subjects foresaw a new descent of foreigners on the court and the public offices. The Congress, reflecting public opinion, assumed a certain aggressive attitude and was dissolved in September, 1829. The people muttered angrily, and the emperor was forced to hesitate. After much vacillation, he selected a ministry composed of republicans, for the most part Brazilians. It was too late. Suddenly changing his tactics, he presented a bill, at the opening of the legislative session in May, 1830, restraining the liberty of the press. Every moribund government takes vengeance on the press which exposes its condition. Just at this time the ordinances of Charles X. of France were accomplishing his downfall, and the shock of the revolution of July was felt beyond the Atlantic. The storm burst at last, and on April 6, 1831, the capital rose in arms; the multitude marched through the streets and the troops who were guarding the emperor's palace joined the citizens. Pedro I. understood that his mission in America was concluded forever, and only endeavored to disappoint the republicans and save the monarchical principle. The next day he abdicated in favor of his son, Pedro II., who was then in his sixth year; and on the 13th of the same month embarked for Europe with the intention of commanding in person an expedition against the usurper Miguel and disputing with him the crown of Portugal by arms.

He left as guardian to his son, Pedro II., Bonifacio José de Andrada e Silva, late head of the Democratic party, and author of the remarkable pamphlet, "The Brazilian Awakening," who had been exiled to France since the year 1823. Andrada, who was at Bordeaux, accepted the difficult office, but the old revolutionary minister, though his selection was a guarantee of liberty, was soon suspected by the popular party. He was deprived of his office in 1833 and ejected from the imperial palace by the public forces. Pedro II. was put under the direct guardianship of a council of regency.

The Congress of 1834 made important modifications in the constitution by giving each province a legislature of its own and leaving to it the management of local business, whether administrative, judicial, financial, or municipal. This bold step saved the unity of the Brazilian Empire in a critical moment when a very powerful party endeavored to divide it into small states in order to form a federal republic similar to that of the United States. This act, which was generally well received, served afterward as a pretext to certain districts to rise in insurrection; a movement which was easily suppressed, except in Rio Grande do Sul, where it had acquired large proportions, prolonging the civil war for ten years. Garibaldi fought for some time among the partisans of the independence of Rio Grande. A decree of amnesty wisely promulgated put an end to the bloody struggle which had cost so many lives.

In 1835 the Congress of Deputies elected as regent Father Antonio Feijo, Bishop of Mariana, a senator and formerly Minister of Justice, at the same time that it excluded from the succession to the Crown Doña Maria, Queen of Portugal, and appointed as

immediate successor to the throne, in case of the decease of
Pedro II., his sister, Doña Januaria. After two years of effort,
Feijo lost hope of reconciling the contending parties and resigned.
The former Minister of War, Pedro Araujo de Liam, took his
place, and was able to maintain himself until July, 1840. But
when he desired to dissolve the Cortes, it declared the majority
of Pedro II., who was then fifteen years of age. The young
emperor was solemnly crowned July 18, 1841. Some insurrectionary movements broke out in the provinces of San Paulo and
Minas Geraes, which were strongholds of republicanism. General
Caxias put them down in San Paulo, but the war dragged on in
Minas Geraes, where the Senator Feleciano had collected a force of
6000 men. In 1842 Caxias won a decisive victory at San Lucia
and broke the strength of the Federal Republicans. Six years later
the proud and fiery province of Pernambuco made a last attempt.
Amnesty was granted after all these uprisings, and resulted in a
thorough pacification, so that peace was restored without the sacrifice of liberty, an eloquent proof of the folly of hangings, shoot-
ings, and bloodshed. This policy of oblivion, wisdom, and generosity secured the greatness of Brazil. The military commis-
sions, summary executions, and bloody revenges of 1817 and 1824
under John VI. and Pedro I. had led to nothing but disasters.

Pedro II. was gentle and just, liberal and enlightened. He
wielded his power with intelligence, and never took advantage of
the difficulties made for him by the reactionary and radical parties
to transform his government into a military dictatorship. His business ability, high character, tact, and moderation saved him from
the reefs where so many other sovereigns have suffered shipwreck.
Martial law was unknown in Brazil; liberty of conscience and of
writing was complete, so that many republican journals were published there without fear of prosecution. Pedro II. had grasped the
idea that liberty was the surest and best means of perpetuating his
power and consolidating his throne. He won the esteem of the
people by always treating parliamentary government with respect.
He reigned but did not govern. But though in political affairs he
was careful to be nothing more than the first representative of " the
political association of all Brazilian citizens, in strict accordance
with the spirit of the constitution," he none the less exercised
a considerable influence on the affairs of the nation. He above
all tried to develop the agricultural, commercial, and maritime re-

sources of Brazil, and assure its national preponderance in South America.

He faithfully observed the constitution which was the fundamental law granted by the edict of Pedro I. on March 25, 1824, as amended by the additional acts of August 12, 1834, and May 12, 1840. It gave to the head of the state the title of Constitutional Emperor and Perpetual Defender of Brazil. He was the first representative of the nation, but the nation was the sovereign. The legislative power was vested in a Chamber of Deputies of one hundred and twenty-two members elected for four years by an indirect vote, and a Senate of fifty-eight members appointed for life; but bills for taxation, army enrollment, impeachment of ministers, and the choice of a new dynasty in case of the extinction of the imperial family, were to originate in the Chamber. Elections were " indirect." The people chose electors, and these chose the deputies and named three persons for each vacant senatorship, one of whom was chosen by the emperor. The princes of the imperial family became senators *ex officio* at the age of twenty-five. The two houses together formed the General Assembly, which had powers distinct from those of each house considered separately. No measure adopted by the two houses could become a law without the approval of the emperor. The judicial power was vested in judges and juries; the judges applying the law and the jury determining the facts. No suit could be begun until all means of conciliation had been exhausted, for which purpose justices of the peace are elected in each parish directly by the people. The sovereign's power of pardoning, of convoking the two houses in the interval of their sessions, and of approving laws, constituted what was called the " Moderator's " power. The executive power belonged to the head of the state. Ministers were responsible to the legislature. The constitution guaranteed to the citizens personal and religious liberty, the inviolability of property, the freedom of labor and the absolute liberty of the press. Titles of nobility were not hereditary.[4] Public in-

---

[4] The Brazilians were very fond of titles. Agassiz shows this in his "Journey to Brazil." When a splendid insane asylum was to be built at Botafogo the government offered titles to such citizens as were willing to loosen their purse strings in aid of this charitable institution so that *commendadores* and barons were created, the importance of the title corresponding to that of the gift which had purchased it. In this manner large sums were raised and many of the titled men of Rio Janeiro got their patents of nobility. Manoel de Macedo also speaks of honorary distinctions granted to citizens of the capital and the provinces who build or by their subscriptions aid the building of schoolhouses.

struction was gratuitous. Slavery was not recognized in the constitution and was tolerated only as a right of property acquired in colonial times.

The provinces into which Brazil was divided had their local legislatures, elected every two years and empowered to create, abolish, and change the seat of government and the area and boundaries of parishes, boroughs, and districts. Each province had a president, appointed by the central power as its representative, who executed the will of the provincial assembly. Each parish was subdivided into *comarcas* or districts, with municipal assemblies, administrative, judicial, and police tribunals. These municipal assemblies were elected for four years, and consisted of nine members or *ecbevins* in cities and seven in boroughs, the one who headed the poll being president. They were charged with the administration of municipal police, and have their independent revenues. All these provinces and *comarcas* were in touch with the capital, a city not subject to any province, which was governed by the senate and the ministry of the empire. The general government had exclusive control over higher education, the postoffice, the financial system in general, diplomatic and consular business, the police, and the military and naval forces. In the ecclesiastical order it nominated the metropolitan archbishop and the bishops.

A strong political centralization resulted from this system, which had a broad administrative decentralization as a regulator or counterpoise, since each province had its own special revenue, which it administered itself, and a general revenue went to the central treasury. In fact, it was the federal system of the United States, allied to a constitutional monarchy, hereditary in the male line.

Brazil had two foreign wars under the rule of Pedro II., one (1851) against Rosas, who armed and supported Oribe, with the manifest object of incorporating Uruguay with the Argentine Confederation, and the other (1865-1869) against Paraguay and its president, Lopez. After what we have already said, we need not again recount the details of these wars. It is sufficient to say that this intervention of the Lusitanian empire in the affairs of La Plata has been variously judged. Some have suspected that Brazil desired to continue the colonial traditions of the Portuguese and to expand at the expense of the neighboring republic. On this point, the apprehensions of Lopez seem to be justified in a measure by a secret note emanating from the foreign office of Montevideo and cited by the author of "*Brésil Contemporain*" (page 312, note). Portuguese authors [5] undertake to refute these accusations. "Brazil," they say, "has too great an extent of territory, and though she wishes to retain it, she realizes that it is a cause of weakness so long as she cannot people her deserts, cover her immense plains with flourishing cities, open roads through all her uninhabited forests, cover the streams and rivers with steamboats and thus carry

industrial progress, life and civilization to the uninhabited interior and its uncultivated lands."

Nevertheless, it is certain that Brazilian statesmen have constantly looked toward the La Plata with ambition, but they know that very great obstacles oppose them. What they secretly think certain publicists openly assert. Such territorial adjustments seem to these pen and ink conquerors an inevitable consequence of the

[5] Perièra da Silva, "*Situation de l'Empire du Brésil.*"

antagonism between the Anglo-Saxon and the Hispano-Portuguese races. "These modifications are inevitable," they say, "because Brazil will not be able to resist the United States effectively until it has extended to its natural boundaries. Since the River Paraguay forms the natural boundary on the west, the state of that name ought to disappear, as well as Corrientes, Entre Rios, and the Banda Oriental, which prevent the empire extending itself to its natural limit, which is the Paraná. This necessity has been proclaimed a hundred times, and the Brazilian government has always responded by energetic disavowals; but, notwithstanding these protests and some excellent promises, if it were only a question of Brazil, they would merely prove the extreme repugnance of the sovereign and of his responsible advisers to accomplish a task which may be difficult but is indispensable." [6]   That is easily said, but this "extreme repugnance" may be wisdom or at least honesty.

Here is another pronouncement: "Perhaps there is no country in either hemisphere that has more right to expansion than Brazil has to extend its boundaries on the side of the La Plata. It is more than a political want; it is an indispensable necessity for the prosperity of the country. The streams that form the La Plata, that is, the Paraná, the Uruguay, the Paraguay, etc., all have their sources in Brazilian territory; besides, these are and will be for a long time the only means of communication that will permit the outflow of the productions of the province of Matta Grosso to the ocean and furnish communication with the capital. Let a war break out among the peoples along these rivers and one of the most extensive provinces of the empire is immediately deprived of its communications and isolated from the rest of the world in the midst of a terrible wilderness." [7]   The author of these lines hastens to point out, nevertheless, that he does not think that "the law of history by which the large states expand, live, and renew themselves at the expense of the small ones can as yet be applicable to Brazil." If ever that hour strikes, Brazil may have to consider her mighty neighbor, the Anglo-Saxon. "The obstacles that arrested Pedro I. before Montevideo still exist," he justly adds. The enormous distances, the want of communications, the swamps which overflow the country, and, above all, the foreign origin of the

[6] Dutot, "France et Brésil."
[7] D'Assier, "Brésil Contemporain."

population, Spanish in the Banda Oriental and Indian in Paraguay, make the conquest almost impossible.

Brazil must have thought so, when, after her dear-bought victory, she allowed the Republic of Paraguay to live. It is true that some extension of territory was won, but an annexation on the frontier has not in unpeopled countries the hostile character that it would have in Europe. The conqueror had claimed this acquisition for a long time past, and even after having confined the enemy to the territory situated between the Rivers Paraguay and Paraná, the conquerors thought that they could prove that their reasons for fighting were solely the interests of liberty and civilization so often alleged in such cases. On that occasion the imperial government put in practice the doctrines of honest international politics, and conducted itself in the best manner possible for the advantage of peace and tranquillity, instead of abusing its victory.

Violence had no part in the proceedings of that government which showed itself merciful in the hour of triumph at home as well as abroad. Hence, that internal tranquillity in contrast with the endless and almost always barren disturbances of some neighboring countries. This does not mean that the empire was free from crises. If it did not drag on from revolution to revolution like Bolivia, it suffered political shocks like Chili. It is only dead nations that never move. Although political parties have been broken up to a considerable extent, and opinions have formed new combinations, the mere difficulty of establishing a certain equilibrium between Liberal aspirations and Conservative tendencies raised parliamentary storms, overturned ministries, and sometimes led to a dissolution of the chambers, but Pedro II. showed himself little inclined to sanction acts of this importance. The stormy year 1862 ran its course through many such crises. The ministries, which were overthrown almost as soon as they were formed, had to prepare for the consequences of a conflict with England, which had its origin in the month of June of the previous year. On the opening of the session of May, 1863, all the elements of a hostile majority were united. In view of foreign complications the emperor consented to that which he had refused to two previous ministries. On May 12, before any debate, the chambers were dissolved, but only after all other means had been exhausted, and the same relief had been denied to the two preceding Cabinets.

This measure seemed a direct blow at the Conservative party, which bitterly attacked the policy of the ministry, and, considering the circumstances, it was a step toward the Liberal party. The electoral campaign opened, and the Conservative party was overthrown; the Liberals, united to the ministerialists by the necessities of the moment, and composing with them a coalition party called the league, were successful in the final balloting on September 8; but the Olinda ministry, sharply attacked by its allies of yesterday, fell in January, 1864, and was replaced on the 15th of the same month by the Cabinet presided over by Zacarías de Goes e Vasconcellos. Zacarías had been the head of the short-lived ministry that had given place to the Marquis de Olinda. This government, being formed of elements of all shades of opinion, had not sufficient strength to win the support of the country. In the month of September it disappeared in its turn, and Furtado was commissioned to form a new Cabinet of a more strictly Liberal character.

The position of the country was full of difficulty, and the treasury showed a deficit. It had been necessary to spend large sums of money on the army, first, because of the differences which arose with Great Britain, and then as a consequence of the war against Montevideo and Paraguay. The failure of one of the first banking houses of Rio Janeiro and other financial disasters brought on a panic, and commerce was at a standstill. The levying of new army contingents and naval expansion exhausted all the resources of the state. Fortunately the quarrel with England had a pacific termination. The Treaty of the Triple Alliance of May 8, 1865, was received with rejoicing. The people showed by warlike manifestations that they approved of the campaign against Paraguay. The nation hoped for an extension of territory, and influence. No one dreamed of condemning the expense, nor the exceptional measures adopted, such as forced enlistment. Nevertheless, the star of the Furtado ministry was waning, and a vote of censure on certain matters of administration overthrew it on May 24, 1865, and brought back to power the Marquis de Olinda. He chose his colleagues from the two factions of the Liberal party, the Moderates and the Radicals. In the period now opening the financial distress and general misery increased. From 1866 the government lacked men and money. What new expedient could be adopted for relief? The whites were not sufficient for the needs of the army, so the blacks were enlisted; and liberating the slaves to convert them into soldiers opened the question of emancipation. Freedom of navigation was perforce adopted at the same time. An attempt to place a loan in London failed. Another was tried in Brazil with little more success, and insolvency was complete. In the Cabinet harmony was at an end. Some reverses before Humaita brought about the dismissal of all the ministers, and Zacarías returned to power, and took charge of the finances.

Such was the situation when the year 1867 opened in the midst of an electoral campaign, in which the government won an uncertain majority. It, like its predecessors, was blamed for the slow progress of the war. When would it be finished? What would be the reward for so much bloodshed and expense? The government was sharply accused by the Conservatives for prematurely raising the question of the emancipation of the negroes, and had to face the unpopularity caused by increased taxation. In July, 1868, the emperor called a Conservative ministry, and there was an explosion of wrath in Parliament.

Pedro II. recurred again to a dissolution, and a new Chamber was elected; but the same story was repeated. Indeed, it was the inevitable consequence of the situation that Brazil had created for herself by entering upon a policy of distant adventure. In spite of everything the government was decided to prosecute with energy the struggle begun with Paraguay, and refused all offers of mediation, nor could the greatest sacrifices make it desist from its purpose. At length the death of President Lopez gave it the victory, but that difficult campaign, which lasted five years, had cost the treasury $255,600,000, not to speak of the blood spilled and the thousands of men who perished in a foreign land.

The ministry which came into power at this time promised reforms with regard to the liberation of the slaves. These promises were renewed in the speech from the throne in 1871, on the opening of the new legislature, and were fulfilled by a law which was passed the same year.

The time was not far distant in which the nation was to pass through another kind of excitement. The attitude of the higher clergy in opposition to the constitutional laws produced one of those religious crises which always excite men's minds and lead them to intolerance and hatred. Things were carried to such a point that the government had to punish the ultramontane faction, and in March, 1874, the Supreme Court condemned the Bishop of Pernambuco to four years' imprisonment. The Bishops of

Olinda and Pará were arrested and prosecuted for similar offenses, and the Jesuits were expelled from the province of Pernambuco. This was enough to arouse the anger of the Clerical party. In the session of September 2, 1874, the Rio Branco Ministry was suddenly attacked by some fanatical deputies, who went so far as to demand its immediate impeachment for treason and conspiracy against the religion of the state. This ministry had to suppress an insurrection in the district of San Leopoldo, and the clergy thundered against it, calling it the "Excommunicated Ministry" and the "Freemason Ministry." The sovereign vacillated, and the Liberals saw with pain the fall of the ministry that had fought with so much courage against the unreasonable demands and aggressions of an ignorant and overbearing sect, which is a continual menace to the young nations of America.

We have already spoken of the abolition of the slave trade. It resulted in turning speculation to a more legitimate and honorable field for the employment of capital. The more important ameliorations that Brazil now enjoys date from the suppression of that crime. The railways, those life-giving arteries of industry, agriculture, and commerce, laid their first rails and soon were established and extended with a species of patriotic ardor; the electric telegraphs stretched their civilizing wires from the great markets of the coast to the fertile fields of the interior, and at the present time the submarine cable has placed Brazil in constant communication with Europe. Many public roads have been made, conveyances are more rapid and commodious, and gas illuminates the towns. Since 1867 the great River Amazon has been open to the commerce of the world, and the admission of the merchant ships of all nations to free navigation in the Brazilian waters of the great river has exercised a very great influence on the civilization of those uncultivated regions. Lines of steamers bind in close relations the maritime and riverside provinces and towns; enterprises are multiplied, and the general prosperity is increased by the competition of private businesses and interests. Public education receives a strong stimulus and the liberty of teaching is coming to be a reality. The assembly of the province of Rio Janeiro, in 1871, made instruction obligatory for children between seven and fourteen years of age. Poor scholars were clothed at the expense of the provincial budget. The higher education had two schools of medicine, two of law; one military school, a central school and a naval school. The French astronomer, M. Liais, was selected to organize the observatory of Rio Janeiro in 1874; and Pedro II., knowing that the future of his empire must rest chiefly on the progress of agriculture, founded two agricultural institutes during his journey through the immense Brazilian provinces, one at Bahía and the other in Pernambuco. A third was founded in the capital in 1860.

According to Audiganne ("*La lutte industrielle des peuples,* 1868") in the Universal Exhibition of 1867 there was hardly any better classified and arranged department than that of Brazil. which contained 3558 articles, exhibited by 684 persons. They had been chosen from over more than 20,000 exhibitors in an exhibition opened at Rio Janeiro in 1866. In 1873 Brazil obtained 202 prizes in the Vienna Exhibition. A National Exhibition, opened at Rio on December 2, 1875, was very successful. In 1876 the Emperor and Empress of Brazil were present at the opening of the Philadelphia Exhibition, in which Brazil was worthily represented. The products of Brazil which occupy the principal place in international commerce are coffee, cotton (the cultivation of which received a great impulse in 1860), sugar, cacao, tobacco, tapioca, hides, and morocco leather. Woods of every species abound in the interior in easy reach of the streams.

Pedro II., who traveled over the country in 1860 to learn its needs at first hand, went to examine the European civilization, and thus was able to judge of the improvements that might be introduced into Brazil. In December, 1871, he remained for a considerable time in Paris, where he carefully inspected the principal scientific and literary institutions.[8] On his return to Rio Janeiro he submitted various bills to the Chambers for the development of primary instruction, the establishment of new railways, and the reform of the electoral law so that it should become "the authentic expression of the popular will." In his message of 1873 he expressed himself thus: "Electoral reform will secure the first necessary condition of our form of government, whose chief strength must emanate from public opinion and the authority of the law."

A broader and more vital administrative decentralization for the provinces was demanded by enlightened minds, and legislation calculated to secure the rights of immigrants. The good fortune and the future of the country might be said to depend on these questions of administrative decentralization and of European emigration. It

[8] He became a member of the French Geographical Society in 1868.

must be confessed that the native free population rarely engages in industrial labor and these occupations are almost exclusively in European hands. Unfortunately, the low wages of slave labor made the position of foreign workmen precarious; good agricultural laborers who immigrate with their families are in an insecure position, since generally the colonist is almost entirely in the power of the proprietor who employs him. The government, nevertheless, decided to coöperate with energy in all efforts tending to make the emigrant who starts for the New World take the road to Brazil. In 1872 it opened a large lodging house, called *Hospedaria do Governo,* which could lodge and feed 500 persons and give hospitality to those who arrived without resources and were obliged to wait until work was given them to provide for their maintenance. Every adult, eighteen years of age, might obtain gratuitously from two to seven and a half acres of land, or from 50 to 200 acres simply by making application to the government. Domestic animals were very cheap. A horse cost $35, a cow $20, a fat pig $2, and a fowl ten cents, so that stock-raising is a growing industry, especially among the Scotch, who are masters of this branch of agriculture.

Numerous groups of English, Swiss, and German colonists formed what may be called separate colonies, which were in a really flourishing condition. Their inhabitants constructed commodious houses; some established manufactures, and others devoted themselves to the cultivation of the fields, or the exploitation of the forests, and many English miners were employed in extracting the wealth buried in the earth.[9]

We conclude this chapter as we began it, by saying that from the point of view of its economic problems the empire of Brazil, which has grown out of the old Portuguese colony, bears a close resemblance to the old Spanish colonies which are now the republics of the New World.

[9] Unfortunately most of the colonists whom speculators send to Brazil with fine promises are cruelly undeceived on their arrival. "Many requirements, of which they are probably not informed in advance, are necessary to enable a colonist to make a profit in agriculture in a new country like Brazil. Several years must pass before he can get any return from his labor and unless he is carried over this period, his failure is certain." (Biard, "*Voyage au Brésil, 1858, 1859; le Tour du Monde, 1861,*" 2d Semestre.)

Chapter XII

BOLÍVAR AND BOLIVIA. 1825-1876

BOLIVIA is shut up in the center of the southern continent with Peru and Chili on the west, Brazil on the
north and east, and the Argentine Republic on the south.
Its obscurity has not sheltered it from political storms. Insurrections have followed one another with discouraging frequency,
and have resulted in chronic instability and the paralysis of all
development, thus affecting the most important interests of the
people and devoting them to ignorance and misery.

Yet Bolivia is endowed with exceptional conditions of fertility.
The valleys and plains present the magical wonders of the tropical
flora, the Cordillera holds in its depths all the valuable metals—gold,
silver, copper, and lead. The famous mountain of Potosí, which
in three centuries has produced $448,000,000, is but the culminating
point of a silver-bearing chain whose boundless wealth has never
been seriously calculated.

Sucre or Chuquisaca, 7000 feet above sea level, is on the watershed of the Amazon and the La Plata. At the foot of two hills of
porphyry, which resemble gigantic sphynxes looking down upon the
town from the Cordilleras, there rise two little rivulets. They flow
in different directions and soon become the two mighty rivers of
South America, flowing toward the ocean, one northward, the other
southward, and inviting Europe to exploit the field that lies waiting
on their banks for modern industry. Here are the outlets of
Bolivia, but unfortunately there is, as yet, little river traffic, and the
only industries are mining and gathering Peruvian bark (cinchona).

The five provinces of La Paz, Potosi, Charcas, Cochabamba, and
Santa Cruz were known as Upper Peru before forming themselves
into an independent state under the name of Bolivia, and had first
been a part of the united provinces of La Plata. This country, after
Colombia, suffered most in the cause of emancipation, and every
one of its towns was several times given up to pillage and slaughter.
" Upper Peru," says its Declaration of Independence, " has been the

181

altar on which flowed the first blood shed for liberty, and the land
where the last tyrant lies buried. . . .   The barbarous burning
of more than a hundred villages, the destruction of towns, the
scaffolds raised everywhere for the partisans of liberty, the blood
of a thousand victims who suffered torments that would have made
the Caribs themselves shudder; the forced contributions and exactions, as arbitrary as they were inhuman; the insecurity of the
honor and lives of persons, and of property, and, lastly, an atrocious
and savage inquisitorial system have not been able to extinguish
the sacred fire of liberty and the just hatred of the Spanish power."
The fifty deputies who formed the Congress, which met in Chuquisaca on August 6, 1825, representing the sovereign power of
Upper Peru, expressed themselves in these terms, barely four
months after the remains of the Spanish forces, commanded by
Olaneta, had been finally defeated at Potosí.   The battle of Tus-
mula, fought on April 1, 1825, had put an end to a struggle, which,
after Ayacucho, could be no longer sustained by the royalists.
Bolívar, when he appointed Sucre provisional head of the recently
liberated provinces, advised them to shape their own destiny.   Peru,
by a decree of February 23, and Rio de la Plata, by the law of
May 9, left them "the free and spontaneous decision of what was
most suitable to their prosperity and government."   Under these
conditions the Congress decided for independence, and on August
11, 1825, a new republic was formed in South America, with more
inhabitants than Chili, and even than La Plata.   It took the name
of the Republic of Bolívar, in honor of its liberator, and shortly
after that of Bolivia, which it has preserved.

Working with all the enthusiasm of triumph, carried away
by a species of patriotic delirium and the necessity of noisy expressions, the Congress voted a series of measures, in which the creole
character is clearly revealed.   The slave noisily shaking off the
chains which he has at last broken, hastens to made a parade of the
freedom bought at so dear a price, and with the overflowing ardor
of the neophyte couches his decrees and proclamations in the
most emphatic and declamatory terms.   It was announced "to the
whole continent" that Upper Peru recognized in Bolívar "her
good father," and the supreme executive power of the republic was
conceded to the hero of South America, with the titles of Protector
and President.   The Congress resolved that the anniversary of the
battle of Junin and the birthday of the Liberator should be annually

celebrated with public rejoicings; that the portrait of Bolívar should be placed in all courts of justice, town halls, universities, colleges, schools, and places of public instruction, in order that the sight of it should keep up the remembrance of the father of his country and be a stimulant to imitate his great virtues, and that his equestrian statue should be placed " on a column " in all the provincial capitals. General Sucre, decorated with the title of Grand Marshal of Ayacucho, was ordered to have struck, and to present to the Liberator, a gold medal surrounded with diamonds, on which were shown the mountain of Potosí and the Liberator high on a trophy of muskets, swords, cannon, and banners, placing the liberty cap on the summit of the mountain. Sucre was equally well treated. Congress willed that the anniversary of his birth and that of the battle of Ayacucho should be celebrated each year, that his portrait should be placed everywhere at the left hand of that of the Liberator, and that a pedestrian statue of him should be erected in each provincial capital. He was acknowledged as the first general of the nation, with the title of captain-general, besides enjoying the title of " Defender and Great Citizen of the Republic of Bolívar." At the same time the province of Chuquisaca and the capital also received the name of Sucre, and it was resolved to present to him a gold medal set with diamonds, representing the grand marshal delivering Peru, under the form of a lama, from the claws of a lion, with the following inscription: " The Republic of Bolívar to her Defender, the Hero of Ayacucho." Nor was this all; a large gold medal was to be struck representing as the symbol of America, an Indian girl, seated on a lion's skin under a tent formed of the banners of the states of the continent. She was to embrace the Liberator with her right hand and the Grand Marshal with her left. These two heroes were to be represented decorating her with a liberty cap, and heaping up at her feet broken chains and shackles. On each side the names of the other generals and chiefs who had taken part in the battles of Junin and Ayacucho were to be engraved, and below those of the commandants and officers who had distinguished themselves there. This medal was to be placed in the Hall of Congress. Lastly, everyone who fought in those battles received the title of citizen of the republic, and $1,000,000 was put in Bolívar's hands, at least on paper, for distribution among the army of liberation.

By another decree of August 31 the government was declared

to be representative republican, and (we quote word for word) centralized, uniform and indivisible.   Bolívar, whose authority appears to have been more absolute in Bolivia than in Peru and Colombia, was petitioned to draw up the social compact, and the result of his labors was that frame of government, the object of so much criticism, known under the name of the Bolivian Code, which his admirers considered a model constitution.   According to proofs that he has left in his own handwriting, he intended from that time to apply this production of his political thought first to Peru and then to Colombia.   This document, then, is of great historical interest and gives the measure of the Liberator's ideas of organization.   The discourse or exposition of principles which accompanied its promulgation deserves minute consideration.   The advantages of a permanent, and, we may say, hereditary government are demonstrated in it, with a conviction very surprising in a republican who professed to be weary of power, but who without doubt dreamed of holding the supreme and irresponsible presidency of an immense republic of the United States of South America.

After laying down the principle that tyranny and anarchy are like an immense ocean of oppression beating against a small island of liberty and continually threatening to submerge it by the violence of its waves, the Liberator establishes four political powers: every ten citizens appoint an elector whose authority lasts four years; the electors elect three Chambers: that of the tribunes, also elected for four years, has the exclusive privilege of legislating on the imposts, peace and war; the Senate, which lasts eight years, watches over the tribunals and religion, and the Chamber of Censors, whose members hold their seats for life, has a political and moral power which has a certain likeness to that exercised by the Areopagus at Athens and the Censors of Rome, and is the guardian of the constitution and the fulfillment of public treaties.   Bolívar doubtless knew Franklin's witty fable on the vaunted bicameral system: " A snake with two heads and one body was going to the brook to drink, and on her way was to pass through a hedge, a twig of which opposed her direct course: one head chose to go on the right side of the twig, the other on the left, so that time was spent in the contest, and, before the decision was completed, the poor snake died of thirst." [1]   That is why Bolívar gave the monster a third head, whose functions as arbitrator and balance he explains thus: " Every difference between two of these chambers

[1] Franklin, Works, ed. by V. Bigelow, v. x, p. 186.

is decided by the intervention of the third. A question examined
and discussed by both sides will then be submitted to the impartial
judgment of the third, so that no useful law can remain without
effect, or at least, before being rejected, will have been put to the
proof two and sometimes three times." And being convinced of
the excellence of his idea, he adds with an air of triumph: " In all
the affairs of life, when difficulties arise between two parties, a
third is named to settle them; would it not be absurd that so simple
a means should be ignored and despised when the most important
interests of society are in question?" But by an important provision
Bolívar confers the executive power upon a president for life, aided
by a vice-president appointed by him and *ex officio* his successor.

In May, 1826, the Congress, elected under the influence of
Colombian bayonets, voted this constitution by acclamation; but
outside the Assembly a veritable tempest broke out against its
author. Bolívar, invested with the power that he himself had
created, left it provisionally in the hands of the grand marshal.
On December 9, which was the day on which the constitution came
into force, and the anniversary of the battle of Ayacucho, Sucre
gave in his resignation, and on being reëlected accepted the presidency for two years only.

The Colombian influence caused secret discontent in Bolivia
and Peru which soon burst forth openly. The two countries agreed
to drive out the foreigner and overturn the institutions and governments that Bolívar had created. Sucre attempted to reëstablish the
prestige of the Colombian name in Lima; but he had enough to do
to maintain his authority in Bolivia. The enormous contributions
that he laid upon the country and the absolute power that he exercised alienated the sympathies of the people from him. There were
conspiracies even in his little army and he shot several of his best
officers. In 1827 some Colombian soldiers, mercenaries of the
republic, rose, headed by Lieutenant-Colonel Guerra. Sucre attacked them and received so severe a wound in the left arm that
amputation was necessary. Other popular risings took place; the
Colombian troops were expelled in April, 1828, and Sucre, after a
desperate resistance, had to give way to numbers. He left the
country; and we know how he perished two years afterward, a
victim to his fidelity to the cause of the Liberator.

A new Congress, which met on August 3, remodeled the constitution from top to bottom, and elected to the presidency General

Santa Cruz, who was then thirty-four years old and had held supreme power in Peru for a short time. As he hesitated to accept the honor, Velasco seized the dictatorship, which he was able to hold for four months, until Congress deposed the usurper and elected General Blanco in his place. This man perished in a revolt on the night of January 1, 1829, and then a provisional government offered the presidency again to Santa Cruz, who accepted it.

On June 24, 1831, the first legislative assembly opened. The chief point in the president's message related to the recognition of Bolivia by France, which, "being the first European power to recognize our national existence, is justly entitled to be preferred in our markets and in all our international relations." In the same year Santa Cruz promulgated the code that bears his name, and from that time some degree of order began to be established in the public finances. According to a ministerial report presented to the Chambers in August, 1832, the budget of expenses amounted to $1,486,026, and of income to $1,700,719. Certain difficulties which arose with Peru were amicably arranged, and a treaty of peace and commerce was signed between the two countries. Santa Cruz, desiring to stimulate agriculture, industry, and the sciences, endeavored to attract Europeans by offering them certain favors and advantages. The army of Bolivia at that time was the best organized, disciplined, and equipped in all South America.

Some passing disturbances did not interfere with the prosperity of the republic, and the neighboring states might envy the relative tranquillity that was enjoyed there. It was even then called in Europe the Switzerland of South America. The simple manners of its inhabitants, their honesty, their desire for education, and also the steepness of their mountains, which formed a natural defense, really justified the comparison. Then it was that Santa Cruz, who was appointed arbitrator between the claimants to the presidency of Peru, realized for his own advantage the immortal tale of "the Oyster and the Litigants." [2] Two pilgrims see an oyster on the beach and, to settle a dispute as to its ownership, choose an arbitrator who eats the oyster and gives each a shell. Compare the story of Daniel O'Connell's arbitration of the ownership of a sovereign in a like case and his pocketing the coin as his fee.

Santa Cruz entered Peru at the head of 5000 men in May, 1835, and made himself master of the country by the end of the following

[2] La Fontaine "Fables," ix. 9.

February. The conqueror divided Peru into two states, forming one out of the provinces of the North, and the other out of those of the South; he gave each a constitution which guaranteed its independence in internal matters, but subjected them both to a central government of which he was the head with the title of protector. These two states united with Bolivia formed the Peru-Bolivian Confederation.

These events were not of a nature to tranquilize the neighboring republics. Chili especially was uneasy, and soon found a pretext for war. The struggle lasted nearly three years, and was ended on January 20, 1839, by the defeat of Santa Cruz. This confirmed the defection of Ballivian, the commander of the army of the Center, and of Velasco, who held the command in Bolivia. The latter got himself recognized as provisional president by a Congress which met in Chuquisaca on June 16, 1839, and Ballivian obtained the vice-presidency. This was a death-blow for the confederation; Velasco made peace with Chili. Santa Cruz escaped the fury of his enemies only by the protection of the British agent, and embarked for Guayaquil March 13, after resigning the authority which his own soldiers would have taken from him.

The protector left many friends behind him who soon got the upper hand again; his administration was declared irreproachable by Congress, and in a short time a revolution was got up in his favor. Colonels Agreda and Goitia seized Velasco, whom they found at card-play in the house of a lady of the city. At the same time the commander of a battalion who had come from Guayaquil with a handful of men endeavored to raise the north of Peru; but he was taken and shot. Santa Cruz did not appear, and Ballivian, who had gone to Peru, learning of these events, undertook to subdue the party of the protector. Gamarra, the President of Peru, lent his aid to this project, expecting to obtain the province of La Paz as the reward of his coöperation; but when Ballivian had obtained power he ordered his ally to evacuate the territory. This did not please Gamarra, who occupied La Paz and took possession of Viacha in the autumn of 1841; but on November 18 of the same year his army of 5200 men was defeated on the plain of Ingavi by 3800 Bolivian soldiers commanded by Ballivian in person. Gamarra lost his life in that battle, and his men, pursued by the enemy's lancers, were almost all killed. Strengthened by his victory, Ballivian entered Peru in order to seize a part of it, taking

advantage of internal quarrels.   On June 7, 1842, peace was signed
in Pasco through the intervention and under the guarantee of Chili.
During this period Santa Cruz, who was meditating in Guayaquil
on the means of regaining power after all his attempts to revolutionize Peru in his favor had failed, ventured to return to Bolivia
in 1844, but was arrested in the Cordilleras and afterward handed
over to Chili.

Ballivian also fell in his turn and retired to Valparaíso. Velasco, who recovered power, did no more than appear and disappear.   At the end of 1848 the Minister of War, Belzu, put himself at the head of a movement whose object was to obtain the
presidency for himself or to aid Santa Cruz, who was exiled in
Europe.   The army pronounced in favor of Belzu.   This violent
and capricious dictator, supported by military demagogy, subjected
Bolivia to the caprices of his despotism.   During his administration, nevertheless, the irritating question of the boundaries between
Upper and Lower Peru was settled at last (1855) ; the port of
Arica was declared common to the two republics, and the waters
of Bolivia were opened to navigation under all flags.   General
Cordova succeeded Belzu in the presidency in 1855, disappeared
in 1858, after a revolt, and perished by a violent death three years
later in a rash enterprise.   Dr. Linares, who was raised to the
presidency by the Liberals, was a man of talent and struggled
against the military party; but fell, without tumult or effusion of
blood, in consequence of a palace revolution, excited by a few
generals, under the pretext that he had not convoked the Congress (January 14, 1861).   A Council of State, composed of Ruperto Fernandez, José María Acha, and Manuel Antonio Sanchez,
undertook the direction of affairs, put Linares on trial, exiled him,
decreed a general amnesty, and convoked an assembly to recon-
stitute the republic once more.   The fall of Linares excited some
movements in the provinces which were quenched in blood.   In
La Paz Colonel Yañez, enraged against the Spaniards and their
half-breeds with that mortal hatred of the pure Indian race to
which he belonged, had 100 persons shot at one time, among whom
were ex-President Cordova, another general, several colonels, and
three priests (October 23).   Two hundred Cholos or Indian half-
breeds were murdered in the streets.

In the meanwhile the usurpers could not agree upon the division of the presidential spoils, and disorder reached such a height

in this year (1861) that in Chili and Peru the partition of Bolivia
was openly discussed. At last, in May, 1862, the National Convention elected General Acha president. Ruperto Fernandez, who
was thus thrown aside, could not contain his resentment. The portfolio of the Interior and of Justice was not sufficient to satisfy his
ambition. By the help of Colonel Balza, whose regiment was in
garrison at Oruro, he resolved to acquire by force of arms the title
which had slipped through his hands. Balza made a *pronunciamiento* in favor of the pretender, marched on La Paz and raised
the mob, which rushed tumultuously against the palace. Yañez, the
author of the horrors of October 23, had taken refuge there, and,
when attacked on all sides, tried to escape by the roof, but a discharge of firearms killed him and his body was given up to the
populace and hacked to pieces. The president arrived with superior
forces and Fernandez had to abandon the field and take refuge in
Argentine territory. A new attempt arranged by some generals
in favor of Belzu, who had taken refuge on the frontiers of Peru,
failed no less miserably, and General Perez, who had been sent
against the rebels, proclaimed himself president in Chuquisaca, but
was defeated by Acha between Oruro and La Paz.

While these events were taking place Linares perished miserably in Valparaíso. In him Bolivia lost a man of good intentions,
who at least wished to deliver his country from militarism, the
plague of the South American states. About the same time the
president, Acha, obtained the ratification of his powers in an election which gave him a considerable majority. He brought into his
administration a spirit of conciliation and enlightened ideas, endeavoring to reëstablish friendly foreign relations, especially with
France, which had had no dealings with Bolivia for ten years on
account of the wrongdoing of Belzu. Santa Cruz was accredited
to Paris to renew diplomatic relations.[3] Early in 1861 the republic had a serious controversy with Chili over the territory of
Mejillones, both countries claiming its rich deposits of guano, and
the Congress, sitting at Oruzo, authorized the president to declare
war if pacific measures failed. The attitude of Bolivia in the
Hispano-Chilian conflict brought some concessions on the part of
Chili, and a treaty was signed on August 10, 1866.

[3] Santa Cruz had been successively appointed minister plenipotentiary to
London (1849), Paris, Rome, and Brussels. In 1851 he had negotiated a
concord with Pius IX. In 1854 he was again a candidate for the presidency
but was defeated by Cordova. He died at Saint-Nazaire in 1865.

In the meanwhile the presidency had changed hands. Acha, constantly attacked by the partisans of Belzu, had been wounded in an encounter where Belzu commanded in person (January, 1865). Some days later Lieutenant-Colonel Melgarejo excited his soldiers to rebellion in Cochabambu, installed himself in the Government House after a combat of twelve hours and took the title of provisional president, which Belzu wished to dispute with him. But Belzu was attacked by Melgarejo in La Paz and killed. The victor might very well consider himself master of the situation; he had already formed a ministry whose first acts were to proclaim a general and complete amnesty and reduce the duties on the exportation of the copper of Corocoro, a measure which would very much favor the export trade, when Colonel Casto Agueda succeeded in seizing La Paz by a bold stroke (May 25). An indecisive struggle followed. In July, 1865, Melgarejo had made himself master of the most important provinces, but La Paz and Cobija defied him until the sixth of the month, when the former fell into his hands. He was now sure of future victory, convoked the citizens in order to proceed to the regular election of a president, and was confirmed as head of the republic until February, 1869. Melgarejo had, by his energetic character, risen from the ranks to the position of general. He laid it down as his system of government to firmly maintain internal tranquillity, preserve the integrity of the territory, draw closer the relations of Bolivia with foreign powers, and give an impulse to industry and internal commerce by liberal legislation. He was more fortunate than his predecessors and maintained himself in power; but the country continued its deplorable habit of political disturbances. A constitution drawn up in August, 1868, was abolished in 1869, when the term of office of Melgarejo expired. Another constitution, the work of an assembly which met in Sucre, was promulgated November 22, 1871.

Colonel Agustin Morales, who was raised to the provisional presidency for a year on June 20, 1871, and promoted by Congress to be general of division, received extensive powers from the chambers. These he used to raise a loan for the construction of railways and to appoint a commission to provide means of communication for Bolivia. Morales promised besides to establish telegraphs and form centers of colonization, two things that Bolivia completely lacked. He had just been proclaimed constitutional president for four years by the legislature assembled at La Paz, when his death, in January, 1873, put an end to his projects. One railway, the only one that Bolivia possesses, was finished; the rest were abandoned for want of money. Frias, the president of the Congress, occupied the presidency of the republic for a short time. Ballivian also died just after he had been elected for the second time. He had found the country a prey to the rivalry of the generals who competed in arms for the dictatorship, and was replaced by Dr. Tomás Frias, February 14, 1874. He also had to fight against insurrectionary bands and to contend with extemporized governments. In January, 1875, he had to expel from La Paz a "Directory" which had set itself up there.

But we are impatient to leave these broils. The pen tires of writing about exploits whose heroes are the everlasting office-seekers, in which the vanquished to-day are sure to be the victors to-morrow. In this rapid succession of governments and parties, men and ideas, the national conscience has been obscured and seems to have entirely disappeared. He who controls the army wields the national power, and the nation counts for nothing. The caprice of the conqueror is the only law; there is no truth other than force, and no justice other than violence. We may say of a nation in this condition that its honor, peace, and fortune [4] are destroyed. Let the republic relegate the unruly generals to their quarters and call the civil element to the head of affairs. It alone can bring in an era of peace and industry, the two indispensable conditions of all regeneration and progress.

[4] The budget of 1873-1874 shows receipts of $2,929,574 and expenses of $4,505,504, a deficit of $1,575,930. Expenses are divided as follows: Interior, $597,458; foreign affairs, $153,940; finances (including the domestic debt), $2,-072,018; justice and education, $399,167; war, $1,126,916; extraordinary items, $155,019. Comment is needless. We may add that in June, 1873, the public debt (according to an official report) amounted to $16,428,329.

Chapter XIII

PERU. 1825-1876

ON December 9, 1826, the anniversary of the victory of
Ayacucho, an oath was taken throughout Peru to the
constitution which the Liberator had already caused to
be adopted by Bolivia. Thus the two peoples received the same
semi-monarchical charter, or in other words, were subjected to
the same yoke. A like fate would have been reserved for Colombia
if the situation had not developed too rapidly. For Lower Peru, as
well as Upper Peru, Bolívar's constitution was the cause of serious
difficulties. The Peruvians saw with uneasiness their country occupied by a numerous, turbulent, and somewhat undisciplined army,
whose commander seemed to act as if he were dealing with a conquered people. Bolívar had hardly departed when the explosion
took place. His hated soldiers were expelled in March, 1827. General Santa Cruz governed then as president of the Supreme Council;
a provisional Cabildo (a municipal magistracy suppressed by the
new constitution), declaring that the Bolivian frame of government
had been "imposed by violence against the will of the people,"
petitioned this Council to convoke "a Congress of the legal representatives of the nation to deliberate on what it might be most
proper to do under the circumstances." Elections were held, and in
the month of June the Congress thus elected abolished the constitution of Bolívar, appointing General La Mar president of the republic. Santa Cruz had insisted that his resignation be accepted.

The new government had not only to resist the sharp attacks
of the Bolívarists, but also to make head against the efforts of
Sucre, who, from Bolivia, endeavored to reëstablish the Colombian influence in Lima. The Peruvian government was soon master of the situation, and did not hesitate to go to the aid of the
Bolivians, who in their turn endeavored to shake off the yoke.
Bolívar published a manifesto in August, 1828, to which La Mar
energetically replied, casting all the blame, and especially that of
aggression, on "the sworn enemy of Peruvian independence." The

army of Peru committed the error of invading the Colombian territory and was almost entirely destroyed February 25, 1829, at Tarqui, in the province of Quito. The Liberator did not abuse his victory; he consented to a treaty highly honorable to the conquered, and left to them the free administration of their affairs.

La Mar paid dear for his defeat. His chief of staff, Agustin Gamarra, taking advantage of the discredit into which he had fallen

through so serious a reverse, came to an understanding with another officer, Lafuente, to oust him from power. The former seized the unfortunate president and put him aboard a ship in Piura, while in Lima the audacious Lafuente took away from Salazar y Baquijano the power that he exercised provisionally in the absence of the president, declared himself supreme head, and called an Assembly to appoint a successor to La Mar. The election disappointed the calculations of Lafuente, since it only conferred the vice-presidency on him and the chief authority fell (1830) into the hands of Gamarra.

This man was a reserved and astute Zambo, and owed his rapid rise to his wife, a beautiful and intrepid Amazon, who had guided him from the lowest to the most brilliant position. Drawing-room triumphs were not sufficient for Señora Gamarra. She was always on horseback among the soldiers, inspiring them by her endurance of fatigue on the march and by unflinching self-exposure to the greatest dangers of battle. She roused enthusiasm bordering on delirium when, in the reviews which she loved, she galloped over the field of maneuvers sword in hand, the feathers of her hat floating in the wind.

At the end of 1831 Gamarra made two proclamations, one to the country and the other to the army, congratulating them on the reëstablishment of friendly relations with Bolivia, and also on the wished-for termination of internal disturbances, which, as he said, had been succeeded by order and concord. But that order and concord were not to be very lasting. We will mention only one plot formed against the life of the president. Its chief author was a captain, who, on March 18, 1832, commanded his soldiers to fire upon Gamarra in Lima, but they refused to obey. The captain was executed, and the conspiracy went no farther, the year ending without any incident worthy of mention. The term of office of the president was about to expire; Gamarra assembled a Congress, on whose good will he reckoned to obtain the revision of the constitution and a continuation of his powers, but his hopes were not realized. He had been raised to power by a woman and was overthrown by women. The fair sex of Lima turned the electoral scales in favor of D. Luís Orbegoso, a young and restless gentleman, a descendant of one of the first families of the city, and belonging to the white race. Gamarra, indeed, did not present himself ostensibly as a candidate, but put forward General Bermudez in opposition to the *protégé* of the ladies and of the upper classes of society, behind whom he thought he would govern. Seeing that the power was slipping from his hands when he used legal means, he resolved to recover it by violence. In January, 1833, he carried through a military revolution which obliged the recently elected president to take refuge in Callao, while Bermudez received the investiture of supreme head in Lima. A short-lived triumph! The people rose, defeated the soldiers of Gamarra, and put them to flight. Orbegoso himself pursued them and gave battle near Jauja. He was repulsed and owed the victory which he at last won to the defection of Colonel Echenique, who commanded one of the chief corps of the insurgents.

But while the legal president was returning to Lima and Gamarra sought refuge in Bolivia, a third claimant appeared in the person of Lafuente, of whom we have already spoken. He had been condemned to exile, but had broken the terms of his sentence and hastened from Chili to seize the dictatorship. On January 1, 1835, the garrison of Callao rose at his call; but the troops commanded by General Salaberry arrived from Lima to fight him, ten insurgents were shot, and Lafuente escaped and reached Valparaíso once more. Salaberry, young, daring, rash and proud of his victory, instantly conceived the idea of profiting by it on his own account. Two months had scarcely elapsed when he marched on the capital at the head of 318 men. At his approach the Vice-President Salazar fled precipitately, followed by a few generals and about 100 soldiers. Orbegoso was then traveling through the provinces, and Salaberry took possession of Lima without striking a blow. He proclaimed himself supreme head and prepared to resist the attacks of the " ambulatory government." He seized all authority, and setting aside the constitution and the laws, wrung forced contributions from the capitalists and the principal inhabitants. His recruiting officers had orders to enroll all who fell into their hands, and everybody sought safety in flight or in hiding. All communication with the outside world was suspended and the roads were full of robbers, who even came into the city and discharged their firearms against the windows of the palace. Orbegoso had been able to hold the city of Arequipa, whence he implored the assistance of Bolivia. Santa Cruz crossed the frontier at the head of an army corps. The result has been told; we have related in the preceding chapter how a confederation was formed between Bolivia and Peru under the protectorate of Santa Cruz, as well as how it terminated with the battle of Jungay, which was won by the Chilian army January 20, 1839. In the previous year this same army, commanded by General Bulnes, had entered Lima and placed the authority in the hands of Gamarra, while Orbegoso, who had continued president of the northern Peruvian state, retired from the fortress of Callao, refusing to recognize that dictatorship imposed by the foreigner or to join it in order to fight Santa Cruz. The fall of the protector left Gamarra in tranquil possession of the presidency of Peru, and the republic enjoyed some degree of tranquillity until 1841.

At that date a revolution took place in Arequipa. A Colonel Vivanco had himself proclaimed under the title of regenerator, and the provinces of Cuzco and Punó and a part of the army supported him. Gamarra sent against him General Castilla, who defeated him and drove him into Bolivia, where at the moment regenerators abounded. Gamarra feared a counter attack from Santa Cruz and suddenly invaded Bolivia, intending to give the last blow to the partisans of the protector. We already know that he was killed a few leagues from La Paz, November 18, 1841. The Bolivians in their turn entered Peru, and after some negotiations a treaty was arranged and peace was signed, June 7, 1842, between the two countries, through the mediation and under the guarantee of Chili.

Now Lafuente appears again. He had been placed at the head of the army of the South, and San Roman, who commanded a division under him, separated from him and accused him of aspiring to the dictatorship. The two generals came to blows, and in this conflict Manuel Menendez, President of the Council of State, who carried on the government during the vacancy in the presidency, declared Lafuente a rebel and a traitor to the country, collected the forces which were scattered over the country and which had remained faithful, and put General Torrico at their head. The first act of Juan Crisóstomo Torrico was to depose Menendez and proclaim himself dictator by a decree dated at Lima on August 16, 1842, beginning in this style: " I decree: Article I. I take upon myself the executive authority of the republic until the civil war, excited by General Antonio Gutierrez de Lafuente, shall be ended, and the national representatives convoked." . . .

Another pretender got the start of him, nevertheless. Very soon the news arrived in Lima that, on July 29, General Vidal had proclaimed himself supreme head in Cuzco by a decree no less alluring than that of his competitor, and that he had been supported in Arequipa by Vivanco, whom we see reappear in command of this province with the rank of general. Vidal, to be sure, was not acting on his own account; the restless Lafuente was concealed behind him, keeping up appearances of legality and of attaining to power only by means of an election which he expected to control at pleasure. Under these circumstances Orbegoso, who had taken refuge in

Ecuador, sent a certain Colonel Hercelles to revolutionize the province of Paita, but Hercelles entered into communication with Colonel Arrieta, who was sent against him, and the attempt failed. Then it was that Vidal and Torrico met in Agua Santa; the latter had to beat a retreat, and the former, after defeating him, made his entry into Lima.

The saying that the Tarpeian Rock is close to the Capitol is the sober truth about Peru and its presidents during this strange period. Vivanco has not renounced his old ambition; he had never submitted to Vidal, and he accepted the command of the province of Arequipa from Lafuente only to play a secret game and to remain near his partisans. Vivanco, like Gamarra, had an ambitious and resolute wife. One night, while all the city was sleeping, Doña Cipriana Latorre de Vivanco mounted a horse and with no weapons but youth and beauty, rode hurriedly to the quarters of two regiments encamped a few leagues from Arequipa. Their colonels were fascinated by her beauty and daring and by her ardent words and extraordinary action. They fell at her feet, declared themselves ready to follow her, and swore to die for her. The assembly is sounded; the soldiers rush together, surround her, and acclaim her. Firm and upright in the stirrups, she addresses them by the light of torches; hurrahs drown her voice; oaths of fidelity and shouts of enthusiasm fill the air. She starts her horse, the detachment moves forward and will follow the enchantress to the world's end. The authorities in Arequipa, who were peacefully sleeping, were seized in their beds and guarded by sentinels, and then, amid the loud ringing of bells, the irresistible lady had Vivanco proclaimed by the troops and the notables of the city assembled in the great square. Vivanco, who was at Cuzco, received the news of his romantic proclamation by a messenger. He took the title of supreme director and set out for Lima. Vidal decided to yield, and left his post quietly. Peru had registered one more revolution in her annals.

Ardent Lima received the president who had fallen to it by such an extraordinary adventure with joyous feasting and noisy demonstrations. Chimes, the blare of trumpets, and salvos of artillery saluted the husband of Doña Cipriana, an elegant young man of distinguished manners, who personified the civilization of his country in its most agreeable qualities. Bullfights, gay cavalcades and processions reappeared in the city of the sun and of

flowers, and poets took up their pipes to celebrate the event. Doña
Cipriana turned the heads of all the men, and the women and the
mob were in love with the brilliant Vivanco. Under these circumstances the supreme director thought he could seize the dictatorship
with impunity, and in consequence he put off for a year the meeting
of Congress, disbanded the numerous and useless staff of the army,
dismissed dishonest officials, and publicly reproved a venal and corrupt magistracy. Useful reforms were in the way of being carried
out when a conspiracy, whose chief instigator was the inevitable
Lafuente, forced the adoption of violent and reactionary measures.
Some honored and influential party leaders were exiled, among them
Castilla, Minister of War in the time of Gamarra, and his chief of
staff at Yngavi. Castilla hastened to the south, raising it in the
name of constitutional principles, and marched on the capital. Lima,
which idolized the magnificent Vivanco and the seductive Cipriana
more than ever, armed itself for resistance in the midst of the wildest manifestations. All the citizens enlisted. Castilla halted and
awaited reinforcements. Vivanco sent off a division which allowed
itself to be surprised; he himself took the field, and several months
passed, during which the two armies sought each other without
meeting, and the crisis threatened to become chronic when an un-
foreseen event gave it a new turn. Everything is unexpected in
those countries born only yesterday into the world of politics. The
prefect of Lima at this time was D. Domingo Elias, a man of influence by his social position and his wealth. He quietly laid his hand
on the power while Vivanco and Castilla played at hide and seek in
the plains and the mountains of the south. One fine morning (June
17, 1844) he marched to the palace, escorted by some thirty soldiers,
and by a *pronunciamiento* declared himself president of the republic.
The drums beat in his honor and the revolution was over.

This *coup d'état,* carried through almost without attracting the
attention of Lima, resulted in the return of Castilla to power after
a year of civil strife. Don Ramon Castilla, a native of Javacapa, on
the frontiers of Bolivia, was at that time forty-eight years old. He
was a captain in the Spanish army when the War of Independence
broke out, but embraced the cause of the patriots and fought at
Ayacucho. About 1830 he entered politics and was always openly
in favor of the power that offered the best conditions of stability.
He long remained faithful to Orbegoso, who had appointed him
general of brigade; then he joined Salaberry when the latter put

Peru into the hands of Santa Cruz, and, after taking part in the unfortunate combats of Yanacocha and Socoboya, he took refuge in Chili (1835). When this country took up arms against Santa Cruz Castilla took the command of the cavalry and was present at the battle of Jungay. He was forced to go into exile a second time after the defeat and death of Gamarra, and attempted to rally all the opponents of the usurper round the constitution, which was openly despised. With the aid of Generals Nioto and Yguain, he defeated Vivanco near Arequipa and entered Lima, where, in order to keep up the appearance of legality, Menendez, provisional president by right, after the death of Gamarra, again took the conduct of business while awaiting the elections. As might be expected, they resulted in calling the victorious Castilla to power (August 19, 1845).

Under his administration Peru was peaceful; order was reëstablished in the public finances; the standing army was reduced, its organization modified, and impressment replaced by conscription. There was some increase in the navy, and the construction of steam vessels gave excellent results. The establishment of the cannon foundry of Bellavista dates from this period. The different branches of national industry and commerce engaged the attention of the government, which, by the exploitation of the guano deposits, opened hitherto unknown sources of general prosperity; and finally the first railway was opened between the capital and Callao.

On March 20, 1851, Castilla gave an account of the condition of the republic to Congress and resigned his authority to D. José Rufino Echenique, who had been elected to succeed him. This was the first time that the supreme power had changed hands without disturbance or revolution. General Echenique pronounced in favor of a reduction of customs duties and invited European emigrants. He had to oppose an insurrection which was attempted by the ex-dictator Vivanco and General San Roman, but public opinion was against him when he favored the enlistments that Flores, the ex-president of Ecuador, made in Peru, and for this reason had to dismiss the ministry. In 1852 a controversy arose between the United States and Peru respecting the possession of the Lobos Islands, which are very rich in guano; this was terminated through the mediation of France and England, who decided against the claims of the government at Washington.

In the meanwhile the policy of the new president appeared to threaten the country with a counter revolution. Castilla issued a new call to arms, and marched against Echenique at the head of a numerous party, and the latter, deserted by the troops, had scarcely time to return to Lima and put himself under the protection of the English flag (January 5, 1855). At the same time his rival was proclaimed by the mob. The elections of 1858 restored Castilla, called the "Grand Marshal," to the presidency of the republic. A conflict soon arose between him and the Congress elected to revise the constitution. He dissolved it under the pretext that it wasted its time and went beyond its rights in fixing the time for its reassembling. The fact is that the Congress had intended to depose him because he showed sinister and despotic instincts in his government, both in domestic and foreign affairs. New elections were held on December 10, 1859, and Castilla met the new Assembly with the firm intention of taking advice only from his own will. His well-known projects of conquest and annexation had gained him a popularity that he hoped to make use of if necessary. About this time Castilla attempted to dismember the republic of Ecuador and to annex that of Bolivia, taking advantage of the dissensions that he had himself helped to create in those two countries. The appearance in March, 1860, of a French vessel in the bay of Callao to demand reparation and satisfaction for injuries to French subjects overthrew his hopes, and lessened his military prestige. He could only make empty threats and for consolation vainly protest against the annexation of San Domingo by Spain.

At last, on November 10, 1860, the constitution was proclaimed which modified the compact of 1858. It distributed the powers of the state among three separate and independent bodies: the executive, the legislative (a senate of 44 members and a house of 110 representatives), and the judicial. The presidential term remained fixed at four years. A few weeks before the grand marshal had been fired upon and wounded in the arm. This attempt, in which 150 men of a single regiment had been associated, led to certain rigorous measures affecting Echnique, Rivas, and some other prominent persons.

When the deplorable intervention of the French in Mexico took place, which the minister Rouher insolently called "the finest thought of the reign," and which was one of the most shameful deeds of the imperial *régime* in France, Castilla launched a violent

manifesto against the government that set out to destroy a republic
in the New World, and offered assistance in arms and money to
Juarez. It is said that Frenchmen residing in Peru were insulted
at the instigation of the president.

Castilla transmitted the supreme authority to General Miguel
San Roman, who was elected in June, 1862. The electoral campaign had been very lively and resulted in the victory of the government candidate and the defeat of the Opposition represented by
Echnique, whom the courts had set at liberty, General La Mar,
and Lopez Lavalle. Castilla, who had been suspected of the intention of retaining power for himself indefinitely, quietly retired into
private life. About this time died Manuel La Mar, leader of the
Opposition. San Roman, who was then about sixty years old, and
an honorable man of good intentions, took the presidency without
any cloud on the title, and found the country peaceful and entering fully on the path of economical and material prosperity. Under
his leadership the Congress set apart $2,000,000 for public works
and made a law to promote the immigration of Asiatics. His
predecessor had, nevertheless, left the republic involved in a certain
number of international controversies, partly due to his dominating and quarrelsome character. Relations with France and
England had become strained, and Peru was on the point of
breaking with the republic of Bolivia, and also with Ecuador, whose
president was considered a traitor to America because of his ideas
in favor of a European protectorate. San Roman, fearing some
domestic attack, exaggerated the danger, which he believed imminent, and on January 2, 1863, asked Congress to invest him with
extraordinary powers. This meant the dictatorship, and Congress
would not accede to his demands. San Roman gave way and made
every effort to appease and conciliate and to unite all minds in
behalf of the public good. His programme, contained in his message of February 3, promised an economical and effective administration, but he died on April 3 after a long illness, leaving such
remembrances of his probity that Congress voted his family a gift
of $100,000.

General Juan Antonio Pezet, the first vice-president elected
under the constitution, was at that time traveling in Europe. General Canseco, the second vice-president, undertook the government
until his return, and Castilla the command of the army. The
policy of the government was not changed. Pezet reached Lima

at the beginning of August, and from the first moment appeared very
zealous for material interests, showing in his addresses that he earnestly desired peace both at home and abroad.　He had lived a long
time in France, and there had made himself acquainted with the
progress of public administration.　He undertook to make the government of his country benefit by his information.　The difficulties
with Ecuador, Bolivia, and the United States had been smoothed
over; and a more serious dispute with Brazil with respect to the
Brazilian navigation of the River Amazon had been peacefully settled, when another question arose in which France intervened.　It
was a question of putting a stop to a poorly disguised slave trade, or
to speak plainly, of protecting certain unhappy Polynesians who
were captured by trickery and treated with revolting cruelty.　Once
more a peaceful agreement was obtained.　In this affair also a
good understanding was reached, and the government of Peru, to
its honor, cleansed itself from all complicity in this shameful
traffic.

Another cause of difficulty with France was the unfortunate
war with Mexico, which, coinciding with the recovery of San
Domingo by Spain, was looked upon as a threat against the independence of the New World.　Public excitement reached an extreme
point and showed itself by manifestations hostile to European action
and in subscriptions in aid of the wounded Mexican patriots.　Pezet
abstained from any act of interference or provocation, but did not
remain indifferent to this attempt at repression.　He then took the
first step in a proposition to unite all the American republics in a
congress, by which a defensive alliance might be formed against
every enterprise that menaced their liberty.　The proposition of
a peace congress was made when the greater number of the nations who should meet in it were at war among themselves.　Peru
itself was about to be involved in serious complications on account
of the sudden occupation of the Chincha Islands by the Spanish
squadron, and, as a consequence, this idea had no better success in
South America than it has met with in Europe whenever some generous men have tried to bring it forward without being able to get
a hearing.　Nevertheless, it is worthy of note that the rulers of
Peru at this time made every effort to establish a good understanding with the neighboring states as well as with those of
Europe, to calm men's minds at home and to direct the efforts of
the country toward agricultural and industrial production.

From this period dates the establishment of a school of arts and trades in Lima, of a breakwater and jetty at Callao, and various concessions for railways planned to place the ports of the Pacific in connection with the mines and the regions still unexplored of the interior. At this time guano became one of the chief resources of the treasury, causing a remarkable increase in the proceeds of the customs duties. Nevertheless the public finances continued in a bad state owing to the increase it was necessary to make in the military forces, which circumstances rendered more and more necessary. The law of February 14, 1853, had established the decimal system, and in consequence the country was free from a great handicap in monetary affairs.

Such was the position of Peru when the sudden and violent seizure of the Chincha Islands by the Spanish Pacific squadron, April 14, 1864, involved it again in complications. That act of unqualified robbery, carried out by the " Extraordinary Special Commissary of Her Catholic Majesty," D. Eusebio Salazar y Mazarredo, with the assistance of Admiral Pinzon, was so much the more serious as Spain had always refused to recognize the independence of Peru. The very title of " commissary," conferred on the agent of the queen, appeared to signify that Peru was still a Spanish colony, and the seizing a part of its territory took the character of a claim upon the whole. The position of the Minister of Foreign Affairs, Ribeyro, was firm and dignified. " The declaration which you have been pleased to send me," he wrote to Admiral Pinzon, " will be deposited in the archives of this ministry as a testimony of the insult offered to the republic, as a document destined to stimulate in the government and in the heart of every Peruvian who shall read it the sentiments of national pride which have been so impudently wounded. It would be unworthy of the government of Peru to discuss the assertions made in the said document as long as he who wrote it holds possession of a part of the national territory.

" Whatever your conduct may be now or in future, you may be assured that the Spaniards residing in Peru will continue to enjoy the most complete security in their persons as long as they continue attending to their affairs peaceably and honorably.

" Peru has progressed too far in civilization since she declared herself independent of the mother country to need to take hostages from her as security. It is you who have revived in modern warfare the customs of the barbarous ages, unworthy of the high officer of a nation that boasts of being civilized."

The *Mercurio,* a journal published in Lima, thus expressed the public opinion of Peru: " The government and people of Peru burn to avenge the insult committed against the nation. Never has such enthusiasm been seen in all classes of society. The various ministries, learned bodies, colleges, societies, and business organizations have offered life and property to the government for the defense of the country. The municipalities and the representatives of judicial power have protested against the crime committed by the Spanish flotilla. The clergy also have given remarkable proofs of patriotism upon this solemn occasion, and the head of the Peruvian Church, the Archbishop of Lima, with his chapter, have condemned that unjust occupation, offering their physical and moral coöperation with the greatest self-denial, not excepting any kind of sacrifice, until Peru should obtain complete satisfaction. The rectors of various parishes in Lima and the neighboring towns have shown no less patriotism and indignation."

The government of the republic had from the first moment taken all necessary means for the defense of Peru and for the assertion of its rights. Congress authorized the president to borrow $50,000,000 in order to increase the army by 20,000 men and the fleet by twenty vessels of war. In England and France the press was unanimous in censuring such an abuse of strength committed by a European nation. The whole of America was indignant on learning the fact, and especially Chili, in which republic the mob made several manifestations hostile to Spain. Before such a strong expression of public opinion the Spanish government no doubt hesitated; and the fact that Pinzon was replaced by Pareja in the command of the squadron of occupation, together with the moderation from which the government of Peru never departed in these difficult circumstances, led to a solution of that extraordinary conflict without effusion of blood, and the preliminaries of peace were signed January 28, 1865, on board the frigate *Villa de Madrid,* which was anchored in the roads of Callao.

Nevertheless the president was accused of weakness on all sides. A riot occurred on May 25 at the gates of his palace, and by the advice of Castilla squadrons of cavalry dispersed the mob, which was howling for war; but the grand marshal himself was not long in joining the party which desired an armed conflict. He was elected president of the Senate July 26, and his warlike ardor was displayed with all its force. He questioned Pezet with great energy, demanded that the government take the initiative in forming an offensive league of the American states against Spain, and begin hostilities at once. Under these conditions the chamber of deputies, making use of a subterfuge which was certainly undignified, hastened to suspend its sittings in order not to have to approve the treaty of January 28, which General Vivanco, who had charge of the negotiations, had just brought to Lima. The president signed the provisional treaty, as was prescribed by the constitution, subject to ratification at the next session. Unfortunately, that document, which had to be signed in view of the scanty means of defense that Peru relied on, became a weapon in the hands of the enemies of the government. On the 29th cries of death were uttered against the Spaniards, and on February 5 some sailors from the Spanish squadron were attacked in Callao and one of them was killed. The president arrived with the cavalry; in Lima the mob thronged the streets, crying " Death to the Spaniards! " and while the troops were repressing the tumult and blood was flowing in the streets, Castilla censured the president in violent terms for signing the treaty with Spain. Castilla was arrested in open session and carried on board a war brig sailing for Pará. There was no less excitement in the provinces; Colonel Prado, the governor of Arequipa, proclaimed himself dictator and established his government in Arica. Punó, Cuzco, and the populous intermediate provinces also organized themselves in rebellion, and the second vice-president, Canseco, escaped from the capital to go and join the insurgents. On May 7 the troops of the president recovered Arica. In Lima an attempted revolt of the municipal guard which was on duty at the palace on the night of May 10 and 11 was repressed; but on that of June 23 and 24 the marines, obeying some of the subaltern officers, rose in revolt in the port of Arica, murdered Rear-Admiral Janizo, part of his staff, and the sub-prefect.

President Pezet, remaining faithful to his policy, received the minister plenipotentiary of Spain on August 5. A month later Prado had notified all the diplomatic representatives in Lima except the Spanish minister, of General Canseco's accession to power. These events coincided with the blockade of the Chilian ports by the Spanish squadron. The firmness with which the Valparaíso government accepted the struggle made the weakness with which Pezet had been so much reproached appear more clearly, and he was even accused of selling himself to Spain. The populace became enthusiastic at the idea of aiding Chili in a conflict born of the sympathy she had shown to Peru. The army of revolt marched on the capital, led by the same idea, and Pezet went out to meet it with 10,000 well-equipped men and sixty guns; but when, on November 6, he arrived in sight of the enemy, his generals refused to obey him, and Canseco entered Lima without difficulty. Pezet, nevertheless, fought on with a handful of men, commanded by Colonel Gonzalez, disputing the streets foot by foot, shut himself up in the palace, and there stood a siege of six hours against more than 12,000 men, with whom the populace of the slums had joined. Prado saved that brave officer from the fury of the insurgents by claiming him as his personal prisoner; but the palace was taken. Pezet fled to Callao, where he took refuge on board an English corvette. On the 7th of the same month the revolution had triumphed everywhere, and Canseco, without claiming any other authority than that of second president, which legally belonged to him, formed his ministry. A decree of the 13th impeached the fallen president, the ministers and public officials, denouncing them all as thieves and assassins. When Pezet was demanded for extradition, the English minister replied that he was on the way to Panama.

Canseco had no intention of breaking off relations with Spain, and thus it was that he entered into secret negotiations with the representative of that nation, calculating that the popular excitement would soon subside. He did not wish to act outside the constitution and the law, nor to exercise any greater power than that which universal suffrage had conferred on him, which shows how much political habits were tending to change. This is far from saying that the era of violent dictatorships had terminated forever. Canseco, the man of legitimate measures, very soon learned that he did not suit the interests of the military chiefs, always greedy, in Peru as elsewhere, of immoderate rewards and of employments such as only an absolute ruler could offer them. On November 25 they deposed Canseco and conferred the dictatorship on Colonel Prado. The populace was called together on the next day in the great square, and there some hundreds of persons acclaimed the colonel, who deemed this a sufficient ratification of his appointment and accepted " the burden of power." The edict relating to his accession, published on the 28th with great pomp and a parade under arms of all the troops, set forth that he only accepted the dictatorship, " indispensable for the salvation of the country," according to the formula always used in similar cases, because Canseco had refused to exercise it.   Canseco protested in vain that he only yielded to force; the military bands, salvos of artillery, and the peals of bells drowned his voice.   Amid all this uproar a reactionary movement which broke out in Ica, a town of 12,000 inhabitants 62 miles distant from the capital, passed unnoticed.

The new government declared that it would be frankly revolutionary: a strange abuse of words, since there was no pretense of consulting the will of the people.   A tribunal was created to try without appeal those who had negotiated, signed or executed treaties or conventions contrary to the national honor.   The Spanish question, which had hurled Pezet and Canseco from power, continued to be the great difficulty of the situation.   Nor did Prado appear desirous of risking a rupture, although, on the other hand, he feared the unpopularity which had made his predecessors succumb.   He knew that the revolution which had raised him to power had sprung chiefly from the desire of resisting the demands of Spain, and eighteen days had passed since the deed of November 25 without the diplomatic body receiving the usual notification; but all hesitation disappeared on receipt of the news of the capture of a Spanish ship by a Chilian corvette and the suicide of Admiral Pareja.   On December 13 the Minister of Foreign Affairs addressed the expected circular to all the members of the diplomatic body except the Spanish minister.   This was equivalent to considering the treaty of January 28 as void, and the Spanish representative embarked on December 21 with all the members of the legation.   At the end of the same month Peru made a treaty of alliance, offensive and defensive, with Chili, to which shortly afterward Bolivia and Ecuador adhered, and war was declared against Spain, January 14, 1866.   On March 21 the bombardment of Valparaíso took place.   On May 2 eleven Spanish ships in order of battle opened fire on the batteries of Callao.   The attack was fruitless, and on the 10th the badly damaged squadron was forced to leave the harbor, after losing some 300 men.   It is true that the Peruvians counted about 1000 slain, and among them the Minister of War, José Galvez; but it was nevertheless a success for the republican arms, and was celebrated with transports of patriotic pride.   The defenders of Callao made a triumphal entry into Lima; they all received promotion, and the construction of a fountain was decreed in commemoration of the victory.

When the Spanish war was ended the government met with difficulties at home, which arose from the modifications it had introduced into the fiscal and administrative system. Canseco, who had been expelled from the presidency, reckoned on the popularity of the old marshal, Castilla, his brother-in-law, for reinstatement. A decree regulating the manner of ringing the church bells and the manner of carrying the sacraments in public excited the clergy, produced a certain emotion among the women, and caused a sort of riot. Religious fanaticism augmented the number of those who, tired of the dictatorship, demanded a return to the regular processes of the constitution. The presence of Castilla gave a chief to the malcontents, and at the same time that a mutiny in the squadron, at that time anchored at Valparaíso, was put down, another conspiracy was organized in the provinces, at the head of which was Colonel Baltá, late head of the Cabinet. The dictator decided at last to order an election for deputies to the Congress which was to draw up a new constitution and for president. The voting, which was terminated at the end of 1866, gave the majority to Colonel Prado. Congress was opened February 15, 1867; it refused to sanction the new personal tax, passed a vote of censure on the acts of the dictator, and forbade the president to commence or continue any negotiation with Spain without the previous authorization of the Chamber. The Cabinet resigned in a body. While this was going on the Indians were devastating the South and Castilla landed a force and declared himself against Prado. Arequipa rose at his call, and Canseco claimed power in a violent manifesto.

The sudden death of Castilla (May 30) exposed to fatigues that he was unable to bear at his age, gave a respite to the president. The old marshal was the most popular leader in Peru, and his death was generally mourned. The fall of the Mexican Empire was another diversion, and was received with enthusiasm; a medal of honor was offered to Juarez, and Prado approved the vote of the Chambers which expelled from the schools the lay brothers who came from France, and the French Sisters of Charity from the hospitals. After much hesitation Congress definitely confirmed the election of the president, and adopted a new constitution (August 31, 1867) which fixed the presidential term at five years. The

Catholic religion was the only one recognized by the state, and the public exercise of any other form of worship was prohibited.

The position of the executive power continued to be very critical; the treasury was exhausted, distress was general, and discontent was more evident every day. In September Arequipa rose once more' for Canseco. The first riot was suppressed after a struggle in which even the women took part; but the garrison soon made common cause with the populace, and recognized Canseco as legal president of the republic. The garrison of Trujillo rose in October and killed the prefect; the north was disturbed by the insurrection which Colónel Baltá organized; and President Prado, leaving the government provisionally with General La Fuerta, marched gainst Arequipa. In his absence the crisis became acute in Lima, and the representatives of foreign powers had to organize their subjects as militia to maintain order. The same thing happened at Callao. On December 27 Prado, after conciliatory measures failed, assaulted Arequipa. The fight, which was sanguinary on both sides, lasted more than six hours, when the presidential troops fled. Prado, who succeeded with difficulty in rallying 800 men, returned to Callao on board two ships of his squadron. In the north also the insurrection was successful, and the president, crushed by these reverses, opposed by a hostile Congress, in effect driven out of Lima, was forced to resign. His fall was not long delayed.

The constitution of 1860 was restored; Baltá was elected president for four years and took the oath on May 1, 1868. A firm, although a hot-tempered man, he displayed great activity in the development of public works; vigorously pushed on the construction of means of communication, and conceived the idea of financing railway construction by pledging the guano deposits. The waters of the interior were opened to ships of all classes and all countries, and an interesting industrial exhibition was held in Lima in July, 1869. Under his administration Peru remained tranquil; but unfortunately the country suffered from several inundations and earthquakes, and a terrible epidemic of yellow fever. The discovery of the gold mines of Huacho, in October, 1871, caused great excitement. The end of the president's term of office coincided with the election of a new Congress; the electoral contest, therefore, was very keen, and the squadron was disarmed as a measure of precaution. Arequipa, which at that period was the alarm bell of revolutions, caused some uneasiness, and the candidates there discussed their claims with arms in hand. The government openly supported Echenique; Manuel Pardo had the sympathy of the populace; and Ureta also had many partisans. Baltá made an appeal to the electors, and requested them, in consideration of the violence of the contest, to give their votes in favor of Dr. Antonio Arenas. Echenique retired, and agreed to support the new candidate; but Pardo and Ureta persisted in their design, and the former, a sincere Democrat, gained a considerable majority. Baltá, following bad advice, declared at first that he would not give up his post, but afterward, seeing that he could not resist the current of public opinion, he announced that he was ready to retire on August 2, the day on which his term expired. The man who had most strongly endeavored to induce him to make a *coup d'état* was Colonel Tomás Gutierrez, Minister of War, who, seeing that Baltá, respecting legality, consented to relinquish power, now decided to violate the constitution on his own account. On July 22, 1872, he arrested the president, pronounced the dissolution of the Congress, which immediately declared him an outlaw, and proclaimed himself Supreme Head. Baltá attempted to escape and was assassinated in prison by Colonel Marcelino Gutierrez, brother of the usurper. On receiving news of this crime Lima rose in arms, and on the 26th of the month the lawful authorities were reinstated after a short struggle. The mob killed the brothers of Gutierrez, and he himself was killed while attempting to escape in disguise and his body was hanged on a lamp-post. A splendid funeral was made for Baltá; the vice-president, Ceballos, took the direction of affairs, and on August 2 Manuel Pardo was proclaimed by Congress.

The civil element triumphed in the person of the new head of the state. His message indicated this in the plainest terms, and public opinion emphasized and applauded his words. He declared that the municipal and electoral organization, " those two corner-stones of the constitutional edifice," and similar questions imperatively demanded the support and protection of the legislators; reform of the army should follow and the horrible crime of impressment should be ended by a just conscription law. The previous administration maintained a considerable number of officers and functionaries who lived at the expense of the Treasury. Pardo, a man of clear intelligence and resolute character, thought it his duty to suppress those parasites and at the same time oppose certain finan-

ciers who took advantage of the necessities of the government to
fleece and ruin it.   This roused much enmity, but also attracted
many supporters.   On August 21, 1874, a captain of artillery, who
had been been retired on half-pay, attempted to assassinate the
president; but nevertheless he persisted in his loyal and patriotic
enterprise.

Pardo had found the national finances pitifully overburdened
with debt; Baltá had made haste too quickly and had been carried
away beyond prudence by the railway fever, which turned all
heads.   To meet pressing needs it had been necessary to resort to
measures which were sure to produce a permanent annual deficit;
loans had been multiplied; the pledging of the guano deposits as
security for the foreign debt left the treasury only the internal
revenue, which was notoriously insufficient to meet the expenses of
the state.   As a consequence of all this the work on the railways was
threatened with paralysis, and a strike of 20,000 workmen was
feared.   The emission of a new loan of $184,000,000 overcame
the difficulty.   The needs of the administration were provided for
by increased receipts under a new tariff and by the profits of the
monopoly of saltpeter.   Municipal expenses were charged upon the
communes, which were granted the right of electing their own
municipal governments.   The double task to which the government
bent all its energies was to insure peace at home and to reëstablish
its credit abroad.   Negotiations were set on foot with China and
Japan in order to guarantee the good treatment of the coolies employed in agriculture and other work.   China, which boasted of not
having known slavery except in the most remote period of her history, was, nevertheless, in some sort the successor of the great
slave market of Africa, and the exportation of the coolies, as it was
practiced in certain ports, almost equalled the horrors of the slave
trade.   The enrollment of these unfortunate men was not much more
free than was the catching of the negroes of the Congo.   By
force or fraud they are made to contract to work for eight years
at least in the plantations oversea for an initial wage of four dollars, and emancipated slaves would nowhere be content with the
highest wages ever paid to the coolies.   The managers of this
traffic are called in China " pig-dealers," and the cruelty with which
the Asiatic laborers were treated in Peru, Cuba, and other places
perfectly justifies the insulting name.[1]   Peru, like all the neighboring republics, should make a constant appeal to immigration.   Pardo

[1] L'Economiste français, November, 1875.

understood this, and attracted many Chinese colonists to Peru. They are laborious, economical, intelligent, docile, peaceful, steady, and fit for any kind of work in the hottest climates. Many thousands of laborers from the Celestial Empire were employed in the construction of railways and the working of estates.

From what has been said it will be understood that Peru, since its independence, has been the theater of many adventures and disasters. It, more than any other country, has produced military chiefs, plumed heroes who appear for a moment on the stage, shoot their adversaries and are shot in their turn; a masquerade, sometimes grotesque and at others sinister, where all the types of the Spanish repertory meet, and where the chief part is played by nose-slitting bullies and swashbuckling captains. Confusion, treachery, intrigue, sword thrusts—nothing is wanting in this history of half a century, not even the disguised gentleman and the veiled lady of the old comedies.

But how can we doubt of the future of this magnificent country which is bathed on the west throughout its whole extent of 1400 miles by the Pacific Ocean? Bounded on the north by Ecuador, on the east by Brazil, and on the east and south by Bolivia, Peru has, according to the latest official data, a territory of about 700,000 square miles admirably fitted for agricultural production, the raising of stock, and for navigation, without reckoning the inexhaustible mineral riches hidden in the soil. When this country, so celebrated for the memory of the civilization of the incas, is spoken of, our thoughts dwell first upon those magical mines whose subterranean galleries hide the richest treasures of the world. These mines, which for three centuries loaded the adventurers who arrived from Spain with gold, are far from being exhausted; but the Peruvians at the present time neglect mining to employ themselves in more productive and less fatiguing labors. Nevertheless, very considerable quantities of silver are still extracted from the Cerro de Parso. The progress of industry, the new scientific processes, the perfection to which the methods of exploitation have been carried, will multiply a hundredfold the already fabulous results obtained in the past with less perfect agencies. And as if nature had desired to heap up riches on Peru she has placed the auriferous and argentiferous deposits in the sterile lands and in the arid tracts of sand unfit for cultivation, where the hand of man is powerless to make them productive. The beds of the rivers, the depths of the rocks hide gold in enormous quantities; the flanks of

the Andes are rich in silver and yield nuggets of the pure metal of
the largest size. The highest valleys abound in mercury, and the
average production of the celebrated mines of Huancavelica, in the
department of Ayacucho, was, during the colonial period, more than
550,000 pounds a year. We might also mention many inexhaustible deposits of copper, tin, lead, iron, sulphur, asphalt, and nickel.
Saltpeter, under the influence of certain atmospheric causes, is reproduced as fast as it is collected. Salt abounds in the neighborhood of the sea, at the bottom of some lakes and of certain rivers.
To these many and various products must be added stone for building and sculpture, brick and porcelain clays, borax, asbestos, etc.

However brilliant this picture may appear, we must rank it
lower than that which the vegetable kingdom offers. Wheat, rice,
coffee, and sugar-cane flourish in the temperate regions of the mountains; excellent wines are produced in Moquegua, Pisco, and the
province of Arequipa, and cacao grows abundantly on the plains of
the interior. Cotton produces as many as three crops a year, and
flax and hemp yield their seeds for medicine and their fibers for industry. Tobacco of superior quality, as well as the nutmeg, ginger,
pepper, and allspice, abounds in all the mountainous districts. The
forests produce valuable woods for shipbuilding, cabinet-work, and
dyeing, and a multitude of plants of pharmaceutical value, such
as coca, which has become indispensable to the laborers of the Andes,
but whose virtues have been rather exaggerated in Europe.

But what has enriched Peru much more than its once boasted
gold mines is guano, that valuable manure which the sea-birds
deposit on the islands near the coast, whose exploitation has been
monopolized by that state since 1842. The Peruvian guano owes
its superiority over other guanos to the peculiarity that there are
no rains on the coast, and thus the ammoniacal salts, which constitute the principal virtue of this manure, are not washed out.

Lima, the principal seat of the Spanish colonial power, the
abode of luxury whence the royal octopus continually drew the
wealth of a whole world, still preserves something of the coquetry,
the lightness of manners, and the satirical spirit of the viceregal
courts. Spain has left her traces in this land of mildness, refinement, elegance, and frivolity. The foreigner is impressed with the
strange contrast of sensual ardor and religious fanaticism, of extravagance and devotion, of indifference and passion.[2] In Lima
the people are generally gallant and witty, and in the opinion of the
women devotion is but another word for love. They are much

[3] Radiguet. "*Souvenirs de l'Amerique Espagnole.*"

adored and delight in it. Their attractions are irresistible when they are dressed in the fashion of the country. They are always seen alone in the streets, shod with blue satin, dressed in the *saya* or clinging skirt. The first man who meets them may address them, sometimes even they make the advance, and with the veil thrown over the face and covering it completely save a narrow opening for one eye, they take delight in inflaming the curiosity of the passer-by. Lima, "the paradise of women," is the place devoted to amorous intrigues, equivocal adventures, and toothsome scandals. Its squares, surrounded by public monuments, fine houses and arcades, and refreshed by fountains; its wide streets, through the middle of which runs a deep and clear rivulet; and its vast promenades have, in broad daylight, the keen attraction and charming mystery of a masquerade. It seems like a Spanish city of the seventeenth century, rejuvenated and modernized by some ingenious decorator who has been careful to multiply the gaslights and to fill the shops with the most delicate and dazzling productions of Parisian industry; or like an opera scene enlivened by conventional figures, and not a capital harassed by a long and unbroken anarchy.

Nevertheless, Lima is something more than a luxurious and worldly capital. If the city of the viceroys has preserved the impress of its former lords, as Cuzco, the ancient city of the incas, preserves its Indian character and also its Indian population, it is none the less a center of labor and instruction. Its poets have nothing in common with the versifiers of the old times, who were educated by the Jesuits and Franciscans, and condemned to sterile imitation of the classical works which were not prohibited. Its authors picture society skillfully, are close observers, have keen wit, and handle satire with ability. Many of them have even won distinction in the drama, and Lima and Cuzco has each its university, and the former has also an institute organized on the German system, of which the foundation-stone was laid January 1, 1873. An industrial school for the training of artisans, founded by Pardo when he was mayor, was consecrated on the same day. Beside its classrooms there are workshops for carpentry, cabinet-making, iron-working, and printing. When the pupils have finished their education they receive a sum of money to procure the means of setting up for themselves.

Chapter XIV

CHILI. 1825-1876

OF all the republics sprung from emancipated Spanish colonies, Chili has had the least disturbed existence. A period of prolific tranquillity long since succeeded the first and inevitable crisis. The stability so early introduced into its institutions made Chili a prosperous commercial and industrial nation, with a natural inclination for material progress. The character of its inhabitants, calm, reflective, little inclined to excitement, too punctilious perhaps, has been favorable to internal peace. Among the nations of South America the Chilians most resemble Europeans; their customs and institutions, still rather aristocratic, have a certain analogy with those of England.

It may be said, on the other hand, that the nature of the country, whose climate and products also resemble those of temperate Europe, protects it against both civil war and foreign invasion. It is a narrow strip enclosed between the sea and the mountains, and offers few resources to the conquered for hiding, taking breath, and forming again. Insurrections last but a short time, and the first battle is almost always decisive. For this reason there has never been chronic civil war in Chili as in the neighboring republics, Bolivia, for instance, whose southern border it touches, where vast deserts offer a secure refuge to the defeated but not discouraged parties.

San Martin, O'Higgins, and Freyre, who won fame in the war of independence, were the ephemeral presidents of the first years of freedom. Here as elsewhere the Unitarians and Federalists disputed for power. From the first the republic experienced shock after shock, insurrection after insurrection, and was in turmoil because of continual changes of president and constitution. A Congress met on February 24, 1828, at Santiago and then at Valparaíso, to form a constitution. The document was the work of the Radicals or Federalists, was based on democratic principles, and served to excite rioting at Concepcion in the following year.

The Opposition, that is, the Unitarians, known, in allusion to their reactionary tendencies, by the permanent nickname of "*Pelucones,*" or the "Wigs," had General Joaquin Prieto at its head, and in its ranks a citizen named Diego Portales, who was very soon to play an important part. General Pinto, who was invested with the executive power after the fall of Freyre, resigned in order to promote harmony, and the Federalists put General Lastera in his place. Party strife waxed hot. An insurrectionary junta was formed in Santiago. The *Pelucones* won the battle of Larcay, declared the constitution "null and void," and proscribed its principal defenders.

A policy of compromise prevailed in the councils of the government, designed to resist the Radicals, under the well-known pretext that the country was not yet ripe for liberty, and to oppose an obstacle to the abuses that the triumph of the upper classes and the clergy could not fail to cause or revive. This was the political philosophy that inspired the authors of the constitution of 1833, in which they made visible efforts to reconcile liberty and republican forms with a very strong and almost independent executive power, giving a large place to the advantages of fortune if not of birth, at the same time acknowledging the rights of the people.

The constitution of 1833 recognizes three powers—the legislative, the executive, and the judicial. The first is exercised by the National Congress composed of a chamber of twenty senators, elected for nine years by special electors, and a chamber of deputies elected for three years by direct vote, at the ratio of one deputy for every 20,000 inhabitants. Senators must be thirty-six years of age and possess an income of $2000, and deputies an income of $500. The executive power is exercised by a president, the supreme head of the nation and of the administration, elected by indirect suffrage for a term of five years, and reëligible only once. This reëligibility was abolished in 1871. The president has the command of the land and sea forces and can proclaim martial law. The judicial power has the exclusive right of deciding suits, and a jury is allowed only in cases involving the press. The constitution guarantees liberty of writing. A decree of September 25, 1846, established a special tribunal for press offenses, composed of a judge of first instance, and jurors taken from a list which is drawn up every year by the municipal council of each town in which any periodical is published. The constitution also guarantees inviolability of domicile, proclaims liberty of industry, prohibits unusual judicial sentences, and abolishes slavery.

Portales, one of the framers of this document, insured its enforcement during the years that he was at the head of the ministry. When the term of office of Prieto, whom Congress had raised to the presidency, expired in 1835, the election of Portales was discussed; but he would not accept the nomination which his numerous political friends and admirers offered him, and made every effort to bring about Prieto's reëlection.

It was about this time that Santa Cruz, who had become the head of the Peruvio-Bolivian Confederation, furnished arms and vessels of war to the Chilian exiles led by Freyre. Public opinion attributed ambitious views to Santa Cruz, whose intervention might have appeared necessary if there had been a civil war. Freyre descended as far as Chiloè, where he remained for a fortnight, supported by the enthusiasm of the inhabitants of San Carlos, but was defeated and obliged to fly in the boat of a fisherman, who was to take him on board an American whaler. Freyre said to his conductor: " I have not a real, but I will never forget you, and some day you shall be rewarded "; but the fisherman, not trusting much to the future, sold the fugitive for an ounce of gold. War was declared against Santa Cruz, and the army was organized. It lay at Quillota, near Valparaíso, awaiting the signal to start, when four companies, instigated by Colonel Vidaurre, revolted while Portales was holding the last review. The minister was made prisoner, and the revolted troops marched on Valparaíso. The governor of the city, supported by the national guard and the seamen, posted himself in a position easy to be defended and blocked the road against the troops of Vidaurre. The encounter took place in the middle of a night in the month of June, which is winter in that country. A well-escorted *birlocho* or cabriolet went in the rearguard of the insurgent army. A man descended from this carriage and walked steadily to the side of the road; shots were heard, and the man fell. When the first light of dawn illumined the field of battle the national guards carried away a body pierced by four bullets. It was that of Portales. The first shot fired by his friends had been his death warrant. The heads of the movement who fell into the hands of the conquerors were taken to Valparaíso to be shot. They all bravely faced death. The tragical end of Portales awakened many keen regrets. He left to his country an honored memory and many institutions that he himself was far from considering as perfect and final. The reformation of the clergy and of the courts of justice; the creation of the national guard; the organization of the police; and, above all, the assured confidence of the country in the government, give this enlightened administrator a claim to public remembrance.[1]

The first attempt of the Chilians against Santa Cruz produced no result, but the second ended in the defeat of the Protector and destroyed his political edifice. Chili, thanks to the good financial administration of Rinjifo, the intelligent and active friend to Portales, was able to provide for the expenses of the expedition without a loan. This triumph of the Chilian arms attained the double advantage of making the republic respected abroad and of securing that tranquillity at home which it has since enjoyed.

Prieto retired from power in 1841, but his policy of moderation was continued by his successor, General Bulnés. Under his administration Spain at length recognized the independence of Chili (1844). The successor of Bulnés, in 1851, was an old professor of the University of Chili, a man of distinguished talent, named Manuel Montt, attached, like himself, to the Conservative party. After the elections, which had caused great excitement, insurrectionary movements broke out in various places. In San Felipe a Junta of Equality was established. The new president gave the command of the army to his predecessor, who secured the final triumph of the government, and by retiring into private life set an example, certainly very new in South America, but glorious everywhere, of a victorious soldier laying down his sword before a civil magistracy. Fresh disturbances broke out in 1858. This time the enemies of the president were the reactionary Conservatives, or *Pelucones,* and the Radicals. Their coalition almost overthrew him. The establishment of a Protestant chapel in Valparaíso was the pretext for the revolt of the ultraconservatives, incited by the Catholic clergy. The Radicals, taking advantage of the circumstances, demanded reforms in the constitution and opened a Constituent Club in Santiago, which the government put under the ban, as a menace to public order; but the order was not obeyed. Force was used, many arrests were made, and martial law was proclaimed in the cities of Santiago and Valparaíso. As a consequence of these measures Copiapo rose in revolt, and the urban guard took up arms and expelled the lawful authorities. A young man named Pedro Leon

[1] Radiguet. *"Souvenirs de l'Amerique Espagnole."*

Gallo was proclaimed intendant and military commandant. A little later (January, 1859) the victorious Radicals seized Talca and occupied it for about a month.

Important reforms were carried out even in the midst of all these complications. Chili, like the rest of the South American colonies, had inherited from her old masters a confused collection of laws and customs taken from the Roman law, the laws of Alfonso the Wise, the Siete Partidas, the ordinance of Bilbao, and the old colonial jurisprudence. A scheme for recasting all these documents was submitted to Congress at the suggestion of the president, was approved in all its parts, and had the force of law from January 1, 1859. European jurisconsults recognize in this a simple and profound method, a happy alliance of Roman law, Spanish law, and the French laws that were begotten by the spirit of 1789.

The position of Montt was becoming more difficult. The generals lent their assistance unwillingly to a civilian president. Though he tried to get on with them he got the Congress to give him extraordinary powers, defeated the insurgent army on the plain of Penuelos, and obliged his adversaries to have patience at least until the regular election of another president, to give legal force to their pretensions and votes. In reality, these attempts had not affected institutional foundations. José Joaquin Perez was called into power by the elections of July, 1861. No disorder accompanied his accession, which took place in the following September. His presidency was the result of the fusion of all parties, for all had united to secure his triumph. He was a man of upright motives, inclined to conciliation, and began his administration by an act of clemency. He induced the Chambers to sanction a complete amnesty for all political crimes committed since 1851; and later, in March, 1863, restored to the officers who were compromised in the insurrection of 1859, the rank which they held in the army. The advantage of the combination which had raised him to power was that it did not mean the victory of one of the two parties over the other; it had nevertheless the disadvantage of obliging him to carry out a policy of counterpoise and compromise. This policy, which put off the time for self-assertion, had no other result at last than to diminish the influence of the government. The advanced party accused Perez of weakness; the Conservatives blamed him for not conforming to their programme, for favoring the Liberals, and accused him of ingratitude. In the Congress the Conservative opposition had ex-President Montt for their leader. The government, nevertheless, secured an almost complete triumph in the elections of March and April, 1864.

At the same time that the executive power was thus consolidating itself at home, very grave complications arose abroad. On April 14, 1864, the Spanish squadron seized the Chincha Islands. Chili, on account of her proximity to Peru, was greatly excited on learning that Spain claimed the possession of those islands, and that she looked upon the cessation of the war since 1825 as a sort of truce. Before the danger which threatened Peru, the Chilians desired to take up arms and be ready to help her, and for this purpose energetic and patriotic manifestations took place all over the republic. When the Treaty of Callao had put an end to the Hispano-Peruvian war, Spain turned against Chili and addressed certain demands to her because of her attitude during this war. Apologies were made which satisfied the representative of Madrid at Santiago, as he declared (May 20, 1865). A good understanding appeared to be reëstablished when the news was received, on September 12, that the resident minister of Spain, Tavira, was recalled; that the arrangement signed by him was disavowed; and that orders had been given to Admiral Pareja to sail for Chili escorted by five vessels of war.

The Chilian nation was celebrating the annual festivals of its independence when the new Spanish negotiator, to whom a deep hatred and mean prejudices against Chili were attributed, presented himself (September 17) on board the *Villa de Madrid* before Valparaíso, a large and opulent commercial city and port of deposit for the Pacific Ocean. On the next day Pareja addressed an ultimatum to the Minister for Foreign Affairs, demanding immediately a salute of twenty-one guns to the Spanish flag, and, within four days, full explanations on the principal points of the old demands. The minister, Alvaro Covarrubias, gave an energetic, dignified, and decidedly negative reply to this unreasonable demand. He protested solemnly against the measures, contrary to the spirit of the treaties, which were employed against Chili, and threw all the responsibility for this scandalous abuse of strength on the aggressor: " The Republic, strong in the justice of her cause, supported by the heroism of her sons, taking God for judge and the civilized world for witness of the strife, will defend her honor and privileges to the last extreme, and will wage war by all the means permitted by the law of nations, however extreme and painful they may be." Pareja replied by a second ultimatum, dated at night on the 22d, but sent on the morning of the 23d, in which he fixed six o'clock in the morning of the 24th as the time when he should appeal to force. At the same time he refused all friendly intervention of the diplomatic body resident in Santiago. The attitude of the government was firm and resolute; the president, by means of an address, which was posted up everywhere, let the people know that he was resolved to face the consequences of the struggle provoked by Spain. Congress voted by acclamation $20,000,000 to arm the country by sea and land; the declaration of war was solemnly proclaimed in the whole republic, and produced an admirable outburst of patriotism. In the meanwhile Pareja, taking up positions with his vessels, declared the ports of Valparaíso, Coquimbo, Caldera, Herradura, Tome, and Talcahuano in a state of blockade. To counteract this measure, which directly affected foreign commerce and raised sharp protests from the neutral powers, the government of the republic opened thirty-eight new ports and abolished the customs duties.

There was no serious encounter between the two countries until November 26. The Chilian corvette *Esmeralda* had left Valparaíso on the night of the 17th just when the enemy's squadron was entering it. On the 26th she was near Papulo, anchored near the coast a few miles from Valparaíso. At dawn of the same day the Spanish gunboat *Virgen de Covadonga,* coming from Coquimbo and steering a course toward the south, was going to pass on the other side of Papulo, when the *Esmeralda,* by a bold maneuver, attacked and took her after a fight of twenty minutes. On receipt of the news of this reverse, Pareja, who had distinctly heard the cannonade on board his flagship, retired to his cabin, wrote this request: "I ask as a favor that my body be not thrown into the waters of Chili," and killed himself with a revolver. The newspapers of that period printed a letter, which he had written to a friend in those last moments, declaring that the errors of judgment, not of will, that had caused him to mislead the government of the queen could only be expiated by his death. He confessed that he had been unjust to Tavira, and declared that the interest of Spain required her to take advantage of the first opportunity and make peace with Chili. We refer to this document with due reserve and without guaranteeing its authenticity. Whatever the truth may be, the *Villa de Madrid* left the roads of Valparaíso (January 1, 1866)

for twenty-four hours, taking the body of the suicide, whose tragical
end was kept secret until the brigadier Mendez Nuñez, commander
of the frigate *Numancia,* which was in the waters of Callao, had
taken command of the squadron.   As soon as the government of
Chili knew of the death of its enemy, it offered to receive the remains of the admiral in the cemetery of Valparaíso and hold them
at the disposal of the family, but the body of Pareja had by that
time been buried at sea.   The new Spanish commander, perceiving
the impossibility of effectively guarding more than 1250 miles of
coast, reduced the blockade to the ports of Valparaíso and Cardela.
Besides, one part of his force was about to be employed against
Peru, which had given orders to hold its ships in readiness.   The
blockade of Valparaíso had been a mortal blow for the treasury,
and, besides, had ruined private individuals, because Valparaíso is
the commercial center of Chili, as Santiago is its agricultural center.
Mendez Nuñez caused a new injury to the finances by declaring that
coal from the mines of the republic, which is an article of considerable exportation, would be considered as contraband of war, and
seized, although it were found on board neutral vessels.   However
much she suffered by the war, Chili was not disposed to withdraw.
The capture of the *Covadonga* had raised her hopes, which were
raised still higher by another advantage gained by the Chilian navy
in the roads of Abtoa.

   Besides the alliance with Peru, which was settled by the treaty
of December, 1865, Chili relied on the assistance of Ecuador,
Colombia, and Venezuela, and hoped for the powerful intervention
of the United States, since the representative of the great republic
was certainly working in favor of peace.   This was the position
of affairs when one of the most odious deeds of the century was
done.

   Valparaíso (Vale of Paradise), the principal port of Chili, was
then a city of about 80,000 inhabitants.   It is situated at the head
of a deep circular inlet enclosed by hills 400 meters high.   One
of these heights, Mount Allegro, was covered with elegant country
houses, belonging for the most part to Englishmen.   The city is
divided into two sections, the port and the *Almendral* (place of al-
mond trees) east of the port.   The port is the true center of the
commerce and activity of Valparaíso and the most considerable
district of the city, which also extends for some distance through
gaps in the hills called *quebradas.*   In the port, in a long line,

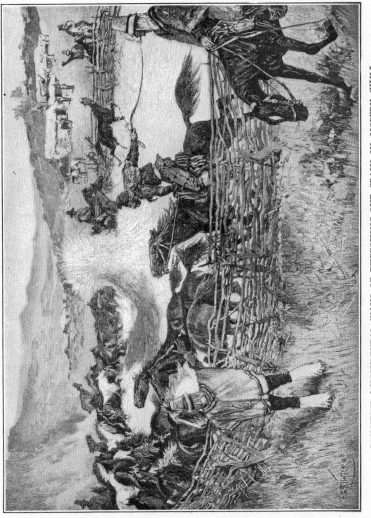

PRIMITIVE AGRICULTURAL WAYS OF THRESHING OUT GRAIN IN MODERN CHILI

Painting by Albert Richter

—page 230

were situated the warehouses and counting-houses of the merchants, who are almost all foreigners.   This line of buildings
was overlooked by the vast and magnificent customs house, and the
residences of the consular authorities were also there.   Two forts
commanded the harbor, and a citadel defended the city.   In reality
Valparaíso was a defenseless town.   The Chilian government had
even withdrawn some guns from a battery, which without being
useful for defense, might give a shadow of a pretext for an attack.
Valparaíso is the great depot of Chilian commerce.   Most of the
vessels that come round Cape Horn or from the northern regions

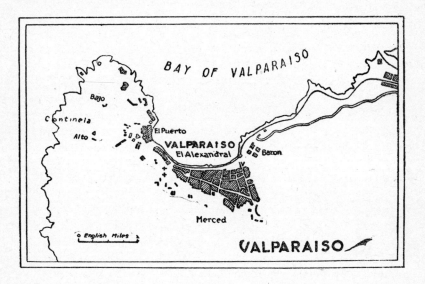

put in at the port, and this causes a great mercantile activity and
animation.   But the bay, which is semicircular, does not offer a
good anchorage except from December to April.   From the beginning of May until the end of August it is constantly lashed by the
northwest winds, which very often occasion disasters.   The Spanish
squadron took advantage of the last days in which it was possible
for it to be stationed before Valparaíso to bombard, burn, and ruin
that defenseless city.

Mendez Nuñez had prepared for the operation coolly.   He
gave notice that if after four days the Chilian government did
not adhere to the terms of arrangement established on the bases
proposed by France and England, which in reality differed very

slightly from those of Pareja, he would bombard Valparaíso.[2] On March 31, 1866, a little before eight o'clock in the morning, the frigate *Numancia* fired two guns as if to warn the inhabitants. They were given an hour to put themselves under shelter from the bombs. Soon all the heights situated behind the city were covered with men, women, and children, who were flying from death, and who abandoned the greater part of what they possessed. Line of battle was formed by the ships and the firing began with shouts of "Long live the queen." A shower of bombs fell on the customs house, the commissariat, the hospital, the house for the poor, and the quarters surrounding these buildings. At noon, after a cannonade of three hours, the Spanish ships ceased firing and retired toward the entrance of the roads; their work was done. Merchandise worth $8,400,000 was destroyed, the greater part of the city was in ruins, and the conflagration ended by devouring the principal wards. The white flag hoisted on the hospital had been thrown down; the national standard, with its single star, alone remained standing over the smoking ruins of the Vale of Paradise. The neutral vessels looked on passively at the destruction of such a beautiful seat of commerce and the ruin of their fellow-countrymen. This was the last act of the Spanish squadron. The blockade of Valparaíso was raised on April 14, and very soon the barbarous Mendez Nuñez finally left the Pacific without making any kind of arrangement with the republic.

The result of foreign aggression was a better understanding between Chili and the neighboring republics. Their treaty of quadruple alliance against Spain led to great intimacy between Chili, Peru, Bolivia, and Ecuador, and in this manner the differences which for a quarter of a century had produced continual conflicts between Chili and Bolivia respecting the northeastern boundary were adjusted. The disputed territory was amicably divided by a treaty signed at Santiago.

On the other hand, nothing had disturbed home politics. The constitution came out intact from that severe trial, and the president could proudly say, on the opening of the session of 1866, that, even in the midst of the hazards of war, the country continued in the

---

[2] The real weight of the Spanish complaints can be determined by reference to the "*Contre-manifesto de M. Alvaro Cervarrubias, Ministre des Affaires Etrangeres au Chili, à propos de la presente guerre entre le Chili et l'Espagne,*" published by the Chilian consulate at Paris, January, 1863.

enjoyment of all its liberties.   Thus a fine example was set by the
republic of Chili to those powerful nations of Europe, where all
guarantees are suspended at the caprice of the governments for six
years at a time, and where, on the slightest pretext, the severities
of martial law are called for and applied.   By this time the period of
the elections was drawing near, and the president declared: " They
shall be the true expression of the opinion of the country.   The
government, whatever may be the position in which it is placed, will
be no more active in the elections than it. has been in the past."
Perez did not disguise the damage that the blockade had caused, but
at the same time he enumerated the efforts that had been made to
repair it.   The salaries of the government employees had been
reduced, the citizens had given free gifts to the treasury, and
a loan without interest had been oversubscribed.   Besides, in spite
of the preoccupations of the war, the government had accomplished
economic improvements, had extended the telegraph lines and
opened sections of railway between Currico and. San Fernando.
Nevertheless, new sacrifices must be made; it was necessary to
secure Valparaíso from another aggression, to increase the naval
forces, to improve the artillery, and provide coast defenses.   In addition to raising new loans the government suggested a modification
of the system of taxation.   The nation did not complain.   The president who thus addressed it had completed his five years of office,
but was reëligible by the terms of the constitution, and he was
reëlected July 25, 1866, in spite of the efforts of the partisans of
General Bulnés.   Congress confirmed the election August 31, 1866,
and dissolved on January 15, 1867, after voting a tax of $5,000,000
on the actual or approximate. income of private individuals and cor-
porations.   The congressional elections of March 31 and April 1,
1867, showed that however heavy this burden may have been,
the popularity of the government had not suffered, since the opposition succeeded in electing only four of its candidates.   The
new Congress was opened on June 1, and the presidential message proved the happy influence of Chili's institutions by showing its steady moral and material progress, the reëstablishment
of its commerce, and the strengthening of its finances.   The
Anglo-Chilian loan of March and the internal loan of August
5, 1866, had covered the extraordinary expenses occasioned by
the war.   In 1867 a new loan, destined to pay off the Anglo-
Chilian loan of 1866 and to acquire war material, was made

in London. The reformed tax on patents and the income tax yielded excellent results. Though the work of fortification, the preparation of material for heavy artillery, and the casting of bronze cannon went on constantly, the effective strength of the battalions of militia, organized at the beginning of the war, was reduced. At the same time the national territory was increased by a large district acquired at the expense of the natives of Araucania, and secured against the treacherous attacks of these savages by the establishment of the two fortresses of Quidico and Collico.

France and England had several times offered their mediation to Chili as well as to Peru in the questions at issue with Spain. The Chilian government appeared inclined at least to discuss the matter, but they thought otherwise in Peru, and the press at Santiago, as at Lima, violently attacked the conciliatory tendencies of certain statesmen. The attempts made under the auspices of the two European powers, and the proposition to make a truce for an indefinite time between the two belligerents, had no result; the unjust and exaggerated pretensions of Spain were, according to the words of the Minister of Foreign Affairs of Chili, Alvaro Covarrubias, an insuperable obstacle to an understanding. The United States on their side saw their good offices refused for the same reasons. Nevertheless, a convention was signed at Lima, January 2, 1867, for the purpose of concluding an armistice first and afterward discussing the bases of a definite peace, and Chili ratified it in 1871. In consequence of this agreement the commerce of the allies and of neutrals was freed from all restraint. In the interval Chili, following the example of Peru, recognized the patriots of Cuba as belligerents.

In the meantime a reform of the constitution was desired to abolish the president's right to reëlection, and Congress effected this reform in July, 1871. Thereafter Federico Errásuriz was elected to succeed Joaquin Perez in the presidency. He took the oath on September 18, the anniversary of the independence of Chili, and the outgoing president immediately handed him the scarf of the national colors, which was the emblem of the power he was called upon to exercise.

Errásuriz had successively discharged the duties of intendant of the province of Santiago, deputy, minister, and senator. During the war he had taken the portfolio of Justice and, temporarily,

that of Foreign Affairs. He kept in the Ministry of the Interior and
in that of Foreign Affairs Eulogio Altamirano, a member of the
late cabinet, who had scarcely taken possession of his office when a
conflict arose with the Argentine Confederation. Both countries
had long disputed the sovereignty of Araucania and Patagonia,
regions which until then had preserved their independence. The
Argentine Senate having declared the territory of Magallanes to be
included in the limits of the confederation, Chili, in order to assert
her rights, hurriedly granted authority to one of her subjects to
take 3000 tons of guano from the Islands of Santa Magdalena, in
the Straits of Magellan. At the same time the government took
possession of all the coast of Arauco and distributed the land in
those regions, in shares, to Chilian and foreign colonists. It is
true that few dared to profit by these concessions because of the
danger to life and property at such distances from the settled parts.
The Indians made frequent incursions into the territory in question
to carry off the women, children, and cattle.

The excitement produced by these neighborhood quarrels fortunately passed away, and political, financial, or commercial relations were not affected. Other complications arose with Bolivia
and lasted until the beginning of the year 1873, when a treaty
signed at La Paz fixed the boundaries of the two nations and put
an end to their differences.

Although the economic position of Chili had progressed remarkably in the years immediately preceding 1876, and the country had always been the most industrious and progressive of all
the Spanish-American republics, no comparison could be made between this state of South America and the United States. The
superstitious, ignorant, and narrow-minded Castilian race lacks the
unconquerable energy and courage of the Anglo-Saxons. Chili,
nevertheless, had one of the most advantageous geographical positions; its soil is fertile and rich in minerals, and in spite of
the scantiness of its population it is a district wonderfully suited
for the importations of the Old World. The public works pushed
on with activity, new railways opened for working, the telegraph crossing the Andes and uniting Santiago and Valparaíso
with Buenos Ayres and Rio Janeiro, the direct communication
with Europe, established August 4, 1874, by a submarine cable,
were substantial achievements, and had been obtained without losing
sight of intellectual interests. The statesmen of Chili justly con-

sidered education as the principal guarantee for the future of their country, and therefore the organization of teaching was carefully provided for by the government. Primary instruction was divided among fiscal, municipal, private, and monastic schools, and was gratuitous even in many private establishments. The number of schools in 1873 was 1190, of which 726 were public and 464 private, attended by not less than 81,162 pupils, not including infant schools. There were regimental schools in most of the army corps; and in the large cities night schools are open for adults. Unfortunately, the population could not benefit equally by the sacrifices made for it by the state because it is widely scattered over a vast territory. While in the cities there was one school for every 1759 inhabitants, in the country, where the population is three-quarters of the total of the republic, the proportion was not more than one school for every 3020 inhabitants.[3]

Normal schools for teachers of both sexes have been founded to raise the standard of education. In the towns primary instruction included linear drawing, geography, and an outline of the history of Chili. The pupils were drilled in the metric system of weights and measures, which had been adopted throughout the republic. Secondary education had not been neglected; in addition to a large college, incorporated with the National Institution of Santiago as its preparatory section, there were in the provinces lyceums or high schools assisted by the state. Santiago also had a practical School of Arts and Trades, endowed for the education of 100 pupils, and superintended by engineers from Europe. In the mining district, in Copiapo, a School of Mines had been established. The Conservatory of Music and the School of Fine Arts are also worthy of mention. The National Institute was organized like the College de France and corresponds to the French universities for advanced instruction. A national literature had been formed, modeled on that of Spain, France, and England. Chili has distinguished poets, but is especially famous for its scholars, economists, and financiers.

But much remained to be done. Much progress was still needed among a people where, as late as the close of 1874, the bishops dared to excommunicate the government in a body. The struggle with the episcopate, which is going on almost everywhere in South America, will no doubt terminate by the triumph of the

[3] Report to the Congress by the Inspector-General of Public Instruction, 1873.

lay spirit; but in the meantime, as it actually presents itself, it testifies to an alarming moral condition.

Chili, which had not exhibited at Paris in 1852, figured notably in the Universal Exposition at Paris in 1867, sending large colored fabrics that were not without merit, engravings on coins and medals, lithographs, which were very curious from an ethnographical point of view, remarkable geographical works made at government expense, geological maps, due to the engineer Plessis, who was appointed to study the geology of the whole republic, glazed pottery of very brilliant colors, magnificent furs, delicate hand-made cotton laces, the reproduction of an ancient art which has revealed the extreme dexterity of the Chilians, the curious wool yielded by a cross between the goat and the sheep, hides prepared in various ways, harness and saddlery very ingeniously made, dried meat, salted provisions, and other articles. Beautiful specimens from her mines—gold, silver, copper, iron, nickel, cobalt, lapis-lazuli, marbles, and coal—demonstrated the superiority of Chili over the other South American republics from the point of view of mining and metallurgy. An international exhibition of raw and manufactured products opened in Santiago in 1875 was very successful. It showed that imports from France had for several years steadily decreased, while those from Germany, though not then equal to the French, had increased at a remarkable rate. Nevertheless, English commerce continued predominant. Moreover, the Chilian has a marked liking for England and claims to be the Englishman of South America. The national sentiment which animates him, the mercantile instinct which more especially distinguishes the inhabitants of Valparaíso, their liking for comfort, their ready adoption of British customs, and the lack of sympathy of the people in general for the French appear to support this pretension; but studying more closely the domestic life of the Chilian, it will appear that he is more of a Netherlander than an Englishman.[4]

To sum up, Chili, one of the richest countries of South America, gave promise of a prosperous future. From an economic point of view it had an interest analogous to that of the Argentine Republic. The sea facilitates the working of the mines, near which is found the fuel for smelting the ores. The exploitation of the forest and agricultural resources has the same advantages. It was unfortunate, nevertheless, that landed property remained concen-

[4] Max Radiguet. "*Souvenirs de l'Amerique du Sud.*"

trated in too few hands.   Possessions of 50,000 acres of cultiva-
ble land were met with on the coast plains, and of from 250,000
to 500,000 acres, with virgin forests, in the valleys of the Cordilleras.   Wheat was sown abundantly, but the most primitive
methods were employed for threshing it.   The sheaves were opened
on the ground in fenced enclosures, wild mares were let loose and
excited by shouts and lashes, and the stamping of these irritated
animals replaced the threshing flail.   There were proprietors who
employed 1000 mares for two months in various enclosures of this
kind, for the harvest gathered from 6500 acres.[5]

Thus in Chili also there was a want of laborers that prevented
the most profitable exploitation of the productive elements of the
soil.   The Germans seemed to emigrate willingly to Chili in large
numbers.   The arrival of 4000 of them was announced during the
single month of June, 1871.

[5] Audiganne, " *La lutte industrielle des Peuples,*" 1868.

PART III

THE PRESENT SOUTH AMERICA
1876-1910

Chapter **XV**

THE WAR OF THE PACIFIC—THE ANDINE
STATES AND VENEZUELA. 1876-1910

THE great historical event of the Andine region during the last thirty years was the war waged by Chili against Bolivia and Peru, and the resultant civil war among the victors, which is still fresh in memory.

About 1878 Chili was in a prosperous condition. Twenty-five years of peace had induced the investment of foreign capital in the country, and the consequent development of agriculture. The mineral resources of the nation had begun to be exploited and were yielding good profits. The finances were in good condition, the fleet and army were well recruited and disciplined, and the public credit among foreign financiers was excellent. The republic, shut in between the wall of the Andes and the sea, was ambitious of expansion, and its strength enabled it to satisfy the ambition. To the north lay the desert of Atacama, belonging to Bolivia, and possessing subterranean wealth which was the immediate cause of the conflict.

The dominant trait of the present age is the controlling influence of economic questions in domestic and foreign politics. The struggles of parties within each state and of states with each other are carried on to defend economic privileges and rights already acquired, or to obtain and divide such privileges. Other questions upon which the union of parties and states were formerly based are now subordinated to this. The bloody war, whose story we are about to tell, was due to the exploitation of nitrate of soda deposits.

In the Desert of Atacama when the soil is dug up there appears, under the upper stratum of sand, a pure stratum formed of small stones, which the prospectors for nitrate of soda call crusts (*costras*). This stratum lies at a depth of from two to four decimeters. It lies in a very irregular deposit varying in thickness from four inches to six and a half feet (Varigny). After the war of 1866 against Spain a convention had been made between Chili and

Bolivia fixing the frontier at the twenty-fourth degree of latitude; but the region between the twenty-third and twenty-fifth degrees was subjected to a peculiar system of dual economic control: The two states were to exploit it in common, and share equally the right of prospecting for minerals. Difficulties were certain to arise from a system which subjected a political dependency of Bolivia to economic dependence upon Chili. To be sure all concessions for exploitation must be granted by the Bolivian government, but the advent of large numbers of immigrants from Chili in the vacant territory created a delicate situation. Chilian capitalists financed the exploitation, and Chilian laborers carried on the industry. Soon 20,000 Chilian emigrants had gone to Antofagasta. Public opinion in the Bolivian capital soon became sensitive to this state of affairs, and the president was accused of favoritism toward these southern neighbors. Nevertheless the suggestion of war against Chili came from a foreign nation. It was Peru that sought and brought about the conflict.

Peru had exhausted its financial resources, and was on the verge of bankruptcy. The revenue from the guano deposits had been alienated, and the government devised an export duty on nitrate of soda. The result of this economic policy was soon manifest in the competition between the untaxed product of Chili and the tax-burdened product of Peru. An easy victory fell to Chili; the European ships deserted the Peruvian and flocked to the Chilian ports. Peru, in desperation, demanded that Bolivia levy a tax upon the nitrate of soda of Atacama, and Bolivia yielded, though a treaty concluded by the La Paz government with Chili, in 1874, forbade such a tax. This was war. After part of the year 1878 had been spent in fruitless negotiations Chili recalled its minister from Bolivia. Peru tendered its good offices, but Chili declined them, and denounced the treaty of 1866, thus reviving its claim to all territory south of the twenty-third degree of latitude, because of the breach of the treaty of 1874.

The war began in 1879 with the Chilian occupation, first of Antofagasta and then of the whole Bolivian coast with the towns of Cobija and Calama. The Bolivians had retired to Calama under the command of Ladislas Cabrera, and were dislodged by the troops of the Chilian commander, Sotomayor, who had made a painful march across a region without water or vegetation (March 23).

Then ensued a memorable naval campaign. The Chilian fleet

detached two ships to blockade the Peruvian port of Iquique, bombarded Pisagua and Mollendo, and laid waste the Peruvian coast. Thus far the advantage was evidently upon the side of Chili. Two Peruvian ships, the monitor *Huascar,* commanded by Grau, and the armored frigate *Independencia,* sailed from Callao, proceeded to Iquique, and engaged in a double naval duel before that town, with the two blockading ships, in which the *Huascar* sunk its Chilian adversary the *Esmeralda,* but the *Independencia* was wrecked. On land the Bolivian army, under President Daza, effected a junction at Arica with the Peruvians, under President Prado, but the chief interest in the war was transferred to the sea, where the intrepid Grau, now admiral, undertook a heroic campaign. He slipped through the line of the blockading fleet before Iquique and began a cruise of devastation on the coasts of Chili. The Chilian government put Don Riberos in command of its fleet, and a squadron composed of the *Blanco Encalado,* the *Cochrane,* the *O'Higgins,* and the *Covandaga* sailed in search of the *Huascar.* They found and fought her on October 8, off Cape Agamos, near Antofagasta. After a heroic struggle, in which Grau was killed, the *Huascar* was beaten and destroyed. No fleet remained to dispute the mastery of the sea by Chili within the zone of hostilities, and the Chilians prepared to conquer Peru by land.

Peru and Bolivia had good armies. The men were well disciplined, temperate, and inured to fatigue. The Peruvians were enthusiastic soldiers and confident of success. The Bolivians were more numerous, and could stand fire, but lacked warlike ardor. The allied army was in two divisions at Iquique and Arica. The Chilians landed at Pisagua, to the number of 10,000. Thus the enemies were isolated from each other, but the landing had not been accomplished without a struggle, for detachments of the allies had defended Pisagua for five hours. The plan of the general staff of the coalition was to drive back to the sea the Chilian expeditionary force, and for this purpose to effect a junction of the two armies in the interior of the country in the strong position of Dolores, whence they were to march to the coast. But the Chilians discovered this plan, and got the start of their enemies by sending 6000 men with artillery to occupy the heights. The Chilian army reached the position first and threw up intrenchments. When the enemy appeared he was routed by a terrible cannonade, and fled, leaving his cannon and baggage in the hands of the Chilians.

Buendia, the Peruvian general, rallied his troops at Tarapaca, where the garrison of Iquique joined them, and Sotomayor, the victor at Dolores, tried in vain to dislodge them. After a long day of battle the Peruvians remained masters of the field, but the retreat was renewed. " The retreat of Buendia was terrible and pitiable. The thin columns took twenty days to cover the distance of forty leagues to Arica. Forced to proceed along the steep slopes of the Cordillera to avoid the Chilians, who were masters of the plain, marching by night in intense cold, camping by day without shelter, under a burning sun, rarely finding a spring where they could quench their thirst, compelled to drink the infected water of stagnant swamps, passing here and there plundered villages, whose inhabitants had fled with their miserable stock of provisions, these columns reached Arica in a pitiful condition. Half their number had perished on the march. Some had killed themselves to put an end to their terrible sufferings, and others had died of hunger, thirst, and disease. In spite of the costly victory at Tarapaca the Desert of Atacama, the ports of Antofagasta, Cobija, Iquique, and Pisagua, with 120 leagues of coast, remained in the hands of Chili " (Varigny).

These military reverses were followed in the two defeated countries by political disturbances. President Prado, who had not stirred from Arica, fled the country, leaving his powers to be exercised by the vice-president, General La Puerta; but La Puerta was forced to resign in favor of General Pierola, who was recognized at home and by the army. A revolution also took place in Bolivia; General Daza was deposed, Colonel Carmancho was made general-in-chief in his stead, and General Narciso Campero president of the republic.

The Peruvian and Bolivian armies were concentrated in the neighborhood of Arica and Tacna. The Chilians attempted to cut them off from their respective capitals, Lima and La Paz, by occupying Ylo, Pacocha and the valley of Moqueja with 14,000 men (February 15, 1880). The Peruvians hoped to defeat this plan by establishing themselves in a strong position on the heights of Los Angeles, but the Chilians took the position by a night attack. The road to the north was closed to the allies. The victors marched against the allied army at Tacna and Arica, a laborious march across a desert where everything had to be carried, even water for the troops.

The little Chilian army of 13,000 men, 40 Krupp guns, 550 artillerymen, and 1200 cavalry camped for several days at Buena Vista on the further edge of the desert, and then resumed its march against the enemy. It won a bloody battle at Tacna (May 25, 1880), and occupied all Peru south of Ylo. The vanquished

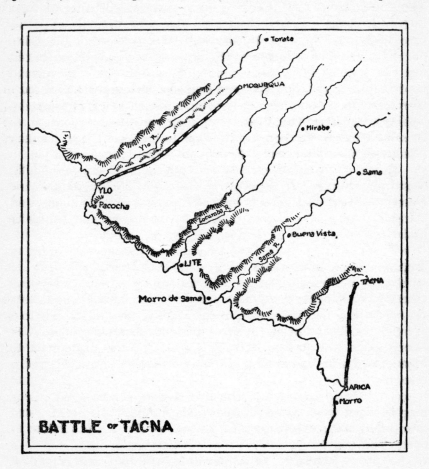

BATTLE of TACNA

retreated into the interior toward Lake Titicaca. The town of Arica, caught between the fire of the fleet and the Chilian army, capitulated June 7.

The Chilian fleet was then sent to harass the northern coast of Peru. The Peruvian army was concentrated near the capital, between Lima and the coast. Behind the intrenchments at Chorillos and Miraflores 22,000 men were gathered in positions which the Peruvians believed to be impregnable, but the Chilians took them in a two days' fight, January 13 and 15, 1881, and then entered Lima.

The struggle continued for two years in the Peruvian territory, which was not yet subdued. A truce was signed in April, 1884, between Bolivia and Chili, not to be broken without one year's notice, leaving in the hands of Chili all the territory which gave Bolivia access to the sea; and Peru, by the Treaty of Ancon, signed October 23, 1883, gave up to the victors the provinces of Tacna, Arica, and Tarapaca, rich in guano and saltpeter. Tarapaca was ceded in perpetuity, and the other two provinces for ten years, at the end of which a plebiscite should determine their permanent possession, the possessor to pay $10,000,000 in silver to the loser. The plebiscite has never been taken, and Chili still holds these provinces.

Since the peace internal affairs take the first place in Chilian history. President Errásuriz had first been a Clerical, but later came to terms with the Liberals. The Liberal party made great progress after 1881. In that year President Santa Maria established the civil status of citizens and in 1885 abolished article 5 of the constitution, by which Catholicism had been recognized as the state religion. Civil strife began with President Balmaceda. He wished to name his successor, and had chosen for the honor Sanfuentes, the minister of industry and public works, who was devoted to his chief. This pretension offended the Liberal party, and to be sure of the last word in the discussion the president prorogued the Congress. The opposition to his measures was renewed by the committee of the two houses (*Comisión Conservadora*), charged by the constitution with the duty of supervising the exercise of the executive power, deliberating upon it, and in urgent cases demanding from the president the convocation of Congress. This committee began the struggle, summoned the people to rise against the president, and took charge of the military operations.

Balmaceda's reply to the committee's remonstrance against the dissolution was an increase in the pay of the army, the proclamation of martial law, the suppression of the liberty of meeting and of the press, and a summons to the electors to choose a constitutional convention. These dictatorial measures of Balmaceda were followed by revolutionary measures on the part of the committee. It released the army and navy from its oath of fidelity to the president, and, on January 26, twenty-five ships of the fleet abandoned his cause and offered an asylum to the committee, which had now become a junta of government. The army, 30,000 strong, remained faithful to him, and he also held a fund of $30,000,000. The large cities also remained loyal to him, and he took steps to collect a fleet from the dockyards of Europe.

Between February and April Tarapaca, Iquique, Arica, and Tacna fell into the hands of the Congressionalists; the northern provinces were lost to the president; the Congressionalist capital was fixed at Iquique; and in June, 1891, a part of Balmaceda's troops went over to them. The country was cut in two. The central and southern provinces elected Claudio Vicuna, the Balmacedist candidate for the presidency, but the Congressionalists, who held the northern provinces, refused to recognize him and entrusted the command of the troops to Errásuriz. The control of the fleet gave the advantage to the Congressionalists and after one indecisive battle near Valparaiso, General Canto, their leader, was victorious. Balmaceda was deserted by his defenders. Santiago surrendered, and the president, who had sought asylum in the Argentine legation, committed suicide after writing a letter to the *New York Herald.* The news of his death was received with joy in the capitol.

The Liberal party, having conquered the dictator, returned to power. The new Congress which met November 10 continued the powers of the insurrectionary junta until after the election of a new president. Señor Jorje Montt was unanimously chosen President of the republic November 18, 1891. He was a Liberal, and in March, 1892, a ministry composed of five Liberals and a Radical took charge of affairs. The Conservatives were excluded from power; and the Clericals were driven from public office by the ministry of Matto; the Liberal press denounced the " Clerical peril " and gave out that the return of the Conservatives to power would result in the revocation of the Liberal reforms, such as registration of civil status.

A serious difference with the United States was the sequel of the civil war. The *Itata,* laden with war material for the Congressionalists, escaped from the port of San Diego, California, after seizure under the process of a federal court, and the demand for the return of the vessel and her cargo had to be complied with at a great sacrifice of Congressionalist interests. The attitude of the American minister and naval commander had also been considered as too friendly to the Balmacedists, and popular feeling against the northerners was strong. Under these circumstances 116 petty officers and men of the U. S. S. *Baltimore* were granted shore liberty at Valparaiso on October 16, 1891. A quarrel between some of these men and some Chilian sailors brought on a formidable riot in which two of the *Baltimore's* men lost their lives. After some controversy on this subject the United States, on January 22, 1892, delivered an ultimatum demanding indemnity, which was complied with. The relations of Chili with Argentina, Bolivia, and Peru are dealt with in a subsequent chapter.

In home politics the results of the civil war were important. The real issue of that struggle was between parliamentary government by a ministry responsible to the legislature, on the English model, and a representative system with an independent executive like that of the United States. The Congressionalist victory secured the triumph of the parliamentary system, which has not worked satisfactorily because of the tendency of parties to split up into small hostile groups, no one of which has been strong enough to control the Congress. Thus a coalition of discordant factions, which is in its nature ephemeral, is necessary to form a ministry; and the result has been frequent changes of ministry, instability, and a lack of continuity in policy and effectiveness in administration. In 1892 a formal amendment to the constitution empowered the committee of the two houses (*Comisión Conservadora*) to call an extraordinary session of Congress without the assent of the president. Local self-government was accorded to municipalities in 1891.

President Montt's administration was moderate and conciliatory. He declined to stand again, and in 1896 Federico Errásuriz was elected to that office by the Conservatives and a faction of Liberals, whereupon Montt returned to his duties as admiral. In 1901 the Conservative and Liberal-Democratic coalition was defeated by the election of Jerman Riesco, upon whom the Liberal factions had combined.

The educational system of the country is deficient if judged by Northern standards. In 1895 seventy-two per cent. of the population was illiterate, and even in Santiago the percentage was fifty-five. Of 675,000 children between five and fifteen years of age there were but 97,000 at school in the whole country, and the figures in Santiago were 47,000 children and 13,000 scholars. Primary education is free but not compulsory; schoolhouses are few and teachers poorly paid, except among the German immigrants in the south. Secondary and higher education is on a better footing. There are numerous colleges and lyceums under state control giving free tuition, and a state university; also church seminaries and a church university. As a whole, the educational system is top-heavy, and the elementary schools have been neglected for the benefit of the higher schools. Religious liberty prevails, but the Roman Catholic Church is specially favored, receives substantial financial aid from the government, possesses great wealth of its own, and exerts great influence. Protestantism is practically confined to the small foreign population.

Chili has not fulfilled the economic promise of thirty years ago. For this, war and its cost is partly responsible. First, the war with Spain and the destruction of Valparaiso, then the war with Peru and Bolivia and its heavy draft on the men and resources of the nation, then the civil war of Balmacedists and Congressionalists, and, lastly, heavy naval and military armaments to secure Chilian claims in case of a rupture with the Argentine Republic over the Andes boundary, have checked economic development. The total area is about 300,000 square miles. The census of 1895 showed an annual average increase of population for the preceding ten years of less than seven-tenths of one per cent. The death rate is very high, especially in the cities; in 1895 34 for the whole country, 72 in Santiago and 67 in Valparaiso. In the former city there were 1678 more deaths than births and in the latter only 152 more births than deaths. Immigration is small and the total foreign population was only 72,000, of whom 29,000 were from other South American countries. The distribution of population is abnormal. Of the total (2,712,000 in 1895), more than forty-five per cent. (1,240,000) were urban. Alcoholism is alarmingly prevalent among the people, and jobbery at the expense of the government is common. In the rural districts organized brigandage, a heritage from the civil war of 1891, flourishes unchecked, and in consequence of this and of purely economic causes, agriculture has in the last thirty years lost the place it once held as the most important industry. Landed proprietors congregate in the cities, leaving the management of their estates to agents, and the mass of the rural population tends to follow them. Agricultural products (including live stock) have fallen to twelve per cent. of the total exports in 1899, and wheat had to be imported in 1901. Stock-raising is increasing under the stimulus of protective duties levied upon cattle imported from the Argentine Republic.

Mining is the main industry and its chief product is nitrate from the north. In this industry $60,000,000 is invested. Other mineral products are borax, silver, copper, and coal, and valuable iron ores are found near the coal beds. Minerals made up 84 per cent. of the exports in 1899. Manufacturing is in its infancy, but economic conditions are favorable for its growth and protective duties have been laid to stimulate it. Railroads are few (2890 miles in 1891, of which half was owned by the state), and roads are poor. Chili suffered a severe commercial crisis in the early 'nineties and adopted the gold standard of currency in 1895.

In contrast with the country as a whole, the region on both sides of the Straits of Magellan has made rapid progress. Sheep-farming is the prevalent industry here, and the thriving city of Punta Arenas, which has grown to a population of 10,000 in ten years, attests the general prosperity of this part of the country.

The history of Peru since her defeat by Chili is a monotonous record of political turmoil and industrial stagnation. General Miguel Iglesias was made president by the help of the Chilian army of occupation. In 1886 Carceres led a successful revolution against him and ruled in person until 1890, and through Morales Bermudez from 1890 to 1894, when he again took the office himself. A new revolution in the following year gave the presidency for the second time to Nicolas de Pierola. His successors were Romaña (1889-1903), Manuel Caudamo (1903-1904), José Pardo (1904), Augusto B. Lequia (1910). The country is characterized by an educational system having, in an exaggerated form, all the faults mentioned in the case of Chili, by corrupt courts, and an all-powerful church. The population is variously estimated at from 1,500,000 to 4,000,000. By the census of 1876 it was 2,660,881. The Indians are the most numerous race and other important elements are Spaniards, negroes, and Chinese. These races are much mixed in blood, but are divided by mutual hatred. There is no immigration of importance. Infant mortality is very high and alcoholism very prevalent.

Commerce and industry have been stagnant since the Chilian

war, but now give some promise of improvement. A heavy load of foreign debt, $270,000,000, was liquidated in 1889 by a lease of the state railways and other concessions with an annual payment of $400,000. The credit of the government is poor. In 1898 the gold standard of currency was adopted by taking the pound sterling (*libra*) as a unit and valuing the current silver as decimal parts of the standard coin. The chief agricultural products are sugar, cotton, coffee, cacao, rice, hides, and wool, including that of llamas and alpacas. Mining yields copper, silver, petroleum, and borax, and from the tropical forest east of the Andes come rubber, Peruvian bark, and dyewoods. There are a few small manufactories. Railroads are few, 917 miles in 1901, and roads almost entirely lacking.

Bolivia by the war with Chili was cut off from access to the sea, and has at various times sought the help of the Argentine Republic for the recovery of her lost territory, but thus far to no purpose. There remain some 700,000 square miles subject to her jurisdiction. Her politics have been simple. President Campero negotiated the peace and dictated the election of his successor Pacheco (1884). In like manner the office was transferred to Arce (1884), Baptista (1892), and Alonzo (1896). It was now the turn of the Outs, and a revolution (1899) placed Paredo in power, who was followed by Ysmael Montes (1904). Elections are a farce and there are but two political elements: office-seeking creoles and apathetic Indians. The population is about 2,000,000, of whom about 250,000 are whites, 500,000 half-breeds, and the rest Indians. There are only 36,000 pupils enrolled in the primary schools, but the country boasts six universities, attended by 500 students. The chief cities are La Paz, with 62,000 inhabitants, and Sucre with 27,000. Geographically the country consists of tropical forests on the eastern slope of the Andes, the high peaks and ranges, the temperate plateau, and the subtropical valleys on the Pacific slope. Agriculture is unimportant. Mining is the chief industry, and there are exported 15,000,000 ounces of silver, 7000 tons of tin, and 3000 tons of copper annually, besides small quantities of antimony, bismuth, and borax. Rubber to the amount of 5000 tons a year is exported through Peru, also some Peruvian bark.

Means of communication are almost non-existent. The courts are corrupt, as in Peru, but the general conditions of Bolivia are more promising. The public debt is small and taxation light. Natural resources are abundant, especially minerals. Peru has decayed. Bolivia has not begun to grow.

Upon the assassination of Moreno in 1875 Dr. Borrero succeeded to the presidency of Ecuador, but was driven from power in the following year by General Veintemilla. Then followed thirty years of alternate tyranny and revolution, the victorious chief of the moment sometimes masquerading as a constitutional president and again ruling frankly as dictator. An exception was Dr. Antonio Flores (1888-1892), who made an earnest effort to infuse honesty and efficiency into the conduct of public affairs, and declined reëlection at the end of his term. Veintemilla was dictator 1876-1878, "president" 1878-1882, dictator 1882, and fugitive in 1883. His successor, Dr. Placido Caamaño (1884-1888), struggled successfully throughout his term against conspiracies and insurrections. The four years of peace and order under Flores was but a breathing spell. Under Dr. Luis Cordero the old methods of corruption and oppression returned, bringing the country to bankruptcy in 1894. In 1895 Cordero was driven from power by General Eloy Alfaro, who forthwith became dictator until 1897, and "president" until 1901, when he secured the election of General Leonidas Plaza as his successor. Plaza was followed by Lizardo Garcia. The revolutions and other political activities are carried on by the whites, who are only seven per cent. of the population. Their lack of stability is illustrated by the ten constitutions successively proclaimed for the republic since 1830.

Ecuador has an area of 116,000 square miles, and a population of about 1,400,000, of whom perhaps 100,000 are whites, 400,000 half-breeds, and the rest Indians. The low coast lands are very unhealthful, but in the mountain valleys at elevations of 4000 feet and more the climate is temperate. There is one railroad into the interior from Guayaquil. The road between these two cities has fallen into decay and there are no other roads worthy of the name. The chief exports are cocoa, coffee, and rubber. On April 14, 1909, an infamous plot was discovered and checked. There was a definite plan to overthrow President Alfarro, and the present government, and to establish instead a triumvirate.

In Colombia President Parra was succeeded by General Tru-

jillo (1878-1880), who had recently led the Liberal army to victory.
The evil consequences of war now became apparent. The federal
bond was greatly weakened; the finances were in bad condition,
and in 1879 the public creditors could not be paid. In this state of
affairs a jurist, Dr. Rafael Nuñez, came into power (1880). He
was one of the most prominent Liberal leaders. In his first term
he undertook the economic restoration of the country. He was
reëlected in 1884, and in January, 1885, seven states rose in insurrection against him. With the moral support of the United States,
a Colombian man-of-war drove the insurgents from Panama and
their ships were captured in July. After this Nuñez left the Au-
tonomist party and went over to the Centralists. In pursuance of
this new policy he overthrew the constitution, and in the following
year procured the ratification of a new one, which reëstablished a
centralized republic. The majority in Congress was of the same
mind as the president, and assisted him in carrying out this transformation on August 5, 1886. To insure the stability of the new
order Nuñez was elected in 1886 for a further term of six years,
and reëlected for six years more in 1892. He died in September,
1894, and was succeeded by Vice-President Miguel Caro (1892-
1898). The aged Sanclamente was elected by the Conservatives
in 1898, but the real power was in the hands of Vice-President
Marroquin, who formally deposed Sanclamente in 1900, after
putting down a Liberal insurrection which had been marked by
severe fighting on the Isthmus of Panama. The most important
event of his administration was the secession of Panama in November, 1903, and the recognition and protection of its independence by the United States. General Reyes was elected president in
1904 and his term was extended for ten years by an act passed in
1905. The resignation of President Rafael Reyes, on July 26,
1909, inaugurated a new order of things. His successor was appointed on August 3rd, being Gonzales Tremau.

The mountainous region enjoys a temperate climate, and the
vast plains of the interior are tropical in character. The mountains
are rich in minerals and their valleys are very fertile, but the obstacles to internal communication offered by these ranges, 12,000
to 14,000 feet in altitude, are enormous. The total area of the
country is about 500,000 square miles and the estimated population is 4,000,000.

In Venezuela Guzman Blanco's power lasted from 1870 to

1889. He held the presidential office in person during the years 1870-1877, 1879-1884, and 1886-1887, and placed his creatures in it for the other years of the period, controlling Venezuelan affairs from Paris, where he resided as minister to France. His rule was favorable to the economic development and financial strength of the country, for under his absolutism Venezuela enjoyed the longest period of internal peace in her history. In 1889 his nominee, Dr. Rojas Paul, was driven from power by General Palacios, and in 1892 Palacios was defeated in battle and deposed by General Joaquin Crespo (1892-1898). Crespo was peaceably succeeded by Andrade (1898) and was killed in battle in the following year while defending Andrade's government against a new insurrection. His death ensured the success of the insurgents and the succession of their leader, Cipriano Castro, who held the presidential office, against repeated attempts to displace him by force, until April 16, 1906, when he was succeeded by General Gomez.

Venezuela has held a prominent place in international affairs during the last decade. The boundary dispute with British Guiana and the intervention of the United States are described in a subsequent chapter. The chronic revolutionary turmoil had given rise to many claims by foreign residents to damages for injury to their property.

Castro would give no satisfaction, and in 1902 Great Britain, Germany, and Italy blockaded La Guayra and seized the customs house. The United States secured an agreement by all parties to refer the dispute to The Hague Tribunal, all other nations to be allowed to prove their claims also. The award (February 22, 1904) gave to the three powers who had used force a preferential right to 30 per cent. of the customs duties. After their claims should be fully satisfied the fund could be applied to other claims. The United States was requested to execute the award.

Venezuela is a federal republic. The Congress is composed of a Senate and a House of Representatives chosen in the same manner as in the United States, but the president is elected by a Federal Council of nineteen members who are appointed by Congress for a term of two years. The president must be chosen from among the members of the council, and holds his office for six years. The constitution encourages revolution by according belligerent rights to insurgents, and exempting their property from confiscation. That these prerogatives have been fully exercised, witness half a hundred insurrections in seventy years. The revolutionary habit receives similar encouragement in other South American states.

The narrow strip of low-lying coast lands, and the plains of the interior, are unhealthful; but between them is a region of mountain and valley well fitted for European settlement. The total area of the country is about 600,000 square miles and the population is estimated at 2,500,000.

Trouble between Venezuela and the United States was brought to a focus, when that country refused to accept the answer of Castro to American demands for arbitration, in July, 1907. In January, 1908, Castro continued his headlong career towards ultimate destruction by annulling the contract between his government and an English corporation known as the Venezuelan Salt Monopoly, and he further aroused the United States, by continuing to refuse to arbitrate. In the meanwhile, Venezuela was crippled by the payment to Mexico of the first installment of a loan which was originally made by that country to Colombia, but assumed later by Venezuela. On April 21, 1908, Venezuela was visited by bubonic plague, and the port of La Guayra was closed. The relations between the United States and Venezuela had by this time become so strained that on June 23, 1908, the secretary of the American legation left Caracas, and on July 9, the Venezuelan charge d' affaires in Washington was recalled. Not content with having estranged the United States and England, the government made things so atrocious for the Dutch settlers that on July 5, 1908, they appealed to their home government for redress. This resulted in the expelling of the minister of the Netherlands from Caracas by Castro, on July 22, 1908, and the Dutch government immediately responded by sending a government cruiser for him. Castro, seeing in this an insult, demanded an apology from Holland, but on August 23, the Dutch foreign office refused to agree to any kind of compromise. Castro made himself still more unpopular by stopping passenger traffic between his country and the West Indian ports. As this was very disastrous, especially to the Dutch merchant vessels, Holland demanded that Castro revoke this embargo before November. This he refused to do, but he later modified his trans-shipment decree, so as to permit ships to leave Parian ports for Trinidad. As Castro refused to comply with her demand, Holland on November 7, 1908, revoked her treaty of 1894. This resulted in the flight of Castro, who landed in France on December 10. On December 11, the Netherlands sent a warship from Willemstad, cleared for action, but reassured by the promise and action of acting-president Gomez, the warship was recalled on December 25. Gomez took immediate action against the partisans of Castro, arresting a number, and cancelled Castro's letter of credit. With the inauguration of Gomez on February 28, 1909, a new condition of affairs commenced, and March 6, 1909, he signed a general amnesty treaty, and forbade Castro to return to Venezuela. He appointed Señor Rojas to represent his country at Washington, and cordial diplomatic relations were resumed between the United States and Venezuela.

Other countries took measures to show their disapproval of Castro, and on April 6, 1909, Great Britain refused to permit the exile to land at the port of Pjani. On April 10 Castro was expelled from Martineau and on the 11th of the same month, Denmark declared he must not land at any of her West Indian ports. Castro was finally repudiated by the rejection on July 30, by the congress of his country, of his report in which he endeavored to justify himself for his arbitrary actions. In spite of the prompt and salutary action of President Gomez, Venezuela continued to be in a state of unrest, and many of the citizens were arrested during the latter part of 1909. During December, Venezuela brought to a termination the diplomatic mission to France; that country having insisted upon arbitration of matters relating to the claims French citizens had against the country on account of having been expelled by Castro. In spite of his many defeats and the general execration of him by other countries, Castro has not yet given up hope of regaining his power, and is at the present time continuing his intrigues for re-instatement.

The term of President Gomez who had endeavored to give the country an honest administration expired on April 10, 1914. He was succeeded by General V. Marquez Bustelle as Provisional President for one year.. Measures for the development of the country were taken, which included an extensive system of national highways and the opening of manual training schools.

Good progress was made in 1914 in the work of national sanitation. Under the new regulation the Department of Health made such advancement that it has practically stamped out yellow fever and the bubonic plague.

BRAZIL, 1876-1910

Chapter XVI

BRAZIL. 1876-1910

THE history of Brazil for the last thirty years is dominated by three great facts: the gradual abolition of slavery, the encouragement of European colonization, and the establishment of republican government.

The slavery question was raised in 1850, and remained unsolved until 1888. Emperor Pedro favored abolition from humanitarian motives, but as a constitutional sovereign he had to reckon with powerful interests, and only by degrees did Portuguese America rid itself of the shame of continuing slavery in the full light of the nineteenth century. In 1852 the slave trade was abolished and the minister, Eusebio de Quieroz, took measures to suppress it. But though officially abolished, the trade was in fact kept up with the Portuguese colonies in Africa until 1858. Not until that time did it entirely cease.

The abolitionist party, of which the emperor was in fact an ally, was not satisfied with having cut off one of the sources of slave labor. Measures favorable to the slaves were taken, beginning in 1864, and Dom Pedro's initiative secured the passage of a law abolishing slavery in principle, but continuing it temporarily until a method of gradual emancipation should be devised. Its devising was postponed (April, 1866) by the war with Paraguay. But the emperor did not dare to assume the responsibility for the complete abolition which he would have welcomed. Perhaps he feared the loss of his empire. In any case the three acts emancipating the negroes were adopted during his absence in Europe. Nevertheless, when the French Society for the Abolition of Slavery sent him an address in July, 1866, Pedro replied that his government would take up, as soon as circumstances would permit, a measure " demanded by the spirit of Christianity."

In 1871 the government won its first success. The prime minister, J. M. da Silva Paranhos, Viscount of Rio Branço, on September 21 secured the passage of a law which abolished slavery in principle and removed certain taxes on the emancipation of ne-groes. This law of Rio Branco was also called the law of " free birth," for all children thereafter born of negro mothers were to be free, though they were to remain under the power of the mother's master until twenty-one years of age to compensate him for the expense of their education.

Thus the two sources of the institution, the slave trade and slave birth, were removed; but there were many people in Brazil who thought it unjust to allow the distinction to continue between slave parents and free children in negro families. A great number of proprietors liberated their blacks, two provinces freed all their slaves, and negroes still held in slavery in adjoining provinces fled thither amid the applause of the abolitionists, and in spite of the efforts of the authorities to prevent it. Then, in 1885, the ministry decreed that all slaves under sixty years of age were free. One last step remained, and on May 13, 1888, the speech from the throne of the Princess Regent gave notice that this step was to be taken. She added: " To the honor of Brazil, under the influ-ence of national sentiment and individual liberality, the extinction of the servile element has made such progress that it is to-day a hope acclaimed by all classes and by admirable examples of un-selfishness on the part of the owners." In the chamber of deputies Joaquin Nabuco said with some exaggeration: " The present gen-eration has never been so powerfully moved, and for a parallel we must recall the emotion our fathers experienced at the proclama-tion of our independence. For us, Brazilians, 1888 is a greater date than 1789 for France. Literally a new country is beginning for us."

On May 13 the Senate followed the lower house in voting for emancipation and the Princess signed the act with a pen of gold which had been offered to her for that purpose. The Argentine Republic and all the great cities throughout America celebrated the event as joyfully as the population of Rio, and distant France took part in the rejoicing occasioned by this advance of civilization. The abolition of slavery has not had such important economic re-sults as might have been expected. It is true that for the moment the blacks flocked to the cities and coffee culture was abandoned, but in general they dreaded the competition of white laborers and entered the service of their old masters as wage earners. As a result of the abolition of slavery the Brazilian government has encouraged foreign immigration, and strong "colonies" have been formed on Brazilian soil and subject to Brazilian rule, chiefly by Italians and Germans.

German immigration to Brazil, though important only in recent years, began early in the nineteenth century. German officers and soldiers who had entered the service of Pedro I. against Portugal remained in the country after its independence was secured. From 1820 to 1830 7000 immigrants arrived. After non-Protestants acquired civil rights (1861) and slavery became a tottering institution soon to be suppressed, this immigration increased. Companies were formed at Hamburg (1853) and Rio (1855) to aid the movement. In 1857-1858 33,000 Germans from Pomerania, Prussia, and the Rhine Provinces landed in South America. But the companies exploited the emigrants without mercy and raised a powerful opposition against themselves among the members of the German families, so that the Prussian and Brazilian governments were forced to interfere and suppress what had become a sort of white slave trade.

The Italian immigration is equally large. In 1887 Brazil received 31,445 Italians; in 1888, 97,730; in 1889, 65,000; in 1902, 29,000. There are to-day 1,100,000 Italians in the country. Unlike the Germans, they do not form compact agricultural colonies, but are scattered, and for the most part employed in the industries. In the province of San Paulo they are more compact and cultivate the soil, forming a colony of 650,000. Italian immigration is recruited in Lombardy, Venetia, Tuscany, Calabria, and at Palermo. Not all the immigrants are in the same economic condition. Some are enrolled by contracts of service with Brazilian masters and are miserably lodged and nourished. Others settle in colonies which they found in coöperation with the government. These are relatively well off and receive an allotment of land 45 to 62 acres in area, and worth $60 to $100. The Bureau of Statistics at Rome tries to direct Italian emigration to the southern states of the republic.[1]

Hereafter immigration may become more important. From 1864 to 1866 the number of immigrants rose from 1500 to 1800 a

[1] See the *Bulletin de l'Institut International de Statistique de Rome* for Italy; and for Germany the *Monatsheft zur Statistik des deutschen Reichs;* also the article "*Brésil*" in the "*Grande Encyclopédie.*" M. Meuriot's article in the *Revue de Geographie* for January, 1892, has been drawn upon in preparing a part of this chapter.

year. In 1862 there were 54,000 persons of German blood in Brazil; in 1876, 110,000; in 1892, 240,000 (half Catholics, half Protestants). This group is rather compact and includes colonies:

(1) In Rio Grande do Sul, a region where the average temperature is 62° to 84° Fahrenheit, and hence can be easily endured by Europeans. Two German newspapers are published here. In this province alone there are 160,000 Germans, forming a colony with an area of granted lands equal to that of a French department. Some Westphalians exploit the coal mines at San Jeromnio.

(2) In the province of Santa Catharina. Here the two principal centers are Blumenan and Doña Francisca. A German newspaper has been published here since 1881, and the German population is about 60,000.

(3) In Parana, San Paulo, Minas Geraes, and Matto Grosso, 30,000 Germans in the midst of Brazilians, Spaniards, Portuguese, and Italians.

The German settlements in Brazil have created a commerce with Germany, and are in close relations with the mother country. This ethnic element, modern in character and new in Brazilian history, may some day become a separatist element. The Cologne *Gazette* remarked in 1890 that there might one day be an independent Brazilian German state and that in that event there were 25,000 fellow-countrymen in Uruguay to join it.

To sum up: Brazil was in a prosperous condition. Although it had assumed a part of the Portuguese debt at the time of independence, the finances were on a good basis, expenses were moderate, the army and navy were neither large nor expensive, public education and public works did not impose ruinous burdens, and the well-adjusted budget showed a surplus. Foreigners readily gave financial credit to this state, the most orderly and without doubt the best administered in all South America. Such was the condition of Brazil in 1889 when a sudden revolutionary outbreak overthrew the monarchy.

The old emperor was a Liberal in politics and was popular, but it was generally felt that under a successor the imperial form of government might be irksome. Moreover, Pedro gave but little attention to the public business, which was therefore not well administered. Malcontents formed combinations. The army officers, who had been neglected by the emperor and were hostile to Count d'Eu, heir presumptive to the crown; provincials who desired decentralization; many landed proprietors who resented the abolition of slavery; and finally republican and federalist states rights doctrinaires; all agreed in dreading the accession of Count d'Eu.

There were many converts to liberalism in the empire, and they had shown their strength in the anti-slavery agitation. Along with liberalism the positivism of Auguste Compte had won wide acceptance through the works of Benjamin Constant, the chief apostle of this political sect. Its doctrines spread in the military institutes, and their influence on the eve of the revolution was shown by decrees looking to the separation of church and state, the institution of a national holiday on July 14, and the adoption of the mottoes: "Order and progress" inscribed on the flags and "greetings and brotherhood" in official correspondence.[2] The revolution was preceded by a parliamentary contest. A Conservative ministry under João Alfredo was in office at the beginning of 1889. Though it had, in the preceding year, brought about the abolition of slavery, it was sharply attacked by the Liberals. Dom Pedro refused to dissolve the Congress at the request of the ministry, the Conservatives were unable to form a government, and power passed into the hands of the Liberals, who got rid of their adversaries by dissolution, which they had known how to get from the emperor.

The Republican party profited by this state of things, and prospered under the leadership of two journalists, Ruy Barbosa and Quintino Bocayuva, the editors of the *Diario de Noticias* and *O Pais*. There were Republican demonstrations on the street, and the prefect of Rio was obliged to make an order forbidding shouts of "Long live the Republic, Down with the Monarchy" in public. The Liberals carried the elections, leaving only seven seats to the Conservatives and two to the Republicans.

Apparently there was nothing to criticise in an emperor who had favored the Liberals, and had called them to power in response to public opinion. But the army was very hostile to the dynasty and was distrusted. It was proud of its achievements in the war with Paraguay, but the emperor showed it no favor and was influenced to take the fatal step of exiling the discontented regiments whose officers were opposed to him to distant and some-

[2] Adapted from "*Apostolat Positiviste au Brésil*," by Miguel Lamos.

times unhealthful provinces, as in Matto Grosso or on the upper Amazon. The Republicans took advantage of the sentiment of the army and made allies of the military chiefs. A large number of general officers had already been sent off when the turn of Admiral van den Kolk came. At last Marshal Deodora da Fonseca, who had long been in opposition, was under orders to embark with several battalions under his command. After an understanding had been reached, the revolution was quickly accomplished. Marshal Fonseca, Benjamin Constant, and the Republicans seized the ministers and forced Dom Pedro, who had come from Petropolis, to sign an act of abdication. The imperial family was put on board a ship bound for Lisbon, where they arrived December 17. The people had not stirred. A provisional government, composed of Marshal Deodora da Fonseca (President), B. Constant (War), Admiral van den Kolk (Navy), Ruy Barbosa (Treasury), and Q. Bocayuva (Foreign Affairs), proclaimed the republic.

One of the first acts of the new government was to dismiss public officers who had been appointed under the empire. More than half the governors of provinces in 1893 were soldiers. The country was governed by soldiers, or rather by officers, the only element of political importance in a volunteer force composed chiefly of mulattoes. The government hastened to raise the pay of the army. To satisfy the Republicans universal suffrage was proclaimed and notice was given that a constitutional convention would be called. The ministry, composed of soldiers and men of revolutionary ideas, took energetic measures and executed them rapidly. Like every new government it met resistance, which it crushed by arrests, banishments, the suppression of newspapers, and the establishment of a military court. It recognized civil marriage and decreed the separation of church and state.

The provisional government, declaring that it "was created by the army and navy in the name of the nation," promulgated (June 22) a constitution modeled on that of the United States. The head of the nation is responsible for his official acts. Cabinet ministers are excluded from Congress. The president is elected by indirect vote for a term of five years and the two houses by universal suffrage for three years. In the lower house there is one member for 70,000 inhabitants. There are three senators from each state, and members of both houses are paid for their services.

The Congress of 1890, composed of members summoned by

the government, worked upon the constitution. It decided that the president should not be reëligible and that no member of his family could be a candidate to succeed him. The judiciary power is vested in a supreme court. The constitution is federal, democratic, and non-sectarian. The style of the nation is " The United States of Brazil." (There are twenty-one states in the Union, including the federal district of Rio de Janiero.) State legislatures and governors are elected by direct vote. Each state adopts its own democratic constitution as it pleases. To exclude the negroes from the exercise of the right to vote, the ability to read and write is required.

Fonseca did not long remain in power. On June 15 he opened the session of Congress, but dissension soon arose between him and the legislative power. On November 3 he dissolved Congress and proclaimed martial law; the provinces were disaffected; Rio Grande do Sol rose in arms; the navy declared against the president, and in view of these grave difficulties Fonseca resigned. General Floriano Peixoto, vice-president of the republic and president of the senate, succeeded to the presidency in accordance with the constitution. He had supported the provisional government, had been elected as a representative of the province of Alagoas, and in 1891 had become vice-president of the republic.

Peixoto followed the evil example of his predecessor and ruled despotically. On September 6, 1893, the naval squadron in the harbor of Rio de Janeiro revolted, under Admiral Custodio de Mello, and with the aid of a rising in the south menaced the city and defied the president for six months. The turning point of the struggle was the action of Admiral Benham, U. S. N., who by a show of superior force compelled the insurgents to permit merchant ships of the United States to unload at the wharves of Rio. The rebellion was finally suppressed in March, 1894, and Peixoto took a terrible vengeance on his enemies, who were summarily tried by court martial and shot wholesale.

While the insurrection was still active Dr. Prudente de Moraes Barros had been elected to the presidency by the influence of Peixoto, and was inaugurated November 15, 1894. He reversed the policy of his predecessor, restored constitutional methods, granted amnesty to the late rebels, and by 1896 had pacified the country. He was bitterly opposed by former partisans of Peixoto, and his life was attempted November 4, 1897. He united firmness with conciliation and did not hesitate to put down revolutionary outbreaks. A costly episode of his administration was a war with the mixed bloods of the interior called Jagunços. They were led by a white man, Antonio Maciel or Conselheiro, a strange figure, half renegade and half prophet, who roused his people to such a pitch of fanaticism that the national government had to use against them 14,000 men and sacrifice over 5000 lives before they could be suppressed. Barros chose as his successor Dr. Manuel Campos Salles (1898-1902) whose title received formal sanction by popular election in the usual course. He was followed (1902-1906) by Dr. Francisco Rodriguez Alves. Dr. Alfonso Penna was elected March 1, 1906, and inaugurated November 15; one of his first acts after coming into power, being to authorize the loan of $50,000,000 to Rio Janeiro. In March, 1907, some trouble arose because of the heavy immigration from the Baltic provinces to Brazil, but it was eventually settled. President Penna reduced the tariff upon a number of United States products in return for considerable favors extended the coffee exporters, and also as a mark of esteem to the American fleet, which reached Brazil in January, 1908. On October 2nd of that same year, Penna signed a general treaty with Argentina, and this received the ratification of the United States on December 10th. Brazil and Uruguay signed a treaty on November 7, 1909, which gave the latter country valuable concessions. Another ratification of boundary lines was made January 11, 1910, when Peru sanctioned the boundary treaty with Brazil.

In July of the same year a Pan-American Conference took place in Rio Janeiro, representatives from all the American republics being present. Elihu Root, Secretary of State of the United States, was making an official visit to South America at the time, and, though present at but one meeting, and that an extraordinary session, summoned to hear his speech, directed the policy of the United States delegates. Many measures for the development of the wonderful resources of South America were discussed, and the old feeling of distrust for the policy of the United States seemed to pass away.

Economic progress in Brazil has been checked by war and political turmoil. Financial stress was induced by the long period of war (1908-1894), and by mismanagement. The currency was depreciated, new and heavy taxes were laid, and in 1898 an extension of credit was granted to the republic by the Rothschilds. Brazil has an area of 3,200,000 square miles, and the population is: whites, 5,000,000; half-breeds, 6,500,000; negroes, 3,500,000; Indians, 400,000. Immigration is very large. There are now 1,000,-000 Italians in the country, many thousands of Germans, and numerous Portuguese. The Italians and Germans adhere to their several customs, but the Portuguese are readily assimilated. There are only 9,000 miles of railway in the vast territory, and these are poorly equipped and administered, as are the telegraph lines. The magnificent system of communication afforded by the navigable rivers is neglected. In 1889 there were only 300,000 children in the primary schools, and in 1890, 8,300,000 of the population were illiterate. The people are superstitious, the courts corrupt, and the local governments expensive and inefficient.

The election in March, 1914, resulted in the election of Dr. Wenceslao Braz to succeed Marshal Fonseca as President of the Republic. He was inaugurated on November 15, 1914, for the full term of four years.

During the year the government endeavored to straighten out the tangled and financial situation. In June, 1914, a new loan was authorized by the Chamber. The outbreak of the European War in August, 1914, put a stop to negotiations for a loan in Europe. A new issue of 300,000 contos of paper money was made to partly relieve the financial crisis.

STATES OF THE LA PLATA, 1876-1910

Chapter XVII

THE STATES OF THE LA PLATA. 1876-1910

GENERAL MITRE, who had revolted against President Sarmiento of Argentina (1868-1874), repeated the offense against his successor, Avellaneda, who put down the insurrection and captured its leader. But Buenos Ayres rose in behalf of the Nationalists (the old Unitarian party) and the government was driven from that city to Belgrano, whence it established a blockade of the port of Buenos Ayres and thus compelled the rebels to submit. When General J. A. Roca (1880-1886) succeeded Avellaneda the strife between Buenos Ayres and the provinces broke out again, but was promptly suppressed. Roca was succeeded (October 12, 1886) by the former governor of Cordoba, Dr. Miguel Juarez Celman, who was forced by a popular uprising to resign (July 30, 1890), leaving the vice-president, Carlos Pellegrini, to complete the unexpired term. During Pellegrini's presidency the country suffered from a great economic crisis, which followed a period of great prosperity and heavy immigration aided by subsidies from the government to immigration companies. In this manner the government had spent considerabe sums. The number of European immigrants, chiefly Italians, Spaniards, and Basques, was: 6300 in 1883; 77,000 in 1884; 108,000 in 1885; 180,000 in 1886; 290,000 in 1889; 57,000 in 1902, and 125,000 in 1904.

At first all went well; agricultural colonies were founded, sheep were raised in large numbers, railway building was undertaken on a large scale, and numerous mining concessions were granted. But business ran into speculation and became unsound. In 1890 gold disappeared from circulation and rose to a premium of 250. European countries, which had accepted Argentina paper in vast quantities, were uneasy, became cautious, and refused further credit. Matters went from bad to worse in Argentina. To prevent disorder the government took measures that were often inconsistent.

It closed the stock exchange, sold the public lands, required the payment of customs duties in gold, etc. Meanwhile the foreign speculation in Argentine railway enterprises, mines, and industries brought on financial catastrophes which aggravated the situation.

The shock of the economic crisis in the Argentine Republic was quickly felt in Europe. The famous and long-established English banking house of the Barings, which had floated most of the Argentine loans in Europe, was forced into liquidation in November, and all the financial markets of the world felt the shock in turn. An international financial syndicate was formed to secure from the Argentine government the fulfillment of its obligations. Pellegrini had not retained the public confidence and the latter part of his term was marked by political unrest and threats of revolution. In 1892 Dr. Luis Saenz Peña, with the powerful aid of Pellegrini's influence, was elected to the presidency. He was a highly respected jurist with no political connections and attempted to give the country a non-partisan administration. The experiment was a failure, the president was utterly without support in Congress, government became impossible, and Peña resigned in 1895. He was succeeded by the vice-president, Dr. José Uriburu, who also had no political connections, having been absent from the country as a diplomat for twenty years before his election to the vice-presidency. But he received the powerful support of Roca and Pellegrini, and thus gave the country a firm and moderate administration. In 1898 General Julio Roca was elected to the presidency for the second time. His administration was dignified, firm, and on the whole very successful. In 1904 he was succeeded by Dr. Miguel Quintana and at the same time Dr. José Figueros Alcorta became vice-president. Quintana died in March, 1906, and Alcorta then became president.

The financial difficulties of the country continued. Paper money was issued as a measure of relief, but the notes were at a discount and the situation was soon worse than ever. In January, 1891, the country could not meet payments due on account of the public debt. In April wild panic ensued and important local banks failed, including the Banco Nacional. A new national bank was created in October, authorized to issue notes to the value of $50,000,000. Nevertheless the finances slowly improved, and in 1898 the foreign debt of the provinces was assumed by the federal government. The survival of unsound financial principles is attested by a law passed in 1899 to prevent a fall in the price of gold by fixing the premium at 127.

Argentina has an area of about 1,100,000 square miles, and a population of 6,000,000, which is centered in the middle part on account of its extreme fertility. Large areas, as large as the states of Illinois or Wisconsin, contain not more than 10,000. The forests are producing an export trade of $6,000,000; the cattle products are worth from $80,000,000 to $90,000,000 annually; the agricultural exports equal $158,000,000, while other exports are about $3,000,000. The total imports are $318,000,000 annually, while the total exports are $268,000,000, or a per capita exportation of $65, which is twice as large as that of the United States. Great Britain is the largest buyer of these exports; the United States second; Germany third, and France fourth. There is soft coal and petroleum in abundance, although but little has as yet been produced. England has invested largely in railroads in Argentina; France is also interested in them and there are the following trunk lines; Buenos Ayres and Rosario, the Central Argentina and Central de Cordova, the Buenos Ayrès & Pacific and the Southern Railway. Argentina is ranked among the first wheat producing countries of the world.

Buenos Ayres, the capital, ranks as one of the large centers of the world, its population being 1,146,865. Italy, Spain, Russia, Syria, France, Austria, Germany, Great Britain, Portugal, China, Japan and Africa as well as Latin-American states all sending their quota to swell the population. The birth rate is also very high. There are less than 300 Americans in Buenos Ayres, for prior to the extradition treaty of the United States with Argentina, which was signed September 26, 1896, approved December 29, 1898, and exchanged June 2, 1900, this city was the refuge of those under the ban of the law. The present president is Dr. José F. Alcorta.

January 26, 1908, was a memorable day at Buenos Ayres for it was on that date that the American fleet arrived in its harbor. On May 1, 1909, in the midst of the May day festivities, five persons were killed, and many wounded in a riot. Naturally, there were a number of arrests, and as a protest against the action, a strike was called two days later and on the following day, six hundred people were arrested. Trouble continued and the chief of police and the police secretary were killed on November 14, 1909. On August 8, 1909, a treaty was signed by Argentina and the United States which provided for reciprocity and naturalization. During the early part of 1910, Argentina signed contracts with American ship builders for the construction of two first class battleships to add to her navy.

In Uruguay the dictatorship of Latorre lasted for three years (1876-1879). He then tried to rule as a constitutional president, but resigned in disgust March 13, 1880, declaring that the country was ungovernable. Dr. Francisco A. Vidal was elected to succeed him, but the real power was General Maximo Santos, who was formally made president when Vidal resigned, March 1, 1882. Santos procured the second election of Vidal in 1886, and within a few months these two statesmen reënacted the comedy of Vidal's resignation and Santos's election to fill the unexpired term. Santos's government was a military despotism, and aroused such discontent that he was forced to resign on November 18, 1886, after being wounded by a would-be assassin in August. Maximo Tajes, who filled out the term of Santos, ruled wisely and maintained order until March 1, 1890, when Dr. Julio Herrera y Obes was chosen to succeed him.

Under Herrera and Juan Idiarte Borda, who followed him in office (March 21, 1894), the old *régime* of extravagance, inefficiency, and corruption was renewed, bringing forth the inevitable insurrection in 1897. In these two administrations Uruguay suffered from the economic crisis which overwhelmed Argentina. The two nations had been guilty of like sins and now paid like penalties. The interest on the public debt was defaulted by Uruguay in 1891. Borda was at last assassinated (August 25, 1897), and the president of the senate, Juan Lindolfo Cuestas, who succeeded him, had to face a difficult situation. The insurgents were still in arms, and discontent was general. Cuestas ruled with moderation and firmness. Peace was restored by granting amnesty to the insurgents, and the flagrant abuses which had prevailed in the two preceding administrations were reformed. He met with much factional opposition and did not hesitate to proclaim himself dictator in 1898, but resigned the office in the following year and was reëlected president. He reduced the strength of the army, thus provoking a revolt among the troops, which was suppressed July 1, 1899. An unsuccessful insurrection occurred in 1903. The present president is Dr. Clodio Willimau.

Uruguay is a well-watered rolling country, 72,210 square miles in area. The climate is mild and healthful for the European races. In 1907 the population was 1,140,799. Of these 72,280 were Italians, 57,865 Spaniards, and 12,879 Frenchmen. The population of Monteveideo is about 316,000. The chief industries are agriculture and grazing. In 1904 there were 1,210 miles of railroad in operation. Roads are poor at a distance from the cities, but are being improved. The government is a centralized republic, under a president elected for four years and a congress of two houses. The Roman Catholic Church is established, but complete toleration is accorded to other beliefs. As in many South American countries, there is a compulsory education law, which is not enforced. Of 138,200 children of school age in 1898 only 72,242 attended school. The University of Montevideo had in the same year 684 students.

The little state of Paraguay, since the death of Lopez, has been the sport of scheming politicians and military chieftians. When President Gill took office in 1874 the Brazilian army of occupation had been withdrawn and the country was left to enjoy the "liberty" guaranteed by the constitution of 1870. Gill's determination to enforce honesty in public affairs led to his assassination in 1877. With this example before his eyes Vice-President Uribe, who succeeded Gill, took care not to offend the corruptionists. Baredo, elected in 1878, died within a few months, and was believed to have been poisoned. Saguier, who was thus promoted from the vice-presidency, dared to resist the will of the army and was accordingly deposed in 1881. The administrations of Caballero (1881-1886) and Escobar (1886-1890) were controlled by the military politicians in their own interest. Gonzalez, who became president in 1890, was another reformer, and was accordingly ejected by force and exiled a few months before the expiration of his term, which was filled out by Vice-President Moriñigo. Egusquiza (1894-1898) was a skilful politician, and accomplished what seemed impossible by carrying through some administrative reforms for the public good and holding his office for the full term. He was succeeded by Emilio Aceval (1898-1902), Juan B. Escurra (1902), and Dr. Baez (1905). The present president is Dr. Don Emiliano Gonzalez-Navero.

The area of Paraguay is 157,000 square miles, and the population in 1905 was about 631,347, of whom about 60,000 were wild Indians. The largest town is Asuncion, the capital, with a population of 60,251. The country lies partly within the tropics; the climate is ill suited to white settlement, and there are less than 3,000 European residents. The economic ruin caused by the war has been somewhat repaired since 1870. The industries of the country are pastoral and agricultural, and tobacco, Paraguay tea (*yerba maté*), and fruits are the crops exported. There are 156 miles of railway in operation. The war increased the public debt. In 1882 there was a deficit of $25,000 and in 1892 the English bond-holders got no interest. Thus the country fell into economic and financial dependence on foreigners. In 1895 the interest was scaled.

The law requires all children between eight and fourteen to attend school, but it is not enforced, and in the country districts the population is too much scattered for its carrying out. The actual number of pupils in 1898 was 23,000. There is a national college at Asuncion with 205 students. Roman Catholicism is the established religion, but other forms of worship are tolerated.

President Eduardo Schaerer inaugurated during 1914 an epoch of peace which had a most beneficial influence on the country. Numerous reforms were instituted and a general betterment of conditions was apparent.

The budget of 1914 estimated the receipts at 3,525,300 pesos gold and 20,093,400 pesos paper, with an estimated expenditure of 1,630,133 pesos gold and 61,440,592 pesos paper, the pesos paper being worth 10 cents as against 96 cents for the pesos gold.

Chapter XVIII

BOUNDARY DISPUTES. 1890-1910

THE boundaries of the South American nations are ill defined. Civilization and European settlement have gradually penetrated inland from the coasts, and for a long time the back country was little known; but as the wilderness was explored the several nations whose territories were thus enlarged came into conflict and it became necessary to mark the boundaries accurately. The war between Chili and Peru was a frontier war, and there were other disputed boundaries between Venezuela, Colombia, Ecuador, Peru; between Brazil and Peru, the Argentine Republic and Chili, etc. But the disputes of the greatest importance are those caused by the claims of France and England for their colonies in Guiana, and those of the Argentine Republic and of Chili.

The Chili-Argentine [1] dispute arose over the interpretation of the treaty of 1884, which had fixed the international boundary at the crest of the chain of the Andes and the line of the watershed; but this diplomatic agreement did not accord with the facts of geography, for the summit of the Andes does not coincide with the watershed. Hence came conflicting claims by the two republics. The Chilians claimed the watershed as the dividing line, for this would extend their territory to the east; but the Argentines would hear of nothing but the line of highest peaks, which would extend their territory toward the west. Each country prepared to maintain its supposed rights by force, and from 1895 till 1902 each tried to outdo the other in warlike preparations, which put a heavy financial burden on both. An attempt was made in 1899 to restrict this ruinous competition by an understanding between the presidents, and a treaty for the same purpose was signed in June, 1902. Arbitration had been agreed upon in 1898. The northern boundary was settled in 1899 by a commission composed of one representative of each country and Mr. Buchanan,

---

[1] See Gallois, "*Bibliographe des Annales de Geographie,*" 1896; and Stephen, "*Geografische Zeitschrift,*" 1895.

United States Minister to the Argentine Republic. The line proposed by Mr. Buchanan was a compromise and was accepted by both his colleagues and by their respective nations. The southern boundary was referred to the arbitration of the British Crown, which gave its award in 1902.

French Guiana also had ill-defined boundaries. The Franco-Dutch frontier was in dispute from the Treaty of Utrecht to 1891, and the Franco-Brazilian frontier until 1899. The Treaty of Utrecht had simply given the Maroni River as the Franco-Dutch boundary, but the upper course of that stream is formed by the junction of two rivers, the Awa and the Tapahonic, and the question was which of the two should be taken as the upper course of the Maroni. The discovery of gold-bearing deposits between the Awa and the Tapahonic caused each nation to press its claims more vigorously and made the solution of the question more difficult. A sound basis for serious argument upon historical and geographical lines was lacking, and the task of fixing the boundary was by common consent entrusted to the czar, who decided for the Awa and thus awarded the disputed territory to Holland.

The Franco-Brazilian dispute was more complicated. The French government claimed as a boundary on the west the Rio Negro and Rio Bramo and on the south the Amazon, alleging the following facts: In 1551 the French built the Fort de Brest on the Amazon near Macapa; Henry IV. in 1605 granted to the Count of Soissons the viceroyalty of the country lying between the Orinoco and the Amazon; Albuquerque, in behalf of Portugal, recognized the northern bank of the Amazon as French territory in 1614.

By the Treaty of Utrecht, Louis XIV. abandoned his claim to the free navigation of the Amazon and the possession of its northern bank. But here arose two difficulties in interpretation. (1) Did this abandonment of the northern bank include the abandonment of the northern half of the Amazon valley? (2) The river Vincent Pinson, designated as a boundary, was not marked on the map. Was it the Araguary, as the French said, or the Oyopock, as the Brazilians claimed? Over this question floods of ink were shed to no purpose, notwithstanding the wishes of Choiseul, Talleyrand, Guizot, Napoleon III., Jules Ferry, etc. The Brazilians obstinately contended that their territory extended to what is now the Oyopock, that is to say, to Cape Orange.

The disputed territory was as large as the French colony of Guiana and contained gold-bearing deposits. In 1836 Louis Philippe established a port at Mapa to assert the rights of France. In 1804 the Brazilian government strengthened the port of Dom Pedro II. upon the Araguary. In 1860 Brazilian officials were installed in the district of Apurema and the Rio government paid the school teachers of Mapa and Coumani. In 1890 the provisional republican government of Brazil decided to create a commission for Brazilian Guiana, which was finally constituted and began its work in 1892. It was granted $247,500 a year and two small ships of war, the *Cabedello* and the *Cacador*.

The French government sent expeditions into the country under Dr. Crevaux (1876-1888) and Condreau (1883-1894), but it respected the disputed territory. In 1890 the Brazilians planned an attack upon Mapa, but it failed. A like attempt in 1885 upon the same place had resulted in bloodshed and the recall of the Governor of Cayenne.[2] In 1899 the question was submitted for arbitration to the President of the Swiss Republic, who gave his award (December 1, 1900) in favor of Brazil.

Similar difficulties attended the fixing of the boundary between British Guiana and Venezuela. In 1814 Great Britain forced the Netherlands to cede the eastern part of Dutch Guiana, and between 1810 and 1822 Venezuela succeeded to the rights formerly held by the Spanish captain-generalcy of Caracas. In 1840 the British government sent Sir Robert Schomburgh on a mission to the country. He claimed that the rights of the Netherlands, which England had inherited, carried the English territory to the watershed of the Orinoco, but he proposed a more easterly line which bore his name in the later discussions. In 1814 Lord Aberdeen consented to remove the frontier still further toward the east, and in 1850 both nations agreed to respect the *status quo*.

Nevertheless British subjects invaded the disputed territory, which contained rich gold deposits, and in 1886 Guzman Blanco demanded the evacuation of the territory west of the Pomaron. The British government refused this and diplomatic negotiations were broken off (February, 1887). On December 1, 1895, the Venezuelans sacked a British post that had been established on the contested ground and the queen's government sent an ultimatum full of threats for Venezuela in case it did not pay an indemnity. This incident almost caused an Anglo-American war. The gov-

[2] From articles of M. Crevau, B. S. G., Com. de Paris.

ernment of the United States had urged Lord Salisbury to submit the boundary question to arbitration, arguing that England's appropriation of any of the disputed territory by superior force would be a violation of the Monroe Doctrine. This the British government refused, and on December 18, 1895, President Cleveland reported the situation to Congress and urged that the true divisional line be determined, after careful investigation, by a commission of American citizens. The message produced great excitement in the United States and caused a heavy fall in the price of American securities on the New York Stock Exchange. Congress adopted the President's proposal with unanimity, the commission was organized, and Venezuela submitted her claims and proofs to it. The British press and public were unmoved and had no mind for war with the United States over the method to be chosen for reaching a just decision of the boundary dispute. Lord Salisbury's government, after its first misstep, displayed self-restraint and good judgment. Though it did not formally submit proofs to the American commission, it published its evidence, which thus became accessible to the commission. On June 14, 1897, a treaty was signed by Great Britain and Venezuela submitting the question to arbitration, as the United States had originally demanded. The decision of the arbitrators was more favorable to the British than to the Venezuelan claims. President Cleveland's commission made no report.

The Treaty of Ancon, which ended the war between Chili and Peru, was ratified May 8, 1884. By it the Peruvian provinces of Tacna and Arica were left in the possession and under the control of Chili for a period of ten years, a plebiscite was to decide whether they were to remain permanently under the Chilian sovereignty or be returned to Peru, and the country to which the provinces should be thus adjudged was to pay to the other $10,000,000 in Chilian silver. When the ten years expired Peru was in revolution and could not have found this sum of money. The decision was therefore postponed by mutual agreement. When negotiations were renewed Peru claimed that only Peruvian citizens could vote on the question, and Chili that all residents of the two provinces had a right to vote. A proposal to submit the question to the arbitration of the queen regent of Spain was rejected by the Chilian Congress in 1898, and Chili has since remained in possession with this cloud on her title.

Bolivia would not agree to the Chilian proposals for a treaty of peace after the Treaty of Ancon, so a truce, known as the *" Pacto de Tregua "* was signed April 4, 1884. By the terms of the truce one year's notice was to be given by either party of its determination to resume hostilities, and Chili was to hold and govern the coast territory it had won by arms. Bolivia had repeatedly tried to recover this territory by diplomacy, using the Chili-Argentine boundary dispute as a means of bringing pressure upon Chili in this matter, but Chili still remains in possession and Bolivia is in no position to recover the province by force of arms.

Other boundary questions have been settled as follows: Bolivia-Brazil in 1903, by treaty; Brazil-Argentina, by the arbitration of President Cleveland in March, 1895; Brazil-British Guiana in 1904 by the arbitration of the king of Italy; Peru-Colombia, submitted to the arbitration of the Spanish Crown in 1895; Colombia-Venezuela, in April, 1891, by arbitration of the Spanish Crown; Colombia-Costa Rica, in July, 1880, by treaty. The boundary dispute of Peru with Brazil, was finally settled on January 11, 1910, when the Peruvian congress sanctioned the treaty with that country. On July 22, 1909, another of these boundary disputes arose between Peru and Bolivia, in which Chili became involved to the extent of requesting Bolivia to recall her minister because of alleged misrepresentation regarding the matter. August 8, 1909, Bolivians stoned the houses of the people of Peru and Argentina, then residing at Guapai. With the inauguration, August 12th, of Ellidore Vallazon, successor to Ismail Montes, a new element was introduced into the government, and on August 13th, the new president suggested that the matter be settled by diplomacy. On November 29, 1909, Chili joined the United States in requesting King Edward to act as arbitrator regarding the Alsop claims. The worst fire Chili has ever known raged December 13, 1909, during which eighteen blocks of Valdivia were destroyed, entailing a loss of $2,500,000, and thousands were made homeless.

Chapter XIX

CONCLUSION

IT was for a long time the fashion to laugh at South America. Brazilians, Argentines, Colombians, and Peruvians seemed like the characters of melodrama or vaudeville, and the unenlightened public had no wish to remember anything more than some striking events in the bloodstained life of the young republics and certain grotesque traits of well-known low-bred millionaires whose wealth had been acquired in vast speculations on the exchanges of the great South American cities. Such absurd and ill-considered opinions were long since shown to be unjust. Much of the present is explained by the past, and if we wish to give a just judgment upon the young Southern republics and determine the degree of their progress, we must glance backward over their history.

As yet science throws but an imperfect light upon the condition of South America before the coming of the Spanish. Only as to Peru have we any considerable information. When the ethnography of the wild Indians is better known, it will enable us to understand the customs, religion, and, perhaps, the history of the tribes living in the valley of the Amazon, which still number several hundred thousand persons.

The conquest was marked by many massacres and persecutions of the natives, the extermination of tribes, the pitiless exploitation of the vanquished, the destruction of the native civilizations; the colonial system of popular ignorance fostered by the clergy; administrative despotism and economic isolation. At the end of the eighteenth century some light had begun to penetrate the darkened minds of the South Americans. The half-breeds who had acquired some education, but still lacked all legal rights, understood the importance of those two great historical events, the independence of the United States and the French Revolution. The force of the blow struck by the French Revolution and the Napoleonic wars at the monarchies holding South America, was felt in the American colonies of Spain and Portugal.

Then began the fight for independence, which gave fine examples of courage, love of liberty, and fraternity among the enslaved Americans. What wonder that these peoples, made up of different races—Indians, half-bloods, negroes, and whites—did not enter upon peaceful political life immediately after their liberation? But were not the days of revolution in France, 1793, July 1, 1830, February and June, 1848, and 1871, marked by mob violence and bloodshed? And this in spite of the advantages of the French people, enlightened by philosophy, literature, books, and newspapers, as contrasted with these primitive peoples where only a small number of chosen men had acquired a certain degree of education. This difference of customs and of previous training is enough to explain the cruelty of the civil wars, the odious despotisms, and the bloody revolutions which stain the history of these American republics during the nineteenth century.

To-day there are proofs of social progress. Political life, if not peaceful, is at least more humane. The noisy civil wars do little damage and this progress is certainly due to European influence. It is generally true that many of those who become party leaders have been educated abroad, in the United States, England, or France, and the increase of European immigrants with the influence of European financiers has not been without results. To secure the esteem of Europe and credit from European financiers, South Americans must become more humane.

Moreover, the South American republics have each had a liberal party modeled on the liberal parties of Europe, devoted to civilization and enlightenment and striving to separate the state from the church, to spread knowledge, and to establish primary education. In the nineteenth century all the South American states displayed equal zeal in the promotion of art, science, and literature. All have tried to introduce the material civilization that western Europe and the United States together created during the century: railroads, gas lighting, electricity, telegraphy, etc. In the last twenty years slavery and monarchy, the only survivals of the old order in America, were entirely eliminated by the transformation of Brazil into a republic shortly after the liberal empire of Dom Pedro II. had freed its slaves.

In a word, the South Americans have thrown off the several

tyrannies imposed by their masters in the sixteenth century, and have transformed their governments into modern states, republican in form, in accordance with the examples set them by the history of the United States and the liberal political doctrines professed in that country, in England, and in France. To be sure, not all

CHIEF SOUTH AMERICAN COMMERCIAL CENTERS

South Americans are citizens who know their rights and duties, and some voters fail to act wisely and righteously in political life. In truth, there are among the mulattoes men who blindly follow their chiefs and who will not contend for a political platform or an idea; but in most of the South American republics there are vigorous minorities which are conscientious in their political actions. And it must be admitted that in most European countries political life is no more intense or logical, and no more guided by ideas rather than by attachment to the person of a leader, than it is in South America.

Such facts must be noted and such parallels drawn to judge truly and without prejudice young nations, and races newly brought to civilization.

The place which South America holds in the world, when all its political groups are considered together, is not large. The vast continent has a population no greater than that of France, and this population is so scattered that it has not been possible to establish any great power. There is to-day no South American nation whose army, fleet, or diplomacy has any weight in general world politics. Recent events have shown that Europe must take account of the United States, but it cannot be influenced by any South American nation. Though these new states have their writers, poets, scholars, and artists, some of whom have achieved personal distinction, there has not yet arisen in South America any intellectual center of which contemporary thought must take notice. Whether from the political or scientific point of view these republics play a modest part.

The real importance of the continent lies in its economic wealth. Agriculture, grazing, and mining are its strength. South America is still rich in gold. The exploitation of its fertile soil has only just commenced: cotton, coffee, cacao, sugar, tobacco, wheat, and manioc are its true riches. Its pampas have pasturage enough to supply cattle for the greatest markets of Europe. Valuable woods abound, and, taken as a whole, the richness of the soil of this land is beyond comparison. Now that population is becoming more and more dense in the old world and in the United States, in other words, when these consuming countries are tending more and more to form close relations with agricultural countries and promote the exchange of raw materials and food stuffs on the one hand, against manufactured goods on the other, the place of South America in the economic world is becoming more important.

To be sure, the belief sometimes expressed that South America has room for a population numbering hundreds of millions, is ill founded. When we consider the vast areas occupied by mountains with pleasant valleys but inaccessible steep slopes and uninhabitable summits, besides the immense valley of the Amazon with its close-growing forests, where the sun penetrates but feebly through the thick foliage, and the waters of numerous and vast rivers flood the land near their banks, where animal life has no more unconquerable enemy than the vigorous vegetable growth, where the Indian tribes vegetate rather than live, we must doubt whether there are extensive regions open to colonization, at least by the white race.

But the economic value of South America is independent of its fitness for colonization, and thus the question now awaiting solution is: who is destined to exploit the continent? For a long period South America, though independent of Europe in politics, remained in economic dependence on the European market. European capitalists and manufacturers have supplied South America with the capital it lacked and the manufactured goods it desired but could not make for itself. To-day certain nations show a tendency to throw off this dependence; among them Chili, with its rich coal and mineral deposits, desires, and can probably create, a manufacturing system. The other republics, though less fortunately situated, at least have the choice between two markets for manufactures, Europe and the United States, and for some parts of South America the latter is nearer and more attractive. In truth a new phase seems to have begun in the external politics of South America. Its foreign relations may well be transformed into an informal alliance with the United States.

Brazil and Argentina already have the federal form of government on the northern model, and the White House stands ready to defend American republics when they are threatened by a European power. The Anglo-Venezuelan case was symptomatic, and the attitude of President Cleveland was the more interesting because it agrees both with a political dogma, " America for the Americans," and with a commercial tendency, much emphasized of late years, toward a customs union between North and South America. This scheme has aroused keen interest in Europe. If it becomes a reality the economic struggle for existence will become difficult if not impossible for the merchants and manufacturers of the Old World, and it will result in such an economic crisis in Europe that the Baring panic will appear trifling in comparison. But will South America freely choose to take from North America the manufactured articles which it consumes, and give in exchange the products that its fertile soil produces in such abundance? The South American statesmen will probably be at more pains to secure for their country political independence, so closely related to economic independence, than to support a formula of pure geographic chauvinism, and will preserve the right to choose their customers and furnishers as moved by their own wants and those of their fellow-citizens. Moreover, it is likely that the most active part of the South American population, the European immigrants, will keep up their relations with the Old World, relations which are to-day obligatory because of heavy debts contracted with the financiers of Europe. Doubtless it would be unwise to exaggerate the lasting quality of this bond between Europe and South America, for the European emigrants settled in North America and Australia have shown an independence of heart with relation to the mother countries whence they came, which cannot quite be called ingratitude, but is the natural result of new economic conditions, overcoming sentimental considerations as they always do.

It is not our business, in this place, to prophesy, but simply to point out the new state of things, and if we have shown that in the last one hundred years liberal ideas have replaced autocratic doctrines in South America, that the people have progressed from monarchical subjection to independence and the republican form of government, from state-fostered ignorance to a system of intellectual and scientific education, from economic subjection to the beginnings of economic freedom and the ability to buy in the markets of America or Europe according to their desires or interests, the reader can understand what progress the South Americans have made, and that their history has entered upon a new phase.

To the observer in the United States the developments of the last decade suggest some modification of the foregoing views. Increasing political stability and economic progress may be confidently looked for in the portion of the continent south of the Tropic of Capricorn. Here, facing the Atlantic, are Argentina, Uruguay, and the southern provinces of Brazil, which are the heart of the Portuguese republic. To this group of states, Paraguay, the mineral wealth of the Bolivian highlands, and the tropical forests of the Amazon valley, stand in close political or economic relation. The La Plata is the natural outlet of this temperate region, and Buenos Ayres is its metropolis. Here, more than anywhere else in South America, the European race predominates over the Indian, and is

constantly recruited by fresh European immigration. History and
the present movement of population have reserved this portion of the
New World for new nations of the Latin race. Though the German
colonies in Brazil are influential, the industrial prosperity of the
German Empire has dried up the springs of emigration, while
the outpouring of Italians and Spaniards continues, so that the
Germans are far outnumbered already by the newcomers from
southern Europe, who are readily assimilated by the Spanish and
Portuguese creoles. This region is destined to grow in commercial importance with the steady increase of its export of food
stuffs and raw materials to Europe. Immigration and commerce
both work toward political stability, and the habit of revolution
is already being outgrown. International jealousies, the other
enemy of progress in these regions, ought to be removed and closer
commercial and political relations cultivated by the statesmen of
these nations, which may some day realize a part of the dream of
Bolívar, a United States of South America. Chili also belongs
to the temperate zone, but lacks two elements of greatness which
the La Plata region possesses: room for expansion, and large immigration. This country has been the most stable of all the South
American republics, and by the energy and intelligence of its creole
population dominates the western coast to the borders of Colombia, but its domination is irksome and the military and naval
strength of Chili rests on a narrow basis. Hemmed in as she is
between the Andes and the Pacific, and handicapped by the thinly
disguised enmity of Bolivia and Peru, Chili has cause to dread a
contest with Argentina, and such a contest may arise out of the
closer relations which are likely to be established between Argentina and Bolivia. With the completion of the tunnel through the
Andes, now building, Chili will be brought in touch with the
group of Latin nations of the Southern Hemisphere to which she
rightfully belongs.

The tropical portion of the continent, except its high mountain regions, is unfitted for white colonization, and gives as yet
no sure promise of self-development. Colombia and Venezuela,
by geographical position, must be greatly influenced by the United
States, whence will come the capital to develop their resources. If
their governments habitually fail to give reasonable protection to life
and property, it is probable that some means will be found by the
United States to secure it. Peru and Ecuador will also be brought

into closer relations with the United States and with Europe by the Panama Canal, and here, too, law and order must be established from within or imposed from without. The commerce of the western and Caribbean coasts of the continent is likely to be attracted to the United States, while the Atlantic coast, especially the La Plata region, by geographical position and economic conditions, will trade chiefly in European markets.

The official visit of Secretary of State Root of the United States in the fall of 1906 did much for the establishment of a friendly feeling toward his country. Formerly South Americans had distrusted the policy of the United States, believing that the great northern republic desired commercial intercourse with them so that she might make them politically dependent on her. His speech, delivered at Rio Janeiro during a session of the Pan-American Conference, was an official expression from the Washington government and bids fair to be as much quoted as the Monroe Doctrine.

APPENDIX

PROGRAMME OF THE THIRD INTERNATIONAL CONFERENCE OF THE AMERICAN REPUBLICS AT RIO DE JANEIRO, JULY 23, 1906

INTERNATIONAL BUREAU OF THE AMERICAN REPUBLICS

I. (*a*) Reorganization of the International Bureau of the American Republics on a more permanent basis;

(*b*) Enlarging and improving the scope and efficiency of the Institution.

II. A resolution affirming the adherence of the American Republics to the principle of arbitration for the settlement of disputes arising between them, and expressing the hope of the Republics taking part in the Conference that the International Conference to be convened at The Hague will agree upon a general arbitration convention that can be approved and put in operation by every country.

III. A resolution recommending to the different Republics the extension for a further period of five years of the "Treaty of Arbitration for Pecuniary Claims," agreed upon at the Mexican Conference between the different Republics.

IV. A resolution recommending that the Second Peace Conference at The Hague be requested to consider whether, and, if at all, the extent to which, the use of force for the collection of public debts is admissible.

CODIFICATION OF PUBLIC AND PRIVATE INTERNATIONAL LAW

V. A convention providing for the creation of a committee of jurists who shall prepare for the consideration of the next Conference a draft of a Code of Public International Law and Private International Law, and providing for the payment of the expenses incident to such work; especially recommending for the consideration of the said committee of jurists the treaties agreed upon at the Congress of Montevideo in 1889 on "Civil Law," "Commercial Law," "Criminal Law," and "Judicial Procedure."

NATURALIZATION

VI. The advisability of concluding a convention embodying the principle that a naturalized citizen in one of the contracting countries, who renews his residence in the country of his origin, without the intention of returning to the country where he was naturalized, be considered to have renounced his naturalization in the said country, and the intent not to return shall be presumed to exist when the naturalized person resides for over two years in the country of his origin.

DEVELOPMENT OF COMMERCIAL INTERCOURSE BETWEEN THE AMERICAN REPUBLICS

VII. Adoption of resolutions which the Conference may consider proper for:

(*a*) The more rapid communication between the different nations.

(*b*) The conclusion of commercial treaties.

(*c*) The greatest possible dissemination of statistical and commercial information.

(*d*) Measures tending to develop and extend commercial intercourse between the Republics forming the conference.

CUSTOMS AND CONSULAR LAWS

VIII. The simplification and coördination of the customs and consular laws referring to the entry and clearance of ships and merchandise.

PATENTS AND TRADE-MARKS

IX. Consideration of the treaties of Montevideo and Mexico, covering this subject, together with:

(*a*) Recommendations tending toward uniformity in patent laws and procedure.

(*b*) The creation of an International Bureau for the registration of trade-marks.

SANITARY POLICE AND QUARANTINE

X. Consideration of the sanitary convention signed and referendum at Washington, and the one concluded at Rio Janeiro, and such additional recommendations on matters of public health as will most effectively enable each of the Republics to assist the others in the prevention of epidemic, and in the reduction of mortality from contagious diseases.

PAN-AMERICAN RAILWAY

XI. Consideration of the report of the Permanent Committee of The Pan-American Railway, and recommendation, to ———— at the Conference, to the different Republics with regard thereto, and reaffirming the interest of all the Republics in the success of this project.

COPYRIGHT

XII. Consideration of the Treaties of Montevideo and of Mexico regarding copyright, and legislation bearing on the subject in the American Republics.

PRACTICE OF THE LEARNED PROFESSIONS

XIII. Measures which may be deemed necessary to carry into effect the idea embodied in the treaty agreed to in the Second Pan-American Conference with regard to this subject.

XIV. Future conferences.

THE THIRD INTERNATIONAL AMERICAN CONFERENCE [1]

THE Third International American Conference met at Rio de Janeiro on the evening of July 23, 1906, as previously announced. Baron de Rio Branco, Minister of Foreign Relations of Brazil, and temporary president of the Conference, delivered the following brilliant speech:

" In inaugurating the work of the Third International American Conference it is my pleasant duty, in behalf of the Government and people of Brazil, to welcome the delegates of the nations here represented, and to congratulate them on their safe arrival.

" These greetings, expressing the cordial feelings of a people noted for its hospitality, are accompanied by our sincere gratitude that Rio de Janeiro has this time been chosen for the holding of the Conference. Indeed, never before has there been seen in Brazilian territory so large and distinguished an assemblage of foreign statesmen, jurists, and diplomats, and I can assure you that Brazil and its Government know how to appreciate at its full value this great honor which has already been granted to Washington and Mexico, and which must fall successively to the capitals of the other American states.

" It is our earnest wish that this Third Conference may result in establishing the happy conviction, confirmed and expressed in acts and practical measures of common interest, that the time of true international confraternity is not far distant. A pledge of it already is this spirit now being generally manifested of seeking the means of conciliating opposing, or apparently opposing, interests, putting them afterwards to the same service of attaining the ideal, the progress of peace. It already manifests itself in the spirit of farsightedness with which nations are seeking to promote closer political relations, avoid conflicts, and provide for the peaceful solution of international differences by simplifying and making

[1] From the report of the International Bureau of American Republics.

280

uniform the laws of trade and of nations, thereby facilitating greater approximation among them.

"In former times so-called congresses of peace were held to determine the consequences of war, and the conquerors, in the name of a future friendship, based on respect for the stronger, dictated laws to the conquered. To-day congresses assemble without constraint; they are almost always convoked in times of peace, by a wise foresight, for the purpose of regulating the peaceful activities of the nations, and in them the rights of the weakest receive the same consideration as those of the strongest. They give body, form, and authority to international law, which happily is coming more and more to be respected, and therefore constitutes a great step in the history of civilization. They have their origin in a strong public sentiment created by the greater diffusion of education, the increasing importance of economic interests, and the assiduous dissemination of humanitarian and peace sentiments.

"Instead of the difficult and painful negotiations in which one party pleads for justice or generosity, and the other imposes the law of his will alone, we now have calm and friendly discussions, in which each party makes a clear and simple statement of his views on practical questions of general utility. Here, concessions represent conquests of judgment, friendly compromises, or compensations counseled by mutual interests. In them only friendly actions are used, such as true courtesy demands among equals; and by acting thus the national dignity, instead of being lessened, will be enhanced.

"In these diplomatic encounters, where there are neither conquerors nor conquered, such considerations as these are certainly not unfamiliar to the distinguished members of the International Conference; they are familiar to, and thoroughly understood by, all here. Nevertheless, I have thought them necessary as an express declaration of the true and sincere purpose of our meeting.

"That is one of the false ideas that still survive from the past, when history taught only the lesson of pessimism, that men assemble together only to do harm to other men. Perchance our meeting in conference gives rise to the suspicion that it is an international league formed against interests not represented herein. It is necessary, therefore, to declare emphatically that all interests will be respected by us; that in the discussion of the political and commercial problems submitted to the Conference for its consideration, it works against no one; that it has solely in view the greater approximation of the American people, their welfare and progress, with the realization of which Europe and the other parts of the world have but to gain.

"Nations still young, we cannot forget what we owe to the founders of the capital with which we have entered the society of nations. The very vastness of our territory, a large part of which is uninhabited and some parts even unexplored, and the certainty that we have on this continent resources sufficient for a population ten, twenty times larger, would counsel us to strengthen and develop the relations of friendship and of trade with this inexhaustible source of men and wonderful fountain of fruitful energies—Europe. She has created us, she has taught us, from her we receive, incessantly, aid and example, the benefits of her science and art, the products of her industry, and the most profitable lesson of progress. What we, by growing and prospering, can give her in exchange for these inappreciable moral and material benefits will assuredly be a more important field for the employment of her commercial and industrial activity.

"Gentlemen, a few days ago we were under the painful impression that the Conference would open with three sister republics at war. To-day I have the great satisfaction of announcing to you that, thanks to the good offices of the President of the United States and of the President of Mexico, as well as to the patriotism and American sentiment of the three governments and nations that had appealed to the decision of arms, perfect peace now reigns throughout our continent. The Third International American Conference is now open."

Dr. Asención Esquivel, ex-president of Costa Rica, and delegate from that country, was called upon to reply, which he did as follows:

"MR. MINISTER: The delegates to the Third International American Conference have conferred upon me the high honor of replying to the able discourse which you have just delivered, and which is destined to attract the attention of the whole world because of the sound wisdom underlying the declarations made in the name of the distinguished Government of Brazil.

"The history of the Pan-American Conferences shows that

they have always conducted their deliberations within the limits of equity and an enlightened patriotism, and if it is true that their work is slow, and the ideals sought have not yet been realized, yet our sincere applause cannot be withheld from the efforts which in past Conferences have been made to establish peace on a firm basis, and to develop those interests which will contribute to the greater well-being of all the Republics of the Continent.

"This work will be continued by the present Conference. We did not know what the attitude of the Brazilian Government would be with regard to the apprehension which Europe has manifested over the work of our assembly. We could not doubt, however, in view of the high state of culture of the Brazilian people, that the Government would not forget the ties that unite us to Europe, nor did we believe that it would lend its sanction to the formation of leagues against interests not represented in the Conference.

"We have heard with great satisfaction the views expressed by the Minister of State, and we, on our part, wish to express the belief that the advantages we offer to commercial enterprises have been of inestimable benefit to us, because of the important elements which we in exchange have obtained for our progress; we believe we should preserve these advantages, maintaining our doors open to the trade of all nations for mutual benefit, and without other restrictions than those which each country may find necessary to adopt for the safeguard of its interests.

"We begin our task with the faith which our high purposes inspire. If anything is done toward promoting peace and progress it will be mainly due to the esteemed Government of Brazil, which has worked effectively to bring about the Conference, and to which we present our grateful acknowledgments for its cordial welcome and generous hospitality."

His Excellency Señor Nabuco was appointed Permanent President, and upon assuming the duties of his office he, in an eloquent address, expressed his appreciation of the honor conferred upon him.

His Excellency Baron de Rio Branco and the Hon. Elihu Root, Secretary of State of the United States, were unanimously elected Honorary Presidents, and Dr. Assis-Brasil, Secretary-General.

At the second session of the Conference it was decided to hold a special meeting in honor of the Hon. Elihu Root, which took place on the evening of July 31, when His Excellency Señor Nabuco, President of the Conference, and the Hon. Elihu Root, Secretary of State of the United States, delivered the following notable speeches.

MINISTER NABUCO'S SPEECH

MR. SECRETARY OF STATE: It is not as a stranger that you come here this evening to take your place as one of the Honorary Presidents of this Conference. You were the first to express the desire that it should be held this year. It was you who in Washington carried on to its successful conclusion the difficult work of preparing its programme and regulations. Nor can we forget that at one time you even expected to be one of us, a plan which you abandoned only that you might divide your time among the different republics which to-day receive your visit.

The meeting of this Conference is thus largely your work. From the time you assumed your high station there is nothing in which you have taken a more direct and personal interest. In the spirit with which you are animated toward our continent, you seem to foreshadow the high place your name is to take in history.

You and the Conference thoroughly understand each other. The periodical reunion of this body, composed exclusively of American nations, signifies assuredly that America forms a political system different from that of Europe, a constellation having its own distinct orbit.

While working for the common civilization, striving to make the space we occupy on the globe a vast neutral zone of peace, we are working for the benefit of the whole world. In this way we offer to the people, wealth, and, initiative of Europe, a much wider and safer field of action in our hemisphere than we should if we formed a disunited continent, or belonged to the belligerent camps into which the New World may yet be divided. One point will be of great interest to you who so greatly desire the success of this Conference. It is that the Conference is convinced that its mission is not to force any of the states composing it to accept anything which they would not be ready to do of their own free will; it recognizes that its function alone is to give its collective sanction to what has already become the unanimous opinion of the whole continent.

This is the first time that an American Secretary of State makes an official visit to foreign countries, and we rejoice that this first visit has been reserved for Latin America. You will find everywhere the same admiration for your great country, whose influence in the advancement of learning, political liberty, and international law has already begun to counterbalance that of the rest of the world. Mingled with this admiration, you will find the sentiment that you cannot elevate yourselves without raising the whole continent with you, and that in all the progress you make we shall have our share.

There are few lists of names in history as brilliant as that of the men who have occupied your high office. To make any selection from among them because of personal worth would be unjust. A few names, however, which shine out more brightly in history, such as Jefferson, Monroe, Webster, Clay, Seward, and Blaine, are sufficient to show to the foreigner that the United States has always had as much pride and shown as much zeal in the selection of its Secretaries of State as in that of its Presidents. We fully realize the great prominence given to this Conference by the part you are to-day taking in it.

It is with genuine pleasure that we receive you. Here, you may be sure, you are surrounded with the respect of our continent for your great country, for President Roosevelt, who has become, during his administration, and will continue to be in whatever position in public life he may decide to occupy, one of the leaders of humanity, and for you yourself, whose spirit of justice and sincere interest in the prosperity of all the American nations reflect the noblest aspirations of the greatest among your predecessors.

This voyage of yours proves to the whole world your good faith as a statesman, and your sympathy as an American. It shows your scrupulous care in wishing to correctly inform the President and the country with regard to the foundation of our international policy. You are opening up political seas " never before navigated," lands not yet revealed to the genius of your statesmen, and to which they are attracted only, as we are all attracted one to another, by the irresistible gravitation of the continent. We are all certain, therefore, that at the end of your long journey you must feel and confess that in ideals and heart the American republics already form in the world a great political unity.

SECRETARY ROOT'S SPEECH

Mr. President and Gentlemen of the Third Conference of American Republics: I beg you to believe that I highly appreciate and thank you for the honor you do me.

I bring from my country a special greeting to her elder sisters in the civilization of America.

Unlike as we are in many respects, we are alike in this, that we are all engaged under new conditions, and free from the traditional forms and limitations of the Old World in working out the same problem of popular self-government.

It is a difficult and laborious task for each of us. Not in one generation nor in one century can the effective control of a superior sovereign, so long deemed necessary to government, be rejected, and effective self-control by the governed be perfected in its place. The first fruits of democracy are many of them crude and unlovely: its mistakes are many, its partial failures many, its sins not few. Capacity for self-government does not come to man by nature. It is an art to be learned, and it is also an expression of character to be developed among all the thousands of men who exercise popular sovereignty.

To reach the goal toward which we are pressing forward, the governing multitude must first acquire knowledge that comes from universal education, wisdom that follows practical experience, personal independence and self-respect befitting men who acknowledge no superior, self-control to replace that external control which a democracy rejects, respect for law, obedience to the lawful expressions of the public will, consideration for the opinions and interests of others equally entitled to a voice in the state, loyalty to that abstract conception—one's country—as inspiring as that loyalty to personal sovereigns which has so illumined the pages of history, subordination of personal interests to the public good, love of justice and mercy, of liberty and order. All these we must seek by slow and patient effort; and of how many shortcomings in his own land and among his own people each one of us is conscious.

Yet no student of our times can fail to see that not America alone, but the whole civilized world, is swinging away from its old governmental moorings, and entrusting the fate of its civilization to the capacity of the popular mass to govern. By this pathway mankind is to travel, whithersoever it leads. Upon the success of this our undertaking the hope of humanity depends.

Nor can we fail to see that the world makes substantial progress toward more perfect popular self-government.

I believe it to be true that, viewed against the background of conditions, a century, a generation, a decade ago, government in my own country has advanced, in the intelligent participation of the great mass of the people, in the fidelity and honesty with which they are represented, in respect for law, in obedience to the dictates of a sound morality, and in effectiveness and purity of administration.

Nowhere in the world has this progress been more marked than in Latin America. Out of the wrack of Indian fighting and race conflicts and civil wars strong and stable governments have arisen. Peaceful succession in accord with the people's will has replaced the forcible seizure of power permitted by the people's indifference. Loyalty to country, its peace, its dignity, its honor, has risen above partisanship for individual leaders. The rule of law supersedes the rule of man. Property is protected and the fruits of enterprise are secure. Individual liberty is respected. Continuous public policies are followed; national faith is held sacred. Progress has not been equal everywhere, but there has been progress everywhere. The movement in the right direction is general. The right tendency is not exceptional, it is continental. The present affords just cause for satisfaction; the future is bright with hope.

It is not by national isolation that these results have been accomplished, or that this progress can be continued. No nation can live unto itself alone and continue to live. Each nation's growth is a part of the development of the race. There may be leaders and there may be laggards, but no nation can long continue very far in advance of the general progress of mankind, and no nation that is not doomed to extinction can remain very far behind. It is with nations as it is with individual men; intercourse, association, correction of egotism by the influence of others' judgment, broadening of views by the experience and thought of equals, acceptance of the moral standards of a community the desire for whose good opinion lends a sanction to the rules of right conduct—these are the conditions of growth in civilization. A people whose minds are not open to the lessons of the world's progress, whose spirits are not stirred by the aspirations and the achievements of humanity struggling the world over for liberty and justice, must be left behind by civilization, in its steady and beneficent advance.

To promote this mutual interchange and assistance between the American republics, engaged in the same great task, inspired by the same purpose, and professing the same principles, I understand to be the function of the American Conference now in session. There is not one of all our countries that cannot benefit the others; there is not one that cannot receive benefit from the others; there is not one that will not gain by the prosperity, the peace, the happiness of all.

According to your programme, no great and impressive single thing is to be done by you; no political questions are to be discussed; no controversies are to be settled; no judgment is to be passed upon the conduct of any state; but many subjects are to be considered, which afford the possibility of removing barriers to intercourse, of ascertaining for the common benefit what advances have been made by each nation in knowledge, in experience, in enterprise, in the solution of difficult questions of government, and in ethical standards, of perfecting our knowledge of each other, and of doing away with the misconceptions, the misunderstandings, and the resultant prejudices, that are such fruitful sources of controversy.

And there are some subjects in the programme which invite discussion that may lead the American republics toward agreement upon principles, the general practical application of which can come only in the future, through long and patient effort. Some advance, at least, may be made here toward the complete rule of justice and peace among nations in lieu of force and war.

The association of so many eminent men from all the republics, leaders of opinion in their own homes, and the friendships that will arise among you, the habit of temperate and kindly discussion of matters of common interest, the ascertainment of common sympathies and aims, the dissipation of misunderstandings, the exhibition to all the American peoples of this peaceful and considerate method of conferring upon international questions, this alone, quite irrespective of the resolutions you may adopt, and the conventions you may sign, will mark a substantial advance in the direction of international good understanding.

These beneficent results the government and the people of the United States of America greatly desire. We wish for no victories but those of peace; for no territory except our own; for no sovereignty except the sovereignty over ourselves. We deem the independence and equal rights of the smallest and weakest member of the family of nations entitled to as much respect as those of the greatest empire, and we deem the observance of that respect the chief guarantee of the weak against the oppression of the strong. We neither claim nor desire any rights, or privileges, or powers that we do not freely concede to every American republic. We wish to increase our prosperity, to expand our trade, to grow in wealth, in wisdom, and in spirit, but our conception of the true way to accomplish this is not to pull down others and profit by their ruin, but to help all friends to a common prosperity and a common growth, that we may all become greater and stronger together.

Within a few months, for the first time the recognized possessors of every foot of soil upon the American continents can be, and I hope will be, represented with the acknowledged rights of equal sovereign states in the great World Congress at The Hague. This will be the world's formal and final acceptance of the declaration that no part of the American continents is to be deemed subject to colonization. Let us pledge ourselves to aid each other in the full performance of the duty to humanity which that accepted declaration implies, so that in time the weakest and most unfortunate of our republics may come to march with equal step by the side of the stronger and more fortunate. Let us help each other to show that, for all the races of men, the Liberty for which we have fought and labored is the twin sister of Justice and Peace.

Let us unite in creating and maintaining and making effective an all-American public opinion, whose power shall influence international conduct and prevent international wrong, and narrow the causes of war, and forever preserve our free lands from the burden of such armaments as are massed behind the frontiers of Europe, and bring us ever nearer to the perfection of ordered liberty.   So shall come security and prosperity, production and trade, wealth, learning, the arts, and happiness for us all.

Not in a single conference, nor by a single effort, can very much be done.   You labor more for the future than for the present; but if the right impulse be given, if the right tendency be established, the work you do here will go on among all the millions of people in the American continents long after your final adjournment, long after your lives, with incalculable benefit to all our beloved countries, which may it please God to continue free and independent and happy for ages to come.

LATIN AMERICA AND COLOMBIA[1]

By Hon. John Barrett
United States Minister to Colombia

TOO much emphasis cannot be laid upon the character and significance of Mr. Root's tour of South America. It has not been fully appreciated in the United States. The natural modesty of the Secretary of State has kept him from describing the cordiality of the treatment he received at the hands of the South Americans. The press of the United States, while following Mr. Root's trip, failed to catch the spirit and greatness of the reception, as was plainly shown by the South American press. We of North America should be profoundly grateful to all South America for the way it received Mr. Root. It was a splendid compliment to us, which we have failed to reciprocate in any expression of approbation. Many of us remember the honors showered upon Admiral Dewey when he arrived in this country after his Philippine achievements. It is no exaggeration to state that Mr. Root was greeted with a Dewey reception in every capital of South America which he visited. There was no lack of real enthusiasm in the cheers and plaudits of the throngs that bade him welcome. Those of us who have lived in South America know the difference between a reception that is heartfelt and one that is perfunctory. In no place was the reception of our Secretary of State perfunctory.

In each capital and city where he was the guest he was given every attention possible. Had he been the President of the United States, or a European monarch, more could not have been done for him. The South Americans were grateful, and wished to show their gratitude, because we sent to them one of our greatest men. They appreciated the fact that he is the premier of our cabinet; that he is regarded as one of our ablest lawyers, as well as being a high-class and distinguished politician, and that he represents the intellectual, as well as the material, side of our progress. In short, they looked upon him as the best we could send, as an

[1] Contributed through the courtesy of The National Geographic Society.

ambassador of good-will, next to the President himself. Heretofore every South American country had been visited by princes and distinguished statesmen of different European countries, but the United States, in the passing of years, had seemed to neglect South America, as if it were not worthy of the recognition which Europe had given it. When, therefore, the United States, through the sagacity of President Roosevelt, arose to the occasion and sent one of its foremost statesmen, South America returned the compliment with a reception unsurpassed in the history of the western hemisphere. Now it behooves the United States to take advantage of what Mr. Root has done by fostering in every way a movement throughout our country for greater intercourse and acquaintance with Latin America, from Mexico to Argentina.

The time is at hand that calls for what might be termed a widespread Latin-American movement in the United States. The commercial and economic possibilities and social conditions and progress of our southern neighbors invite our immediate and particular attention. To say that it may be " now or never " with North American prestige and trade in Central and South America is not a statement of an alarmist or pessimist. It is a simple and logical conclusion drawn from a thorough study of the actual situation.

There never was a period in the history of the relations of the United States with her sister American republics that afforded such combined opportunity and necessity as the present for the development not only of our moral influence, but of our commercial interests. On the other hand, there never was a time when European nations and business interests put forth such efforts as they are now legitimately exerting to increase their own prestige and trade in South America. Although the situation should be one of closest rivalry, where the United States can and ought to win, if it does not give Europe too long a start, the advantage now is decidedly with the latter. There is no gainsaying the fact that Latin America to-day is strongly inclined to be more sympathetic, in its actual likes and dislikes, with the Old World than with the United States, because of plain reasons of race, language, and association.

Many of our sister republics are now making a progress that challenges the attention and respect of the world. Some of them are going forward with such splendid energy that they are running a close race with the past records of the United States, and the present achievements of Japan. Others are on the verge of a progressive growth that will astonish skeptical critics of the Latin race, and delight knowing admirers of their latent possibilities.

In short, it is safe to predict a forward movement during the next decade for the Latin-American republics that will give them a position and prominence among the nations of the earth not thought possible a few years ago. It will bring to them a commerce for which the United States and Europe will compete with every resource at their command.

I admit that I seem to talk with an element of prejudice. Frankly, I like Latin America, and the Latin peoples! The more I see of them the better I respect them. Would that more North Americans could become better acquainted with South Americans, study more intimately their impulses, ambitions, hopes, achievements, and see things from the Latin-American standpoint. Otherwise expressed, it would be a signal blessing to international Pan-American accord, and it would inaugurate immediately a new era in the relations of the United States with her sister American republics, if, in thinking, writing, and speaking of them, their peoples, and their politics, we could follow the old Biblical adage and remove the beam from our own eye before looking for the moat in that of the Latin-American.

The United States has reached a most critical period in its relations with Latin America. What is done or accomplished during the next two years may determine forever the relative position of North American trade and prestige in Central and South America. The recent Pan-American Conference in Rio Janeiro, and the unprecedented visit of Secretary Root to South America, should awaken sufficient interest throughout the United States in this part of the world to inspire our people in general, and our newspapers, our manufacturers, our merchants, our congressmen, our travelers, and our students of foreign intercourse in particular, to a new and active appreciation of the Latin-American republics.

Without half the reason we have for improving the opportunity, European commercial, financial, and diplomatic interests, with commendable judgment and spirit, which we cannot criticise, but must admire, are alive to the situation and doing everything legitimately in their power to retain a hold of which they cannot be dispossessed. They keenly realize the present and future possibilities of the material and economic exploitation of Latin America, and they are leaving no stone unturned to gain the necessary advantages before the manufacturers and tradesmen of the United States suddenly become aroused to the situation and compete for its control.

A great factor unfavorable to North American trade and influence in Latin America is the essential difference in lineage and language; but this point is little appreciated. The power of similarity in race and tongue is mighty. Kinship in these respects brings men closer together. It makes them more sympathetic, and this counts much in Latin countries. The average North American, instead of carefully studying methods of counterbalancing these adverse conditions to his progress in Latin America and of adapting himself thereto, undertakes an independent line of action, and ultimately fails in his purpose.

A second great factor is corollary to the first, and it is one of which, in our seeming abundance of knowledge and self-confidence, we are lamentably ignorant. Frankly termed, it should be called the "holier than thou" attitude too commonly and persistently assumed by North American statesmen, newspapers, writers, travelers, and business agents, when discussing or dealing with Latin America. In other words, the people of the United States have too often and too persistently and characteristically "patronized" the peoples, customs, institutions, achievements, and governments of their sister American nations. Per contra, we should give Latin America more credit for its actual and praiseworthy progress in developing stable national and municipal government, in promoting both high-class and general education, in making its own excellent literature, historical and romantic, in advancing scientific investigation and invention, in solving grave social and economic problems, and comprehensively striving, under difficult conditions, to reach a higher standard of civilization.

How few North Americans realize that Latin-American history during the last four centuries is replete with incident and event, names and results, that compare creditably with those of the United States, Europe, and Asia! How few know the names of the great heroes, statesmen, writers, and scholars who have figured prominently in evolving the Latin America of to-day!

How few are aware that the principal countries and capitals of Latin America have groups of eminent scholars, scientists, and philosophers, as well as universities and professional schools, which are no less advanced than similar groups and institutions in the United States and Europe!

How few North Americans, moreover, of high position in public life, in literary, scholastic, and scientific circles, visit Latin America, and exchange courtesies with their fellow-statesmen and students, as they do with those of Europe! No greater blessing to Pan-American accord could now be bestowed than an exchange of actual visits and views of the leaders of Pan-American thought and action. Latin America is too much accustomed to seeing and meeting only those North Americans who are intent on making money, securing this and that concession, and thinking only of selfish material considerations and a return, with pockets filled, as soon as possible to the United States.

A change, a renaissance in higher-class association, acquaintance, and friendship, will not only start an era of good-will and better mutual appreciation, but indirectly prove of extraordinary advantage to commerce and trade. European countries long ago realized the distinct advantage of such intercourse with and knowledge of Latin America, and have improved every opportunity to promote more intimate acquaintance.

As to language, it is difficult to speak with patience. So small is the percentage of North Americans visiting Latin America, on business or pleasure, who speak Spanish, Portuguese, or French, that it is a wonder they make any progress in their plans. Ninety-five per cent. of the Europeans who go to Central and South America understand one of these tongues. French is mentioned because nearly all the well-educated Latin Americans speak that language. This subject requires no argument; it is simply impossible for the North American who knows none of these languages to become thoroughly " simpatico," and to master the Latin point of view in either commercial or political relations. I would that both our business schools and regular colleges might make the study of either Spanish, French, or Portuguese compulsory in order to receive a diploma. Portuguese is more important than is generally regarded, because it is the working language of Brazil —and Brazil to-day is taking rank as one of the great nations of the world; but the average well-to-do Brazilian also speaks French.

In studying the causes that act as deterrents to Pan-American accord, we must emphasize the lack of first-class passenger and mail steamship service, such as characterizes the systems of communication between Europe and Latin America. The long-established and well-defined association of Latin Americans with Europe has been immeasurably encouraged by the excellence of steamship facilities, which have given them ready access to the satisfactory conditions found there, in turn for business transactions, education of families, and enjoyment of leisure and travel. If the average merchant and traveler of South America could reach New York with the same comfort and speed that he can proceed to Paris, there would be at once a vast and radical change in the situation favorable to the United States.

This statement is not made as an argument for a " subsidized " merchant marine. I am not discussing the pros and cons of that mooted issue. I am simply stating a fact and describing a situation. That there is not one first-class fast mail and passenger steamer running between New York, in the United States, and such important South American points as Rio Janeiro and Buenos Ayres was given glaring prominence by the experience of the delegates to the recent Pan-American Conference in Rio Janeiro. Only a few could obtain accommodations on the one little vessel that, with its sister boat, makes monthly trips to the great capital of Brazil. All the others were forced to go via Europe, where six different lines provide a score of splendid, modern, up-to-date, fast ships between the principal ports and those of South America.

No Latin-American merchant or capitalist is going to North America on a slow semi-cargo boat, with limited accommodations, when there are numerous fast steamers bound for Europe with as fine arrangements as the transatlantic liners. This is axiomatic; but it means the loss of millions of dollars of trade to the United States every year, according to the direct testimony of South Americans themselves! It is true that there are excellent freight steamship facilities between North and South American ports, but they do not meet the passenger requirements any more than would a purely railway freight service suit the traffic between New York and Chicago.

Too much importance is now attached in the United States to the idea that revolutions prevail all over Latin America, and that therefore commerce and investments are insecure. This conception of Latin America as a whole is entirely erroneous, and does our progressive sister republics a great injustice. The continent of South America to-day is free of serious insurrectionary movements, with few, if any, indications of more civil wars. The tendency of public opinion and the powerful influence of large business interests in such great nations as Mexico, Brazil, Argentina, Chili, and Peru are all against revolutionary movements, and, although now and then some slight sporadic attempt shows itself, it is most difficult for it to grow into dangerous proportions. Then, again, the gridironing of these countries with railways permits the immediate sending of troops to any place and crushing without delay incipient revolts.

Turning now to the direct consideration of Colombia as a land of great possibilities, I wish first to invite your attention to its remarkable location. Colombia is the only South American country that borders on both the Atlantic and Pacific. It therefore holds a position of strategic value in the development of its commerce, and in its relationship to the Panama Canal, possessed by no other Latin-American nation. It is the nearest South American country to the Gulf and Atlantic ports, and to the Pacific ports of the United States. It is the only South American country that has direct access by water to both the Atlantic and Pacific shores of Central America and Mexico. It is the one South American republic that will benefit more than all others by the construction of the transisthmian canal. It has in all a coast line of 1200 to 1500 miles—about 700 miles on each coast, including the windings of its principal bays and sea inlets. Along both the Atlantic and Pacific shores are one or two excellent harbors, with lesser ones that can be improved by dredging, or the building of jetties. In short, it is splendidly equipped by location to develop a large foreign trade. To give a practical idea of the location of Colombia to the United States, it is well to bear in mind the following facts:

(1) The least distance between Colombia and the United States is only 950 miles.

(2) From Cartagena to Tampa, Florida, is less distance by sea than from New York to St. Louis by land.

(3) From Cartagena to New Orleans is only 1400 miles, or four days' easy steaming.

(4) From Barranquilla, another Colombian port, to New

York is almost a straight line, due north, less than 1900 miles, and five days' easy steaming.

(5) Colombia is nearer than Panama to the majority of Atlantic and Gulf ports of the United States.

The average North American does not appreciate the size of Colombia. Inasmuch as there are eighteen Latin republics, there is a tendency to think that all of them must be small. Nothing better proves the material possibilities of Colombia than to consider its great area. The best estimates, based on the most recent surveys, give Colombia an area of nearly 500,000 square miles. The following comparisons may enable you to form a clearer idea of her extent:

(1) Colombia is larger than Germany, France, and Belgium combined.

(2) Larger than all the coast States of the United States from Maine to Florida united.

(3) Larger than Illinois, Indiana, Michigan, Wisconsin, Minnesota, Iowa, Missouri, Kentucky, and Tennessee merged in one State.

(4) As large as California, Oregon, Washington, Idaho, and Nevada, together.

The land conformation of Colombia provides it with a variety of climate that adds immeasurably to its potentialities. Notwithstanding the fact that Colombia is all in the tropical zone and has a considerable portion very near the Equator, there are large sections that have a temperate climate in the real sense of the word, where are raised all the products of the temperate zone, and where men live and work under as healthful conditions as they do in the northern part of the United States. The Andean mountains, or Cordillera, on entering Colombia from Ecuador divide into three ranges, respectively the Eastern, Central, and Western Cordillera. On these are numerous high plateaus, where the principal cities of the interior are located and whose population is prosperous and progressive. There are numerous level and rolling highlands in Colombia where the thermometer seldom goes above 75 degrees Fahrenheit, or below 55 degrees. At elevations of between 5000 and 10,000 feet this temperature and agreeable climate is found, and the area of this section would cover that of the New England States, with New York and Pennsylvania combined.

The traveler who visits either the Atlantic or Pacific coasts of Colombia with their sea-level altitude and their tropical heat gains an entirely wrong impression of what he would find if he journeyed into the interior. Colombia will never be fully appreciated or understood until it is gridironed with railroads, so that visitors can go immediately from the seacoast to the higher sections in the shortest possible time.

Speaking of the conformation of Colombia reminds me to comment on the marvelous scenery that charms one's eyes as he travels over the different parts of the Republic. It has been my privilege to view the best panoramas of the United States and Canada, of Switzerland, and the Himalayas in India, but I have never seen anything to equal the variety, grandeur, and exquisite beauty of the vistas of the Colombian Andes. When, by the construction of the Panama Canal and by favorable conditions of steamboat and railway travel, it will be possible for American tourists to go there with facility and comfort, Colombia will become one of the most-visited countries, both on account of the scenery and climate.

Perhaps it is possible for me to speak on this matter with some authority because of the recent overland journey which I made, accompanied by Mr. Mahlon C. Martin, a prominent American of Bogota, from the capital of Colombia via Quito to Guayaquil, Ecuador. Although the first object of this journey was to meet Mr. Root on the west coast of South America, a secondary purpose was to study, and be able to report upon, an important section of South America never before traveled or visited by a North American official, but which will have a vast material and industrial development upon the opening of the Panama Canal. We traveled in all 1500 miles, of which 1100 miles were on mule back. We spent thirty-one continuous days in the saddle and four days on railroads, in steamboats, and in automobiles.

Naturally one of the first questions asked in regard to Colombia is how one gets there, and how he reaches the capital. The regular route is as follows: One goes from New York to either Barranquilla or Cartagena, on the Caribbean coast. There are at present no steamers running direct to these places without stopping at other ports, but there are two or three lines, notably the Hamburg-American, with the Atlas service, and the Royal Mail, which touch en route south at Kingston, Jamaica, and either at Colon, Panama, or Port Limon, Costa Rica, as well as at Kings-

ton, returning north. The trip usually requires, on account of
stops, about nine days.

At Barranquilla the river-steamer up the river can be taken,
or, as some prefer, it is possible to go to Cartagena, and then
by rail across to a town called Calamar, on the Magdalena River,
where the river boat, in turn, is boarded. Many persons visit
Cartagena in order to see the city, as it is one of the most interesting, historically speaking, in all the western hemisphere. No other
city in North or South America has such wonderful walls as those
constructed in Cartagena by the Spaniards several centuries ago,
at a cost of two or three hundred millions of dollars. They are
still standing, in almost as good condition as when constructed.
The journey up the river consumes from six to ten days, according
to the condition of the river. Navigation stops at a town called
La Dorada, where a short railroad carries the passenger to Honda.
At Honda it is possible to transfer to an up-river, or smaller,
steamer and proceed for a two days' journey to a town called
Giradot, were begins the railroad that will eventually reach Bogota.
At the present time this railroad reaches a point where there
must be a mule-back ride of from seven to eight hours to Fa-
catativa, the railroad station on the plateau of Bogota, which,
after a run of thirty miles across the savanna, lands one in the
capital.

The more common route, however, is that from Honda direct
to Bogota, a distance of about eighty miles, or two and a half
days' traveling on mule back. It is not as difficult as it would
seem, and is interesting because of its novelty, and the beautiful
scenery. Mules can always be obtained in abundance to carry
both passengers and baggage. Trunks and packages should not
weigh altogether, for one mule, more than two hundred and fifty
pounds, and should be arranged so that no one piece would weigh
more than one hundred and twenty-five pounds. In this way
two pieces of baggage are carried on one mule's back. Steamer
trunks should always be taken instead of large, bulky ones. Heavy
trunks and freight must be shipped up the river, to be landed at
a point where they are carried by carts to Bogota. Honda is
approximately 600 miles up the Magdalena River, and Bogota is
practically a 700-mile journey, requiring about two weeks' travel,
from the seacoast. Women make the journey almost as frequently
and easily as men, and there is no reason why American women

wishing to go to that part of the world should not undertake the trip as well as men.

Bogota, the capital of Colombia, is one of the most interesting cities in all Latin America. With a population of 125,000 and beautifully located on the edge of the plateau, in an excellent climate, it always proves an attractive place of residence. The social conditions are particularly pleasing. Nearly all the high-class people with whom one comes in contact live in beautiful homes, are well educated, have traveled abroad, and speak French as fluently as they do Spanish. There is a vigorous literary, artistic, and musical element, which exercises a favorable influence on the refined progress of the nation. There are excellent colleges and general schools. The clubs are centers where the cleverer men of the capital gather. There is opportunity for the enjoyment of sports, especially in such forms as tennis, polo, and riding horse-back. Dinners and balls are given with an elegance that would be a credit to Washington or New York, while the women dress with as much taste and respect for the latest fashions as the women of our home capital. It is not possible for me to speak in too strong terms of the charming hospitality and kindness of association which I experienced during my stay in Bogota as United States Minister.

Considering now some tangible facts about the resources and possibilities of the country, it is well to note the principal products of Colombian soil. In the so-called " hot country " we find coffee, cocoa, sugar, tobacco, indigo, cacao, bananas, vanilla, corn, rice, beans, yucca, oranges, lemons, pineapples, alligator pears, and other tropical fruits growing in splendid abundance. Then in the forests are cedar and mahogany, dyewoods, vegetable ivory, Peruvian bark, rubber trees, sarsaparilla, cocoa, ipecacuanha, gums, resins, and rare orchids. Cotton will grow readily in the open, but so far it is little cultivated, while on the warm uplands are cinchona, wax palms, balsam of tolu, vine of the cross, and the arisa in the forest, and corn, barley, wheat, potatoes, etc., in the plantations.

To describe further the products of the cooler plateaus of Colombia would simply be to name those of northern United States and Europe, but the oddity and advantage of it all to Colombia is that the hot and cold zones are in such remarkable and accessible proximity. We do not think of Colombia as a cattle country, but I have seen as fine beef on the hoof in both the hot and cold sections of the Republic as can be raised on our western plains. The day

is not remote when Colombia will be supplying the New York
market with meat, and it should supply the present and future
demands of the Panama Canal Zone not only with beef, but with
all other kinds of fresh natural products.

Now let us note the ever-fascinating subject of minerals and
mines. Colombia would be a rich country if dependent only on
its agricultural and forest wealth, but it has a vast supply of minerals
and precious stones that alone would make it a land of immense
riches. If coal ever gives out in the United States, there is enough
in Colombia to supply the world for centuries. It is found in many
different parts of the Republic, including Cali, in the Cauca, on the
Pacific, and also near the Atlantic coast, while there is so much
soft, or bituminous, coal in the mountains around Bogota that the
numerous mines running into their sides here and there remind one
of giant gopher holes.

There are also indications of anthracite deposits which may
rival those of Pennsylvania. So far, these have not been developed,
because the natives do not understand or like hard coal.

Gold is mined in the states of Antioquia, Caldas, Tolima, and
Santander in richly paying quantities, and experts declare that some
day there will be a " boom " here like those of the Klondike,
California, and South Africa. Silver is found in Antioquia, Cauca,
and Tolima; copper in Boyaca; platinum in Cauca; petroleum in
Tolima; while lime, alum, chalk, magnesia, sulphur, marble, asphalt,
cinnabar, lead, and quicksilver ore are found in large deposits in
many parts of the country.

At Pradera, not far from Bogota, iron and coal are side by side
in such vast amounts that costly iron works have been erected, and
it is now proposed to undertake the manufacture of steel by the
Bessemer process.

Special mention should be made of the famous Musa Mine,
which provides the best and largest number of emeralds of any mine
or mines in the world. It is one of the principal sources of income of
the Republic, and as it is further developed it will be all the more
valuable. Practically the only sure source of supply for the emerald
demands of the world is the Musa Mine. It is to-day one of the
guarantees which the Colombian government uses for its credit
abroad.

To-day Colombia is selling to the United States such exports as
coffee, hides, alligator skins, goat skins, gold bars and dust,

rubber, tobacco, and balsam of tolu, heron plumes and other feathers, straw hats, bananas, cocoanuts, chocolate, ivory nuts, quina, platinum, dyewoods, cedar, mahogany, orchids, etc. The value of these exports to the United States in 1905 approximated $6,300,000 in gold. This amount will be tripled when Colombia is started on an era of permanent peace and the national productiveness is accordingly increased.

Colombian imports from the United States include flour, kerosene oil, agricultural implements, mining and sugar refining machinery, railroad and steamboat equipment, novelties of all kinds, shoes, matches, arms, sporting goods, hardware, dyes and chemicals, toilet articles, some lines of cotton cloth and clothing, paper and printing supplies, etc.; but, excepting the first of these items, the greatest quantities are supplied by Europe. Imports from the United States in 1905 amounted in value to only $3,700,000, although the grand total of foreign imports amounted approximately from $12,000,000 to $15,000,000.

The true American who loves sportsmanship and hunting for the exercise and rest, or the professional explorer and hunter who seeks new fields and prey, will find in Colombia unrivaled opportunities for pleasure or adventure. In the tropical and semi-tropical forests roam the jaguar, puma, bear, amarillo, tapir, peccary, sloth, deer, opossum, and cary. In the trees can be seen monkeys and a multitude of bird species, like condors, parrots, cockatoos, toucans, bush turkeys, or grouse, and humming birds. In the rivers are legions of alligators and iguanas, while along the coast there are numerous turtles. Cranes and storks fly over the damp lowlands and boa constrictors crawl through the rank vegetation. In the higher and colder country are deer, foxes, mountain lions, and tigers, and along the lagoons and among the fields duck, snipe, and pigeons.

The geologist, mineralogist, botanist, forester, and average scientist, moreover, can always find abundant lines of study and investigation respectively in the geological formation, mineral deposits, flora and tree growth, and general physical characteristics of Colombia. In this connection it must be remembered that the great Humboldt found this part of South America the most interesting of his travels. The National Museum in Bogota contains rare specimens of fauna, flora, mineral and geological development which interest both the layman and the specialist.

Before this discussion is at a close there are a few different points to which reference should be made. First, I desire to speak feelingly and in the highest terms of the President of Colombia, General Rafael Reyes. He undoubtedly stands out to-day as one of the foremost statesmen in all Latin America. Against heavy odds he is struggling bravely and manfully to evolve Colombia into a condition of permanent peace and prosperity. The terrible heritage that Colombia received from its last civil war, by which her land was reduced to a condition almost of poverty, and more than one hundred thousand able-bodied heads of families were lost in battle, is a heavy handicap; but, if he keeps his health and is backed up by his people, he will be sure to place Colombia in the front rank of Latin America. Many criticisms are continually hurled at him by those who are not familiar with his high policies and with the obstacles that are in his path, but all those who have the best interests of Colombia at heart repose confidence in General Reyes' sincerity, ability, and patriotism.

Another point to bear in mind in connection with Colombia is the establishment of the Pan-American Railway connections. The great need of Colombia is railroads. It is interesting to note that many railroads are now in course of construction, and when these are completed they will do much for the progress of the country. One of the most important lines of approach from the coast to the interior is that from Buenaventura, on the Pacific coast, by the way of Cali and the Cauca Valley, and then on to the Medellin, the prosperous capital of Antioquia, which is being built by two Americans, Messrs. Alfred Bishop and Edward Mason.

Finally, for the benefit of those who wish to study carefully the Republic of Colombia and form a broader idea of the country than this cursory talk has given them, I desire to call their attention to the reports and pamphlets of the International Bureau of American Republics of Washington, which is always doing its best to bring about closer acquaintance and relations between the United States and the Latin-American nations. It is also a pleasure to commend the excellent reports of the United States Consul General at Bogota, and the consuls at Barranquilla, Cartagena, and Cali, which are published in the " Commercial Relations of the United States " and the " Daily Consular and Trade Reports " issued by the Bureau of Manufactures, Department of Commerce and Labor.

A NEW PERUVIAN ROUTE TO THE PLAIN OF THE AMAZON [1]

BY SOLON I. BAILEY

Associate Professor of Astronomy, Harvard College Observatory

The author of this article was sent to the west coast of South America in 1889 to determine the best site for the Southern station of the Harvard College Observatory. He examined the west coast from the Equator to the southern coast of South America, and upon his report Arequipa, Peru, was selected. Professor Bailey had charge of the work there for eight years, and also established a meteorological station on the summit of El Misti, at an elevation of 19,000 feet, where observations have since been carried on. It is by far the highest scientific station in the world.

A COMMERCIAL conquest of the heart of the South American continent is going rapidly forward. While the coast regions have been settled and civilized for centuries, colonization has hardly touched the great plains of the upper Amazon and the lower valleys of the eastern Andes. Only yesterday, indeed, this vast region was almost unknown; to-day little remains which has not been at least partially explored. Nor is it now any thought of the millions who in the future may here make their homes which is working for the development of the country, but simply the desire to be first in the exploitation of its natural wealth, especially rubber.

Commerce naturally follows the lines of great rivers, and nowhere else are there such vast water systems as in South America; nor does it seem improbable that the same law will hold true here, especially after the possibilities of the tributaries of the Amazon have been properly developed, and that the commerce of southeastern Peru and Bolivia will find its way to the Atlantic, thousands of miles distant, rather than to the Pacific, only a few hundred miles away. This has been true in the past, and is strikingly illustrated by Iquitos, in northeastern Peru, which is practically an Atlantic seaport, although in Peruvian territory and 2000 miles from one mouth of the Amazon. From southeastern Peru and Bolivia, however, in the regions of the Madre de Dios and the Beni, communi-

[1] Contributed through the courtesy of The National Geographic Society.

cation with the Atlantic is more difficult. This is due especially to the falls of the Madeira, near the junction of the two rivers named above. These rapids block navigation at a distance of 2000 miles from the mouth of the Madeira. Above the falls steamships may again be used; but the danger and loss in passing the rapids are so great that, until this difficulty is overcome, another route is very desirable. The Pacific is comparatively near, but a journey must be made through dense forests and wild gorges to the crest of the eastern Andes and down to the Titicaca Plateau, where railway transportation to the Pacific is ready. Until recently no direct route had been opened up.

At the present time there are several ways of reaching the Madre de Dios and its tributaries, but the most direct and comfortable route is that which I traversed in 1903 before its completion. Since that time many improvements in the road have been made.

From New York one may reach the Peruvian port of Mollendo in about three weeks. At the present time it is necessary to cross the Isthmus of Panama by rail, but when the canal is completed through steamships from Atlantic cities will doubtless call at all important South American Pacific ports. From Mollendo a railway journey of seven or eight hours takes one across the desert to Arequipa, the chief city of southern Peru. Arequipa lies on the western slope of the Andes, at an elevation of 7500 feet. This elevation within the tropics furnishes an almost ideal climate. The whole region west of the Andes in Peru is, however, desert and capable of cultivation only by irrigation. Arequipa owes its existence to the small River Chili, whose waters are exhausted in irrigating the valley which surrounds the city.

A railway leads from Arequipa to the Titicaca Plateau, which lies between the eastern and western Andes. On the lofty and desolate Puna it reaches an altitude of 14,660 feet before it descends to the plateau. Lake Titicaca has an elevation of about 12,500 feet. This great region between the different ranges of the Andes was the home of the various Indian races that under the domination of the incas made up the semi-civilized population at the time of the Spanish conquest. Their descendants, for the most part full-blooded Indians, still dwell on the same plateaus and lofty valleys, but in a low social condition. They have lost rather than gained by the coming of a higher civilization.

At Tiripata, on this plateau, it is necessary to leave the railway and cross the eastern Cordillera. Through American enterprise, in connection with an enlightened policy on the part of the Peruvian government, a wagon road has been constructed for a portion of the route across the plateau, and will be carried over the mountains to a small Indian town on the eastern slope. From this town a good trail for miles will be built, down to some navigable river on which small steamers can be used. With the railway most of the comforts of civilization are left behind. In four or five days of mule-back travel we mount the eastern Andes, winding our way through the Aricoma Pass at an altitude of about 16,500 feet. Here the scenery, if the weather is fine, repays the hardships of the trip. Snowy mountains and enormous glaciers are mirrored in the waters of lakes, which change their colors with every whim of cloud and sky. More often, however, the traveler is wrapped in blinding snowstorms, which shut out every glimpse beyond the narrow limits of a few feet. Hour after hour he clings half-frozen to his mule, his discomfort heightened by the mountain sickness, which is one of the terrors of these lofty regions. To lose his way under these conditions may mean death.

On reaching the eastern crest of these mountains, if the view is clear, one seems to be standing on the edge of the world. The eye, indeed, can reach but little of the vast panorama, but just at one's feet the earth drops away into apparently endless and almost bottomless valleys. We may call them valleys, but this does not express the idea; they are gorges, deep ravines in whose gloomy depths rage the torrents which fall from the snowy summits of the Andes down toward the plain. We might hunt the world over for a better example of the power of running water. The whole country is on edge. Here all the moisture from the wet air, borne by the trade winds across Brazil from the distant Atlantic, is wrung by the mountain barrier, and falls in almost continual rain.

Near the summit of the pass only the lowest and scantiest forms of vegetable life are seen. In a single day, however, even by the slow march of weary mules, in many places literally stepping " downstairs " from stone to stone, we drop 7000 feet. Here the forest begins, first in stunted growths, and then, a little lower down, in all the wild luxuriance of the tropics, where moisture never fails. The lower eastern foothills of the Andes are more heavily watered, and more densely overgrown, than the great

plain farther down.   Here is a land drenched in rain, and reeking
with mists, where the bright sun is a surprise and a joy in spite
of his heat.   In these dense forests, with their twisting vines and
hanging lianas, a man without a path can force his way with
difficulty a mile a day.

In these foothills, at an elevation of 4000 or 5000 feet, is the
Santo Domingo mine.   Here is an American colony provided
with comfortable, almost luxurious, dwellings, which are flanked
by the unsightly huts of native miners and Indians.

From this abode of comparative luxury we again started mule-
back along a new, but splendid, trail down into the "rubber country."   Four days of this travel, through forests peopled with nothing more frightful than jaguars and monkeys, brought us to the
end of the trail.   Day after day, ten hours a day, in the saddle
is sufficiently tiresome, but it was with regret that we left our
animals to try the forest afoot.   Our first experience involved only
a walk of a couple of hours, but over a trail so narrow, steep, and
blocked with trees and roots that we were soon exhausted.   We
were glad enough to arrive at a clearing on the bank of a recently
discovered stream called the New River.   After a delay of a day
or two at this post, we made our way downstream a few miles
to the junction of the New River with the Tavora, on whose
waters we intended to embark.   Six hours of walking over a path
known in the picturesque language of my companions as "A hell
of a trail," brought us to the junction, where we found another
camp with a group of workmen of various nationalities.

The party which I joined for the trip down the rivers was
under the direction of Mr. Chester Brown, the general manager
of the Inca Rubber Company.   To him and to his genial brother,
"Fred," I am indebted for some of the most interesting experiences
which the present day furnishes.   The route we took to the Madre
de Dios had been traversed but once previously by a white man,
and then only a few weeks before by an engineer in the employ of
the company.   At the place where we embarked on the River
Tavora we were still well up among the foothills of the Andes,
and navigation, even in canoes and rafts, was attended by many
difficulties, and some dangers, owing to the numerous rapids.

The canoes are dugouts shaped from a single log.   They are
from twenty to twenty-five feet long, two or three feet broad, and
readily carry half a dozen men and several hundred pounds of

freight. For the passage upstream only canoes are used, and they are propelled by paddles or by poles, according to the depth and swiftness of the water. For the journey down the river, however, rafts are also used, since the rapid current renders great exertion unnecessary. Many of the native woods are too heavy for rafts; indeed, a number of varieties sink at once, so great is their specific gravity. The variety used for rafts is nearly as light as cork. A number of logs of this raft-wood are fastened together by driving through them long wood pins, made of a kind of palm which is so hard that it takes the place of iron. Cross-pieces are then fastened on in the same way, and the front end is made pointed, so that the craft shall not be stopped by collision with driftwood or boulders. When finished the raft consists entirely of wood, and no tool has been used in its construction except an ax.

With two rafts and two canoes, our party set out one day about noon. The trip began with the running of a swift rapid, which was one of many to follow. The canoes generally led the way and pointed out the best route. In many cases there were sharp curves, with here and there the stranded trunks of great trees and huge boulders. Many of our experiences were sufficiently exciting, and a fall into the river was a common incident of the trip. Our company included a crew of ten men—a motley crowd of various colors and nationalities. A nearly continuous stream of profanity attended the various maneuvers of our fleet, which reached its climax in intensity and picturesqueness when some sudden jar projected one or more of the boatmen into the water. At such times familiarity with the language of the boatmen would have been a misfortune. In the swifter and shallower rapids of the upper streams it was often necessary to lighten the load by wading in the water beside the canoes, which were guided by hand or even by a rope carried along the bank. This sort of travel, together with frequent rains, caused all the party to be soaked with water from morning to night, and we were fortunate when the kits were kept dry, so that the night could be passed in comfort. At one time during the expedition rain fell in prodigious quantities, causing the river to rise nearly ten feet within twenty-four hours. Progress became difficult and extremely dangerous, owing to the swiftness of the current and the trunks of trees carried along on its surface. We were obliged to make camp and

wait. This we did at a place which seemed sufficiently elevated
above the surface of the river. The following night, however,
the water reached our camping ground and compelled us to change
quarters in the darkness. Pitching a new camp at midnight, in
a tropical jungle, in a pouring rain, is a far from cheerful
occupation.

The Tavora, a river found on no map yet published, is one
of the branches of the Tambopata, a stately stream but little known.
The Tambopata is a tributary of the Madre de Dios, which joins
its waters with those of the Beni and other rivers to form the
Madeira. The Madeira is one of the great rivers of the world,
and yet it is only one of the sources of the mighty Amazon.

Until our embarkation we had been continually in deep,
densely wooded valleys, our view always shut in by their lofty
sides. On the second day down the Tavora, however, as we swept
out into the broader waters of the Tambopata, the hills fell away
suddenly, leaving before us only the level Amazonian plain—one
vast forest, extending unbroken, save for the river courses, for
hundreds, even thousands, of miles. At rare intervals the banks
rise in bluffs fifty or a hundred feet above the general level, but
usually it is an unbroken, forest-covered plain, rising only a few
feet above the level of the river, and in time of flood covered for
great distances by the swollen waters. It is a forest, so far as I
saw, without a single natural opening or glade, except along the
banks of the rivers. For days we had longed to see the hills melt
away and the plain appear; a month later, while working our slow
way up the river, we watched with even greater eagerness to
catch again a glimpse of the blue hills outlined against the sky.

In the shade of this ever-present forest live various groups of
savages, known as Chunchos. They dwell in general along the
banks of the rivers, and indeed they seem almost as much at
home on, or even in, the river as on the land. The reputation
which they enjoy is none of the best. We met half a dozen groups
during our expedition, some of whom apparently had never before
seen white men. They impressed me as simple and well-disposed,
if treated fairly, and surprisingly intelligent. Indeed, several times,
while attempting to converse with them by means of signs, I could
not resist the impression that they were merely masquerading under
the guise of savagery. From almost every standpoint, however,
they are mere savages. They are nomadic, roaming up and down

the rivers, and building only the rudest huts. They have no metal implements, so far as I could learn, and few, if any, made of stone. Some of them appear to have no proper household utensils, and such scant pottery as I saw was very rude. Their clothing is made of the fibrous bark of a certain tree, called by them " Ianchama." This is stripped off in large pieces and pounded on flat stones with great patience until the coarser materials are removed, and only the inner, tough, but rather soft and pliable, bark is left. This resembles in texture a coarse cloth. Two pieces of this material are sewed together to form a sleeveless shirt which reaches from the shoulders to the knees. Shawls and loin-cloths are also made from the same bark. These garments are not always worn, however, for when we approached a village unannounced both men and women completely nude were sometimes seen. The Garden of Eden still lingers here. These Amazonian Eves have evidently never heard of The Fall. Like other people, however, they take pride in dress. Jewelry also is worn, made of the teeth of monkeys, or of pretty shells. Nose ornaments are worn, which no doubt add some charm for Chuncho eyes, but which are decidedly inconvenient when eating.

Insects are a great pest, even to these hardy children of the forest, who slip into the water frequently to be free from their stings, and to cool themselves. Men and women, boys and girls, threw themselves into the water, unmindful of our presence, and swam about in unencumbered grace.

Food is abundant with them—plantains and yuccas, as well as game and fish. The weapons of war and those of the chase are much alike, consisting of bows, spears, and arrows, all made of an extremely hard variety of palm. With these they wage war on unfriendly neighboring tribes, and also hunt the tapir, deer, monkeys, wild turkeys, and fish. They roast the flesh of animals and fish, either by placing it directly in the fire, or first inclosing it in hollow pieces of cane or bamboo. The heads of monkeys and of the larger kinds of fish seem to be regarded as dainties, and are simply placed in the fire and roasted or burned to the proper point. Monkey meat, when properly cooked, is palatable enough, but the appearance and manner of a large monkey is so human that when roasted and served whole it gives a cannibal air to the meat somewhat disagreeable to me. No such thought, however, comes to the Chuncho.

They have a curious combination of rather bright and "taking" ways, and of low and filthy habits. Their continual bathing renders them free from personal unpleasantness, though it is doubtful if they enter the water with any idea of cleanliness. Their sense of humor is as quick as that of an Irishman. With no idea of our language, they seemed to catch a joke at once and were frequently laughing. This is in great contrast with the Indians of the Peruvian Plateau, who are slow in thought and movement, and seldom laugh, at least in the presence of strangers. Many of the Chunchos whom we met apparently saw white men for the first time. Certainly no one of them had ever seen a bald man. One of our party was decidedly bald, and when he removed his hat a look of surprise and amusement passed over the faces of the whole group, accompanied by sly, if expressive, remarks. Freedom from the use of hats may account for the absence of baldness among them. It is an interesting fact, however, that among the different groups which we met no person, man or woman, appeared to me over forty years of age. What became of the aged I could not learn.

I have never seen a more interesting affair than a luncheon which a party of Chunchos took with us on our way down the Tambopata. Our limited stores of provisions contained marvelous novelties for them. Sugar was quite unknown to them. Each took some in the palm of his hand and tasted it slowly and cautiously; then a smile of satisfaction lighted up his face, and the sugar disappeared. Men and women, impelled by curiosity, mingled freely and frankly among us, and although among themselves the women are probably accustomed to eat after the men, with us they all came together in apparent equality. For pickles they expressed great disgust. Tea was taken with indifference or contempt, but cocoa with plenty of sugar pleased them extremely. A little confectionery, in the form of rather solid balls, was eaten with emphatic nods of appreciation, with the exception of two or three pieces which one of them saved. He explained, by digging a hole in the ground and pretending to cover up one piece, that these were to be kept for seed, so that in the future they might have plenty of so delicious a fruit.

Of their religious life, or the lack of it, almost nothing could be learned from the bands we met along the Tambopata. At Maldonado, however, the newly established military post of Peru on the Madre de Dios, were two or three Chunchos from another river, who had become residents of the camp, and had learned some Spanish. The commandant of the post and I spent some time trying to find out whether these savages have any idea of religion. The commandant, a good Catholic, attempted to explain to them some idea of God. They listened apparently in vague wonder, and when asked if their people had no such belief replied in the negative. The idea of a future life after death, so far as we could learn, was not familiar to them. At the present time there are several thousands of these savages living in scattered groups of twenty or more along the rivers flowing into the Madre de Dios. Many of them are just coming into intimate contact with the white race. A condition little better than slavery awaits them.

For the present the chief interest in this great, undeveloped region lies in the fact that it is rich in rubber and a few other natural products. But what of its future? Is it "a white man's country"? Parts of it undoubtedly offer favorable conditions for white laborers, so far as climate is concerned. From the crest of the eastern Andes down to the level plains, every climate, from the frigid to the torrid, is passed in succession. This zone, however, is narrow and badly cut up into deep valleys with precipitous sides. Agriculture has its difficulties. It is stated that a farmer arrived one day at the Santo Domingo Mine in very bad condition. Asked what had happened to him, he replied that the night before his farm had fallen on him. Landslides in this region are certainly frequent. Probably enough water power is going to waste on these slopes to do the work of the world. Within a short distance large streams fall in a continuous mass of foam 10,000 feet or more. Nor does it seem to me probable that the lower plains will be found especially unsuited to the white race. At present in these endless forests insects swarm in countless millions, and malaria doubtless is prevalent; but, with the forests cleared away and with the comforts of civilization, the conditions would be much improved. The altitude is some 2000 feet above sea-level, and the heat by no means extreme. During our journey on the rivers the highest temperature recorded was ninety-six degrees Fahrenheit, and a temperature above ninety degrees was extremely rare. One hesitates even in imagination to picture what manifold industries may be found among these foothills in coming centuries, and what millions of prosperous dwellers may be clustered on the plains at their feet.

THE FALLS OF IGUAZU[1]

By Marie Robinson Wright

IN the heart of South America, at the meeting place of three republics, Brazil, Argentina, and Paraguay, Nature has chosen the site for a masterpiece of scenic grandeur, to be compared only to the mighty Niagara in majesty, and pronounced by some of the few travelers who have seen it to be even greater than its North American counterpart.

The Falls of Iguazu occur at the junction of Iguazu River with the Upper Parana, in a territory famous as the original locality of the Jesuit missions, established in the sixteenth century, the ruins of which may still be seen by those who visit the falls. The history of these missions alone makes them sufficiently interesting to warrant a journey thither, and the fact that they have survived centuries of disaster from fire and storm speaks volumes for the enduring character of the work done by the simple natives of what was then a savage country, under the civilizing influence of the celebrated Company of Jesus.

There is no other spot in South America, except the site of the ancient empire of the incas, where historic interest and natural beauty are so allied in attractiveness as in the land of "Las Misiones," where it overlooks the Iguazu Falls on the Upper Parana. In the course of the Upper Parana there are many notable waterfalls, among them the Guayra and the Nacunday, of considerable fame, but none equal the magnificence of the Iguazu. Until recently the inaccessibility of this region prevented its being known to any but daring travelers, willing to bear the fatigue and discomfort of many days' journeys across the pampas and through the forest, under the blaze of a tropical sun and subject to the annoyance of innumerable insects, with no accommodations along the route, nor at the end of it, except such as the traveler himself could provide. But now that the Argentine government has recognized the importance of opening up a route to the missions and

[1] Contributed through the courtesy of The National Geographic Society.

the falls, regular excursions take many visitors to Iguazu from Buenos Ayres and other Argentine cities. The return trip requires about two weeks, and can be made with comparative comfort by train to Posadas, on the Upper Parana, and thence by a small steamer in a few hours to the falls. Occasional excursions are also made all the way from Buenos Ayres to the falls by steamer. The approach to the falls is heralded by the thunder of the cataract, which may be heard many miles away. About twelve miles above the falls the River Iguazu makes a sharp bend, almost at right angles, giving them greater extent and more varied character than those of Niagara, which to some degree they resemble. Indeed, a comparison between the two affords the best means of judging of their relative claims to preëminence, and is, perhaps, necessary in order to give an adequate idea of the appearance of Iguazu.

The cataract of Niagara makes a clear leap in an enormous sheet of water twenty feet thick over a precipice varying from 150 to 180 feet in height. Above the falls is a broad expanse of river, and below them a narrow gorge through which the water is forced in a rapid torrent. The setting of this magnificent *chef d'œuvre* of Nature is a cluster of busy modern towns, with only the intervening parks to put them in harmony with the glorious work they serve to frame.

The Falls of Iguazu offer a notable contrast to Niagara in many important features. As the river makes the sharp bend already mentioned, the main volume of water rushes round the inner bank and is discharged into a long, narrow gorge, at one point making a clear plunge of 210 feet. Not all the volume of the river is received at this place, however, the rest of the water running out past it into the wide elbow formed by the bend, and circling along the further shore among many rocks and islands before reaching the edge of the cliff, over which the descent is made in two great leaps of a hundred feet each, in a vast semicircle of 3000 feet. The total length of Iguazu Falls, if measured at the upper edge of the cliff, through their broken contour, including intersecting islets, is twice as great as that of Niagara, including the intersection of Goat Island.

The double fall of Iguazu is the most striking feature of the cataract, the rocky shelf or platform that divides the leap being in some places over fifty yards wide and in others only a few feet.

The scenery surrounding Iguazu Falls is in peculiar harmony with the solemn grandeur of the cataract and its varied character. The roar of the waterfall is more impressive for the solitude of the spot and the eternal silence that reigns in the dense forests that mark its border, into which the white man has scarcely penetrated. For several miles before the falls are reached the river is a mass of huge frowning boulders and whirlpools, and the first view of the great cataract is often a disappointment, from the fact that it must be seen from many different points to be appreciated in all its beauty.

The outline of Iguazu Falls is so broken that one can hardly gain a correct idea of its immense width, and even the great height of the cataract loses something in effectiveness by being divided into two leaps, instead of forming one stupendous fall. But, on the other hand, the charm of the South American falls as they plunge out of the hidden recesses of a semitropical forest at a hundred different points is unequaled elsewhere, and the traveler may look in vain the world over for a rival to their seductive beauty. Here Nature revels in perfect abandon, and presents a spectacle seldom seen in these days, when the surging tide of travel rolls in upon her most secluded retreats with its " modern improvements." Iguazu remains so free from the meddling of man that one can imagine the picture to be much the same to-day as when it first came from the Creator's hand in the primeval days " when the morning stars sang together."

From the falls to the ruins of the Jesuit missions the route is along forest paths overgrown with tropical verdure. In the heart of a thick wood, covering more than a thousand acres, the ruins of San Ignacio, so named for the founder of the order, stand in persistent survival of all the agents of destruction that have attacked it during the past two centuries. A proof of the remarkable fertility of this region in which the Jesuits established their settlement is shown in the marvelous growth of the forest which now marks the site, most of the trees towering to a height of more than a hundred feet, although it is only about eighty years since the Jesuit capital was burned down. The only open space in this wilderness of woods is in the center of what was formerly the settlement—a public plaza around which the houses were built—and strangely enough no trees have grown on this spot, though they have pushed their way through crevices in the walls that mark where the houses stood, and have buried under their branches the greater part of the ruins. Occupying all one side of the plaza was the church, and the ruins of this edifice present many interesting features. The coat of arms of the Jesuit order is still in evidence, as well as some of the sculptured figures of the portico. The dimensions of this building were about 250 feet long by 150 feet broad. Behind the church was the college, with eight large class rooms, and near it the refectory and cellars.

All the work of the missions was performed by the Indians, under the direction of the Jesuit fathers, and not only the churches but the dwellings of the Indians themselves were so well built by them that the ruins of these houses are as well preserved as those of the temples. Each house was 17 feet long by 14 feet wide, and had a window and a door in front, and a door at the back leading to the garden. In each house was a niche, presumably for the statue of some saint.

It is impossible not to admire the genius of Loyola's followers, who were able to teach the arts of civilization to the savage so successfully that after more than three hundred years the record of their work remains to attest its strength and beauty. There still exist the evidences of good architecture, and creditable sculpture; and though, as is well known, the Jesuit edifices all over the country are remarkable for a lack of technical accuracy in their architectural design, yet they stand a great monument to the persistent energy of the most important civilizing agency in South America for two centuries after the discovery, and they represent an influence that extended from the Amazon to Cape Horn, of which proofs are to be found among the remotest tribes of the interior of the continent, who still preserve in the traditions of their people many of the Christian teachings brought to them by the Jesuits.

THREE OLD PORTS ON THE SPANISH MAIN [1]

By G. M. L. Brown
Member of The National Geographic Society

FEW expressions in English literature have given rise to more confusion than the term "Spanish Main." Applied originally, it would appear, to the waters of the Caribbean Sea and that part of the Atlantic Ocean traversed by the treasure ships of Spain, it gradually included the adjacent coasts of the continent, until, with most modern writers, it has come to mean this alone, and "sailing the Spanish Main," forsooth, will hereafter be an anachronism until such time as airships shall have become popular in Caribbean countries. In these pages, however, with the reader's permission, the term will be applied, in its original sense, to the sea only—to the "golden, tropic sea," which, deserted by its galleons, bereft of its romance and its mystery, deserves, surely, to retain its memories and its ancient glorious name.

But the coast has its historic memories as well—this far-famed coast of Tierra Firme which Columbus declared to be the site of the earthly Paradise, "the most beautiful [lands] in the world, and very populous."

After Columbus came Alonzo de Ojeda, who sailed westward to the Gulf of Maracaibo, where he chanced upon some Indian villages built on piles, and so named the land Venezuela, or "Little Venice." In the next year—the opening year of the sixteenth century—Père Alonzo Nino sailed over the same course, and, besides confirming the reports of his predecessors as to the richness of the vegetation and its numerous inhabitants, was fortunate enough to secure a quantity of pearls. Here, then, was a land yielding pearls, and probably gold, for the treasure-seeker; and Indians, suitable for slaves, so the Spaniards thought. To Tierra Firme, therefore, an adventurous rabble soon found their way, and the horrors of the Spanish conquest began.

[1] Contributed through the courtesy of The National Geographic Society.

318

For a moment, however, the black shadow is lifted, and one Bartholomew de Las Casas steps forth—a simple priest, afterward a bishop, but "a figure," as Fiske eloquently observes, "which is in some respects the most sublime and beautiful in the annals of Christianity since the apostolic age." Las Casas had dedicated his life to the protection and conversion of the Indians, and, securing a grant from the king for a tract of land with two hundred and sixty leagues of seaboard (the whole coast, in fact, from the peninsula of Paria to the province of Santa Marta), he set about organizing a semi-religious expedition, which, had it been successful, might have changed the entire history of Venezuela.

The first settlement was to be made at Cumana, where some Franciscan monks had established themselves in 1515, and was actually begun by Gonzalez Ocampo in 1520, though his cruelty and treachery toward the Indians brought Las Casas' cherished schemes to naught, a fitting prelude to the three—or, shall I say, nearly four—centuries of strife and misery that followed. Las Casas arrived at Cumana in 1521, but during his subsequent absence in Hayti the little colony was driven away by the enraged and deluded Indians, who thus banished from their shores the one man who would, and could, have saved them from their piteous fate.

Apart from the hallowed memories of this devoted priest, Cumana, or New Toledo, as it was formerly called, has the distinction of being the first European settlement in Venezuela, and with the exception of a supposed settlement of the Portuguese upon the Amazon, the first on the continent. Ocampo was preceded just one year by Cortes in Mexico, and it was ten years later that Pizarro set out for Peru. When John Cotton knelt upon the shore at Plymouth, surrounded by his devout pilgrim band, and asked God's blessing upon their enterprise, a century lacking one year had elapsed since his noble prototype had debarked his little following upon the lonely Pearl Coast, and prayed with equal earnestness for divine assistance in establishing a Christian colony. One prayer was answered, and the other was not, and Providence only knoweth why; but certainly no more sacred mission was ever undertaken than that of Las Casas to Tierra Firme. When we read, therefore, of the subsequent misdeeds of the conquistadores, let us not forget that the "Apostle of the Indies" also was a Span-

iard, and, were it not for the one great mistake of his life—his
defense and promotion of negro slavery, though the facts have
been grossly exaggerated and, indeed, perverted—his work would
perhaps be ranked as the greatest moral factor in the early history
of the New World.

It is hard to leave this heroic figure and the desolate little
settlement that marked the failure of his first great project, but
Cumana, in time, became a prosperous town—that is, as prosperity
was understood in the Spanish colonies—and has at least one
other claim upon our notice, viz., that it was here that Humboldt
landed, and remained for a time, with his friend Bonpland, before
beginning those remarkable journeys that added so materially to
all branches of natural science, and, perhaps even more important
at this day, to our knowledge of the economic and social conditions
of colonial Spain—conditions that might never have been understood had this indefatigable traveler and scientist not arrived so
opportunely before the revolutionary struggle began.

Cumana to-day is a humdrum city of about 10,000 inhabitants,
the capital of the State of Bermudez, and an important port in
the " Orient," as the eastern states of Venezuela are called, though
the government of late has been openly hostile to its interests.
It certainly presents a sorry contrast to the town of a century ago,
then the independent capital of a large province, or rather of two,
an important ecclesiastical center, and ranking easily first among
all the cities of the coast in the culture and intelligence of its inhabitants, as indeed a Venezuelan (not a native of Cumana) in-
forms me is still the case.

Cumana is as yet almost unknown to the traveler, partly owing
to the ignorance or lack of enterprise of the steamship companies
that make it a port of call; but some day the tourist tide will set
in, and not only the city itself, but the delightful hill country of
the interior, as well as the neighboring towns of Barcelona—which,
like Cumana, was the scene of many stirring events during the
war of independence—and Carupano, noted for its trade in agricultural products, and for its incomparable rum—all, no doubt,
will in time be " stopped over " at and duly photographed, as will
the extensive *salinas* or salt beds of Araya and the neighboring
island of Margarita, where the famous pearl fisheries are situated.
It is a country well worth visiting.

" So, westward-ho, they ran," writes Kingsley of the good

ship *Rose,* as she skirted the coast between Cape Codera and La Guaira, " beneath the mighty northern wall, the highest cliff on earth, some seven thousand feet of rock parted from the sea by a narrow strip of bright, green lowland. Here and there a patch of sugar-cane or a knot of cocoanut trees, close to the water's edge, reminded them that they were in the tropics; but above, all was savage, rough, and bare as an Alpine precipice. Sometimes deep clefts allowed the southern sun to pour a blaze of light down to the sea marge, and gave glimpses far above of strange and stately trees lining the glens, and of a veil of perpetual mist which shrouded the inner summits, while up and down, between them and the mountain side, white, fleecy clouds hung motionless in the burning air, increasing the impression of vastness and of solemn rest, which was already overpowering."

And so, indeed, as Kingsley so vividly pictures them, do these mighty cliffs appear; and one learns with regret that the talented novelist should never have beheld their awful grandeur, he who alone, perhaps, has done justice to the scene. Inaccuracies, to be sure, have crept into the description, and as the steamer approaches from the north the traveler may fail, through a misjudgment of distance, to appreciate the magnitude of the greenish-brown mass before him; but presently he spies something to measure with, a cluster of buildings, a little toy city, which he is told is La Guaira, while apparently but a stone's throw away lies Macuto, the well-known watering place. Then, perhaps, though almost too late— for the Red D line has a schedule to maintain—does the full impressiveness of the scene burst upon his awakened senses; and if there yet be time, let him gaze intently before him, for the view entirely changes when he lands, and not until he is once more on board, and the vessel well in the offing, can the noble proportions of the " Silla " again be appreciated. In my case, unfortunately, my first view was my last.

La Guaira, for all its fame, or rather notoriety, is a city of but fourteen thousand inhabitants, or about two-thirds the size of Bangor, Maine; but even this seems an overestimate when one climbs the hillside and looks down upon its jumbled mass of dark-red roofs, with a thin line running east and west along the shore and a short spur following a cleft in the otherwise impassable barrier behind it. Prominent at the water front are the market place, the large customs house—practically the *raison d'être* of the city—

the inevitable plaza, and the new shore batteries, erected by President Castro.

Here, also, is the terminus of the La Guaira and Caracas Railway, and jutting out from the shore a distance of two thousand feet or more is the famous breakwater which has done so much to increase the traffic of the port, though the passenger is apt to forget, when charged to set foot upon it and denied the alternative of hiring a boat, that this formerly was one of the most disagreeable roadsteads in the world. Anyway, in a land of habitual " graft," why should the stranger be spared on the day of his arrival? " Why, indeed! " echoes the collector of customs, who incidentally is the proprietor of the Hotel Neptuno, the only decent hostelry in the place, as he delays the inspection of luggage till the Caracas train has departed and complacently watches the passengers stream off for breakfast—wherever they like to go, of course!

La Guaira can boast of several churches (one a rather imposing structure), a bull ring, a large theater, and a diminutive fort, the latter perched high above it, like the turret of a battleship, and provided with the same armament as the shore battery, viz., two Cruezot guns of the latest type. To one side, but below this fort, stand the ruins of the old governor's castle, where the " Rose of Torridge " dwelt, and if the tourist be so inclined he may seat himself upon a crumbling wall, and, with the whole scene before him and the sound of the surf in his ears, may imagine he sees the brave Devon lads fighting their way to the boat, their best loved leader a prisoner, several of their comrades dead, and the daring venture of the *Rose,* so they think, an utter failure.

An American who recently came to La Guaira, and has experienced exceptionally pleasant weather, calls the coast hereabout the " Riviera of the Tropics," while a well-known writer who delights in big phrases styles Macuto the " Saratoga, the Newport, and the Coney Island of Venezuela, all in one." Both comparisons are about as apt as is the term " Paris of South America," applied to Caracas, a comparison, to digress for a moment, that unquestionably aided the floating of a recent continental syndicate, which was capitalized at several million francs, and proposed establishing a large gambling casino in that city. The enterprise, of course, came to grief, though the disappointment of the projector who reached Caracas could hardly exceed that of the Ameri-

can tourist who should travel to La Guaira—hot, ill-smelling old
town that it is!—expecting to find a new Riviera. Nevertheless,
La Guaira has been dealt unjustly with, as well, even in the matter
of smells, which few tropical towns are free from, not excepting
the much-governed city of Port-of-Spain; and while one can
sympathize with the former American consul, who in the elation
of departure wrote:

> "Farewell, ye gloomy *casas*,[2] *mejor dicho*,[3] prison cells;
> Ye narrow, crooked *calles*,[4] reeking with atrocious smells."

and in another stanza:

> "Home of the wailing donkey and the all-abounding flea,
> *Manana*,[5] *gracias a Dios*[6] I bid farwell to thee;"

it does seem as if the final lines, both from a sense of fair play and
for diplomatic reasons, might have been somewhat modified:

> "Good-bye, ye Latin greasers, *su atento servidor;*[7]
> *Que van bien;*[8] *pues adios;*[9]—my boat is on the shore.
> Oh, dirty people, dirty homes, oh, despicable spot,
> Departing I will bless you in your dirtiness and rot!"

Equally unjust is the cool assertion—pardon the seeming
paradox—of the writer above referred to, who gives the town a
steady temperature of "100° Fahrenheit from one year's end to
another." As a matter of fact, the mean temperature is about 84°
Fahrenheit, and the maximum very little over ninety, which,
owing to the moisture of the air, could easily deceive the per-
spiring tourist. "It is generally the duration of a high temperature," observes Humboldt, "and not the excess of heat, or its
absolute quantity, which occasions the sufferings of the inhabitants
of the torrid zone"; and eighty-four degrees with a humid atmosphere is certainly excessive.

Another stigma cast upon La Guaira is its unhealthfulness, and
especially the prevalence of yellow fever. La Guaira, be it known,
is not particularly unhealthful, certainly not so unhealthful as
Caracas, and, while a mild form of yellow fever lurks in the
neighborhood, it is not greatly to be dreaded. "Indeed," the inhabitants might exclaim, "who gave us the yellow fever? Was

---

[2] Houses; [3] better said; [4] streets; [5] to-morrow; [6] thank God; [7] at your
service; [8] good luck to you; [9] so good-bye.

it not communicated to the city originally by a vessel from Philadelphia, after we had enjoyed more than two centuries of im-
munity?" This charge, to be sure, has not been proven, but the
crew of an American vessel in port (in the year 1799) were
actually the first to be stricken, and local historians draw their
own conclusions.

La Guaira was founded in 1558, two years before our ancient
city of St. Augustine, and has shared the usual vicissitudes of the
Spanish settlements upon the coast, having been repeatedly attacked by pirates and foreign fleets, several of which, notably that
of the British commodore Knowles, were successfully repulsed.
The city, furthermore, was destroyed by the great earthquake of
1812, and experienced many exciting events in the war of independence, as, indeed, it has at intervals ever since, not least of
which was the blockade of the powers a few years ago. This
indignity, however, its officials assert, will never be repeated, and
they point to the well-equipped batteries, silent and grim, but
ever ready for the enemy—ready, that is, in a Pickwickian sense!

I have coupled Maracaibo with Cumana and La Guaira in
naming this article, though the situation of the former makes the
title plainly a misnomer. It is difficult, however, in passing to this
western city to resist mentioning a few of the interesting towns in
the intervening region, historic old places, such as Tocuyo, founded
in 1545; Coro, the ancient capital of the province of Venezuela
and the seat of the Welsers, founded in 1527, just seven years
after Cumana, and in reality the first permanent settlement in
Tierra Firme; Carora, founded in 1572, more than half a century
after Cumana, yet a hundred and ten years before William Penn
established his colony on the northern continent; Ocumare—but
why continue the list; no more historic region can be found in the
New World than these southern shores of the Caribbean Sea,
and none, certainly, are more neglected by the traveler.

Maracaibo, as the reader is aware, is situated upon the lake
of the same name, or rather upon the strait connecting the lake
with the outer gulf. Like La Guaira and Puerto Cabello, it has
excellent steamer communications with Curaçao and New York,
an American line having built two vessels of sufficiently light
draft to pass the dangerous sand bars that obstruct the entrance
to the lake. Were navigation entirely unobstructed, and the city
not preyed upon as it has been by every government since the time

of Guzman-Blanco, it would long since have been one of the most important ports in Caribbean countries, for behind it lies a vast lowland region, rich in all manner of tropical products and only rendered inaccessible in places by the very profusion of its wealth. Furthermore, Maracaibo is the port of a considerable section of Colombia, and nearly all of the coffee that bears its name comes either from across the boundary or from the Venezuelan Cordillera region south and east of the lake. At intervals of a year or so, it would appear, President Castro from some fancied grievance prohibits all intercourse with the neighboring republic; whereupon the exports of " Maracaibo " coffee fall to half the usual amount, only to leap to an abnormal figure when his wrath has been appeased. Colombian cities are allowed to discharge their accumulated supply. When I outlined this article the barriers, if I mistake not, were up; at the present writing they have been removed. And yet Colombia, like Curaçao, was at one time a haven of refuge when the President was a fugitive. What unheard-of indignities might they not suffer to-day had they not received him so hospitably!

Maracaibo has the unenviable reputation of being one of the most unhealthful cities in the world, which is sheer nonsense, for its climate is said to be rather agreeable, though moist and hot. Yellow fever is prevalent at times, but of such a mild type that it is seldom fatal, and German commercial houses in Cucuta, where this disease, on the contrary, is most deadly, are said to station their newly arrived clerks in Maracaibo until they have taken the fever before allowing them to enter the interior. I did not believe this story until a gentleman of unquestionable veracity assured me that such is actually the case, and that Maracaibo fever, like the measles, is really welcomed, that the ordeal may be over for all time.

Perhaps Maracaibo's bad name originated in the story of the consul and the coffin, of which many versions are current. Ex-Minister Scruggs gives it as follows:

" A Western politician of some local prominence, who had long been pressed upon the attention of our State Department for a consular position in South America, was finally nominated and confirmed as consul to Maracaibo, much to the disgust and discomfort of the incumbent, who wanted to retain his place. The new consul arrived at his post in midsummer and became the guest of his predecessor, whom he was about to relieve.   Discovering a metallic coffin in an obscure closet of his bedroom, he inquired of his host the next morning why such an article of furniture should be there.   The host was profuse in his apologies, but added by way of explanation that such things were not unusual in Maracaibo, especially during 'the fever season, which,' said he, 'is just now setting in!'   The new consul took the return steamer for New York, leaving his predecessor undisturbed."

Here again I was long dubious about accepting such a good yarn seriously, till I was assured not once, but a dozen times, that it is essentially true; that the wily consul is none other than the present incumbent, and that he himself is nothing loath to admit the fact.   Yet few travelers go to verify either story, perhaps from an unmanly feeling that if they have been misinformed they may pay for the error by taking up a permanent residence there, without the assurance even of a consular coffin.

I am writing of Maracaibo as if it were an out-of-the-way village, instead of an important city and port, with ocean vessels coming and going, and fleets of sailing craft plying to various towns upon the lake, as well as to up-river ports—a city that can boast of electric light, tramway lines, telephones, telegraphs, a submarine cable, a splendid theater, a legislative palace, seven churches, a dockyard, and, to quote verbatim from the official report, "2 clubs, 5 hotels, 17 inns, 24 restaurants, and all modern improvements," which, of course, is equally misleading.

Maracaibo was founded in 1571, and has had its ups and downs, like the other cities upon the coast, the greatest disaster in its history being the raid of the notorious buccaneer, Morgan, in 1669, which, had it been two years later, might have been regarded as a centenary celebration.   To-day, happily, the city enjoys comparative prosperity, and despite the unfortunate reputation for unhealthfulness that it has gained abroad, and, within the republic, the equally unfortunate association in the popular mind with its huge dungeon, crowded with political suspects and the wretched leaders of the last revolution—for Maracaibo and its prison have become almost synonymous terms in Venezuela—its citizens might be excused for boasting of their western metropolis, the only city upon the Venezuelan coast which has refused to be merely a port of call for vessels—an aggregation of buildings, so to speak, surrounding a customs house.

Notwithstanding the drawbacks, from the tourist's standpoint, to many of the places I have mentioned, I believe the trip to and from the Venezuela coast will soon become an attractive one, even to the comfort-loving American. He will visit Caracas, La Guaira, and Macuto, and perhaps Puerto Cabello, returning either by Curaçao and Porto Rico or by Margarita, Trinidad, and the beautiful islands of the Windward group; and if he has read and treasured as a child the strange and terrible stories of the Spanish Main, with its gold-laden galleons, its fierce buccaneers, and the occasional English freebooter from the Drake of history to the Amyas Leigh of fiction, no trip could be more fascinating to him. The invalid, also, will in time be attracted to these southern waters, and will find to his surprise that a voyage through the Caribbean Sea is almost as delightful and quite as beneficial as a tour of the Mediterranean.

SOUTH AMERICA FIFTY YEARS HENCE[1]

By Charles M. Pepper

I N the first Pan-American Conference, which was held in Washington in 1890, one of the most eminent of the delegates from Latin America declared that the twentieth century would belong to South America, just as the nineteenth century had belonged to the United States. This sentiment was reëchoed by the Third Pan-American Conference during the sessions at Rio Janeiro. In the meantime Canada has come forward with rapid strides, and Premier Laurier asserts that the twentieth century belongs to Canada.

In the opinion of many people in the United States, though they know almost as little of Canada as of South America—that is, of the splendid domain which stretches from the maritime provinces to the Pacific and the regions of the Yukon—the Dominion has the better claim. But it is not necessary to quarrel with either prophecy. Both have vast possibilities.

With regard to South America, it may still be difficult to convince North Americans that this continent, whose area comes within a fraction of equaling North America, has a future which should not be measured by the past; or that fifty years hence it will not continue to be the region best known to the rest of the world as the seat of earthquakes and revolutions. There is no need to enter here into political abstractions or theories which involve the political future of the southern continent. In a half century from now, looking backward, it may be interesting to see how speculative principles have yielded to hard economic facts. The point for the present is that South America has a future which is just becoming known to itself. In all its possibilities, industrial and political, this may be described as a geographic future, and the geography is commercial rather than political geography.

The influence of the physical aspects of the continent always must be considered in relation to South America as a whole. The

[1] Contributed through the courtesy of The National Geographic Society.

sixteenth century idea that the precious metals constituted the principal wealth of a nation has been very slowly dissipated. The mineral resources of the Andes and of the other mountain systems of South America will continue a very potent incentive during the next half century, but the greater development is going to come from supplying what mankind eats and wears. South America's productive resources must be considered in relation to the world's cotton crop, wool clip, cereal products, coffee crop, sheep and cattle, and rubber. Thus the Amazon forests, the Brazil coffee plantations, the Argentine wheat fields and grazing ranges, and the Chilian nitrate beds are all to be considered, as well as the mines of Bolivia and Peru.

Some epoch-making economic events will mark the coming half century. There will be an overflow of capital from the United States, and this will be an enormous factor in securing the development of the various countries. Up to this time our capital has been so fully employed at home that it could not be induced to venture abroad. Now a new condition, fully recognized in the circles of high finance, though not appreciated by the people at large, is arising, and this new condition is marked by the investment of large sums of money in railway and similar construction enterprises as well as in mines. These investments are tentative and preliminary, but they recognize the growing necessity of finding an outlet for redundant funds in the South American field.

There is also, of course, the Panama Canal, which has incalculable possibilities for the west-coast countries without in any way impairing the growth of the Atlantic regions.

North Americans are more familiar with the Atlantic coast, and for various reasons those countries already have shown the most marked progress; but the general line of development during the next fifty years may be described as inter-South American and not restricted to any one region.

It was just about half a century ago that the South American countries began to build their first railways. The Argentine Republic in 1907 will hold a railway exposition at Buenos Ayres to commemorate its first railroad, which was a short and unimportant one. Brazil started its lines somewhat later, while on the Pacific coast there were various schemes for piercing the Andes. One of the first railroads constructed in South America was in southern Peru, from Arica to Tacna, and the prediction was that it soon would cross the volcanic coast Cordilleras and reach the great central plain of Bolivia.   Another line was from Valparaiso and Santiago right to the mountain wall of the Cordillera, and this was expected to bore its way through and reach the pampas of Argentina.   But half a century passed and the Andes wall was still unconquered and the skeptics renewed their doubts whether it ever would be pierced.

On the Atlantic slope the engineering difficulties were not so great and both Brazil and Argentina from year to year spread out their systems of railways; yet, considering the resources of the regions to be developed, these extensions were not up to expectation, and the prophets of doubt again raised their distressed voices.   Prophets of this class, however, lacked the sense of proportion and failed to note the really remarkable development that had taken place.   Few of them yet have an idea of the enormous foreign commerce that has been developed by the Atlantic coast countries, which now reaches approximately $800,000,000 annually and soon will be $1,000,000,000.

It may be that fifty years hence northern Brazil—that is, the torrid region of the Amazon—will not have a notably greater population or a greater commerce than now exists, for much of that vast basin is not a white man's country and is not susceptible of permanent settlement by the Caucasian races.   It is fifty years since Alfred Russel Wallace wrote his fascinating description of life on the Amazon, and in another fifty years the civilization may not be markedly different.   It is even possible that in another half century the increasing appetite for crude rubber will have caused the gum forests to be depleted almost completedly; yet the measures adopted by the Brazilian government for preserving this industry and for encouraging new cultivation are taken especially with a view to fifty years and a century hence.   So it is more probable that Para, at the mouth of the Amazon; Manaos, the fluvial capital; and Iquitos, the Peruvian rubber metropolis, to which Commander Todd, of the United States Navy, took the *Wilmington* a few years ago, will show a growth proportionate to that of the last half century.   In the case of Iquitos the half century cannot be taken as the measure mark of growth, since its existence only dates back a quarter of a century.

With Brazil the greatest development is more likely to be in the semitropical and the temperate regions in the southern part of its extensive territory. No reason exists for imagining that in half a century the country's position as the chief source of coffee production will be altered, and there is cause to believe that vast cotton plantations also will exist; but the more rapid growth will be in the states of southern Brazil where the cereals are raised. Brazil is so vast and, except on the fringe of coast, is so undeveloped that it is difficult to guess at this period how far the development will advance inland. It may not progress very far in fifty years, and yet, with the very large area which is contiguous to the coast, even a relatively slight growth would add very materially to the productive resources and the commercial opportunities of the country.

There is almost a certainty that a phase of development which follows the line of least resistance will be realized within the next fifty years by the construction of a railway trunk from Pernambuco to the border of Uruguay. This is the grand conception known as the Interoceanic Railway, whose ultimate purpose is to place Pernambuco in through railway communication with Valparaiso on the Pacific, traversing a total distance of approximately 4000 miles. The sections through other countries may be overlooked temporarily and this proposed trunk line be considered with reference to Brazil alone. It would run from Pernambuco along the course of the San Francisco River, forming a northeast and southwest artery, giving several Brazilian states needed railway communication by branches and by crossing the systems of the states of Bahia, Minas Geraes, San Paolo, Parana, and Rio Grande do Sul. The distance from Pernambuco to the border of Uruguay is 2800 miles and the technical conditions for railway construction are not difficult. The Brazilian government gave the project its indorsement fifteen years ago, and some preliminary studies and surveys of the route have been made. It may lie dormant for a quarter of a century or more, or it may be taken up within the next ten years, but it is certain to come within the next half century and to add enormously to Brazil's development, both in population and in production and commerce.

The Argentine Republic is best known of all the South American countries because it produces cereals and beef, mutton, wool, and hides in competition with the United States, Canada, and European countries; yet it is difficult to keep pace with the enormous growth of Argentine agriculture during the last few years, just as very many persons are still unable to grasp the fact that instead of being a little country somewhere down in South America it is twenty-eight times the size of Ohio, and that while in the northern regions it produces sugar and other tropical products, yet as a whole it is to be viewed as another Mississippi Valley. The Argentine Minister of Agriculture estimates the wheat crop for the year 1906 at 3,882,000 tons, the area under cultivation being 14,028,000 acres. The foreign commerce for the same year exceeded $550,000,000.

The population of the country is not in excess of 5,250,000. Argentina easily has room for 50,000,000 inhabitants. I don't pretend to say that it will have 50,000,000 or anything like that number fifty years hence; yet there must be an appreciable growth, for the country can sustain a dense agricultural population from its northern border clear down through Patagonia, and settlements will spread through all those regions. Buenos Ayres in 1856 had 100,000 inhabitants; to-day it has more than 1,000,000. It is no wild flight of fancy to prophesy that in another fifty years its population will be 2,500,000, and that on the southern continent, 2000 miles south of the Equator, there will be a city which may not be exceeded by more than two cities in the United States.

In considering the industrial and commercial South America of fifty years hence as relates to the Atlantic coast, it would be better to disregard the lines formed by the boundaries of countries and to consider Argentina, Uruguay, southern Brazil, and part of Paraguay as one section, for in this region are the enormous productive resources which constitute it the world's granary, that will be drawn upon as rapidly as the United States and Canada require their own agricultural products for home consumption. The statistics of agricultural output for this central region will be the measure of growth. Another means of measuring it will be the shipping statistics of Buenos Ayres and Montevideo.

To the economic effect of the Panama Canal on the west-coast countries of South America, and to the possibilities of the Pan-American Railway project, I shall give only brief consideration here, starting with the premise that the railways will spread across the Andes and make some of the regions on the eastern side tributary to the west coast. In stating that the efforts to pierce the Andes from Tacna and Valparaiso did not come up to the expectations of a half century ago, I neglected to add that the beginning of the present fifty-year period will be marked by this through communication. The trans-Andine tunnel through the Uspallata Pass from the Chilian side to the Argentine side at Mendoza will be completed within less than three years, and the railway from Arica and Tacna to La Paz, in Bolivia, will be finished within four or five years. These results are to be accomplished under contracts already let.

In the Intercontinental or Pan-American Trunk Line project undoubtedly there will be long halts before all the gaps in such sections as those between Cuzco, in Peru, and Quito, in Ecuador, are completed; but all this is easily within the vista of half a century. The spell of the inca civilization may come over the railway builder in Peru, but from the ruins of that civilization he may take lessons in road construction which can be applied to railway lines.

It is an engaging theme to inquire whether, in addition to the coast development, within half a century the heart of South America will really have the arteries of commerce pulsating through it. Now Bolivia, in the Andes, may be considered as the heart of South America. Here, too, there have been projects almost half a century old for opening up this great interior to the outside world. Thirty years ago Colonel George Earl Church, one of the most distinguished of American civil engineers, entered heartily into the project of railway building in connection with river navigation, which was to insure the through route to the Atlantic by way of the Amazon and its affluents. The plan went down in disaster due to financial and other reasons. But to-day Bolivia has the assurance, probably within ten years, of railway outlets to the Pacific at Arica, at Mollendo, and probably at Callao, while on the Atlantic side there is the certainty of reaching the Plata at Buenos Ayres through the connection with the Argentine systems, and a later possibility of reaching the Atlantic through Paraguay.

For the Amazon there is also now the certainty of realizing Colonel Church's plan, for the Brazilian government will be impelled by the outlets Bolivia is securing in other directions to build the long-deferred railway around the falls of the Madeira to Santo Antonio. It already has made financial provision for this purpose just as Bolivia has made provision by contracts signed within the last few months for the connection of a series of links from Lake Titicaca to the border of Argentina, and also to Puerto Pando, on the Beni River, which is the beginning of navigation to the Amazon. At the very farthest, the opening up of this heart of South America may be placed at a quarter of a century instead of fifty years hence.

There is another phase of river transportation which undoubtedly will be considered within the next fifty years. General Rafael Reyes, the President of Colombia, in his explorations showed the possibility of interfluvial communication through all South America. Other explorers and writers have advanced various propositions for bringing the Mississippi Valley, through the mouth of the Mississippi, and the immense interior of South America, through the mouths of the Amazon and the Orinoco, into more direct communication. It is very fascinating to think of sailing from New York or New Orleans up the Orinoco or the Amazon, and thence in smaller boats, and even canoes, with an occasional portage, dropping down to Buenos Ayres. Fifty years hence it is quite probable that the canal, of less than 1000 feet in length, which the early Portuguese explorers proposed from the headwaters of the Guapore, the largest affluent of the Madeira, in the Brazilian state of Matto Grosso, to connect with the streamlets Aguapey and Estiva, which empty into the Jauru, a tributary of the Paraguay, will be completed and a through means of navigation be obtained. The Portuguese made this canoe voyage without much portage. Some years ago, in Rio Janeiro, I saw the plans for the modern canal connection, and they appeared not only feasible in the engineering sense, but practicable in the commercial view. Yet this general fact is apparent—water transportation by means of inland rivers never reaches its full utility until the railway systems begin to spread a network among the river courses; nor do colonization and immigration follow upstream. There are numerous regions in South America easily accessible by river navigation, yet the efforts to plant colonies at their headwaters have failed. When the railway begins to creep along, then the people appear.

The whole question of immigration has to be considered in discounting the South America of fifty years hence. The movement has been very slow, and even with the better government which is now assured in most of the South American countries, it is not likely to keep pace with the needs of production; yet in time it will be secured, and probably there will be a notable movement within the next few years to Argentina, Uruguay, and southern Brazil, and later to the inter-Andine regions.

It must follow, if the development which is to show that the South America of fifty years hence has made much greater progress than during the preceding half century does not prove an illusion, that the minor streams of immigration will turn into currents. The native Indian stock of the South American countries must be overlapped. The South America of the middle of the twentieth century will be less Spanish also, though possibly not less Latin, for one of the great sources of immigration which is peopling Argentina and some sections of Brazil is from Italy. The Panama Canal is likely to bring this element around to the west-coast countries. The northern races—Scandinavians, Germans, and natives of the British Islands—will find much larger areas of settlement than heretofore they have cared to seek. The Scotch sheep herders already have taken very kindly to Patagonia, while Welsh and Russian colonies also are established in that region. It may even be that from the United States there will be some overflow of our own cosmopolitan population, though the direct ocean routes cannot be changed and Argentina and Brazil must continue closer to Europe than to the United States.

In conclusion, viewing South America fifty years hence, both in relation to the productive regions which will attract immigration and to the conditions of life which insure a permanent population, it may be said that the star of empire takes its way south from the Caribbean to Patagonia. That is the course for the grain-raiser, for the wool-grower, and for the grazer. It is also the course for the miner who follows the trend of the Andes.

AN AWAKENED CONTINENT TO THE SOUTH OF US [1]

By Hon. Elihu Root, Secretary of State

A LITTLE less than three centuries of colonial and national
life have brought the people inhabiting the United States,
by a process of evolution, natural and with the existing
forces inevitable, to a point of distinct and radical change in their
economic relations to the rest of mankind.

During the period now past the energy of our people, directed
by the formative power created in our early population by heredity,
by environment, by the struggle for existence, by individual independence, and by free institutions, has been devoted to the internal
development of our own country. The surplus wealth produced
by our labors has been applied immediately to reproduction in our
own land. We have been cutting down forests and breaking virgin
soil and fencing prairies and opening mines of coal and iron and
copper and silver and gold, and building roads and canals and
railroads and telegraph lines and cars and locomotives and mills
and furnaces and school-houses and colleges and libraries and hospitals and asylums and public buildings and store-houses and shops
and homes. We have been drawing on the resources of the world
in capital and in labor to aid us in our work. We have gathered
strength from every rich and powerful nation and expended it upon
these home undertakings; into them we have poured hundreds of
millions of money attracted from the investors of Europe. We
have been always a debtor nation, borrowing from the rest of the
world, drawing all possible energy toward us and concentrating
it with our own energy upon our own enterprises. The engrossing
pursuit of our own opportunities has excluded from our consideration and interest the enterprises and the possibilities of the outside
world. Invention, discovery, the progress of science, capacity for
organization, the enormous increase in the productive power of

[1] An address before the Trans-Mississippi Commercial Congress, Kansas
City, Missouri, Tuesday, November 20, 1906, printed here by special permission
from Mr. Root.

mankind, have accelerated our progress and have brought us to a result of development in every branch of internal industrial activity marvelous and unprecedented in the history of the world.

Since the first election of President McKinley the people of the United States have for the first time accumulated a surplus of capital beyond the requirements of internal development. That surplus is increasing with extraordinary rapidity. We have paid our debts to Europe and have become a creditor instead of a debtor nation; we have faced about; we have left the ranks of the borrowing nations and have entered the ranks of the investing nations. Our surplus energy is beginning to look beyond our own borders, throughout the world, to find opportunity for the profitable use of our surplus capital, foreign markets for our manufactures, foreign mines to be developed, foreign bridges and railroads and public works to be built, foreign rivers to be turned into electric power and light. As in their several ways England and France and Germany have stood, so we in our own way are beginning to stand and must continue to stand toward the industrial enterprise of the world.

That we are not beginning our new role feebly is indicated by $1,518,561,666 of exports in the year 1905 as against $1,117,-513,071 of imports, and by $1,743,864,500 of exports in the year 1906 as against $1,226,563,843 of imports. Our first steps in the new field indeed are somewhat clumsy and unskilled. In our own vast country, with oceans on either side, we have had too little contact with foreign peoples readily to understand their customs or learn their languages; yet no one can doubt that we shall learn and shall understand and shall do our business abroad as we have done it at home with force and efficiency.

Coincident with this change in the United States the progress of political development has been carrying the neighboring continent of South America out of the stage of militarism into the stage of industrialism. Throughout the greater part of that vast continent revolutions have ceased to be looked upon with favor or submitted to with indifference; the revolutionary general and the dictator are no longer the objects of admiration and imitation; civic virtues command the highest respect; the people point with satisfaction and pride to the stability of their governments, to the safety of property and the certainty of justice; nearly everywhere the people are eager for foreign capital to develop their natural resources and for foreign immigration to occupy their vacant land. Immediately before us, at exactly the right time, just as we are ready for it, great opportunities for peaceful commercial and industrial expansion to the south are presented.

Other investing nations are already in the field—England, France, Germany, Italy, Spain; but the field is so vast, the new demands are so great, the progress so rapid, that what other nations have done up to this time is but a slight advance in the race for the grand total. The opportunities are so large that figures fail to convey them. The area of this newly awakened continent is 7,502,848 square miles—more than two and one-half times as large as the United States without Alaska and more than double the United States including Alaska. A large part of this area lies within the temperate zone, with an equable and invigorating climate, free from extremes of either heat or cold. Farther north in the tropics are enormous expanses of high tablelands stretching from the Atlantic to the foothills of the Andes, and lifted far above the tropical heats; the fertile valleys of the western Cordilleras are cooled by perpetual snows even under the Equator; vast forests grow untouched from a soil of incredible richness. The plains of Argentina, the great uplands of Brazil; the mountain valleys of Chili, Peru, Ecuador, Bolivia, and Colombia are suited to the habitation of any race, however far to the north its origin may have been; hundreds of millions of men can find healthful homes and abundant sustenance in this great territory.

The population in 1900 was only 42,461,381, less than six to the square mile. The density of population was less than one-eighth of that in the State of Missouri, less than one-sixtieth of that in the State of Massachusetts, less than one-seventieth of that in England, less than one per cent. of that in Belgium.

With this sparse population the production of wealth is already enormous. The latest trade statistics show exports from South America to foreign countries of $745,530,000, and imports of $499,-858,600. Of the five hundred millions of goods that South America buys we sell them but $63,246,525, or 12.6 per cent. Of the seven hundred and forty-five millions that South America sells we buy $152,092,000, or 20.4 per cent., nearly two and a half times as much as we sell.

Their production is increasing by leaps and bounds. In eleven years the exports of Chili have increased forty-five per cent., from

$54,030,000 in 1894, to $78,840,000, in 1905. In eight years the exports of Peru have increased one hundred per cent., from $13,-899,000 in 1897 to $28,758,000 in 1905. In ten years the exports of Brazil have increased sixty-six per cent., from $134,062,000 in 1894 to $223,101,000, in 1905. In ten years the exports of Argentina have increased one hundred and sixty-eight per cent., from $115,868,000 in 1895 to $311,544,000 in 1905.

This is only the beginning; the coffee and rubber of Brazil, the wheat and beef and hides of Argentina and Uruguay, the copper and nitrates of Chili, the copper and tin of Bolivia, the silver and gold and cotton and sugar of Peru, are but samples of what the soil and mines of that wonderful continent are capable of yielding. Ninety-seven per cent. of the territory of South America is occupied by ten independent republics living under constitutions substantially copied or adapted from our own. Under the new conditions of tranquillity and security which prevail in most of them, their eager invitation to immigrants from the old world will not long pass unheeded.

The pressure of population abroad will inevitably turn its streams of life and labor toward those fertile fields and valleys; the streams have already begun to flow; more than two hundred thousand immigrants entered the Argentine Republic last year; they are coming this year at the rate of over three hundred thousand. Many thousands of Germans have already settled in southern Brazil. They are most welcome in Brazil; they are good and useful citizens there as they are here; I hope that many more will come to Brazil and every other South American country, and add their vigorous industry and good citizenship to the upbuilding of their adopted home.

With the increase of population in such a field, under free institutions, with the fruits of labor and the rewards of enterprise secure, the production of wealth and the increase of purchasing power will afford a market for the commerce of the world worthy to rank even with the markets of the Orient as the goal of business enterprise.

The material resources of South America are in some important respects complementary to our own; that continent is weakest where North America is strongest as a field for manufactures; it has comparatively little coal and iron.

In many respects the people of the two continents are complementary to each other; the South American is polite, refined, cultivated, fond of literature and of expression and of the graces and charms of life, while the North American is strenuous, intense, utilitarian. Where we accumulate, they spend. While we have less of the cheerful philosophy which finds sources of happiness in the existing conditions of life, they have less of the inventive faculty which strives continually to increase the productive power of man and lower the cost of manufacture. The chief merits of the peoples of the two continents are different; their chief defects are different. Mutual intercourse and knowledge cannot fail to greatly benefit both; each can learn from the other; each can teach much to the other, and each can contribute greatly to the development and prosperity of the other. A large part of their products finds no domestic competition here; a large part of our products will find no domestic competition there. The typical conditions exist for that kind of trade which is profitable, honorable, and beneficial to both parties.

The relations between the United States and South America have been chiefly political rather than commercial or personal. In the early days of the South American struggle for independence, the eloquence of Henry Clay awakened in the American people a generous sympathy for the patriots of the South as for brethren struggling in the common cause of liberty. The clear-eyed, judicious diplomacy of Richard Rush, the American Minister at the Court of St. James, effected a complete understanding with Great Britain for concurrent action in opposition to the designs of the Holy Alliance, already contemplating the partition of the Southern Continent among the great powers of continental Europe. The famous declaration of Monroe arrayed the organized and rapidly increasing power of the United States as an obstacle to European interference and made it forever plain that the cost of European aggression would be greater than any advantage which could be won even by successful aggression.

That great declaration was not the chance expression of the opinion or the feeling of the moment; it crystallized the sentiment for human liberty and human rights which has saved American idealism from the demoralization of narrow selfishness, and has given to American democracy its true world power in the virile potency of a great example. It responded to the instinct of self-preservation in an intensely practical people. It was the result of conference with Jefferson and Madison and John Quincy Adams and John C. Calhoun and William Wirt—a combination of political wisdom, experience, and skill not easily surpassed. The particular circumstances which led to the declaration no longer exist; no Holy Alliance now threatens to partition South America; no European colonization of the west coast threatens to exclude us from the Pacific. But those conditions were merely the occasion for the declaration of a principle of action.

Other occasions for the application of the principle have arisen since; it needs no prophetic vision to see that other occasions for its application may arise hereafter. The principle declared by Monroe is as wise an expression of sound political judgment to-day, as truthful a representation of the sentiments and instincts of the American people to-day, as living in its force as an effective rule of conduct whenever occasion shall arise, as it was on the 2d of December, 1823.

These great political services to South American independence, however, did not and could not in the nature of things create any relation between the people of South America and the people of the United States except a relation of political sympathy.

Twenty-five years ago Mr. Blaine, sanguine, resourceful, and gifted with that imagination which enlarges the historian's understanding of the past into the statesman's comprehension of the future, undertook to inaugurate a new era of American relations which should supplement political sympathy by personal acquaintance, by the intercourse of expanding trade, and by mutual helpfulness. As Secretary of State under President Arthur, he invited the American nations to a conference to be held on the 24th of November, 1882, for the purpose of considering and discussing the subject of preventing war between the nations of America. That invitation, abandoned by Mr. Frelinghuysen, was renewed under Mr. Cleveland, and on the 2d of October, 1889, Mr. Blaine, again Secretary of State under President Harrison, had the singular good fortune to execute his former design and to open the sessions of the first American Conference at Washington. In an address of wisdom and lofty spirit, which should ever give honor to his memory, he described the assembly as—

An honorable, peaceful conference of seventeen independent American powers, in which all shall meet together on terms of absolute equality; a conference in which there can be no attempt to coerce a single delegate against his own conception of the interests of his nation; a conference which will permit no secret understanding on any subject, but will frankly publish to the world all its conclusions; a conference which will tolerate no spirit of conquest, but will aim to cultivate an American sympathy as broad as both continents; a conference which will form no selfish alliance against the older nations from which we are proud to claim inheritance—a conference, in fine, which will seek nothing, propose nothing, endure nothing that is not, in the general sense of all the delegates, timely, wise and peaceful.

The policy which Blaine inaugurated has been continued; the Congress of the United States has approved it; subsequent Presidents have followed it. The first conference at Washington has been succeeded by a second conference in Mexico, and now by a third conference in Rio de Janeiro; and it is to be followed in years to come by further successive assemblies in which the representatives of all American States shall acquire better knowledge and more perfect understanding and be drawn together by the recognition of common interests and the kindly consideration and discussion of measures for mutual benefit.

Nevertheless, Mr. Blaine was in advance of his time. In 1881 and 1889 neither had the United States reached a point where it could turn its energies away from its own internal development and direct them outward toward the development of foreign enterprises and foreign trade, nor had the South American countries reached the stage of stability in government and security for property necessary to their industrial development.

Now, however, the time has come; both North and South America have grown up to Blaine's policy; the production, the trade, the capital, the enterprise of the United States have before them the opportunity to follow, and they are free to follow, the pathway marked out by the far-sighted statesmanship of Blaine for the growth of America, North and South, in the peaceful prosperity of a mighty commerce.

To utilize this opportunity certain practical things must be done. For the most part these things must be done by a multitude of individual efforts; they cannot be done by government. Government may help to furnish facilities for the doing of them, but the facilities will be useless unless used by individuals; they cannot be done by resolutions of this or any other commercial body; resolutions are useless unless they stir individual business men to action in their own business affairs. The things needed have been fully and specifically set forth in many reports of efficient consuls and of highly competent agents of the Department of Commerce and Labor, and they have been described in countless newspapers and magazine articles; but all these things are worthless unless they are followed by individual action. I will indicate some of the matters to which every producer and merchant who desires South American trade should pay attention:

1. He should learn what the South Americans want and conform his product to their wants. If they think they need heavy castings, he should give them heavy castings and not expect them to buy light ones because he thinks they are better. If they want coarse cottons, he should give them coarse cottons and not expect them to buy fine cottons. It may not pay to-day, but it will pay to-morrow. The tendency to standardize articles of manufacture may reduce the cost and promote convenience, but if the consumers on the River Plate demand a different standard from the consumers on the Mississippi, you must have two standards or lose one market.

2. Both for the purpose of learning what the South American people want and of securing their attention to your goods, you must have agents who speak the Spanish or Portuguese language. For this there are two reasons: one is that people can seldom really get at each other's minds through an interpreter, and the other is that nine times out of ten it is only through knowing the Spanish or Portuguese language that a North American comes to appreciate the admirable and attractive personal qualities of the South American, and is thus able to establish that kindly and agreeable personal relation which is so potent in leading to business relations.

3. The American producer should arrange to conform his credit system to that prevailing in the country where he wishes to sell goods. There is no more money lost upon commercial credits in South America than there is in North America; but business men there have their own ways of doing business; they have to adapt the credits they receive to the credits they give. It is often inconvenient, disagreeable, and sometimes impossible for them to conform to our ways, and the requirement that they should do so is a serious obstacle to trade.

To understand credits it is, of course, necessary to know something about the character, trustworthiness, and commercial standing of the purchaser, and the American producer or merchant who would sell goods in South America must have some means of knowledge upon this subject. This leads naturally to the next observation I have to make.

4. The establishment of banks should be brought about. The

Americans already engaged in South American trade could well afford to subscribe the capital and establish an American bank in each of the principal cities of South America. This is, first, because nothing but very bad management could prevent such a bank from making money; capital is much needed in those cities, and six, eight and ten per cent. can be obtained for money upon just as safe security as can be had in Kansas City, St. Louis, or New York. It is also because the American bank would furnish a source of information as to the standing of the South American purchasers to whom credit may be extended, and because American banks would relieve American business in South America from the disadvantage which now exists of making all its financial transactions through Europe instead of directly with the United States. It is unfortunately true that among hundreds of thousands of possible customers the United States now stands in a position of assumed financial and business inferiority to the countries through whose banking houses all its business has to be done.

5. The American merchant should himself acquire, if he has not already done so, and should impress upon all his agents, that respect for the South American to which he is justly entitled and which is the essential requisite to respect from the South American. We are different in many ways as to character and methods. In dealing with all foreign people it is important to avoid the narrow and uninstructed prejudice which assumes that difference from ourselves denotes inferiority. There is nothing that we resent so quickly as an assumption of superiority or evidence of condescension in foreigners; there is nothing that the South Americans resent so quickly. The South Americans are our superiors in some respects; we are their superiors in other respects. We should show to them what is best in us and see what is best in them. Every agent of an American producer or merchant should be instructed that courtesy, politeness, kindly consideration are essential requisites for success in the South American trade.

6. The investment of American capital in South America under the direction of American experts should be promoted, not merely upon simple investment grounds, but as a means of creating and enlarging trade. For simple investment purposes the opportunities are innumerable. Good business judgment and good business management will be necessary there, of course, as they are necessary here; but given these, I believe that there is a vast number of enter-

prises awaiting capital in the more advanced countries of South America, capable of yielding great profits, and in which the property and the profits will be as safe as in the United States or Canada.

A good many such enterprises are already begun. I have found a graduate of the Massachusetts Institute of Technology, a graduate of the Columbia School of Mines, and a graduate of Colonel Roosevelt's Rough Riders smelting copper close under the snow line of the Andes; I have ridden in an American car upon an American electric road, built by a New York engineer, in the heart of the coffee region of Brazil, and I have seen the waters of that river along which Pizarro established his line of communication in the conquest of Peru harnessed to American machinery to make light and power for the city of Lima. Every such point is the nucleus of American trade—the source of orders for American goods.

7. It is absolutely essential that the means of communication between the two countries should be improved and increased.

This underlies all other considerations and it applies both to the mail, the passenger, and the freight services. Between all the principal South American ports and England, Germany, France, Spain, Italy, lines of swift and commodious steamers ply regularly. There are five subsidized first-class mail and passenger lines between Buenos Ayres and Europe; there is no such line between Buenos Ayres and the United States. Within the past two years the German, the English, and the Italian lines have been replacing their old steamers with new and swifter steamers of modern construction, accommodation, and capacity.

In the year ending June 30, 1905, there entered the port of Rio de Janeiro steamers and sailing vessels flying the flag of Austria-Hungary 120, of Norway 142, of Italy 165, of Argentina 264, of France 349, of Germany 657, of Great Britain 1,785, of the United States no steamers and seven sailing vessels, two of which were in distress!

An English firm runs a small steamer monthly between New York and Rio de Janeiro; the Panama Railroad Company runs steamers between New York and the Isthmus of Panama; the Brazilians are starting for themselves a line between Rio and New York; there are two or three foreign concerns running slow cargo boats, and there are some foreign tramp steamers. That is the sum total of American communications with South America beyond the Caribbean Sea. Not one American steamship runs to any South American port beyond the Caribbean. During the past summer I entered the ports of Para, Pernambuco, Bahia, Rio de Janeiro, Santos, Montevideo, Buenos Ayres, Bahia Blanca, Punta Arenas, Lota, Valparaiso, Coquimbo, Tocopilla, Callao, and Carthagena—all of the great ports and a large proportion of the secondary ports of the Southern Continent. I saw only one ship, besides the cruiser that carried me, flying the American flag.

The mails between South America and Europe are swift, regular, and certain; between South America and the United States they are slow, irregular, and uncertain. Six weeks is not an uncommon time for a letter to take between Buenos Ayres or Valparaiso and New York. The merchant who wishes to order American goods cannot know when his order will be received or when it will be filled.

The freight charges between the South American cities and American cities are generally and substantially higher than between the same cities and Europe; at many points the deliveries of freight are uncertain and its condition upon arrival doubtful.

The passenger accommodations are such as to make a journey to the United States a trial to be endured and a journey to Europe a pleasure to be enjoyed. The best way to travel between the United States and both the southwest coast and the east coast of South America is to go by way of Europe, crossing the Atlantic twice. It is impossible that trade should prosper or intercourse increase or mutual knowledge grow to any great degree under such circumstances. The communication is worse now than it was twenty-five years ago. So long as it is left in the hands of our foreign competitors in business we cannot reasonably look for any improvement. It is only reasonable to expect that European steamship lines shall be so managed as to promote European trade in South America rather than to promote the trade of the United States in South America.

This woeful deficiency in the means to carry on and enlarge our South American trade is but a part of the general decline and feebleness of the American merchant marine, which has reduced us from carrying over ninety per cent. of our export trade in our own ships to the carriage of nine per cent. of that trade in our own ships and dependence upon foreign ship-owners for the carriage of ninety-one per cent. The true remedy and the only remedy is the establishment of American lines of steamships between the United States and the great ports of South America adequate to render fully as good service as is now afforded by the European lines between those ports and Europe. The substantial underlying fact was well stated in the resolution of this Trans-Mississippi Congress three years ago:

That every ship is a missionary of trade; that steamship lines work for their own countries just as railroad lines work for their terminal points, and that it is as absurd for the United States to depend upon foreign ships to distribute its products as it would be for a department store to depend upon wagons of a competing house to deliver its goods.

How can this defect be remedied? The answer to this question must be found by ascertaining the cause of the decline of our merchant marine. Why is it that Americans have substantially retired from the foreign transport service? We are a nation of maritime traditions and facility; we are a nation of constructive capacity, competent to build ships; we are eminent, if not preëminent, in the construction of machinery; we have abundant capital seeking investment; we have courage and enterprise, shrinking from no competition in any field which we choose to enter. Why, then, have we retired from this field, in which we were once conspicuously successful?

I think the answer is twofold.

1. The higher wages and the greater cost of maintenance of American officers and crews make it impossible to compete on equal terms with foreign ships. The scale of living and the scale of pay of American sailors are fixed by the standard of wages and of living in the United States, and those are maintained at a high level by the protective tariff. The moment the American passes beyond the limits of his country and engages in ocean transportation he comes into competition with the lower foreign scale of wages and of living. Mr. Joseph L. Bristow, in his report upon trade conditions affecting the Panama Railroad, dated June 14, 1905, gives in detail the cost of operating an American steamship with a tonnage of approximately thirty-five hundred tons as compared with the cost of operating a specified German steamship of the same tonnage, and the differences aggregate $15,315 per annum greater cost for the American steamship than for the German, that is $4.37 per ton. He gives also in detail the cost of maintaining another American steamship with a tonnage of approximately

twenty-five hundred tons as compared with the cost of operating a specified British steamship of the same tonnage, and the differences aggregate $18,289.68 per annum greater cost for the American steamship than for the British, that is $7.31 per ton. It is manifest that if the German steamship were content with a profit of less than $15,000 per annum, and the British with a profit of less than $18,000 per annum, the American ships would have to go out of business.

2. The principal maritime nations of the world, anxious to develop their trade, to promote their shipbuilding industry, to have at hand transports and auxiliary cruisers in case of war, are fostering their steamship lines by the payment of subsidies. England is paying to her steamship lines between six and seven million dollars a year; it is estimated that since 1840 she has paid to them between two hundred and fifty and three hundred millions. The enormous development of her commerce, her preponderant share of the carrying trade of the world, and her shipyards crowded with construction orders from every part of the earth, indicate the success of her policy. France is paying about eight million dollars a year; Italy and Japan, between three and four millions each; Germany, upon the initiative of Bismarck, is building up her trade with wonderful rapidity by heavy subventions to her steamship lines and by giving special differential rates of carriage over her railroads for merchandise shipped by those lines. Spain, Norway, Austria-Hungary, Canada, all subsidize their own lines. It is estimated that about $28,000,000 a year are paid by our commercial competitors to their steamship lines.

Against these advantages to his competitor the American ship owner has to contend; and it is manifest that the subsidized ship can afford to carry freight at cost for a long enough period to drive him out of business.

We are living in a world not of natural competition, but of subsidized competition. State aid to steamship lines is as much a part of the commercial system of our day as state employment of consuls to promote business.

It will be observed that both of these disadvantages under which the American ship owner labors are artificial; they are created by governmental action—one by our own government in raising the standard of wages and living, by the protective tariff, the other by foreign governments in paying subsidies to their ships for the promotion of their own trade. For the American ship owner it is not a contest of intelligence, skill, industry, and thrift against similar qualities in his competitor; it is a contest against his competitors and his competitors' governments and his own government also.

Plainly these disadvantages created by governmental action can be neutralized only by governmental action, and should be neutralized by such action.

What action ought our Government to take for the accomplishment of this just purpose? Three kinds of action have been advocated.

1. A law providing for free ships—that is, permitting Americans to buy ships in other countries and bring them under the American flag. Plainly this would not at all meet the difficulties which I have described. The only thing it would accomplish would be to overcome the excess in cost of building a ship in an American shipyard over the cost of building it in a foreign shipyard; but since all the materials which enter into an American ship are entirely relieved of duty, the difference in cost of construction is so slight as to be practically a negligible quantity and to afford no substantial obstacle to the revival of American shipping. The expedient of free ships, therefore, would be merely to sacrifice our American ship-building industry, which ought to be revived and enlarged with American shipping, and to sacrifice it without receiving any substantial benefit. It is to be observed that Germany, France, and Italy all have attempted to build up their own shipping by adopting the policy of free ships, have failed in the experiment, have abandoned it, and have adopted in its place the policy of subsidy.

2. It has been proposed to establish a discriminating tariff duty in favor of goods imported in American ships, that is to say, to impose higher duties upon goods imported in foreign ships than are imposed on goods imported in American ships. We tried that once many years ago and have abandoned it. In its place we have entered into treaties of commerce and navigation with the principal countries of the world expressly agreeing that no such discrimination shall be made between their vessels and ours. To sweep away all those treaties and enter upon a war of commercial retaliation and reprisal for the sake of accomplishing indirectly what can be done directly should not be seriously considered.

3. There remains the third and obvious method: To neutralize the artificial disadvantages imposed upon American shipping through

the action of our own government and foreign governments by an equivalent advantage in the form of a subsidy or subvention. In my opinion this is what should be done; it is the sensible and fair thing to do. It is what must be done if we would have a revival of our shipping and the desired development of our foreign trade. We cannot repeal the protective tariff; no political party dreams of repealing it; we do not wish to lower the standard of American living or American wages. We should give back to the ship owner what we take away from him for the purpose of maintaining that standard; and unless we do give it back, we shall continue to go without ships. How can the expenditure of public money for the improvement of rivers and harbors to promote trade be justified upon any grounds which do not also sustain this proposal? Would anyone reverse the policy that granted aid to the Pacific railroads, the pioneers of our enormous internal commerce, the agencies that built up the great traffic which has enabled half a dozen other roads to be built in later years without assistance? Such subventions would not be gifts. They would be at once compensation for injuries inflicted upon American shipping by American laws and the consideration for benefits received by the whole American people—not the shippers or the ship-builders or the sailors alone, but by every manufacturer, every miner, every farmer, every merchant whose prosperity depends upon a market for his products.

The provision for such just compensation should be carefully shaped and directed so that it will go to individual advantage only so far as the individual is enabled by it to earn a reasonable profit by building up the business of the country.

A bill is now pending in Congress which contains such provisions; it has passed the Senate and is now before the House Committee on Merchant Marine and Fisheries; it is known as Senate Bill No. 529, Fifty-ninth Congress, first session. It provides specifically that the Postmaster-General may pay to American steamships, of specified rates of speed, carrying mails upon a regular service, compensation not to exceed the following amounts: For a line from an Atlantic port to Brazil, monthly, $150,000 a year; for a line from an Atlantic port to Uruguay and Argentina, monthly, $187,500 a year; for a line from a Gulf port to Brazil, monthly, $137,500 a year; for a line from each of two Gulf ports and from New Orleans to Central America and the Isthmus of Panama, weekly, $75,000 a year; for a line from a Gulf port to Mexico, weekly, $50,000 a year; for a line from a Pacific Coast port to Mexico, Central America, and the Isthmus of Panama, fortnightly, $120,000 a year. For these six regular lines a total of $720,000. The payments provided are no more than enough to give the American ships a fair living chance in the competition.

There are other wise and reasonable provisions in the bill relating to trade with the Orient, to tramp steamers and to a naval reserve, but I am now concerned with the provisions for trade to the South. The hope of such a trade lies chiefly in the passage of that bill.

Postmaster-General Cortelyou, in his report for 1905, said:

Congress has authorized the Postmaster-General, by the act of 1891, to contract with the owners of American steamships for ocean mail service and has realized the impracticability of commanding suitable steamships in the interest of the postal service alone by requiring that such steamers shall be of a size, class, and equipment which will promote commerce and become available as auxiliary cruisers of the Navy in case of need. The compensation allowed to such steamers is found to be wholly inadequate to secure the proposals contemplated; hence advertisements from time to time have failed to develop any bids for much-needed service. This is especially true in regard to several of the countries of South America with which we have cordial relations and which, for manifest reasons, should have direct mail connections with us. I refer to Brazil and countries south of it. Complaints of serious delay to mails for these countries have become frequent and emphatic, leading to the suggestion on the part of certain officials of the government that for the present, and until more satisfactory direct communication can be established, important mails should be dispatched to South America by way of European ports and on European steamers, which would not only involve the United States in the payment of double transit rates to a foreign country for the dispatch of its mails to countries of our own hemisphere, but might seriously embarrass the government in the exchange of important official and diplomatic correspondence.

The fact that the Government claims exclusive control of the transmission of letter mail throughout its own territory would seem to imply that it should secure and maintain the exclusive jurisdiction, when necessary, of its mails on the high seas. The unprecedented expansion of trade and foreign commerce justifies prompt consideration of an adequate foreign mail service.

It is difficult to believe, but it is true, that out of this faulty ocean mail service the Government of the United States is making a large profit. The actual cost to the Government last year of the ocean mail service to foreign countries other than Canada and Mexico was $2,965,624.21, while the proceeds realized by the Government from postage between the United States and foreign countries other than Canada and Mexico was $6,008,807.53, leaving the profit to the United States of $3,043,183.32; that is to say, under existing law the Government of the United States, having assumed the monopoly of carrying the mails for the people of the country, is making a profit of $3,000,000 per annum by rendering cheap and inefficient service. Every dollar of that three millions is made at the expense of the commerce of the United States. What can be plainer than that the government ought to expend at least the profits that it gets from the ocean mail service in making the ocean mail service efficient. One-quarter of those profits would establish all these lines which I have described between the United States and South and Central America and give us, besides a good mail service, enlarged markets for the producers and merchants of the United States who pay the postage from which the profits come.[2]

In his last message to Congress, President Roosevelt said:

To the spread of our trade in peace and the defense of our flag in war a great and prosperous merchant marine is indispensable. We should have ships of our own and seamen of our own to convey our goods to neutral markets, and in case of need to reënforce our battle line. It cannot but be a source of regret and uneasiness to us that the lines of communication with our sister republics of South America should be chiefly under foreign control. It is not a good thing that American merchants and manufacturers should have to send their goods and letters to South America via Europe if they wish security and dispatch. Even on the Pacific, where our ships have held their own better than on the Atlantic, our merchant flag is now threatened through the liberal aid bestowed by other governments on their own steam lines. I ask your earnest consideration of the report with which the Merchant Marine Commission has followed its long and careful inquiry.

The bill [3] now pending in the House is a bill framed upon the report of that Merchant Marine Commission. The question whether it shall become a law depends upon your Representatives in the House. You have the judgment of the Postmaster-General, you have the judgment of the Senate, you have the judgment of the President; if you agree with these judgments and wish the bill which embodies them to become a law, say so to your Representatives. Say it to them individually and directly, for it is your

[2] There would be some modification of these figures if the cost of getting the mails to and from the exchange offices were charged against the account; but this is not separable from the general domestic cost and would not materially change the result.

[3] This bill passed the House in a much mutilated condition, but the revised form failed when brought before the Senate on the closing day of the Session, March 4, 1907.—*Editor.*

right to advise them and it will be their pleasure to hear from you what legislation the interests of their constituents demand.

The great body of Congressmen are always sincerely desirous to meet the just wishes of their constituents and to do what is for the public interest; but in this great country they are continually assailed by innumerable expressions of private opinion and by innumerable demands for the expenditure of public money; they come to discriminate very clearly between private opinion and public opinion and between real public opinion and the manufactured appearance of public opinion; they know that when there is a real demand for any kind of legislation it will make itself known to them through a multitude of individual voices. Resolutions of commercial bodies frequently indicate nothing except that the proposer of the resolution has a positive opinion and that no one else has interest enough in the subject to oppose it. Such resolutions by themselves, therefore, have comparatively little effect; they are effective only when the support of individual expressions shows that they really represent a genuine and general opinion.

It is for you and the business men all over the country whom you represent to show to the Representatives in Congress that the producing and commercial interests of the country really desire a practical measure to enlarge the markets and increase the foreign trade of the United States by enabling American shipping to overcome the disadvantages imposed upon it by foreign governments for the benefit of their trade and by our government for the benefit of our home industry.

BIBLIOGRAPHY

BIBLIOGRAPHY

THE ABORIGINES

Larned, J. N.—"Literature of American History, a Bibliographical Guide."
Boston, 1902.
Contains critical notes of the literature of American archæology and
anthropology (pp. 32-50). In addition to the works there noted see the
following:
Winsor, Justin, ed.—"Aboriginal America" ("Narrative and Critical History
of America," Vol. I). Boston, 1889.
Contains essays by the editor on Mexico and Central America and "The
Progress of Opinion Respecting the Antiquity of Man in America"; and
by Clements R. Markham on "The Inca Civilization in Peru," with critical
bibliographical notes of great value.
Farrand, Livingston.—"Basis of American History, 1500-1900" (American
Nation," Vol. II). New York, 1904.
Chiefly concerned with North America. Contains valuable critical essay on
the authorities.
Boston Public Library.—"America before Columbus"; "Pre-Columbian
Visits"; "Mexican Civilization"; "Peruvian Civilization" (in Bulletins,
1875-1878, Vol. III., pp. 65-69).
Critical lists of the literature on these subjects in the library.
Larned's "Literature of American History" (cited above), contains in Part
VI., "Spanish and Portuguese America and the West Indies."
Critical bibliographical notes, some of which relate to the pre-Columbian
period, prepared by George Parker Winship.

In addition to the works noted in the bibliographies above mentioned, the
following may be noted:

Dellenbaugh, Frederick S.—"North Americans of Yesterday." New York, 1901.
Helmott, Hans Ferdinand, ed.—"History of the World: a Survey of Man's
Record." Vol. I. New York, 1902.
Contains 400 pages on America, including aboriginal culture and history,
Spanish colonial history, and Spanish-American history.

DISCOVERY AND CONQUEST

Bourne, Edward Gaylord.—"Spain in America, 1450-1580" ("American Nation," Vol. III).
Summarizes the results of the best scholarship on the Spanish discoveries,
explorations, colonial system, and the transmission of Spanish culture to
America. Spanish achievement in all lines is represented in a highly
favorable light. Valuable and exhaustive critical essay on the authorities.

Larned, J. N., ed.—"Literature of American History. European Discovery and Early Exploration" (pp. 50-68), prepared by E. G. Bourne.
Critical bibliographical notes of great value by Professor E. G. Bourne. See also Part VI. by G. P. Winship (noted above).

Winsor, Justin.—"Narrative and Critical History of America," Vol. II.: "Spanish Explorations and Settlements."
Essays by special students, with valuable bibliographical notes.

The following titles are given in addition to those mentioned in Larned, Bourne, and Winsor.

"Cambridge Modern History," Vol. I.: "The Renaissance." New York, 1902.
Contains two chapters by E. J. Paine on "The Age of Discovery" and "The New World," describing the course of exploration and the beginnings of Spanish dominion.

"Colección de libros y documentos referentes a la historia de America." Vols. I.-III. Madrid, 1904.

Garcia, Genaro.—"Caractér de la conquista Española en America y en Mexico segun los textos de los historiadores primitivos." Mexico, 1901.

Stevenson, Edward Luther.—"Maps, Illustrating Early Discovery and Exploration in America, 1502-1530." New Brunswick, N. J., 1903-1905.
Photographic reproductions of 12 maps of great value and importance.

Vignaud, Henry.—"Toscanelli and Columbus." New York, 1902.

——"Critical Study of the Various Dates Assigned to the Birth of Christopher Columbus." London, 1903.

——"Études Critiques sur la vie de Colomb avant ses découvertes." Paris, 1905.
Mr. Vignaud writes in depreciation of Columbus, finding him guilty of falsehood as to his ancestry, his birth, and his relations with Toscanelli. The author has made a thorough study of the sources, many of them recently published.

COLONIAL SYSTEM

Bourne, Edward Gaylord.—"Spain in America."
Noted above. Critical essay on the authorities.

Winsor, Justin, ed.—"Narrative and Critical History of America"; Vol. VIII.: "The Later History of British, Spanish, and Portuguese America." Boston and New York, 1889.
Contains the colonial history of South America and the wars of independence, with critical essay on the sources of information by Sir Clements Roberts Markham; bibliographical notes on Brazil and colonial South America, and an essay on the historical chorography of South America by Winsor.

Zimmerman, A.—"Die Kolonialpolitik Portugals und Spaniens." 1896.
A good narrative with a full bibliographical list. Covers Portuguese and Spanish colonization in all parts of the world.

The following works, in addition to those listed by Bourne, Winsor, and Zimmerman, may be noted:

Graham, R. B. Cunninghame.—"A Vanished Arcadia: Jesuits in Paraguay, 1607-1767." New York, 1901.

Leroy-Beaulieu, Paul.—"*De la colonisation chez les peuples modernes.*" 5th edition, Vol. I. Paris, 1902.

This eminent economist gives in chapters i. and ii., brief accounts of the Spanish and Portuguese colonial systems, with special reference to their economic aspects.

Roscher, Wilhelm Georg Friedrich.—"The Spanish Colonial System," edited by E. G. Bourne. New York, 1904.

A translation of a chapter of the author's "*Kolonien, Kolonialpolitik und Auswanderung*" from the third Leipzig edition. Roscher's main source is the "Laws of the Indies," and his work is especially valuable for the economic aspects of colonization. Professor Bourne's bibliographical notes give valuable references to works in English.

THE WARS OF INDEPENDENCE

See: Winsor, "Narrative and Critical History of America," Vol. VIII.; and Larned, "Literature of American History," Part VI., by G. P. Winship (noted above). Also, in addition to the works there listed:

Latané, John H.—"Diplomatic Relations of the United States and Spanish America" ("Albert Shaw Lectures"). Baltimore, 1900.

Paxson, Frederic Logan.—"Independence of the South American Republics, a Study in Recognition and Foreign Policy." Philadelphia, 1903.

Based on unpublished sources. Describes the attitude of the United States and England toward the revolted Spanish colonies. Contains a full bibliography.

NATIONAL HISTORY

See Larned, "Literature of American History"; Part VI. (cited above):

For the different states of South America bibliographies may be found in the "Encyclopædia Britannica," the "*Grande Encyclopedie,*" and in Larisse and Rambaud,"*Histoire générale.*"

ARGENTINE REPUBLIC

Napp.—"*Die argentinische Republik Buenos-Ayres,*" 1876.

Latham.—"The States of the River Plate." London, 1868.

Friederich, Karl.—"*Die La Plata Länder.*" Hamburg, 1884.

Dacraux, En.—"*Buenos Ayres, la Pampa et la Patagonie.*" Paris, 1874.

Latzina, Francisco.—"*Die argentinische Republik als Ziel der Europäischen Auswanderung.*" Buenos Ayres, 1883.

Olasgoaca, Manuel.—"*La conquete de la Pampa.*" Buenos Ayres, 1884.

BOLIVIA

Cortés, Manuel José.—"*Ensayo sobre la historia de Bolivia.*" Sucre, 1861.

Guiterrez.—"*La constituciones politicas que ha tenido la republica Boliviana*" (1826-1868).

Mossbach.—"Bolivia." 1875.

Wiener.—"*Bolivie et Pérou.*" Paris, 1880.

BRAZIL

Azevedo, Morera.—"*Historia do Brazil*" (from 1831 to 1840). **Rio.**
Conty, Dr.—"*Le Brésil en 1884.*" Rio, 1884.
——"*L'esclavage au Brésil.*" Paris, 1880.
Jourdain.—"*Guerra do Paraguay.*" Rio, 1871. 1 vol. and 1 atlas.
Levasseur.—"*Abolition de l'esclavage au Brésil.*" Paris, 1888.
Mossé.—"*Dom Pedro II.*" Paris, 1889.
Pulano.—"*Der Sturm des Kaiserthrons un Brasilien.*" 1892.
Saint-Hilaire, Aug. de.—"*Precis de l'histoire des Révolutions du Brésil.*" Paris, 1832.
Santa-Anna-Nery, Baron J. de.—"*Le pays des Amazone, l' El Dorado, les terres à caoutchouc.*" Paris, 1899: translated by George Humphrey ("Land of the Amazons"). New York, 1901.
    Additions have been made to the text in the translation.
Silva, Pevina de.—"*Historia do Brazil de 1831-1840,*" Rio, 1878.
Varnhagen, F. A. de.—"*Examen de quelques points de l'histoire du Brésil.*" Paris, 1857.
Wright, Marie Robinson.—"The New Brazil: Its Resources and Attractions, Historical, Descriptive, and Industrial." Philadelphia, 1901.

CHILI

Barros, Araua D.—"*Historia général de Chili.*" 9 vols., 1884, 1888.
Wiener.—"*Chili et Chiliens.*" 1888.
Smith, W. Anderson.—"Temperate Chile: a Progressive Spain." New York, 1899.

COLOMBIA

Mosquera.—"*Los partidos en Colombia.*" 1874.

ECUADOR

Cevallos.—"*Resumen de la historia del Ecuador*" (to 1845). 3 vols., 1886.

PERU

Middendorf, E. W.—"*Peru, Beobachtungen und Studien über das Land und seine Bewohner.*" 3 vols. Berlin, 1894-1896.
    This book contains: a short history of the country; a description of Lima, of the coast, of the tableland, of the archæological remains, and of the present economic condition.
Urrutia.—"*Epocas del Peru.*" Lima, 1844.

URUGUAY

Bordoni.—"*Montevideo e la republica del Uruguay.*" 1888 *pon.*
Maria, de.—"*Historia del Uruguay.*" 1875-1876.

VENEZUELA

Rojas, de.—"*Bosquejo historico de Venezuela.*" 1888.
Paez.—"*Autobiografia.*" New York. 2 vols. 1867-1869.

GENERAL

Akers, Charles Edward.—"History of South America, 1854-1904." New York, 1904.

A trustworthy account of the events of the years 1875-1904 by a competent observer. Unsatisfactory for the earlier period. Good maps and illustrations.

Carpenter, Frank G.—"South America: Social, Industrial, and Political." Akron, O., 1900.

Useful description of existing industrial and social conditions. Comments on political matters untrustworthy.

Curtis, William Eleroy.—"Between the Andes and the Ocean." Chicago, 1900.

A sympathetic description of existing conditions.

Dawson, Thomas Cleland.—"South American Republics" ("Story of the Nations"). New York, 1903-1904. 2 vols.

Better for the East Andean than for the Pacific states.

Walton, Clifford Stevens.—"The Civil Law in Spain and Spanish America." Washington, 1900.

INDEX

INDEX

A

7-10-52